M000247486

CHILTON'S
REPAIR & TUNE-UP GUIDE
DATSUN 200SX
510 • 610 • 710 • 810
NISSAN MAXIMA
1973-84

All U.S. and Canadian models, including turbo
and diesel engines.

Vice President and General Manager JOHN P. KUSHNERICK
Managing Editor KERRY A. FREEMAN, S.A.E.
Senior Editor RICHARD J. RIVELE, S.A.E.
Editor A. LINDSAY BROOKE

CHILTON BOOK COMPANY
Radnor, Pennsylvania
19089

R. Calkins

SAFETY NOTICE

Proper service and repair procedures are vital to the safe, reliable operation of all motor vehicles, as well as the personal safety of those performing repairs. This book outlines procedures for servicing and repairing vehicles using safe, effective methods. The procedures contain many NOTES, CAUTIONS and WARNINGS which should be followed along with standard safety procedures to eliminate the possibility of personal injury or improper service which could damage the vehicle or compromise its safety.

It is important to note that repair procedures and techniques, tools and parts for servicing motor vehicles, as well as the skill and experience of the individual performing the work vary widely. It is not possible to anticipate all of the conceivable ways or conditions under which vehicles may be serviced, or to provide cautions as to all of the possible hazards that may result. Standard and accepted safety precautions and equipment should be used when handling toxic or flammable fluids, and safety goggles or other protection should be used during cutting, grinding, chiseling, prying, or any other process that can cause material removal or projectiles.

Some procedures require the use of tools specially designed for a specific purpose. Before substituting another tool or procedure, you must be completely satisfied that neither your personal safety, nor the performance of the vehicle will be endangered.

Although information in this guide is based on industry sources and is as complete as possible at the time of publication, the possibility exists that the manufacturer made later changes which could not be included here. While striving for total accuracy, Chilton Book Company cannot assume responsibility for any errors, changes, or omissions that may occur in the compilation of this data.

PART NUMBERS

Part numbers listed in this reference are not recommendations by Chilton for any product by brand name. They are references that can be used with interchange manuals and aftermarket supplier catalogs to locate each brand supplier's discrete part number.

ACKNOWLEDGMENTS

The Chilton Book Company thanks the Nissan Motor Corporation in U.S.A., Gardena, California 90247 and Marsh Pontiac-Datsun, Ardmore, Pennsylvania, for their assistance in the preparation of this book.

Chilton's Repair & Tune-up Guide: Datsun/Nissan 200SX, 510, 610, 710, 810, Maxima 1973–84
ISBN 0-8019-7478-X pbk.
Library of Congress Catalog Card No. 83-45313

CONTENTS

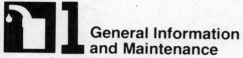

Quick Reference
Specifications For Your Vehicle

Fill in this chart with the most commonly used specifications for your vehicle. Specifications can be found in Chapters 1 through 3 or on the tune-up decal under the hood of the vehicle.

 Tune-Up

Firing Order_____

Spark Plugs:

    Type_____

    Gap (in.)_____

Point Gap (in.)_____

Dwell Angle (°)_____

Ignition Timing (°)_____

    Vacuum (Connected/Disconnected)_____

Valve Clearance (in.)

    Intake_____ Exhaust_____

Capacities

Engine Oil (qts)

    With Filter Change_____

    Without Filter Change_____

Cooling System (qts)_____

Manual Transmission (pts)_____

    Type_____

Automatic Transmission (pts)_____

    Type_____

Front Differential (pts)_____

    Type_____

Rear Differential (pts)_____

    Type_____

Transfer Case (pts)_____

    Type_____

FREQUENTLY REPLACED PARTS

Use these spaces to record the part numbers of frequently replaced parts.

PCV VALVE	**OIL FILTER**	**AIR FILTER**
Manufacturer_____	Manufacturer_____	Manufacturer_____
Part No._____	Part No._____	Part No._____

General Information and Maintenance

HOW TO USE THIS BOOK

Datsun and Nissan 510, 610, 710, 810, 200SX and Maxima models are covered in this book, with procedures specifically labeled as to the particular model when it makes a difference. The purpose of this book is to cover maintenance and repair procedures that the owner can perform with a minimum of special tools or equipment. A lot of attention is given to the type of jobs on which the owner can save labor charges and time by doing it him or her self. Jobs which absolutely require special tools, such as transaxle overhaul, or which the beginner is unlikely to get right the first time, such as differential adjustment, are purposely not covered.

To use the book properly, each operation must be approached logically, with a clear understanding of the theory behind the work involved. *The procedures should be read completely and understood thoroughly before any work is begun.* The required tools and supplies should be on hand and a clean, uncluttered place to work should be available. There is nothing more frustrating than finding yourself one metric bolt short in the middle of your Sunday afternoon repair. So read ahead and plan ahead. To avoid confusion, it is best to complete one job at a time, so that results can be independently evaluated.

When reference is made in this book to the "right side" or "left side" of the car, it should be understood that these positions are to be viewed from the front seat. Thus, the left side of the car is always the driver's side, even when one is facing the car, as when working on the engine.

We have attempted to eliminate the use of special tools wherever possible, substituting more readily available hand tools. However, in some cases the special tools are necessary. These can be purchased from your Datsun/Nissan dealer, or from an automotive parts store.

Always be conscious of the need for safety in your work. Never crawl under your car unless it is firmly supported by jackstands or ramps. Never smoke near or allow flame to get near the battery or fuel system. Keep your clothing, hands and hair clear of the fan and pulleys when working near the engine, if it is running. Most importantly, try to be patient, even in the midst of a problem such as a particularly stubborn bolt; reaching for the largest hammer in the garage is usually a cause for later regret and more extensive repair. As you gain confidence and experience, working on your car will become a source of pride and satisfaction.

TOOLS AND EQUIPMENT

The service procedures in this book presuppose a familiarity with hand tools and their proper use. However, it is possible that you may have a limited amount of experience with the sort of equipment needed to work on an automobile. This section is designed to help you assemble a basic set of tools that will handle most of the jobs you may undertake.

In addition to the normal assortment of screwdrivers and pliers, automotive service work requires an investment in wrenches, sockets and the handles needed to drive them, and various measuring tools such as torque wrenches and feeler gauges.

You will find that virtually every nut and bolt on your car is metric. Therefore, despite various close size similarities, standard inch-size tools will not fit and must not be used. You will need a set of metric wrenches as your most basic tool kit, ranging from about 6 mm to 17 mm in size. High quality forged wrenches are available in three styles: open end, box end, and

FROM TOP: BATTERY TERMINAL TOOL; FEELER GAUGES; OIL SPOUT; FILTER WRENCH

ALLEN WRENCHES

BEAM-TYPE TORQUE WRENCH

JACKSTAND

DWELL TACHOMETER

DWELL/TACHOMETER

VACUUM GAUGE

COMPRESSION GAUGE

TIMING LIGHT

You need only a basic assortment of hand tools and test instruments for most maintenance and repair jobs

combination open-box end. The combination tools are generally the most desirable as a starter set; the wrenches shown in the accompanying illustration are of the combination type.

The other set of tools inevitably required is a ratchet handle and socket set. This set should have the same size range as your wrench set. The ratchet, extension, and flex drives for the sockets are available in many sizes; it is advisable to choose a ⅜ inch drive set initially. One break in the inch/metric sizing war is that metric-sized sockets sold in the U.S. have inch-sized drive (¼, ⅜, ½, etc.). Thus, if you already have an inch-size socket set, you need only buy new metric sockets in the sizes needed. Sockets are available in six and twelve point versions; six point types are generally cheaper and are a good choice for a first set. The choice of a drive handle for the sockets should be made with some care, if this is your first set, take the plunge and invest in a flex-head ratchet; it will get into many places otherwise accessible only through a long chain of universal joints, extensions, and adapters. An alternative is a flex handle, which lacks the ratcheting feature but has a head which pivots 180°; such a tool is shown below the ratchet handle in the illustration. In addition to the range of sockets mentioned, a rubber-lined spark plug socket should be purchased. The correct size for the plugs in your car's engine is ¹³⁄₁₆ inch.

The most important thing to consider when purchasing hand tools is quality. Don't be misled by the low cost of "bargain" tools. Forged wrenches, tempered screwdriver blades, and fine tooth ratchets are much better investments than their less expensive counterparts. The skinned knuckles and frustration inflicted by poor quality tools make any job an unhappy chore. Another consideration is that quality tools come with an on-the-spot replacement guarantee—if the tool breaks, you get a new one, no questions asked.

Most jobs can be accomplished using the tools on the accompanying lists. There will be an occasional need for a special tool, such as snap ring pliers; that need will be mentioned in the text. It would not be wise to buy a large assortment of tools on the premise that someday they will be needed. Instead, the tools should be acquired one at a time, each for a specific job, both to avoid unnecessary expense and to be certain that you have the right tool.

The tools needed for basic maintenance jobs, in addition to the wrenches and sockets mentioned, include:

1. Jackstands, for support;
2. Oil filter wrench;
3. Oil filler spout or funnel;
4. Grease gun;
5. Battery terminal and clamp cleaner;
6. Container for draining oil;
7. Many rags for the inevitable spills.
8. A hydraulic floor jack of at least 1½ ton capacity. This is the only *safe, reliable* jack for raising a car.

In addition to these items there are several others which are not absolutely necessary, but handy to have around. These include a transmission funnel and filler tube, a drop (trouble) light on a long cord, an adjustable wrench (crescent wrench), and slip joint pliers.

A more advanced list of tools suitable for tune-up work, can be drawn up easily. While the tools involved are slightly more sophisticated, they need not be outrageously expensive. The key to these purchases is to make them with an eye towards adaptability and wide range. A basic list of tune-up tools could include:

1. Tachometer;
2. Spark plug gauge and gapping tool;
3. Timing light.

In this list, the choice of a timing light should be made carefully. A light which works on the DC current supplied by the car battery is the best choice; it should have a xenon tube for brightness. Certain 1975–77 models and all 1978 and later models have electronic ignition, and thus the light should have an inductive pick-up (the timing light illustrated has one of these.

In addition to these basic tools, there are several other tools and gauges you may find useful. These include:

1. A compression gauge. The screw-in type is slower to use, but eliminates the possibility of a faulty reading due to escaping pressure;
2. A manifold vacuum gauge;
3. A test light;
4. An induction meter. This is used to determine whether or not there is current flowing in a wire, and thus is extremely helpful in electrical troubleshooting.

Finally, you will probably find a torque wrench necessary for all but the most basic of work. The beam type models are perfectly adequate. The newer click (breakaway) type torque wrenches are more accurate, but are much more expensive, and must be periodically recalibrated.

Special Tools

Datsun special tools referred to in this guide are available through Kent-Moore Corporation, 29784 Little Mack, Roseville, Michigan 48066. For Canada, contact Kent-Moore of Canada, Ltd., 2395 Cawthra Mississauga, Ontario, Canada L5A 3P2.

SERVICING YOUR CAR SAFELY

It is virtually impossible to anticipate all of the hazards involved with automotive maintenance and service, but care and common sense will prevent most accidents.

The rules of safety for mechanics range from "don't smoke around gasoline," to "use the proper tool for the job." The trick to avoiding injuries is to develop safe work habits and take every possible precaution.

Dos

• Do keep a fire extinguisher and first aid kit within easy reach.

• Do wear safety glasses or goggles when cutting, drilling, grinding or prying, even if you have 20–20 vision. If you wear glasses for the sake of vision, they should be made of hardened glass that can serve also as safety glasses, or wear safety goggles over your regular glasses.

• Do shield your eyes whenever you work around the battery. Batteries contain sulphuric acid. In case of contact with the eyes or skin, flush the area with water or a mixture of water and baking soda and get medical attention immediately.

• Do use safety stands for any undercar service. Jacks are for raising vehicles; safety stands are for making sure the vehicle stays raised until you want it to come down. Whenever the car is raised, block the wheels remaining on the ground and set the parking brake.

• Do use a hydraulic floor jack of at least 1½ ton capacity when working on your Datsun or Nissan. That little jack supplied with the car is only designed for changing tires out on the road.

• Do use adequate ventilation when working with any chemicals or hazardous materials. Like carbon monoxide, the asbestos dust resulting from brake lining wear can be poisonous in sufficient quantities.

• Do disconnect the negative battery cable

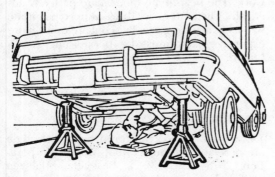

Always support the car securely with jackstands; don't use cinder blocks, tire-changing jacks or the like

when working on the electrical system. The secondary ignition system can contain up to 40,000 volts.

• Do follow manufacturer's directions whenever working with potentially hazardous materials. Both brake fluid and antifreeze are poisonouos if taken internally.

• Do properly maintain your tools. Loose hammerheads, mushroomed punches and chisels, frayed or poorly grounded electrical cords, excessively worn screwdrivers, spread wrenches (open end), cracked sockets, slipping ratchets, or faulty droplight sockets can cause accidents.

• Do use the proper size and type of tool for the job being done.

• Do when possible, pull on a wrench handle rather than push on it, and adjust your stance to prevent a fall.

• Do be sure that adjustable wrenches are tightly closed on the nut or bolt and pulled so that the face is on the side of the fixed jaw.

• Do select a wrench or socket that fits the nut or bolt. The wrench or socket should sit straight, not cocked.

• Do strike squarely with a hammer; avoid glancing blows.

• Do set the parking brake and block the drive wheels if the work requires the engine running.

Don'ts

• Don't run an engine in a garage or anywhere else without proper ventilation—EVER! Carbon monoxide is poisonous; it takes a long time to leave the human body and you can build up a deadly supply of it in your system by simply breathing in a little every day. You may not realize you are slowly poisoning yourself. Always use power vents, windows, fans or open the garage doors.

• Don't work around moving parts while wearing a necktie or other loose clothing. Short sleeves are much safer than long, loose sleeves; hard-toed shoes with neoprene soles protect your toes and give a better grip on slippery surfaces. Jewelry such as watches, fancy belt buckles, beads or body adornment of any kind is not safe working around a car. Long hair should be hidden under a hat or cap.

• Don't use pockets for toolboxes. A fall or bump can drive a screwdriver deep into your body. Even a wiping cloth hanging from the back pocket can wrap around a spinning shaft or fan.

• Don't use cinderblocks to support a car! When you get the car jacked up (with a hydraulic floor jack), support it with jackstands.

• Don't smoke when working around gaso-

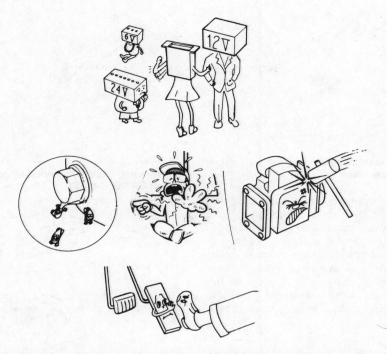

Never work on a car for so long that you begin to lose your sense of reality

line, cleaning solvent or other flammable material.

• Don't smoke when working around the battery. When the battery is being charged, it gives off explosive hydrogen gas.

• Don't use gasoline to wash your hands; there are excellent soaps available. Gasoline may contain lead, and lead can enter the body through a cut, accumulating in the body until you are very ill. Gasoline also removes all the natural oils from the skin so that bone dry hands will suck up oil and grease.

• Don't service the air conditioning system unless you are equipped with the necessary tools and training. The refrigerant, R-12, is extremely cold when compressed, and when released into the air will instantly freeze any surface it contacts, including your eyes. Although the refrigerant is normally non-toxic, R-12 becomes a deadly poisonous gas in the presence of an open flame. One good whiff of the vapors from burning refrigerant can be fatal.

SERIAL NUMBER IDENTIFICATION

Vehicle

The vehicle identification plate is located on the cowl at the rear of the engine compartment. The plate contains the model type, engine ca-

Vehicle identification plate

The vehicle serial number is stamped into the firewall

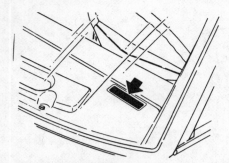

The vehicle identification number is visible through the windshield

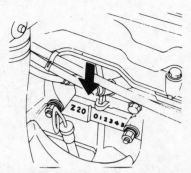

Engine serial number location—all gasoline engines except CA20E, CA18ET

pacity, maximum horsepower, wheelbase and the engine and chassis serial numbers.

The vehicle or chassis serial number is stamped into the firewall at the rear of the engine compartment and is broken down as shown in the illustration. The vehicle identification number is also reproduced on a plate on the upper left surface of the instrument panel and can be seen from the outside through the windshield.

Engine

The engine serial number is stamped on the right side top edge of the cylinder block on all models except the 1980 and later 200SX. 1980–83 200SX engine (Z20, Z22) numbers are

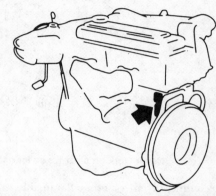

1984 and later 200SX engine (CA20E, CA18ET) serial number location

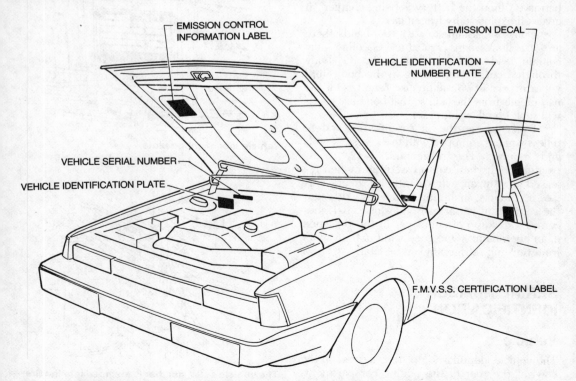

EMISSION CONTROL INFORMATION LABEL

EMISSION DECAL

VEHICLE IDENTIFICATION NUMBER PLATE

VEHICLE SERIAL NUMBER

VEHICLE IDENTIFICATION PLATE

F.M.V.S.S. CERTIFICATION LABEL

1983 200SX showing various identification and emissions label locations. 1984 and later similar

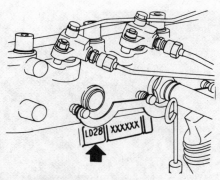

Engine serial number—diesel

stamped on the left side top edge of the cylinder block. 1984 and later 200SX engines (CA20, CA18ET) are stamped on the left side rear edge of the block, next to the bellhousing. The engine serial number is preceeded by the engine model code.

Transmission

The transmission serial number is stamped on the front upper face of the transmission case on manual transmissions, or on the lower right side of the case on automatic transmissions.

ROUTINE MAINTENANCE

Routine maintenance is the self-explanatory term used to describe the sort of periodic work necessary to keep a car in safe and reliable working order. A regular program aimed at monitoring essential systems ensures that the car's components are functioning correctly (and will continue to do so until the next inspection, one hopes), and can prevent small problems from developing into major headaches. Routine maintenance also pays off big dividends in keeping major repair costs at a minimum, extending the life of the car, and enhancing resale value, should you ever desire to part with your Datsun or Nissan.

A very definite maintenance schedule is provided by Datsun and Nissan, and must be followed, not only to keep the new car warranty in effect, but also to keep the car working properly. The "Maintenance Intervals" chart in this chapter outlines the routine maintenance which must be performed according to intervals based on either accumulated mileage or time. Your car also came with a maintenance schedule provided by Datsun and Nissan. Adherence to these schedules will result in a longer life for your car, and will, over the long run, save you money and time.

The checks and adjustments in the following sections generally require only a few minutes of attention every few weeks; the services to be performed can be easily accomplished in a morning. The most important part of any maintenance program is regularity. The few minutes or occasional morning spent on thes seemingly trivial tasks will forestall or elim nate major problems later.

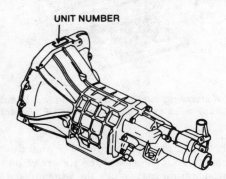

UNIT NUMBER

Location of the manual transmission serial number

AIR CLEANER

An air cleaner is used to keep air-bor and dust out of the air flowing throug gine. Proper maintenance is vital, as element will undesirably richen the ture, restrict air flow and power, an cessive contamination of the oil wit

All models covered in this book with a disposable, paper cartridg element. The filter should be ch tune-up (sooner if the car is ope area). Loose dust can sometim by striking the filter against a eral times or by blowing thr pressed air. The filter should 24,000 miles (30,000 miles,

To remove the filter, uns lift off the housing cover element. The filter shoul four thumb latches whi released before remov Before installing the ment filter, wipe out

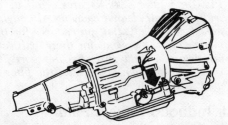

Location of the automatic transmission serial number

Exploded
showing fi

Your engine breathes too, don't strangle it with a dirty air filter

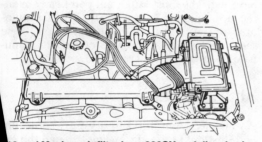

10 and Maxima air filter box. 200SX and diesels similar

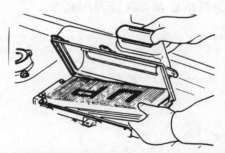

When installing the filter element on fuel injected engines, make sure that the word "UP" is facing up

with a clean rag or paper towel. Install the paper air cleaner filter, seat the top cover on the bottom housing and tighten the wing nut(s). Clip on the thumb latches if so equipped.

NOTE: *Certain models (810, Maxima, and 1980 and later 200SX) utilize a flat, cartridge type air cleaner element. Although removal and installation procedures for these models are the same as for those with round air cleaners, make sure that the word "UP" is facing up when you install the filter element.*

Air Induction Valve Filter

Certain later models use an air induction valve filter. It is located in the side of the air cleaner

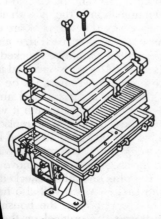

view of the 810 and Maxima air cleaner lter element; 1980 and later 200SX similar

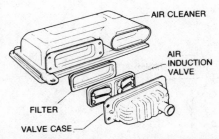

Air induction valve filter—fuel injected engines

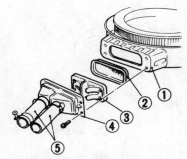

1. Air cleaner
2. Filter K-58
3. Air induction valve
4. Air induction valve case
5. Rubber hose

Air induction valve filter—carbureted engines

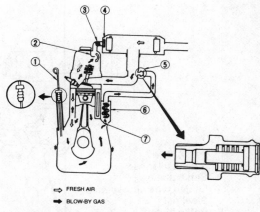

⇨ FRESH AIR
➡ BLOW-BY GAS

1. Seal type oil level gauge
2. Baffle plate
3. Flame arrester
4. Filter
5. P.C.V. valve
6. Steel net
7. Baffle plate

PCV valve location—610, 710, 1978–79 510 and 1980 510 (Canada)

housing and is easily replaced. Unscrew the mounting screws and remove the valve filter case. Pull the air induction valve out and remove the filter that lies underneath it. Install the new filter and then the valve. Pay particular attention to which way the valve is facing so that the exhaust gases will not flow backward through the system. Install the valve case. Replacement intervals are every 30,000 miles.

Positive Crankcase Ventilation Valve

Gasoline Engines

This valve feeds crankcase blow-by gases into the intake manifold to be burned with the normal air/fuel mixture. The PCV valve should be replaced every 24,000 miles. Make sure that all PCV connections are tight. Check that the connecting hoses are clear and not clogged. Replace any brittle or broken hoses.

To check the valve's operation, remove the valve's ventilation hose with the engine idling. If the valve is working, a hissing noise will be heard as air passes through the valve, and a strong vacuum will be felt when you place a finger over the valve opening.

To replace the valve, which is located in the side or bottom of the intake manifold:

1. Squeeze the hose clamp with pliers and remove the hose.

2. Using a wrench, unscrew the PCV valve and remove the valve.

3. Disconnect the ventilation hoses and flush with solvent.

4. Install the new PCV valve and replace the hoses and clamp.

For further details on the positive crankcase ventilation system, please refer to Chapter 4.

Diesel Engines

These engines use a crankcase emission control valve in place of the PCV valve. Although different in shape, it is similar in function.

To replace the valve which is located inline between the cylinder head cover and the intake manifold:

1. Locate the valve. There should be three hoses attached to it.

2. Use a pair of pliers and squeeze the hose clamp on each hose so that you can remove the hose from the valve.

3. Installation is in the reverse order of removal.

For further details on the diesel crankcase emissions control system, please refer to Chapter 4.

Evaporative Emission Control System

Gasoline Engines Only

Check the evaporation control system every 12,000 miles (15,000 miles, 1980 and later). Check the fuel and vapor lines for proper connections and correct routing as well as condition. Replace damaged or deteriorated parts as necessary. Remove and check the operation of

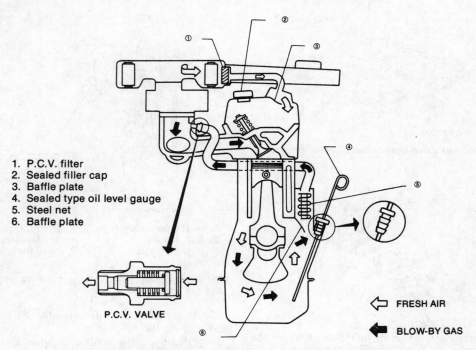

1. P.C.V. filter
2. Sealed filler cap
3. Baffle plate
4. Sealed type oil level gauge
5. Steel net
6. Baffle plate

P.C.V. VALVE

⇦ FRESH AIR

⬅ BLOW-BY GAS

PCV valve location—1980 and later 510 (except Canada)

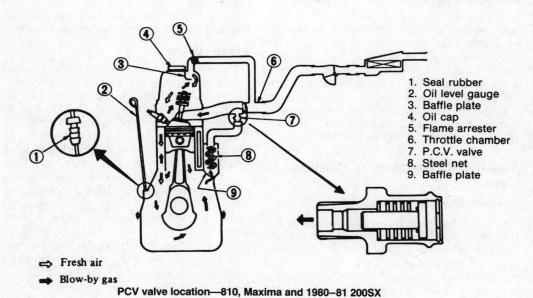

1. Seal rubber
2. Oil level gauge
3. Baffle plate
4. Oil cap
5. Flame arrester
6. Throttle chamber
7. P.C.V. valve
8. Steel net
9. Baffle plate

⇨ Fresh air

➡ Blow-by gas

PCV valve location—810, Maxima and 1980–81 200SX

the check valve on pre-1975 models in the following manner.

1. With all the hoses disconnected from the valve, apply air pressure to the fuel tank side of the valve. The air should flow through the valve and exit the crankcase side of the valve. If the valve does not behave in the above manner, replace it.

2. Apply air pressure to the crankcase side

valve. Air should not pass to either of the two outlets.

3. When air pressure is applied to the carburetor side of the valve, the air should pass through to exit out the fuel tank and/or the crankcase side of the valve.

On 1975 and later models, the flow guide valve is replaced with a carbon filled storage canister which stores fuel vapors until the en-

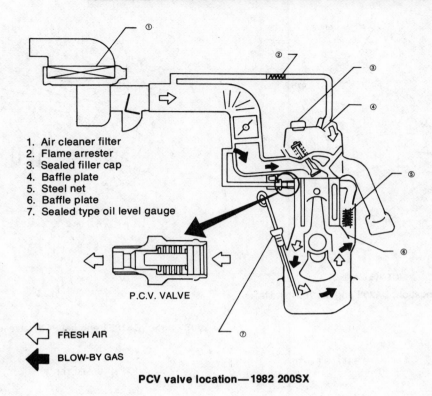

1. Air cleaner filter
2. Flame arrester
3. Sealed filler cap
4. Baffle plate
5. Steel net
6. Baffle plate
7. Sealed type oil level gauge

P.C.V. VALVE

FRESH AIR

BLOW-BY GAS

PCV valve location—1982 200SX

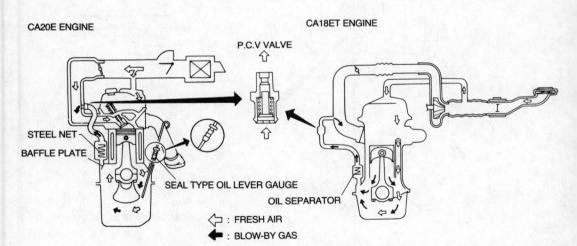

CA20E ENGINE

CA18ET ENGINE

P.C.V VALVE

STEEL NET

BAFFLE PLATE

SEAL TYPE OIL LEVER GAUGE

OIL SEPARATOR

: FRESH AIR

: BLOW-BY GAS

PCV systems, 1984 and later 200SX. Turbo engine on right

gine is started and the vapors are drawn into the combustion chambers and burned.

To check the operation of the carbon canister purge control valve, disconnect the rubber hose between the canister control valve and the T-fitting, at the T-fitting. Apply vacuum to the hose leading to the control valve. The vacuum condition should be maintained indefinitely. If the control valve leaks, remove the top cover

of the valve and check for a dislocated or cracked diaphragm. If the diaphragm is damaged, a repair kit containing a new diaphragm, retainer, and spring is available and should be installed.

The carbon canister has an air filter in the bottom of the canister. The filter element should be checked every two years or 30,000 miles; more frequently if the car is operated in dusty areas. Replace the filter by pulling it out of the

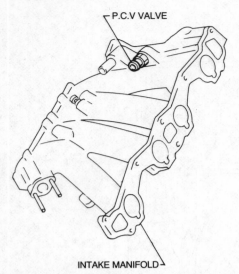

PCV valve location, CA20E engine, 1984 and later

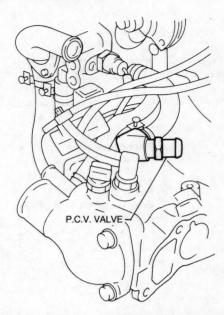

200SX turbo (CA18ET engine) PCV valve location

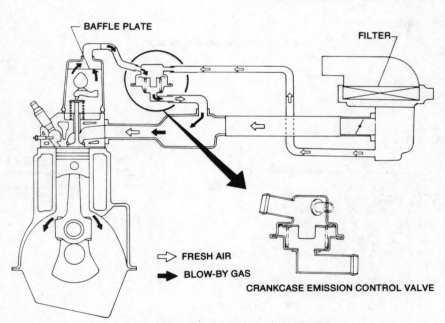

Diesel crankcase emission control valve location

bottom of the canister and installing a new one.

For further details on the evaporative emissions control system, please refer to Chapter 4.

Battery

SPECIFIC GRAVITY (EXCEPT "MAINTENANCE FREE" BATTERIES)

At least once a year, check the specific gravity of the battery. It should be between 1.20 and 1.26 at room temperature.

The specific gravity can be checked with the use of an hydrometer, an inexpensive instrument available from many sources, including auto parts stores. The hydrometer has a squeeze bulb at one end and a nozzle at the other. Battery electrolyte is sucked into the hydrometer until the float is lifted from its seat. The specific gravity is then read by noting the position of the float. Generally, if after charging, the specific gravity between any two cells varies more than 50 points (.050), the battery is bad and should be replaced.

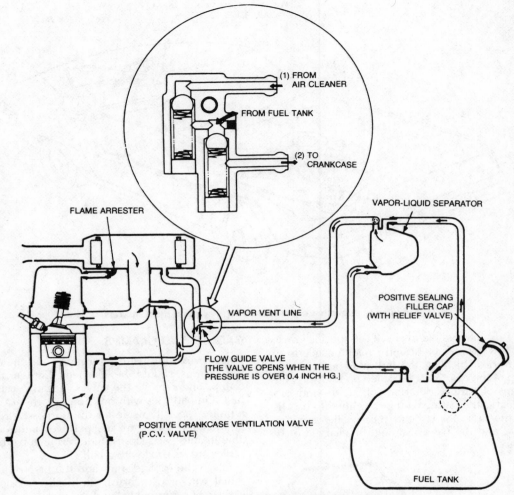

(1) FROM AIR CLEANER

FROM FUEL TANK

(2) TO CRANKCASE

FLAME ARRESTER

VAPOR-LIQUID SEPARATOR

VAPOR VENT LINE

POSITIVE SEALING FILLER CAP (WITH RELIEF VALVE)

FLOW GUIDE VALVE [THE VALVE OPENS WHEN THE PRESSURE IS OVER 0.4 INCH HG.]

POSITIVE CRANKCASE VENTILATION VALVE (P.C.V. VALVE)

FUEL TANK

1973–74 check valve fuel evaporative emissions system

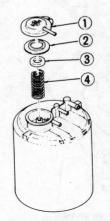

1. Cover
2. Diaphragm
3. Retainer
4. Diaphragm spring

1975 and later carbon canister

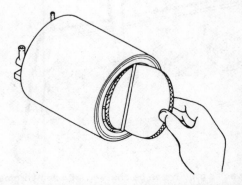

The carbon canister has a replaceable filter in the bottom

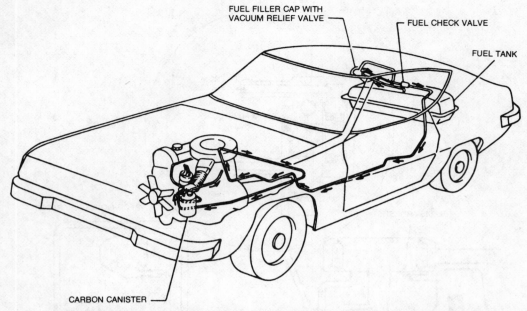

FUEL FILLER CAP WITH
VACUUM RELIEF VALVE

FUEL CHECK VALVE

FUEL TANK

CARBON CANISTER

1975 and later evaporative emissions control system; most models similiar

It is not possible to check the specific gravity in this manner on sealed ("maintenance free") batteries. Instead, the indicator built into the top of the case must be relied on to display any signs of battery deterioration. If the indicator is dark, the battery can be assumed to be OK. If the indicator is light, the specific gravity is low, and the battery should be charged or replaced.

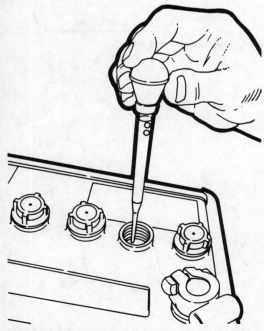

Specific gravity can be checked with an hydrometer

CABLES AND CLAMPS

Once a year, the battery terminals and the cable clamps should be cleaned. Loosen the clamps and remove the cables, negative cable first. On batteries with posts on top, the use of a puller specially made for the purpose is recommended. These are inexpensive, and available in auto parts stores. Side terminal battery cables are secured with a bolt.

Clean the cable clamps and the battery terminal with a wire brush, until all corrosion, grease, etc. is removed and the metal is shiny. It is especially important to clean the inside of the clamp thoroughly, since a small deposit of

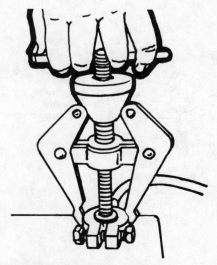

Pullers make clamp removal easier

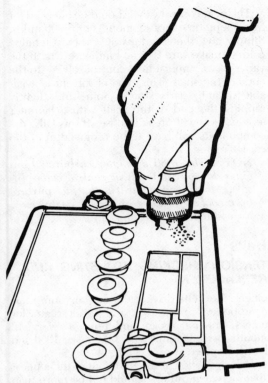

Clean the posts with a wire brush, or a terminal cleaner made for the purpose (shown)

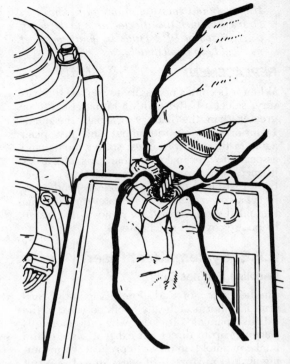

Clean the inside of the clamps with a wire brush, or the special tool

foreign material or oxidation there will prevent a sound electrical connection and inhibit either starting or charging. Special tools are available for cleaning these parts, one type for conventional batteries and another type for side terminal batteries.

Before installing the cables, loosen the battery hold-down clamp or strap, remove the battery and check the battery tray. Clear it of any debris, and check it for soundness. Rust should be wire brushed away, and the metal given a coat of anti-rust paint. Replace the battery and tighten the hold-down clamp or strap securely, but be careful not to overtighten, which will crack the battery case.

After the clamps and terminals are clean, reinstall the cables, negative cable last; do not hammer on the clamps to install. Tighten the clamps securely, but do not distort them. Give the clamps and terminals a thin external coat of grease after installation, to retard corrosion.

Check the cables at the same time that the terminals are cleaned. If the cable insulation is cracked or broken, or if the ends are frayed, the cable should be replaced with a new cable of the same length and gauge.

NOTE: *Keep flame or sparks away from the battery; it gives off explosive hydrogen gas. Battery electrolyte contains sulphuric acid.*

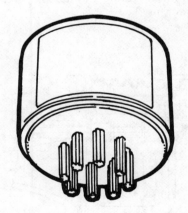

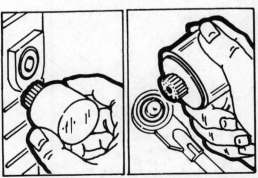

Special tools are also available for cleaning the posts and clamps on side terminal batteries

If you should splash any on your skin or in your eyes, flush the affected area with plenty of clear water; if it lands in your eyes, get medical help immediately.

REPLACEMENT

When it becomes necessary to replace the battery, select a battery with a rating equal to or greater than the battery originally installed. Deterioration, embrittlement and just plain aging of the battery cables, starter motor, and associated wires makes the battery's job harder in successive years. The slow increase in electrical resistance over time makes it prudent to install a new battery with a greater capacity than the old. Details on battery removal and installation are covered in Chapter 3.

E.F.E. System (Heat Riser)

Gasoline Engines Only

The heat riser, or Early Fuel Evaporative System, is a thermostatically operated valve in the exhaust manifold. It closes when the engine is warming up to direct hot exhaust gases to the intake manifold, in order to preheat the incoming air/fuel mixture. If it sticks shut, the result will be frequent stalling during warmup, especially in cold or damp weather. If it sticks open, the result will be a rough idle after the engine is warm.

The heat control valve should be checked for free operation every six months or 6,000 miles. Simply give the counterweight a twirl (engine cold) to make sure that no binding exists. If the valve sticks, apply a heat control solvent to the ends of the shaft. This type of solvent is available in auto parts stores. Sometimes lightly rapping the end of the shaft with a hammer (engine hot) will break it loose. If this fails, the components will have to be removed from the car for repair.

NOTE: *The 1980 and later carbureted engines do not use the heat control valve. Instead, these engines warm the fuel mixture by a coolant passage under the carburetor. No maintenance is required.*

Belts

TENSION CHECKING, ADJUSTING, AND REPLACEMENT

Check the belts driving the fan, air pump, air conditioning compressor, and the alternator for cracks, fraying, wear, and tension every 12 months or 12,000 miles (15,000 miles, 1980 and later). Replace as necessary.

Belt deflection at the midpoint of the longest span between pulleys should not be more than $7/16$ of an inch with 22 lbs. of pressure applied to the belt.

To adjust the tension on all components ex-

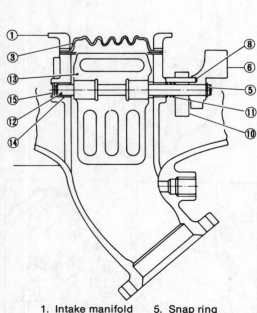

1. Intake manifold	5. Snap ring	9. Screw	13. Heat control valve
2. Stove gasket	6. Counterweight	10. Thermostat spring	14. Bushing
3. Manifold stove	7. Key	11. Coil spring	15. Cap
4. Heat shield plate	8. Stopper pin	12. Control valve shaft	16. Exhaust manifold

EFE system—L-series (both 4 and 6-cyl.) engines

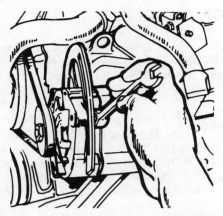

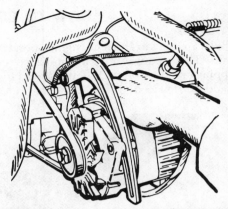

To adjust the belt tension or replace the belts, first loosen the component's (in this case, the alternator) mounting and adjusting bolts slightly

Pull outward on the component while you tighten the mounting bolts. Make sure the belt has proper deflection; a belt too tight will cause premature bearing failure in whatever component it drives, as well as premature belt wear

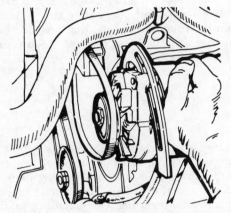

Next, push the component toward the engine and slip off the belt

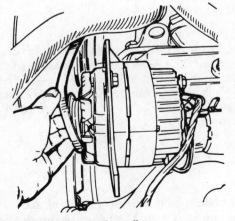

Slip the new belt over the pulleys

cept the air conditioning compressor, power steering pump, and some late model air pumps, loosen the pivot and mounting bolts of the component which the belt is driving, then, us-

ing a wooden lever, pry the component toward or away from the engine until the proper tension is achieved.

CAUTION: *An overtight belt will wear out the pulley bearings on the assorted components.*

Tighten the component mounting bolts securely. If a new belt is installed, recheck the tension after driving about 1,000 miles.

NOTE: *The replacement of the inner belt on multi-belted engines may require the removal of the outer belts.*

Belt tension adjustments for the factory installed air conditioning compressor and power steering pump are made at the idler pulley. The idler pulley is the smallest of the three pulleys. At the top of the slotted bracket holding the idler pulley there is a bolt which is used to either raise or lower the pulley. To free the bolt for adjustment, it is necessary to loosen the lock nut in the face of the idler pulley. After adjusting the belt tension, tighten the lock nut in the face of the idler pulley.

NOTE: *1980 California Datsuns come equipped with special fan belts which, if loose, geneate friction heat by slipping and shrink, taking up the slack.*

The optional air conditioning drive belt is adjusted in a similar fashion.

Cooling System

Dealing with the cooling system can be a dangerous matter unless the proper precautions are observed. It is best to check the coolant level in the radiator when the engine is cold. On early models this is accomplished by carefully removing the radiator cap and checking that the

HOW TO SPOT WORN V-BELTS

V-Belts are vital to efficient engine operation—they drive the fan, water pump and other accessories. They require little maintenance (occasional tightening) but they will not last forever. Slipping or failure of the V-belt will lead to overheating. If your V-belt looks like any of these, it should be replaced.

Cracking or weathering

This belt has deep cracks, which cause it to flex. Too much flexing leads to heat build-up and premature failure. These cracks can be caused by using the belt on a pulley that is too small. Notched belts are available for small diameter pulleys.

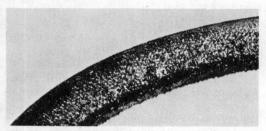

Softening (grease and oil)

Oil and grease on a belt can cause the belt's rubber compounds to soften and separate from the reinforcing cords that hold the belt together. The belt will first slip, then finally fail altogether.

Glazing

Glazing is caused by a belt that is slipping. A slipping belt can cause a run-down battery, erratic power steering, overheating or poor accessory performance. The more the belt slips, the more glazing will be built up on the surface of the belt. The more the belt is glazed, the more it will slip. If the glazing is light, tighten the belt.

Worn cover

The cover of this belt is worn off and is peeling away. The reinforcing cords will begin to wear and the belt will shortly break. When the belt cover wears in spots or has a rough jagged appearance, check the pulley grooves for roughness.

Separation

This belt is on the verge of breaking and leaving you stranded. The layers of the belt are separating and the reinforcing cords are exposed. It's just a matter of time before it breaks completely.

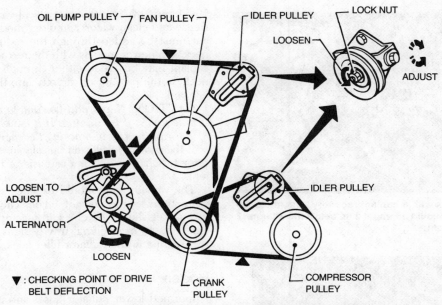

200SX Z-series 4-cylinder engine accessories and belt adjustments

Drive Belt Deflection	Adjust Deflection of Used Belt	Set Deflection of New Belt
Cooling fan mm(in)	12–15 (0.47–0.59)	8–11 (0.31–0.43)
Air conditioner compressor mm(in)	10–13 (0.39–0.51)	7–10 (0.28–0.39)
Power steering oil pump mm(in)	15–18 (0.59–0.71)	12–15 (0.47–0.59)
Aplied pushing force N (kg, lb)	98 (10, 22)	

Z-series 4-cyl. drive belt tensions

coolant is within 3 in. of the bottom of the filler neck. On later models, the cooling system has, as one of its components, a coolant recovery tank. If the coolant level is at or near the "MAX" line, the level is satisfactory. Always be certain that the filler caps on both the radiator and the recovery tank are closed tightly.

In the event that the coolant level must be checked when the engine is hot on engines

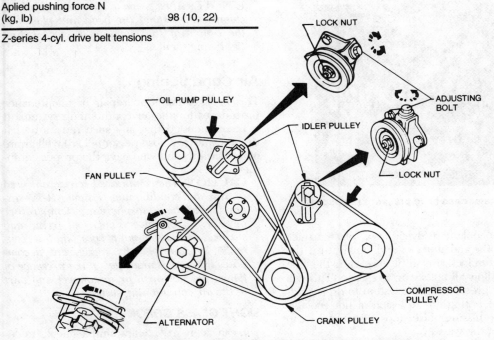

Maxima and 810 fan belt configuration. Note idler pulleys

On models with a coolant recovery tank, the coolant level should be about 3 in. below the filler neck (engine cold)

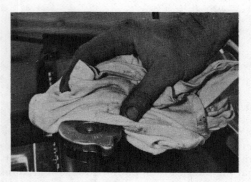

If the engine is hot, cover the radiator cap with a rag

Some radiator caps have pressure release levers

without a coolant recovery tank, place a thick rag over the radiator cap and slowly turn the cap counterclockwise until it reaches the first detent. Allow all hot steam to escape. This will allow the pressure in the system to drop gradually, preventing an explosion of hot coolant. When the hissing noise stops, remove the cap the rest of the way.

If the coolant level is found to be low, add a 50/50 mixture of ethylene glycol-based antifreeze and clean water. On older models, coolant must be added through the radiator filler neck. On newer models with the recovery tank, coolant may be added either through the filler neck on the radiator or directly into the recovery tank.

CAUTION: *Never add coolant to a hot engine unless it is running. If it is not running you run the risk of cracking the engine block.*

If the coolant level is chronically low or rusty, refer to Chapter 11 for diagnosis of the problem.

The radiator cap should be checked at the same time as the coolant level. The radiator cap gasket should be checked for any obvious tears, cracks or swelling, or any signs of incorrect seating in the radiator filler neck.

Hoses

Upper and lower radiator hoses and all heater hoses should be checked for deterioration, leaks and loose hose clamps every 15,000 miles. To remove the hoses:

1. Drain the radiator as detailed later in this chapter.

2. Loosen the hose clamps at each end of the hose to be removed.

3. Working the hose back and forth, slide it off its connection and then install a new hose if necessary.

4. Position the hose clamps at least ¼ in. from the end of the hose and tighten them.

NOTE: *Always make sure that the hose clamps are beyond the bead and placed in the center of the clamping surface before tightening them.*

Air Conditioning

This book contains no repair or maintenance procedures for the air conditioning system. It is recommended that any such repairs be left to the experts, whose personnel are well aware of the hazards and who have the proper equipment.

CAUTION: *The compressed refrigerant used in the air conditioning system (R-12) expands into the atmosphere at a temperature of −21.7°F or lower. This will freeze any surface, including your eyes, that it contacts. In addition, the refrigerant decomposes into a poisonous gas in the presence of flame. Do not open or disconnect any part of the air conditioning system.*

SIGHT GLASS CHECK

You can safely make a few simple checks to determine if your air conditioning system needs

HOW TO SPOT BAD HOSES

Both the upper and lower radiator hoses are called upon to perform difficult jobs in an inhospitable environment. They are subject to nearly 18 psi at under hood temperatures often over 280°F., and must circulate nearly 7500 gallons of coolant an hour—3 good reasons to have good hoses.

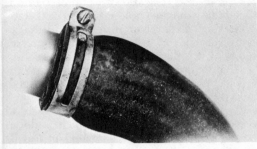

Swollen hose

A good test for any hose is to feel it for soft or spongy spots. Frequently these will appear as swollen areas of the hose. The most likely cause is oil soaking. This hose could burst at any time, when hot or under pressure.

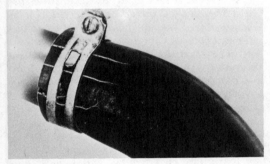

Cracked hose

Cracked hoses can usually be seen but feel the hoses to be sure they have not hardened; a prime cause of cracking. This hose has cracked down to the reinforcing cords and could split at any of the cracks.

Frayed hose end (due to weak clamp)

Weakened clamps frequently are the cause of hose and cooling system failure. The connection between the pipe and hose has deteriorated enough to allow coolant to escape when the engine is hot.

Debris in cooling system

Debris, rust and scale in the cooling system can cause the inside of a hose to weaken. This can usually be felt on the outside of the hose as soft or thinner areas.

The sight glass is located in the head of the receiver-dryer (arrow)

service. The tests work best if the temperature is warm (about 70°F).

NOTE: *If your vehicle is equipped with an after-market air conditioner, the following system check may not apply. You should contact the manufacturer of the unit for instructions on systems checks.*

1. Place the automatic transmission in Park or the manual transmission in Neutral. Set the parking brake.

2. Run the engine at a fast idle (about 1,500 rpm) either with the help of a friend, or by temporarily readjusting the idle speed screw.

3. Set the controls for maximum cold with the blower on high.

4. Locate the sight glass in one of the system lines. Usually it is on the left alongside the top of the radiator.

5. If you see bubbles, the system must be recharged. Very likely there is a leak at some point.

6. If there are no bubbles, there is either no refrigerant at all or the system is fully

charged. Feel the two hoses going to the belt-driven compressor. If they are both at the same temperature, the system is empty and must be recharged.

7. If one hose (high-pressure) is warm and the other (low-pressure) is cold, the system may be all right. However, you are probably making these tests because you think there is something wrong, so proceed to the next step.

8. Have an assistant in the car turn the fan control on and off to operate the compressor clutch. Watch the sight glass.

9. If bubbles appear when the clutch is disengaged and disappear when it is engaged, the system is properly charged.

10. If the refrigerant takes more than 45 seconds to bubble when the clutch is disengaged, the system is overcharged. This usually causes poor cooling at low speeds.

CAUTION: *If it is determined that the system has a leak, it should be corrected as soon as possible. Leaks may allow moisture to enter and cause a very expensive rust problem.*

NOTE: *Exercise the airconditioner for a few minutes, every two weeks or so, during the cold months. This avoids the possibility of the compressor seals drying from lack of lubrication.*

Windshield Wipers

For maximum effectiveness and longest element life, the windshield and wiper blades should be kept clean. Dirt, tree sap, road tar and so on will cause streaking, smearing and blade deterioration if left on the glass. It is advisable to wash the windshield carefully with a commercial glass cleaner at least once a month. Wipe off the rubber blades with the wet rag afterwards. Do not attempt to move the wipers back and forth by hand; damage to the motor and drive mechanism will result.

If the blades are found to be cracked, broken or torn, they should be replaced immediately. Replacement intervals will vary with usage, although ozone deterioration usually limits blade life to about one year. If the wiper pattern is smeared or streaked, or if the blade chatters across the glass, the blades should be replaced. It is easiest and most sensible to replace them in pairs.

There are basically three different types of wiper blade refills, which differ in their method of replacement. One type has two release buttons, approximately one-third of the way up from the ends of the blade frame. Pushing the buttons down releases a lock and allows the rubber blade to be removed from the frame. The new blade slides back into the frame and locks in place.

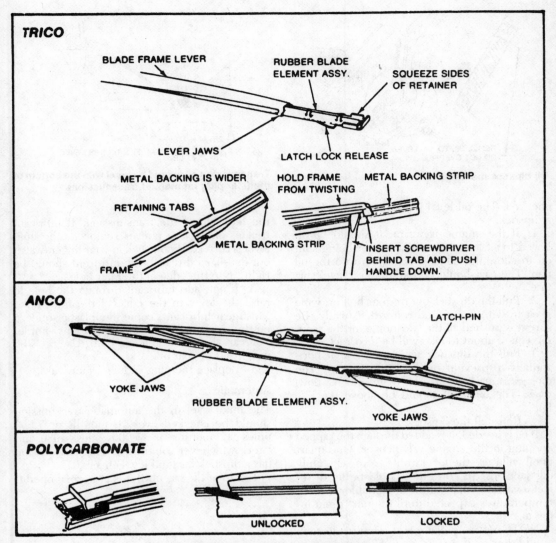

TRICO

BLADE FRAME LEVER

RUBBER BLADE ELEMENT ASSY.

SQUEEZE SIDES OF RETAINER

LEVER JAWS

LATCH LOCK RELEASE

METAL BACKING IS WIDER

HOLD FRAME FROM TWISTING

METAL BACKING STRIP

RETAINING TABS

METAL BACKING STRIP

FRAME

INSERT SCREWDRIVER BEHIND TAB AND PUSH HANDLE DOWN.

ANCO

LATCH-PIN

YOKE JAWS

RUBBER BLADE ELEMENT ASSY.

YOKE JAWS

POLYCARBONATE

UNLOCKED

LOCKED

The three types of wiper blade retention

The second type of refill has two metal tabs which are unlocked by squeezing them together. The rubber blade can then be withdrawn from the frame jaws. A new one is installed by inserting it into the front frame jaws and sliding it rearward to engage the remaining frame jaws. There are usually four jaws; be certain when installing that the refill is engaged in all of them. At the end of its travel, the tabs will lock into place on the front jaws of the wiper blade frame.

The third type is a refill made from polycarbonate. The refill has a simple locking device at one end which flexes downward out of the groove into which the jaws of the holder fit, allowing easy release. By sliding the new refill through all the jaws and pushing through the slight resistance when it reches the end of its travel, the refill will lock into position.

Regardless of the type of refill used, make sure that all of the frame jaws are engaged as the refill is pushed into place and locked. The metal blade holder and frame will scratch the glass if allowed to touch it.

Fluid Level Checks
ENGINE OIL

The engine oil level should be checked at every fuel stop, or once a week, whichever occurs more regularly. The best time to check is when the engine is warm, although checking immediately after the engine has been shut off will result in an accurate reading, since it takes a few minutes for all of the oil to drain back down into the crankcase. If the engine is cold, the engine should not be run before the level is

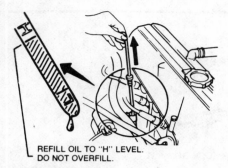

REFILL OIL TO "H" LEVEL.
DO NOT OVERFILL.

Oil dipstick markings

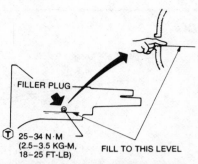

FILLER PLUG

25–34 N·M
(2.5–3.5 KG-M,
18–25 FT-LB)

FILL TO THIS LEVEL

Transmission oil should be level with the bottom of the filler plug on manual transmissions

checked. The oil level is checked by means of a dipstick.

1. If the engine is warm, it should be allowed to sit for a few minutes after being shut off to allow the oil to drain down into the oil pan. The car should be parked on a level surface.

2. Pull the dipstick out from its holder, wipe it clean with a rag, and reinsert it firmly. Be sure it is pushed all the way home, or the reading you're about to take will be incorrect.

3. Pull the dipstick again and hold it horizontally to prevent the oil from running. The dipstick is marked with "H" (high) and "L" (low) lines. The oil level should be above the "L" line.

4. Reinstall the dipstick.

If oil is needed, it is added through the capped opening in the engine valve cover. One quart of oil will raise the level from "L" to "H". Only oils labeled "SE" or "SF" should be used; select a viscosity that will be compatible with the temperatures expected until the next drain interval.

NOTE: *If your car has a diesel engine, in addition to the "SE" or "SF" markings on top of the oil can, you must also look for the letters "CC". The "CC" designation is important for proper diesel lubrication.*

See the "Oil and Fuel Recommendations" section later in this chapter if you are not sure what type of oil to use. Check the oil level again after any additions. Be careful not to overfill, which will lead to leakage and seal damage.

TRANSMISSION

Manual

The fluid level in the manual transmission should be checked every 6 months or 7,500 miles (12 months or 15,000 miles, 1980 and later), whichever comes first.

1. Park the car on a level surface. The transmission should be cool to the touch. If it is hot, check the level later, when it has cooled.

2. Slowly remove the filter hole plug from

the left side of the transmission. If lubricant trickles out as the plug is removed, the fluid level is correct. If not, stick in your finger (watch out for sharp threads); the lubricant should be right up to the edge of the filler hole.

3. If not, add lubricant through the hole to raise the level to the edge of the filler hole. Most gear lubricants come in a plastic squeeze bottle with a nozzle, making additions simple. You can also use a squeeze bulb. Use SAE 90 weight GL-4 gear oil.

4. Replace the plug and check for leaks.

Automatic

The fluid level in the automatic transmission should be checked every 6 months or 7,500 miles (12 months or 15,000 miles, 1980 and later), whichever comes first. The transmission has a dipstick for fluid level checks.

1. Drive the car until it is at normal operat-

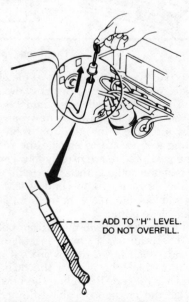

ADD TO "H" LEVEL.
DO NOT OVERFILL.

Remove the automatic transmission dipstick with engine warm and idling in Park

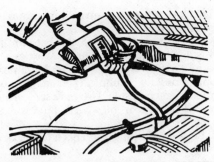

Add automatic transmission fluid through the transmission dipstick tube. You'll probably need a funnel

ing temperature. The level should not be checked immediately after the car has been driven for a long time at high speed, or in city traffic in hot weather; in those cases, the transaxle should be given a half hour to cool down.

2. Stop the car, apply the parking brake, then shift slowly through all gear positions, ending in Park. Let the engine idle for about five minutes with the transmission in Park. The car should be on a level surface.

3. With the engine still running, remove the dipstick, wipe it clean, then reinsert it, pushing it fully home.

4. Pull the dipstick again and, holding it horizontally, read the fluid level.

5. Cautiously feel the end of the dipstick to determine the temperature. Note that on Datsuns there is a scale on each side, HOT on one, COLD on the other. If the fluid level is not in the correct area, more will have to be added.

6. Fluid is added through the dipstick tube. You will probably need the aid of a spout or a long-necked funnel. Be sure that whatever you pour through is perfectly clean and dry. Use an automatic transmission fluid marked "DEXRON®". Add fluid slowly, and in small amounts, checking the level frequently between additions. Do not overfill, which will cause foaming, fluid loss, slippage, and possible transmission damage. It takes only one pint to aise the level from "L" to "H" when the transaxle is hot.

BRAKE AND CLUTCH MASTER CYLINDERS

The brake and clutch master cylinders are located under the hood, in the left rear section of the engine compartment. They are made of translucent plastic so that the levels may be checked without removing the tops. The fluid level in both reservoirs should be checked at least every 7,500 miles (15,000 miles, 1980 and later). The fluid level should be maintained at the upper most mark on the side of the reservoir. Any sudden decrease in the level indicates a possible leak in the system and should be checked out immediately.

NOTE: *Some models may have two reservoirs for the brake master cylinder, while other models (those with an automatic transmission) will not have a clutch master cylinder at all.*

When making additions of brake fluid, use only fresh, uncontaminated brake fluid meeting or exceeding DOT 3 standards. Be careful not to spill any brake fluid on painted surfaces, as it eats the paint. Do not allow the brake fluid container or the master cylinder reservoir to remain open any longer than necessary; brake fluid absorbs moisture from the air, reducing its effectiveness and causing corrosion in the lines.

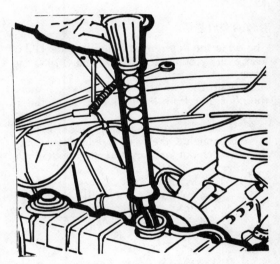

Coolant protection can be checked with a simple, float-type tester

RADIATOR COOLANT

It's a good idea to check the coolant level every time that you stop for fuel. If the engine is hot, let it cool for a few minutes and then check the level following the procedure given earlier in this chapter.

Check the freezing protection rating at least once a year, preferably just before the winter sets in. This can be done with an antifreeze tester (most service stations will have one on hand and will probably check it for you, if not, they are available at an auto parts store). Maintain a protection rating of at least −20°F (−29°C) to prevent engine damage as a result of freezing and to assure the proper engine operating temperature.

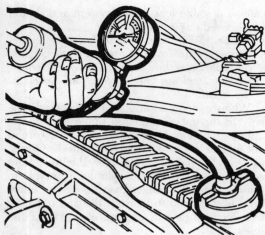

The system should be pressure tested at least once a year

REAR AXLE

The oil in the differential should be checked at least every 7,500 miles (15,000 miles, 1980 and later).

1. With the car on a level surface, remove the filler plug from the back side of the differential.

2. If the oil begins to trickle out of the hole, there is enough. Otherwise, carefully insert your finger (watch out for sharp threads) into the hole

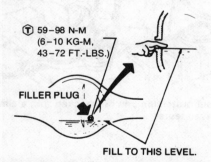

ⓣ 59–98 N-M
(6–10 KG-M,
43–72 FT.-LBS.)

FILLER PLUG

FILL TO THIS LEVEL.

Checking the fluid level in the differential on models with a solid rear axle

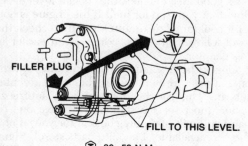

FILLER PLUG

FILL TO THIS LEVEL.

ⓣ 39–59 N-M
(4–6 KG-M, 29–43 FT. LBS.)

Checking the fluid level in the differential on models with independent rear suspension

and check that the oil is up to the bottom edge of the filler hole.

3. If not, add oil through the hole until the level is at the edge of the hole. Most gear oils come in a plastic squeeze bottle with a nozzle; making additions is simple. You can also use a common kitchen baster. Use only standard GL-5 hypoid-type gear oil—SAE 80W or SAE 80W/90.

4. Replace the plug and check for leaks.

STEERING GEAR BOX

Non-Rack and Pinion Type

Check the level of the lubricant in the steering gear every 12,000 miles (15,000 miles, 1979 and later). If the level is low, check for leakage. Any oily film is not considered a leak; solid grease must be present. Use only standard GL-4 hypoid-type gear oil—SAE 80W or SAE 80W/90. The lubricant is added and checked through the filler plug hole in the top of the steering gearbox.

🌢 : CHECK FLUID LEAKS.

🝑 : ADD FLUID.

Check the fluid level in the steering gearbox through the filler hole in the top

POWER STEERING FLUID

The power steering hydraulic fluid level is checked with a dipstick inserted into the pump reservoir cap. The level can be checked with the fluid either warm or cold; the car should be parked on a level surface. Check the fluid level every 6 months or 7,500 miles (12 months or 15,000 miles, 1980 and later), whichever comes first.

1. With the engine off, unscrew the dipstick and check the level. If the engine is warm, the level should be within the proper range on the "HOT" scale. If the engine is cold, the level should be within the proper range on the "COLD" scale (see illustrations).

2. If the level is low, add DEXRON® ATF

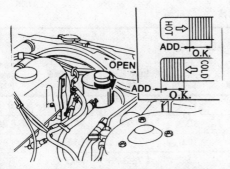

Power steering reservoir dipstick markings on all models but the 1981 and later 200SX

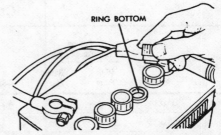

Fill each battery cell to the bottom of the split ring with distilled water

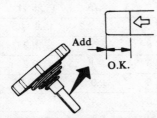

1981 and later 200SX power steering dipstick markings

Tread wear indicators will appear when the tire is worn out

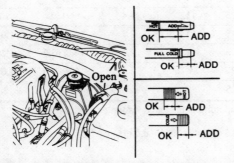

Power steering reservoir dipstick markings on the 1981 and later 810 and Maxima

until correct. Be careful not to overfill, which will cause fluid loss and seal damage.

BATTERY

Check the battery fluid level (except in Maintenance Free batteries) at least once a month, more often in hot weather or during extended periods of travel. The electrolyte level should be up to the bottom of the split-ring in each cell.

Tires

Tires should be checked weekly for proper air pressure. A chart, located either in the glove compartment or on the driver's or passenger's door, gives the recommended inflation pressures. Maximum fuel economy and tire life will result if the pressure is maintained at the highest figure given on the chart. Pressures should be checked before driving since pressure can increase as much as six pounds per square inch (psi) due to heat buildup. It is a good idea to have your own accurate pressure gauge, because not all gauges on service station air pumps can be trusted. When checking pressures, do not neglect the spare tire. Note that some spare tires require pressures considerably higher than those used in the other tires.

While you are about the task of checking air pressure, inspect the tire treads for cuts, bruises and other damage. Check the air valves to be sure that they are tight. Replace any missing valve caps.

Check the tires for uneven wear that might indicate the need for front end alignment or tire rotation. Tires should be replaced when a tread wear indicator appears as a solid band across the tread.

When buying new tires, give some thought to the following points, especially if you are considering a switch to larger tires or a different profile series:

Capacities

Year	Model	Engine Crankcase (qts)		Transmission (pts)			Drive Axle (pts)●	Fuel Tank (gals)●	Cooling System (qts)
		With Filter	Without Filter	4-Spd	5-Spd	Automatic (total capacity)			
1973	610	5.0	4.5	4.25	—	11.8	1.75/2.75	13.8/14.5	9.0
1974	610	4.5	—	4.25	—	10.9	1.75/2.2	14.5/13.5	6.88
	710	4.45	—	4.25	—	10.9	2.75	13.25	7
1975	610	4.5	4.0	4.25	—	11.8	1.75/2.75	14.5/13.7	7.25
	710	5.0	4.5	4.25	—	11.8	2.75	13.2/11.8	7.25
1976	610	4.5	4.0	4.25	—	11.8	1.75/2.2	14.5/13.75	7.25
1976–77	710	4.5	4.0	4.25 ①	—	11.8	2.75	13.25/11.8	7.25
1977–78	810	6.0	5.5	3.6	—	11.8	2.75/2.2	15.9/14.5	11
1977–79	200SX	4.5	4.0	—	3.6	11.8	2.75	15.9	7.9
1978–79	510	4.5	4.0	3.6	3.6	11.8	2.4	13.2	9.4
1979–80	810	5.9	5.25	3.7	4.25	11.8	2.0	15.9/14.5	11
1980	510	4.5	4.0	3.15	3.6	11.8	2.4	13.25	9.25
	200SX	4.4	4.1	—	4.25	11.8	2.4	14/15.9	10
1981	810	5.25	4.75	—	4.25	11.8	2.1	16.4/15.9	11.6
	510	4.6	4.1	3.1	3.6	11.8	2.4	13.25	9.25
	200SX	4.6	4.1	—	4.25	11.8	2.4	14/15.9	10
1982	810	5.0 ②	4.5 ②	—	4.25	11.8	2.1	16.4/15.9	11.6 ③
	200SX	4.5	3.9	—	4.25	11.8	2.1	14.0/15.9	10
1983–84	Maxima	5.25 ②	4.75 ②	—	4.25	14.75	2.1	16.5/16.0	11.5 ③
	200SX	⑦	⑧	—	4.25	⑥	⑤	14	④

● When two numbers are given, first number is sedan and second number is station wagon or hatchback
① 3.6 pts., 1977
② Figures are for gasoline engine. For diesel engine: w/filter—6.5 qts., w/o filter—6.0 qts.
③ Figure is for gasoline engine. For diesel engine: 11.0 qts.
④ 1983: 10 qt. w/heater; 9¼ qts. w/out heater
　 1984: 9⅛ qt.
⑤ Solid rear axle: 2⅛ pt.
　 IRS: 2¾ pt.
⑥ 1983: 11.6 pts.
　 1984: 14.75 pts.
⑦ 1983: 4.5
　 1984: 4.25
⑧ 1983: 3.9
　 1984: 3.75

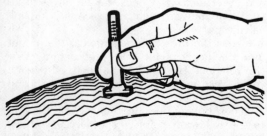

Tread depth can be checked with an inexpensive gauge

1. All four tires must be of the same construction type. This rule cannot be violated. Radial, bias, and bias-belted tires must not be mixed.

2. The wheels should be the correct width for the tire. Tire dealers have charts of tire and rim compatibility. A mistmatch will cause sloppy handling and rapid tire wear. The tread width should match the rim width (inside bead to inside bead) within an inch. For radial tires, the rim width should be 80% or less of the tire (not tread) width.

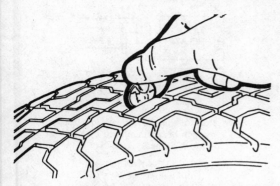

A penny works as well as anything for checking tire tread depth; when you can see the top of Lincoln's head, it's time for a new tire

3. The height (mounted diameter) of the new tires can change speedometer accuracy, engine speed at a given road speed, fuel mileage, acceleration, and ground clearance. Tire manufacturers furnish full measurement specifications.

4. The spare tire should be usable, at least for short distance and low speed operation, with the new tires.

5. There shouldn't be any body interference when loaded, on bumps, or in turns.

TIRE ROTATION

Tire rotation is recommended every 6000 miles or so, to obtain maximum tire wear. The pattern you use depends on whether or not your car has a usable spare. Radial tires should not be cross-switched (from one side of the car to the other); they last longer if their direction of rotation is not changed. Snow tires sometimes have directional arrows molded into the side of the carcass; the arrow shows the direction of rotation. They will wear very rapidly if the rotation is reversed. Studded tires will lose their studs if their rotational direction is reversed.

NOTE: *Mark the wheel position or direction of rotation on radial tires or studded snow tires before removing them.*

STORAGE

Store the tires at the proper inflation pressure if they are mounted on wheels. Keep them in a cool dry place, laid on their sides. If the tires are stored in the garage or basement, do not let them stand on a concrete floor; set them on strips of wood.

Fuel Filter—Gasoline Engines

The fuel filter on all models is a disposable plastic unit. It's located on the right inner fender. The filter should be replaced at least every 24,000 miles. A dirty filter will starve the engine and cause poor running.

REPLACEMENT

510, 610, 710 and 1977–79 200SX

1. Locate fuel filter on right-side of the engine compartment.

2. Disconnect the inlet and outlet hoses from the fuel filter. Make certain that the inlet hose (bottom) doesn't fall below the fuel tank level or the gasoline will drain out.

3. Pry the fuel filter from its clip and replace the assembly.

4. Replace the inlet and outlet lines; secure the hose clamps to prevent leaks.

5. Start the engine and check for leaks.

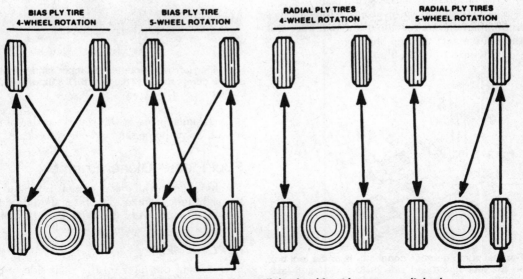

Tire rotation diagrams; note that radials should not be cross-switched

1977–79 810

These models utilize an electric fuel pump. The pressure on these models must be released before removing the fuel filter.

1. Disconnect the negative cable from the battery.

2. Disconnect the cold start valve harness connector.

NOTE: *See "Fuel Pump Testing" in Chapter 4 for illustrations.*

3. Use two jumper wires and connect one side of each to a terminal on the cold start valve connector.

NOTE: *Be sure to keep both terminals separate in order to avoid short circuiting.*

4. Connect the two remaining terminals of the jumper wires to the negative and positive battery terminals in order to release the pressure in the fuel system.

5. Unfasten the clamps securing the fuel lines to the inlet and outlet sides of the fuel filter and then remove the fuel lines.

6. Remove the fuel filter.

7. Installation is in the reverse order of removal. Start the engine and check for leaks.

810, Maxima and 200SX—1980 and Later

These models utilize an electric fuel pump. The pressure must be released on these models before removing the fuel filter.

1. Start the engine.

2. Disconnect the #2 fuel pump relay harness connector with the engine running.

NOTE: *See "Fuel Pump Testing" in Chapter 4 for illustrations.*

3. After the engine stalls, crank it two or three times.

4. Turn the ignition off and reconnect the #2 fuel pump relay harness connector.

5. Unfasten the clamps securing the fuel lines to the inlet and outlet side of the fuel filter and then disconnect the fuel lines.

6. Remove the fuel filter.

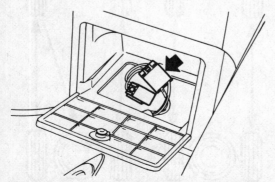

The fuel pump harness connector is in the tool box on the rear right-hand side on the 1984 and later 200SXs

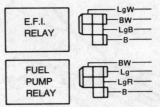

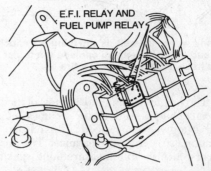

Both of the above relays are green, but can be distinguished by the color of harness.

The Maxima fuel pump relay is located in the engine compartment near the battery

Fuel filter (arrow), mounted on inner fender inside engine compartment. This is a 1978 510; others are similar

7. Installation is in the reverse order of removal. Start the engine and check for leaks.

Fuel Filter—Diesel Engines

The fuel filter on all diesel models is located on the right inner fender. The filter should be replaced at least every 30,000 miles. It should also be drained of water periodically.

REPLACEMENT

1. Locate the filter on the right side of the engine compartment.

Maintenance Intervals Chart

Intervals are for number of months or thousands of miles, whichever comes first.

NOTE: *Heavy-duty operation (trailer towing, prolonged idling, severe stop-and-start driving) should be accompanied by a 50% increase in maintenance. Cut the interval in half for these conditions.*

Maintenance	Service Interval
Air cleaner (Replace)	24,000 miles (38,400 km.) 1973–78 30,000 miles (48,000 km.) 1979 and later
Air induction valve filter (Replace)	30,000 mi. (48,000 km.)
PCV valve (Replace)	24,000 mi. (38,400 km.)
Crankcase emissions control valve (replace)	30,000 mi. (48,000 km.)

Evaporative emissions system
  Fuel and vapor lines (Check)
 	
  Carbon canister filter (Replace)
	
	12,000 mi. (19,200 km.) 1973–79
	15,000 mi. (24,000 km.) 1980 and later
	24 mo./30,000 mi. (48,000 km.)

Battery
  Fluid level (Check)
  Specific gravity (Check)
  Cables and clamps (Check)
	
	Once a month
	Once a year
	Once a year

Belt tension (Adjust)	12 mo./12,000 mi. (19,200 km.) 1973–79 12 mo./15,000 mi. (24,000 km.) 1980 and later
Hoses (Check)	15,000 mi. (24,000 km.)

Radiator coolant
  Check
  Change
	
	Weekly
	24 mo./30,000 mi. (48,000 km.)

Engine oil and filter
  Check
  Change
	
	Weekly
	6 mo./7,500 mi. (12,000 km.)—gasoline
	3,000 mi. (4,800 km.)—diesel
	5,000 mi. (8,000 km.)—200SX Turbo

Manual Transmission
  Check
 	
  Change
	
	6 mo./7,500 mi. (12,000 km.) 1973–79
	12 mo./15,000 mi. (24,000 km.) 1980 and later
	24 mo./30,000 mi. (48,000 km.)

Automatic transmission
  Check
 	
  Change
	
	6 mo./7,500 mi. (12,000 km.) 1973–79
	12 mo./15,000 mi. (24,000 km.) 1980 and later
	24 mo./30,000 mi. (48,000 km.)

Brake and clutch fluid Check	 7,500 mi. (12,000 km.) 1973–79 15,000 mi. (24,000 km.) 1980 and later

Rear axle
  Check
 	
  Change
	
	12 mo./7,500 mi. (12,000 km.) 1973–79
	12 mo./15,000 mi. (24,000 km.) 1980 and later
	24 mo./30,000 mi. (48,000 km.)

Steering gear Check	 12,000 mi. (19,200 km.) 1973–78 15,000 mi. (24,000 km.) 1979 and later
Power steering fluid Check	 6 mo./7,500 mi. (12,000 km.) 1973–79 12 mo./15,000 mi. (24,000 km.) 1980 and later
Tires Rotate	 6,000 mi. (9,600 km.)

Fuel filter
  Change (gasoline)
  Change (diesel)
	
	24,000 mi. (38,400 km.), sooner if necessary
	30,000 mi. (48,000 km.), sooner if necessary

Chassis lubrication	12 mo./15,000 mi. (24,000 km.)

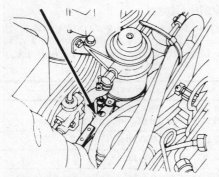

Remove the diesel fuel filter with a strap wrench (arrow)

2. Place a small pan or glass jar under the filter, unscrew the fuel filter sensor on the bottom and drain any fuel that is in the filter.

3. Using Datsun/Nissan special tool SP19320000 or a strap wrench, unscrew the filter from the mount.

4. Connect the fuel filter sensor to the new filter and then install the new filter.

NOTE: *The new fuel filter should be screwed on hand-tight. DO NOT use the wrench to tighten the filter.*

5. Bleed the fuel system as detailed in Chapter 4.

DRAINING WATER FROM THE FUEL FILTER

1. Place a small pan or glass jar under the bottom of the fuel filter.

2. Unscrew the fuel filter sensor and let the filter drain.

NOTE: *There is a round primer pump on top of the filter mount. Pumping it will quicken the draining process.*

3. The diesel fuel and the water will separate themselves in the container. The water is heavier and will therefore be on the bottom.

4. Allow the filter to drain until all the water has dripped out.

5. Replace the fuel sensor and then bleed the fuel system as detailed in Chapter 4.

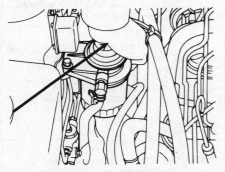

Pump the priming pump (underneath hand at tip of arrow) to speed the draining process

LUBRICATION

Oil and Fuel Recommendations

OIL

The SAE (Society of Automotive Engineers) grade number indicates the viscosity of the engine oil and thus its ability to lubricate at a given temperature. The lower the SAE grade number, the lighter the oil; the lower the viscosity, and the easier it is to crank the engine in cold weather.

Oil viscosities should be chosen from those oils recommended for the lowest anticipated temperatures during the oil change interval.

Multi-viscosity oils (10W-30, 20W-50 etc.) offer the important advantage of being adaptable to temperature extremes. They allow easy starting at low temperatures, yet they give good protection at high speeds and engine temperatures. This is a decided advantage in changeable climates or in long distance touring.

The API (American Petroleum Institute) designation indicates the classification of engine oil used under certain given operating conditions. Only oils designated for use "Service SE" should be used. Oils of the SE type perform a variety of functions inside the engine in addition to the basic function as a lubricant. Through a balanced system of metallic deter-

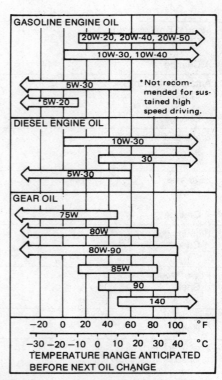

Oil viscosity chart, all except CA20E, CA18ET

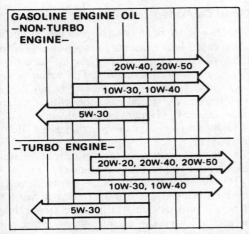

Oil viscosity chart, CA20E and CA18ET (turbo) engines, 200SX

gents and polymeric dispersants, the oil prevents the formation of high and low temperature deposits and also keeps sludge and particles of dirt in suspension. Acids, particularly sulfuric acid, as well as other byproducts of combustion, are neutralized. Both the SAE grade number and the API designation can be found on top of the oil can.

Diesel engines also require SE engine oil. *In addition, the oil must qualify for a CC rating.* The API has a number of different diesel engine ratings, including CB, CC and CD. Any of these other oils are fine as long as the designation CC appears on the can along with them. Do not use oil labeled only SE or only CC. Both designations must always appear together.

For recommended oil viscosities, refer to the chart.

Recommended Lubricants

Item	Lubricant
Engine Oil	API "SE" or "SF" API "SE/CC" or "SF/CC" (diesel)
Manual Transmission	SAE 80W GL-4 or SAE 80W/90 GL-4
Automatic Transmission	DEXRON® ATF
Rear Axle	SAE 80W GL-5 or SAE 80W/90 GL-5
Power Steering Reservoir	DEXRON® ATF
Brake and Clutch Fluid	DOT 3
Antifreeze	Ethylene Glycol
Chassis Lubrication	NLGI #2
Steering Gear	SAE 80W GL-4 or SAE 80W/90 GL-4

NOTE: *As of late 1980, the API has come out with a new designation of motor oil, SF. Oils designated for use "Service SF" are equally acceptable in your Datsun.*
CAUTION: *Non-detergent or straight mineral oils should not be used in your car.*

SYNTHETIC OIL

There are excellent synthetic and fuel-efficient oils available that, *under the right circumstances,* can help provide better fuel mileage and better engine protection. However, these advantages come at a price, which can be three or four times the price per quart of conventional motor oils.

Before pouring any synthetic oils into your car's engine, you should consider the condition of the engine and the type of driving you do. Also, check the car's warranty conditions regarding the use of synthetics.

Generally, it is best to avoid the use of synthetic oil in both brand new and older, high mileage engines. New engines require a proper break-in, and the synthetics are so "slippery" that they can prevent this; most manufacturers recommend that you wait at least 5,000 miles before switching to a synthetic oil. Conversely, older engines are looser and tend to "use" more oil; synthetics will slip past worn parts more readily than regular oil, and will be used up faster. If your car already leaks and/or "uses" oil (due to worn parts and bad seals or gaskets), it will leak and use more with a slippery synthetic inside.

Consider your type of driving. If most of your accumulated mileage is on the highway at higher, steadier speeds, a synthetic oil will reduce friction and probably help deliver better fuel mileage. Under such ideal highway conditions, the oil change interval can be extended, as long as the oil filter will operate effectively for the extended life of the oil. If the filter can't do its job for this extended period, dirt and sludge will build up in your engine's crankcase, sump, oil pump and lines, no matter what type of oil is used. If using synthetic oil in this manner, you should continue to change the oil filter at the recommended intervals.

Cars used under harder, stop-and-go, short hop circumstances should always be serviced more frequently, and for these cars synthetic oil may not be a wise investment. Because of the necessary shorter change interval needed for this type of driving, you cannot take advantage of the long recommended change interval of most synthetic oils.

Finally, most synthetic oils are not compatible with conventional oils and cannot be added to them. This means you should always carry a couple of quarts of synthetic oil with you while on a long trip, as not all service stations carry this oil.

FUEL

All Datsun gasoline-engined models covered in this book have been designed to run on regular low-lead or unleaded fuel, 1973–79, with the exception of those models built for use in California (1975 and later) which require the use of unleaded fuel. All 1980 and later models must also use only unleaded fuel. 1975 and later California cars and all 1980 and later models utilize a catalytic converter; the use of leaded fuel will plug the catalyst, rendering it inoperative, and will increase the exhaust back-pressure to the point where engine output will be severely reduced. The minimum octane requirement for all engines using unleaded fuel is 91 RON (87 CLC). All unleaded fuels sold in the U.S. are required to meet this minimum octane rating.

The use of a fuel too low in octane (a measurement of anti-knock quality) will result in spark knock. Since many factors such as altitude, terrain, air temperature and humidity affect operating efficiency, knocking may result even though the recommended fuel is being used. If persistent knocking occurs, it may be necessary to switch to a higher grade of fuel. Continuous or heavy knocking may result in engine damage.

NOTE: *Your engine's fuel requirement can change with time, mainly due to carbon buildup, which will in turn change the compression ratio. If your engine pings, knocks, or runs on, switch to a higher grade of fuel. Sometimes just changing brands will cure the problem. If it becomes necessary to retard the timing from the specifications, don't change it more than a few degrees. Retarded timing will reduce power output and fuel mileage, in addition to increasing the engine temperature.*

Datsun diesels require the use of diesel fuel. *At no time should gasoline be substituted or mixed with the diesel fuel.* Two grades of diesel fuel are manufactured, #1 and #2, although #2 grade is generally more available. Better fuel economy results from the use of #2 grade fuel. In some northern parts of the U.S. and in most parts of Canada, #1 grade fuel is available in the winter or, if not, a winterized blend of #2 grade is supplied. When the temperature falls below 20°F (−7°C), #1 grade or winterized #2 grade fuel are the only fuels that can be used. Cold temperatures cause unwinterized #2 to thicken (it actually gels), blocking the fuel lines and preventing the engine from running.

Diesel Cautions:

• Do not use heating oil in your car. While in some cases, home heating finement levels equal those of diesel fuel, times they are far below diesel engine requirements. The result of using "dirty" home heating oil will be a clogged fuel system, in which case the entire system may have to be dismantled and cleaned.

• Do not use ether or "Starting assist" fluids in your car.

• Do not use any fuel additives recommended for use in gasoline engines.

It is normal that the engine noise level is louder during the warm-up period in winter. It is also normal that whitish-blue smoke may be emitted from the exhaust after starting and during warm-up. The amount of smoke depends upon the outside temperature.

Lubricant Changes
ENGINE OIL AND FILTER

The mileage figures given in the "Maintenance Intervals" chart are the Datsun recommended intervals for oil and filter changes assuming average driving. If your Datsun is being used under dusty, polluted, of off-road conditions, change the oil and filter sooner than specified. The same thing goes for cars driven in stop-and-go traffic or only for short distances.

NOTE: *Diesel-engined and turbocharged cars require much more frequent oil change intervals than do conventional gasoline engined-cars. Follow the oil change intervals for those engines very closely.*

Always drain the oil after the engine has been running long enough to bring it to operating temperature. Hot oil will flow easier and more contaminants will be removed along with the oil than if it were drained cold. You will need a large capacity drain pan, which you can purchase at any store which sells automotive parts. Another necessity is containers for the used oil. You will find that plastic bottles, such as those used for bleach or fabric softner, make excellent storage jugs. One ecologically desirable solution to the used oil disposal problem is to find a cooperative gas station owner who will allow you to dump your used oil into his tank.

Datsun recommends changing both the oil and filter during the first oil change and the filter every other oil change thereafter. For the small price of an oil filter, it's cheap insurance to replace the filter at every oil change. One of the larger filter manufacturers points out in its advertisements that not changing the filter leaves one quart of dirty oil in the engine. This claim is true and should be kept in mind when changing your oil.

CHANGING YOUR ENGINE OIL

1. Run the engine until it reaches normal operating temperature.

2. Jack up the front of the car and support it on safety stands.

3. Slide a drain pan of at least 6 quarts capacity under the oil pan.

4. Loosen the drain plug. Turn the plug out by hand. By keeping an inward pressure on the plug as you unscrew it, oil won't escape past the threads and you can remove it without being burned by hot oil.

5. Allow the oil to drain completely and then install the drain plug. Don't overtighten the plug, or you'll be buying a new pan or a trick replacement plug for stripped threads.

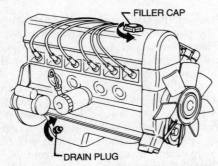

Oil filler cap and drain plug locations, six cylinder engines shown. Four cylinder engines similar. Note filter location on side of block

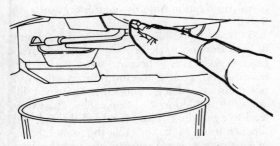

By keeping an inward pressure on the plug as you unscrew it, oil won't escape past the threads

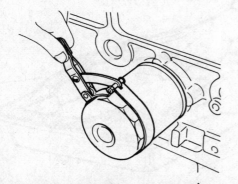

Remove the oil filter with a strap wrench

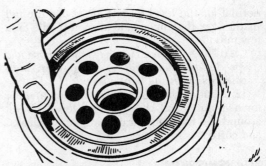

Coat the new oil filter gasket with clean oil

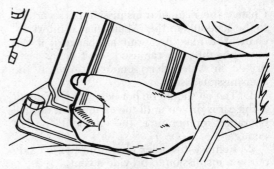

Install the new oil filter by hand

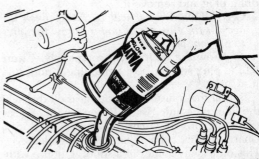

Add oil through the capped opening in the camshaft (valve) cover

6. Using a strap wrench, remove the oil filter. Keep in mind that it's holding about one quart of dirty, hot oil.

7. Empty the old filter into the drain pan and dispose of the filter.

8. Using a clean rag, wipe off the filter adapter on the engine block. Be sure that the rag doesn't leave any lint which could clog an oil passage.

9. Coat the rubber gasket on the filter with fresh oil. Spin it onto the engine *by hand;* when the gasket touches the adapter surface give it another ½–¾ turn. No more, or you'll squash the gasket and it will leak.

10. Refill the engine with the correct amount of fresh oil. See the "Capacities" chart.

11. Check the oil level on the dipstick. It is

normal for the level to be a bit above the full mark. Start the engine and allow it to idle for a few minutes.

CAUTION: *Do not run the engine above idle speed until it has built up oil pressure, indicated when the oil light goes out.*

12. Shut off the engine, allow the oil to drain for a minute, and check the oil level. Check around the filter and drain plug for any leaks, and correct as necessary.

TRANSMISSION

Manual

Change the manual transmission oil according to the schedule in the "Maintenance Intervals" chart. You may also want to change it if you have bought your car used, or if it has been driven in water deep enough to reach the transmission case.

1. The oil should be hot before it is drained. If the car is driven until the engine is at normal operating temperature, the oil should be hot enough.

2. Remove the filler plug from the left side of the transmission to provide a vent.

3. The drain plug is located on the bottom of the transmission case. Place a pan under the drain plug and remove it.

CAUTION: *The oil will be HOT. Push up against the threads as you unscrew the plug to prevent leakage.*

4. Allow the oil to drain completely. Clean off the plug and replace, tightening it until it is just snug.

5. Fill the transmission with gear oil through the filler plug hole. Use API service GL-4 gear oil of the proper viscosity (see the "Viscosity Chart" in this chapter for recommendations). This oil usually comes in a squeeze bottle with a long nozzle. If yours isn't, you can use a rubber squeeze bulb of the type used for kitchen basting to squirt the stuff in. Refer to the "Capacities" chart for the amount of oil needed.

6. The oil level should come right up to the edge of the filler hole. You can stick your finger in to verify this. Watch out for sharp threads.

7. Replace the filler plug. Dispose of the old oil in the same manner as old engine oil. Take a drive in the car, stop, and check for leaks.

Automatic

The fluid should be changed according to the schedule in the "Maintenance Intervals" chart. If the car is normally used in severe service, such as start-and-stop driving, trailer towing, or the like, the interval should be halved. The fluid must be hot before it is drained; a 20 minute drive should accomplish this.

1. There is no drain plug; the fluid pan must

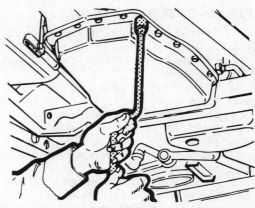

Remove the pan to drain the automatic transmission

be removed. Partially remove the pan screws until the pan can be pulled down at one corner. Place a container under the transmission, lower a rear corner of the pan, and allow the fluid to drain.

2. After draining, remove the pan screws completely, and remove the pan and gasket.

3. Clean the pan thoroughly and allow it to air dry. If you wipe it out with a rag you risk leaving bits of lint in the pan which will clog the tiny hydraulic passages in the transmission.

4. Install the pan using a new gasket. If you decide to use sealer on the gasket apply it only in a very thin bead running to the outside of the pan screw holes. Tighten the pan screws evenly in rotation from the center outwards, to 3–5 ft. lbs.

5. It is a good idea to measure the amount of fluid drained to determine how much fresh fluid to add. This is because some part of the transmission, such as the torque converter, will not drain completely, and using the dry refill amount specified in the "Capacities" chart may lead to overfilling. Fluid is added through the dipstick tube. Make sure that the funnel, hose, or whatever you are using is completely clean

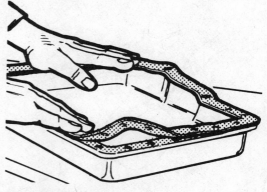

Install a new gasket

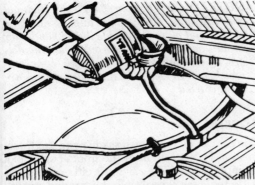

Add fluid through the transmission dipstick tube

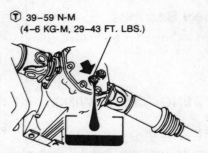

ⓣ 39–59 N-M
(4–6 KG-M, 29–43 FT. LBS.)

Draining the differential fluid on models with independent rear suspension

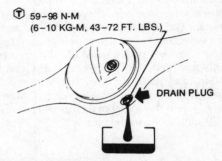

ⓣ 59–98 N-M
(6–10 KG-M, 43–72 FT. LBS.)

DRAIN PLUG

Draining the differential fluid on models with a solid rear axle

and dry before pouring transmission fluid through it. Use DEXRON® automatic transmission fluid.

6. Replace the dipstick after filling. Start the engine and allow it to idle. Do NOT race the engine.

7. After the engine has idled for a few minutes, shift the transmission slowly through the gears, then return the lever to Park. With the engine idling, check the fluid level on the dipstick. It should be between the "H" and "L" marks. If below "L", add sufficient fluid to raise the level to between the marks.

8. Drive the car until the transmission is at operating temperature. The fluid should be at the "H" mark. If not, add sufficient fluid until this is the case. Be careful not to overfill; overfilling causes slippage, overheating, and seal damage.

NOTE: *If the drained fluid is discolored (brown or black), thick, or smells burnt, serious transmission problems due to overheating should be suspected. Your car's transmission should be inspected by a transmission specialist to determine the cause.*

REAR AXLE

The axle lubricant should be changed according to the schedule in the "Maintenance Intervals" chart; you may also want to change it if you have bought your car used, or if it has been driven in water deep enough to reach the axle.

1. Park the car on a level surface. Place a pan of at least two quarts capacity underneath the drain plug. The drain plug is located on the center rear of the differential carrier, just below the filler plug on some models, on others it can be found at the bottom of the carrier. Remove the drain plug.

2. Allow the lubricant to drain completely.

3. Install the drain plug. Tighten it so that it will not leak, but do not overtighten. If you have a torque wrench, recommended torque is 29–43 ft. lbs.

4. Refill the differential housing with API GL-5 gear oil of the proper viscosity. The correct level is to the edge of the filler hole.

5. Install the filler plug. Tighten to 29–43 ft. lbs.

Chassis Greasing

Lubricate the accelerator linkage every 6,000 miles (7,500 miles, 1980 and later). Lubricate the foot pedal bushings every 12,000 miles (15,000 miles, 1980 and later).

Every 30,000 miles or 24 months, whichever comes first:

1. Lubricate the steering and suspension ball joints and the rear axle shaft joints as follows: Remove the grease plug and install a grease fitting. Install the grease gun connector and *slowly* feed grease into the joint to avoid forcing it out of the join except at the grease bleeder. Lubricate the joint with multipurpose grease until new grease emerges at the bleeder point.

2. Apply multipurpose grease to the ball splines of the driveshafts and repack the universal joints on the driveshaft and axle shafts. This will require major disassembly operations—see Chapter 7.

Body Lubrication

Lubricate all locks and hinges with multipurpose grease every 6,000 miles (7,500 miles, 1980 and later).

Wheel Bearings

Clean and repack wheel bearings every 30,000 miles. See Chapter 9.

PUSHING AND TOWING

Push Starting

This is the last recommended method of starting a car and should be used only in an extreme case. Chances of body damage are high, so be sure that the pushcar's bumper does not override your bumper. If your Datsun has an automatic transmission it cannot be push started. In an emergency, you can start a manual transmission car by pushing. With the bumpers evenly matched, get in your car, switch on the ignition, and place the gearshift in Second or Third gear—do not engage the clutch. Start off slowly. When the speed of the car reaches about 15–20 mph, release the clutch.

NOTE: *Although they may have manual transmissions, 1976 and later California models and all models made in 1980 and later should never be push started. These models are all equipped with a catalytic converter which will be severely damaged if they are push started.*

Towing

The car can be flat-towed safely (with the transmission in Neutral) from the front at speeds of 20 mph or less. The car must either be towed with the rear wheels off the ground or the driveshaft disconnected if: towing speeds are to be over 20 mph, or towing distance is over 50 miles, or transmission or rear axle problems exist.

When towing the car on its front wheels, the steering wheel must be secured in a straight-ahead position and the steering column unlocked. Tire-to-ground clearance should not exceed 6 in. during towing.

SEDAN

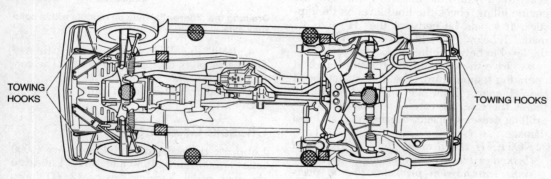

TOWING HOOKS

TOWING HOOKS

WAGON

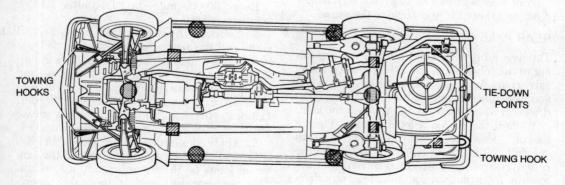

TOWING HOOKS

TIE-DOWN POINTS

TOWING HOOK

⬤ : JACK-UP POINT FOR PANTOGRAPH JACK

⬤ : JACK-UP POINT FOR GARAGE JACK

▨ : SUPPORTABLE POINT FOR SAFETY STAND

810 and Maxima jacking points

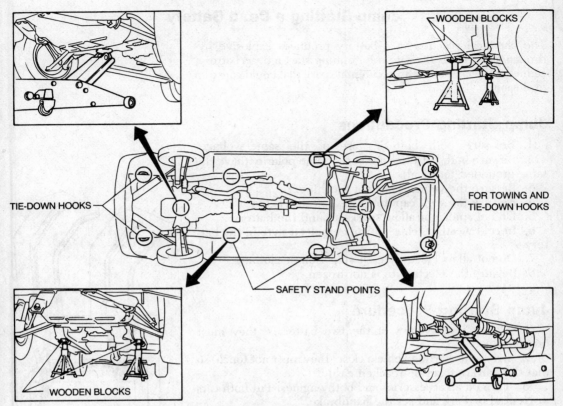

200SX jacking points, 1984 independent rear suspension (IRS) model shown

JACKING

Never use the tire changing jack (the little jack supplied with the car) for anything other than changing a flat out on the road. These jacks are simply not safe enough for any type of vehicle service except tire changing!

The service operations in this book often require that one end or the other, or both, of the car be raised and safely supported. For this reason a hydraulic floor jack of at least 1½ ton capacity is as necessary as a spark plug socket to you, the do-it-yourself owner/mechanic. The cost of these jacks (invest in a good quality unit) is actually quite reasonable considering how they pay for themselves again and again over the years.

Along with a hydraulic floor jack should be at least two sturdy jackstands. These are a necessity if you intend to work underneath the car. Never work under the car when it is only supported by a jack!

Drive-on ramps are an alternative method of raising the front end of the car. They are commercially available or can be fabricated from heavy lumber or steel. Be sure to always block the wheels when using ramps.

CAUTION: *NEVER use concrete cinder blocks to support the car. They are prone to break if the load is not evenly distributed—something you should never trust when you are underneath the car.*

HOW TO BUY A USED CAR

Many people believe that a two or three year old used car is a better buy than a new car. This may be true; the new car suffers the heaviest depreciation in the first two years, but is not old enough to present a lot of costly repair problems. Whatever the age of the used car you might want to buy, this section and a little patience will help you select one that should be safe and dependable.

TIPS

1. First decide what model you want, and how much you want to spend.

2. Check the used car lots and your local newspaper ads. Privately owned cars are usually less expensive, however you will not get a warranty that, in most cases, comes with a used car purchased from a lot.

Jump Starting a Dead Battery

The chemical reaction in a battery produces explosive hydrogen gas. This is the safe way to jump start a dead battery, reducing the chances of an accidental spark that could cause an explosion.

Jump Starting Precautions

1. Be sure both batteries are of the same voltage.
2. Be sure both batteries are of the same polarity (have the same grounded terminal).
3. Be sure the vehicles are not touching.
4. Be sure the vent cap holes are not obstructed.
5. Do not smoke or allow sparks around the battery.
6. In cold weather, check for frozen electrolyte in the battery.
7. Do not allow electrolyte on your skin or clothing.
8. Be sure the electrolyte is not frozen.

Jump Starting Procedure

1. Determine voltages of the two batteries; they must be the same.
2. Bring the starting vehicle close (they must not touch) so that the batteries can be reached easily.
3. Turn off all accessories and both engines. Put both cars in Neutral or Park and set the handbrake.
4. Cover the cell caps with a rag—do not cover terminals.
5. If the terminals on the run-down battery are heavily corroded, clean them.
6. Identify the positive and negative posts on both batteries and connect the cables in the order shown.
7. Start the engine of the starting vehicle and run it at fast idle. Try to start the car with the dead battery. Crank it for no more than 10 seconds at a time and let it cool off for 20 seconds in between tries.
8. If it doesn't start in 3 tries, there is something else wrong.
9. Disconnect the cables in the reverse order.
10. Replace the cell covers and dispose of the rags.

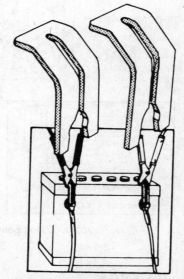

Side terminal batteries occasionally pose a problem when connecting jumper cables. There frequently isn't enough room to clamp the cables without touching sheet metal. Side terminal adaptors are available to alleviate this problem and should be removed after use.

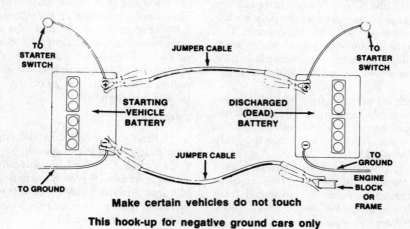

TO STARTER SWITCH

JUMPER CABLE

TO STARTER SWITCH

STARTING VEHICLE BATTERY

DISCHARGED (DEAD) BATTERY

JUMPER CABLE

TO GROUND

TO GROUND

ENGINE BLOCK OR FRAME

Make certain vehicles do not touch

This hook-up for negative ground cars only

3. Never shop at night. The glare of the lights make it easy to miss faults on the body caused by accident or rust repair.

4. Try to get the name and phone number of the previous owner. Contact him/her and ask about the car. If the owner of the lot refuses this information, look for a car somewhere else.

A private seller can tell you about the car and maintenance. Remember, however, there's no law requiring honesty from private citizens selling used cars. There is a law that forbids the tampering with or turning back the odometer mileage. This includes both the private citizen and the lot owner. The law also requires that the seller or anyone transferring ownership of the car must provide the buyer with a signed statement indicating the mileage on the odometer at the time of transfer.

5. Write down the year, model and serial number before you buy any used car. Then dial 1-800-424-9393, the toll free number of the National Highway Traffic Safety Administration, and ask if the car has ever been included on any manufacturer's recall list. If so, make sure the needed repairs were made.

6. Use the "Used Car Checklist" in this section and check all the items on the used car you are considering. Some items are more important than others. You know how much money you can afford for repairs, and, depending on the price of the car, may consider doing any needed work yourself. Beware, however, of trouble in areas that will affect operation, safety or emission. Problems in the "Used Car Checklist" break down as follows:

1–8: Two or more problems in these areas indicate a lack of maintenance. You should beware.

9–13: Indicates a lack of proper care, however, these can usually be corrected with a tune-up or relatively simple parts replacement.

14–17: Problems in the engine or transmission can be very expensive. Walk away from any car with problems in both of these areas.

7. If you are satisfied with the apparent condition of the car, take it to an independent diagnostic center or mechanic for a complete check. If you have a state inspection program, have it inspected immediately before purchase, or specify on the bill of sale that the sale is conditional on passing state inspection.

8. Road test the car—refer to the "Road Test Checklist" in this section. If your original evaluation and the road test agree—the rest is up to you.

USED CAR CHECKLIST

NOTE: *The numbers on the illustrations refer to the numbers on this checklist.*

1. *Mileage:* Average mileage is about 12,000 miles per year. More than average mileage may indicate hard usage. 1975 and later catalytic converter equipped models may need converter service at 50,000 miles.

2. *Paint:* Check around the tailpipe, molding and windows for overspray indicating that the car has been repainted.

3. *Rust:* Check fenders, doors, rocker panels, window moldings, wheelwells, floorboards, under floormats, and in the trunk for signs of rust. Any rust at all will be a problem. There is no way to check the spread of rust, except to replace the part or panel.

4. *Body appearance:* Check the moldings, bumpers, grille, vinyl roof, glass, doors, trunk lid and body panels for general overall condition. Check for misalignment, loose holdown clips, ripples, scratches in glass, rips or patches in the top. Mismatched paint, welding in the trunk, severe misalignment of body panels or ripples may indicate crash work.

5. *Leaks:* Get down and look under the car. There are no normal "leaks", other than water from the air conditioning condenser.

6. *Tires:* Check the tire air pressure. A common trick is to pump the tire pressure up to make the car roll easier. Check the tread wear, open the trunk and check the spare too. Uneven wear is a clue that the front end needs alignment. See the troubleshooting chapter for clues to the causes of tire wear.

7. *Shock absorbers:* Check the shock absrobers by forcing downward sharply on each corner of the car. Good shocks will not allow the car to bounce more than twice after you let go.

8. *Interior:* Check the entire interior. You're looking for an interior condition that agrees with the overall condition of the car. Reasonable wear is expected, but be suspicious of new seatcovers on sagging seats, new pedal pads, and worn armrests. These indicate an attempt to cover up hard use. Pull back the carpets and look for evidence of water leaks or flooding. Look for missing hardware, door handles, control knobs etc. Check lights and signal operations. Make sure all accessories (air conditioner, heater, radio etc.) work. Check windshield wiper operation.

9. *Belts and Hoses:* Open the hood and check all belts and hoses for wear, cracks or weak spots.

10. *Battery:* Low electrolyte level, corroded terminals and/or cracked case indicate a lack of maintenance.

11. *Radiator:* Look for corrosion or rust in the coolant indicating a lack of maintenance.

12. *Air filter:* A dirty air filter usually means a lack of maintenance.

13. *Ignition Wires:* Check the ignition wires for cracks, burned spots, or wear. Worn wires will have to be replaced.

14. *Oil level:* If the oil level is low, chances are the engine uses oil or leaks. Beware of water in the oil (cracked block), excessively thick oil (used to quiet a noisy engine), or thin, dirty oil with a distinct gasoline smell (internal engine problems).

15. *Automatic Transmission:* Pull the transmission dipstick out when the engine is running. The level should read "Full", and the fluid should be clear or bright red. Dark brown or black fluid that has distinct burnt odor, signals a transmission in need of repair or overhaul.

16. *Exhaust:* Check the color of the exhaust smoke. Blue smoke indicates, among other problems, worn rings; black smoke can indicate burnt valves or carburetor problems. Check the exhaust system for leaks; it can be expensive to replace.

17. *Spark Plugs:* Remove one of the spark plugs (the most accessible will do). An engine in good condition will show plugs with a light tain or gray deposit on the firing tip. See the color Tune-Up tips section for spark plug conditions.

ROAD TEST CHECK LIST

1. *Engine Performance:* The car should be peppy whether cold or warm, with adequate power and good pickup. It should respond smoothly through the gears.

2. *Brakes:* They should provide quick, firm stops with no noise, pulling or brake fade.

3. *Steering:* Sure control with no binding, harshness, or looseness and no shimmy in the wheel should be expected. Noise or vibration from the steering wheel when turning the car means trouble.

4. *Clutch (Manual Transmission):* Clutch action should give quick, smooth response with easy shifting. The clutch pedal should have about 1–1½ inches of free-play before it disengages the clutch. Start the engine, set the parking brake, put the transmission in first gear and slowly release the clutch pedal. The engine should begin to stall when the pedal is one-half to three-quarters of the way up.

5. *Automatic Transmission:* The transmission should shift rapidly and smoothly, with no noise, hesitation, or slipping.

6. *Differential:* No noise or thumps should be present. Differentials have no "normal" leaks.

7. *Driveshaft, Universal Joints:* Vibration and noise could mean driveshaft problems. Clicking at low speed or coast conditions means worn U-joints.

8. *Suspension:* Try hitting bumps at different speeds. A car that bounces has weak shock absorbers. Clunks mean worn bushings or ball joints.

9. *Frame:* Wet the tires and drive in a straight line. Tracks should show two straight lines, not four. Four tire tracks indicate a frame bent by collision damage. If the tires can't be wet for this purpose, have a friend drive along behind you and see if the car appears to be traveling in a straight line.

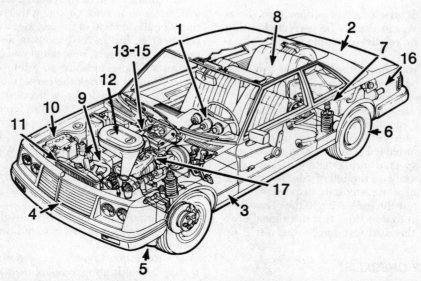

You should check these points when buying a used car. The "Used Car Checklist" gives an explanation of the numbered items

TUNE-UP PROCEDURES

In order to extract the full measure of performance and economy from your engine it is essential that it is properly tuned at regular intervals. A regular tune-up will keep your Datsun's engine running smoothly and will prevent the annoying breakdowns and poor performance associated with an untuned engine.

NOTE: *All 1973–77 models use the conventional breaker point ignition system except for 1975–77 California cars and 1977 810's which use an electronic system. All models made in 1978 and later (except diesels) utilize this system also.*

A complete tune-up should be performed at least every 15,000 miles (12,000 miles for early models) or twelve months, whichever comes first.

NOTE: *1980 and later models have increased their interval to 30,000 miles.*

This interval should be halved if the car is operated under severe conditions such as trailer towing, prolonged idling, start-and-stop driving, or if starting or running problems are noticed. It is assumed that the routine maintenance described in Chapter 1 has been kept up, as this will have a decided effect on the results of a tune-up. All of the applicable steps of a tune-up should be followed in order, as the result is a cumulative one.

If the specifications on the underhood tune-up sticker in the engine compartment of your car disagree with the "Tune-Up Specifications" chart in this chapter, the figures on the sticker must be used. The sticker often reflects changes made during the production run.

Other than the periodic changing of oil, air and fuel filters as outlined in Chapter 1, diesel engines do not require a tune-up *per se*, as there is no ignition system.

Spark Plugs—Gasoline Engines

A typical spark plug consiss of a metal shell surrounding a ceramic insulator. A metal electrode extends downward through the center of the insulator and protrudes a small distance. Located at the end of the plug and attached to the side of the outer metal shell is the side electrode. This side electrode bends in at 90° so its tip is even with, parallel to, the tip of the center electrode. This distance between these two electrodes (measured in thousandths of an inch) is called spark plug gap. The spark plug in no way produces a spark but merely provides a gap across which the current can arc. The coil produces 20,000–25,000 V (transistorized ignition produces considerably more voltage than the standard type, approximately 50,000 volts), which travels to the distributor where it is distributed through the spark plug wires to the plugs. The current passes along the center electrode and jumps the gap to the side electrode and, in so doing, ignites the air/fuel mixture in the combustion chamber. All plugs used in Datsuns have a resistor built into the center electrode to reduce interference to any nearby radio and television receivers. The resistor also cuts down on erosion of plug electrodes caused by excessively long sparking. Resistor spark plug wiring is orignal equipment on all Datsuns.

Spark plug life and efficiency depend upon the condition of the engine and the temperatures to which the plug is exposed. Combustion chamber temperatures are affected by many factors such as compression ratio of the engine, fuel/air mixtures, exhaust emission equipment, and the type of driving you do. Spark plugs are designed and classified by number according to the heat range at which they will operate most efficiently. The amount of heat that the plug absorbs is determined by the length of the

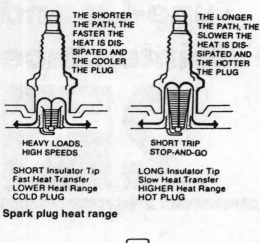

THE SHORTER THE PATH, THE FASTER THE HEAT IS DIS-SIPATED AND THE COOLER THE PLUG

THE LONGER THE PATH, THE SLOWER THE HEAT IS DIS-SIPATED AND THE HOTTER THE PLUG

HEAVY LOADS, HIGH SPEEDS

SHORT TRIP STOP-AND-GO

SHORT Insulator Tip
Fast Heat Transfer
LOWER Heat Range
COLD PLUG

LONG Insulator Tip
Slow Heat Transfer
HIGHER Heat Range
HOT PLUG

Spark plug heat range

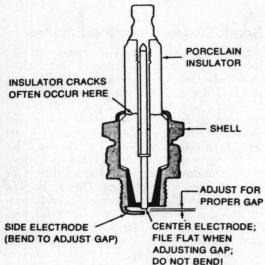

PORCELAIN INSULATOR

INSULATOR CRACKS OFTEN OCCUR HERE

SHELL

ADJUST FOR PROPER GAP

SIDE ELECTRODE (BEND TO ADJUST GAP)

CENTER ELECTRODE; FILE FLAT WHEN ADJUSTING GAP; DO NOT BEND!

Cross section of a spark plug

lower insulator. The longer the insulator (it extends farther into the engine), the hotter the plug will operate. A plug that has a short path for heat tranfer and remains too cool will quickly accumulate deposits of oil and carbon since it is not hot enough to burn them off. This leads to plug fouling and consequently to misfiring. A plug that has a long path for heat transfer will have no deposits but, due to the excessive heat, the electrodes will burn away quickly and, in some instances, pre-ignition may result. Preignition takes place when plug tips get so hot that they glow sufficiently to ignite the fuel/air mixture before the spark does. This early ignition will usually cause a pinging (sounding much like castanets) during low speeds and heavy loads. In severe cases, the heat may become enough to start the fuel/air mixture burning throughout the combustion chamber rather than just to the front of the plug as in normal operation. At this time, the piston is rising in the cylinder making

its compression stroke. The buring mass is compressed and an explosion results producing tremendous pressure. Something has to give, and it does—pistons are often damaged. Obviously, this detonation (explosion) is a destructive condition that can be avoided by installing a spark plug designed and specified for your particular engine.

A set of spark plugs usually requires replacement after 10,000 to 12,000 miles depending on the type of driving (this interval has been increased to 30,000 miles for all 1980 and later models). The electrode on a new spark plug has a sharp edge but, with use, this edge becomes rounded by erosion causing the plug gap to increase. In normal operation, plug gap increases about 0.001 in. in every 1,000–2,000 miles. As the gap increases, the plug's voltage requirement also increases. It requires a greater voltage to jump the wider gap and about two to three times as much voltage to fire a plug at high speeds and acceleration than at idle.

The higher voltage produced by the ignition coil is one of the primary reasons for the prolonged replacement interval for spark plugs in later cars. A consistently hotter spark prevents the fouling of plugs for much longer than could normally be expected; this spark is also able to jump across a larger gap more efficiently than a spark from a conventional system.

Worn plugs become obvious during acceleration. Voltage requirement is greatest during acceleration and a plug with an enlarged gap may require more voltage than the coil is able to produce. As a result, the engine misses and sputters until acceleration is reduced. Reducing acceleration reduces the plug's voltage requirement and the engine runs smoother. Slow, city driving is hard on plugs. The long periods of idle experienced in traffic creates an overly rich gas mixture. The engine isn't running fast enough to completely burn the gas and, consequently, the plugs are fouled with gas deposits and engine idle becomes rough. In many cases, driving under right conditions can effectively clean these fouled plugs.

NOTE: *There are several reasons why a spark plug will foul and you can usually learn which is at fault by just looking at the plug. A few of the most common reasons for plug fouling, and a description of the fouled plug's appearance, can be found in the color insert of this book.*

Accelerate your car to the speed where the engine begins to miss and then slow down to the point where the engine smooths out. Run at this speed for a few minutes and then accelerate again to the point of engine miss. With each repetition this engine miss should occur at increasingly higher speeds and then disappear altogether. Do not attempt to shortcut this procedure by hard acceleration. This approach will compound problems by fusing deposits into a hard permanent glaze. Dirty, fouled plugs may be cleaned by sandblasting. Many shops have a spark plug sandblaster. After sandblasting, the electrode should be filed to a sharp, square shape and then gapped to specifications. Gapping a plug too close will produce rough idle while gapping it too wide will increase its voltage requirement and cause missing at high speeds and during acceleration.

The type of driving you do may require a change in spark plug heat range. If the majority of your driving is done in the city and rarely at high speeds, plug fouling may necessitate changing to a plug with a heat range number one lower than that specified by the car manufacturer. For example, a 1980 810 requires a BP6ES-11 plug. Frequent city driving may foul these plugs making engine operation rough. A BP5ES-11 is the nest hottest plug and its insulator is longer than the BP6ES-11 so that it can absorb and retain more heat tan the shorter BP6ES-11. This hotter BP5ES-11 burns off deposits even at low city speeds but would be too hot for prolonged turnpike driving. Using this plug at high speeds would create dangerous pre-ignition. On the other hand, if the aforementioned 810 were used almost exclusively for long distance high speed driving, the specified BP6ES-11 might be too hot resulting in rapid electrode wear and dangerous pre-ignition. In this case, it might be wise to change to a colder BP7ES-11. If the car is used for abnormal driving (as in the examples above), or the engine has been modified for higher performance; then a change to a plug of a different heat range may be necessary. For a modified car it is always wise to go to a colder plug as a protection against pre-ignition. It will require more frequent plug cleaning, but destructive detonation during acceleration will be avoided.

REMOVAL

NOTE: *Some 1980 Calif. and all 1981 and later 510 and 200SX models equipped with the Z20, Z22, CA20E and CA18ET engine have two plugs for each cylinder. All eight plugs should be replaced at every tune-up for maximum fuel efficiency and power.*

When you're removing spark plugs, you should work on one at a time. Don't start by removing the plug wires all at once because unless you number them, they're going to get mixed up. On some models though, it will be more convenient for you to remove all the wires before you start to work on the plugs. If this is necessary, take a minute before you begin and number the wires with tape before you take them

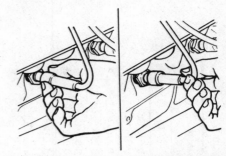

Twist and pull on the rubber boot to remove the spark plug wires; never pull on the wire itself

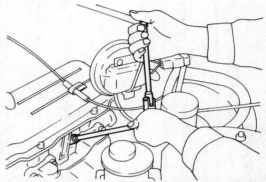

Plugs are removed using the proper combination of socket wrench, universals, and extensions

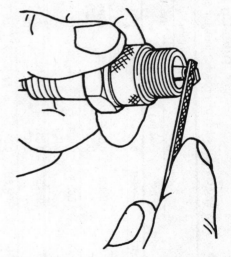

Plugs that are in good condition can be filed and re-used

off. The time you spend here will pay off later on.

1. Twist the spark plug boot and remove the boot from the plug. You may also use a plug wire removal tool designed especially for this purpose. *Do not pull on the wire itself.* When the wire has been removed, take a wire brush

Tune-Up Specifications

When analyzing compression test results, look for uniformity among cylinders, rather than specific pressures.

Year	Model	Spark Plug Type	Spark Plug Gap (in.)	Distributor Point Dwell (deg)	Distributor Point Gap (in.)	Ignition Timing (deg)● MT	Ignition Timing (deg)● AT	Fuel Pump Pressure (psi)	Idle Speed (rpm) MT	Idle Speed (rpm) AT▲	Valve Clearance (in.) In	Valve Clearance (in.) Ex	Percentage of CO at Idle
1973	610	BP-6ES	0.028–0.031	49–55	0.018–0.022	5B	5B	2.6–3.4	800	650	0.008 COLD 0.010 HOT	0.010 COLD 0.012 HOT	1.5
1974	610	B6ES	0.028–0.031	49–55	0.018–0.022	12B	12B	3.0–3.8	750	650	0.008 COLD 0.010 HOT	0.010 COLD 0.012 HOT	3.0
	710	B6ES	0.028–0.031	49–55	0.018–0.022	12B	12B	2.6–3.4	800	650	0.008 COLD 0.010 HOT	0.010 COLD 0.012 HOT	1.5
1975	610	BP-6ES	0.031–0.035	49–55①	0.018–②0.022	12B	12B	3.8	750	650	0.010 HOT	0.012 HOT	2.0
	710	BP-6ES	0.031–0.035	49–55①	0.018–②0.022	12B	12B	3.8	750	650	0.010 HOT	0.012 HOT	2.0
1976	610	BP-6ES	0.031–③0.035	49–55①	0.018–②0.022	12B	12B	3.8	750	650	0.008 COLD 0.010 HOT	0.010 COLD 0.012 HOT	2.0
	710	BP-6ES	0.031–③0.035	49–55①	0.018–②0.022	12B	12B	3.8	750	650	0.008 COLD 0.010 HOT	0.010 COLD 0.012 HOT	2.0
1977	710	BP-6ES	0.039–④0.043	49–55①	0.018–②0.022	12B	12B	3.8	600⑤	600⑥	0.008 COLD 0.010 HOT	0.010 COLD 0.012 HOT	1.0⑦
	810	BP-6ES	0.039–0.043	ELECTRONIC	②	10B	10B	36 EFI	700	650	0.008 COLD 0.010 HOT	0.010 COLD 0.012 HOT	1.0⑧
	200SX	BP-6ES	0.039–④0.043	49–55①	0.018–②0.022	9B⑨	12B	3.8	600⑤	600⑥	0.008 COLD 0.010 HOT	0.010 COLD 0.012 HOT	1.0⑦
1978	510	BP-6ES	0.039–④0.043	ELECTRONIC	②	12B	12B	3.8	600	600	0.010 HOT	0.012 HOT	1.0
	810	B6ES	0.039–0.043	ELECTRONIC	②	8B⑩	8B⑩	36 EFI	700	650	0.010 HOT	0.012 HOT	1.0⑧
1979	200SX	BP-6ES	0.039–④0.043	ELECTRONIC	②	12B	12B	3.8	600	600	0.010 HOT	0.012 HOT	1.0
	510	BP-6ES	0.039–④0.043	ELECTRONIC	②	11B⑨	12B	3.8	600	600	0.010 HOT	0.012 HOT	1.0

Year	Model	Spark Plug	Gap (in.)	Ignition	Dwell	Timing	Timing	Fuel Pump	Idle	Idle	Intake	Exhaust	CO%
	810	B6ES	0.039–0.043	ELECTRONIC	②	10B	10B	37 EFI	700	650	0.010 HOT	0.012 HOT	2.0 ⑧
	200SX	BP-6ES	0.039–④ 0.043	ELECTRONIC	②	9B⑨	12B	3.8	600	600	0.010 HOT	0.012 HOT	1.0
1980	510 (L20B)	BPR6ES	0.031–0.035	ELECTRONIC	②	12B	12B	3.8	600	600	0.010 HOT	0.012 HOT	1.0
	510 (Z20S)	BP-6ES	0.031–0.035	ELECTRONIC	②	8B⑪	8B⑪	3.8	600	600	0.012 HOT	0.012 HOT	1.5⑫
	810	BP6ES-11	0.039–0.043	ELECTRONIC	②	10B	10B	37 EFI	700	650	0.010 HOT	0.012 HOT	1.0⑫
	200SX	BP-6ES	0.031–0.035	ELECTRONIC	②	8B⑪	8B⑪	37 EFI	700	700	0.012 HOT	0.012 HOT	1.3⑫
1981	510	BP-6ES⑬	0.031–0.035	ELECTRONIC	②	6B	6B	3.8	600	600	0.012 HOT	0.012 HOT	⑭
	810	BP6ES-11	0.039–0.043	ELECTRONIC	②	10B	10B	37 EFI	700	650	0.010 HOT	0.012 HOT	⑭
	200SX	BP-6ES⑬	0.031–0.035	ELECTRONIC	②	6B⑮	6B⑮	37 EFI	750	700	0.012 HOT	0.012 HOT	⑯
1982–84	810, Maxima	BPR-6ES-11	0.039–0.043	ELECTRONIC	②	8B	8B	37 EFI	700	650	0.010 HOT	0.012 HOT	⑭
	200SX	⑰	0.031–0.035⑳	ELECTRONIC	②	8B⑲	8B⑲	37 EFI	750	700⑱	0.012 HOT	0.012 HOT	⑭

● At idle
▲ In drive
① California cars are equipped with electronic ignition—dwell is pre-set and non-adjustable
② Electronic ignition—Air gap: 0.008–0.016 in. (1975–78) 0.012–0.020 in. (1979 and later)
③ All models with electronic ignition—0.039–0.043 in.
④ 0.031–0.035 in.—Canada
⑤ 750—Canada
⑥ 650—Canada
⑦ 2%—Canada
⑧ 0.5%—California
⑨ 12B—California and Canada
⑩ 10B—California

⑪ 6B—California
⑫ Idle mixture screw is pre-set and nonadjustable on California cars
⑬ BPR6ES—Canada
⑭ Idle mixture screw is pre-set and nonadjustable
⑮ 8B—Canada
⑯ U.S.A.—idle mixture screw is pre-set and nonadjustable. Canada—1.3%
⑰ 1982–83: Intake side BPR-6ES; exhaust side BPR-5ES
    1984 and later: Intake side BCPR6ES-11
        Exhaust side BCPR5ES-11
⑱ 630 rpm high altitudes
⑲ CA20E (1984 and later): 0° BTDC w/vacuum hose disconnected
    CA18ET (1984 and later): 15° BTDC
⑳ 0.039–0.043 in.—1984 and later

Diesel Tune-Up Specifications

Year Model	Engine Displacement cu. in. (cc)	Warm Valve Clearance (in.)		Intake Valve Opens (deg)	Injection Pump Setting (deg)	Injection Nozzle Pressure (psi)		Idle Speed (rpm)	Compression Pressure (psi)
		In	Ex			New	Used		
1981–83 Diesel	170 (2,793)	0.010	0.012	NA	align marks	1,920– 2,033	1,778– 1,920	650	455 @ 200 rpm

and clean the area around the plug. Make sure that all the grime is removed so that none will enter the cylinder after the plug has been removed.

2. Remove the plug using the proper size socket, extensions, and universals as necessary. The Datsun cylinder head is aluminum, which is easily stripped. Remove plugs ONLY when the engine is cold.

3. If removing the plug is difficult, drip some penetrating oil on the plug threads, allow it to work, then remove the plug. Also, be sure that the socket is straight on the plug, especially on those hard to reach plugs.

INSPECTION

Check the plugs for deposits and wear. If they are not going to be replaced, clean the plugs thoroughly. Remember that any kind of deposit will decrease the efficiency of the plug. Plugs can be cleaned on a spark plug cleaning machine, which can sometimes be found in service stations, or you can do an acceptable job of cleaning with a stiff brush. If the plugs are cleaned, the electrodes must be filed flat. Use an ignition points file, not an emery board or the like, which will leave deposits. The electrodes must be filed perfectly flat with sharp edges; rounded edges reduce the spark plug voltage by as much as 50%.

Check the spark plug gap before installation.

The ground electrode (the L-shaped one connected to the body of the plug) must be parallel to the center electrode and the specified size wire gauge (see "Tune-Up Specifications") should pass through the gap with a slight drag. Always check the gap on new plugs, too; they are not always set correctly at the factory. Do not use a flat feeler gauge when measuring the gap, because the reading will be inaccurate. Wire gapping tools usually have a bending tool attached. Use that to adjust the side electrode until the proper distance is obtained. *Absolutely never bend the center electrode.* Also, be careful not to bend the side electrode too far or too often; it may weaken and break off within the engine, requiring removal of the cylinder head to retrieve it.

INSTALLATION

1. Lubricate the threads of the spark plugs with drop of oil. Install the plugs and tighten them hand-tight. Take care not to cross-thread them.

2. Tighten the spark plugs with the socket. Do not apply the same amount of force you would use for a bolt; just snug them in. If a torque wrench is available, tighten to 11–15 ft. lbs.

3. Install the wires on their respective plugs. Make sure the wires are firmly connected. You will be able to feel them click into place.

Always use a wire gauge to check the electrode gap

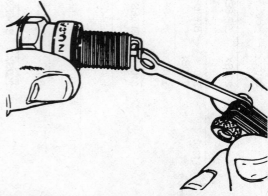

Adjust the electrode gap by bending the side electrode

CHECKING AND REPLACING SPARK PLUG WIRES

Every 15,000 miles, inspect the spark plug wires for burns, cuts, or breaks in the insulation. Check the boots and the nipples on the distributor cap. Replace any damaged wiring.

Every 45,000 miles or so, the resistance of the wires should be checked with an ohmmeter. Wires with excessive resistance will cause misfiring, and may make the engine difficult to start in damp weather. Generally, the useful life of the cables is 45,000–60,000 miles.

To check resistance, remove the distributor cap, leaving the wires in place. Connect one lead of an ohmmeter to an electrode within the cap; connect the other lead to the corresponding spark plug terminal (remove it from the spark plug for this test). Replace it from the spark plug for this test). Replace any wire which shows a resistance over 30,000 ohms. A chart in Chapter 10 gives resistance values as a function of length. Generally speaking, however, resistance should not be over 25,000 ohms, and 30,000 ohms must be considered the outer limit of acceptability.

It should be remembered that resistance is also a function of length; the longer the wire, the greater the resistance. Thus, if the wires on your car are longer than the factory originals, resistance will be higher, quite possibly outside these limits.

When installing new wires, replace them one at a time to avoid mixups. Start by replacing the longest one first. Install the boot firmly over the spark plug. Route the wire over the same path as the original. Insert the nipple firmly onto the tower on the distributor cap, then install the cap cover and latches to secure the wires.

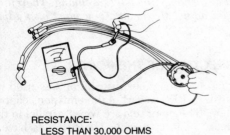

RESISTANCE:
LESS THAN 30,000 OHMS

Checking the spark plug wire resistance. 30,000 ohms is the absolute limit of acceptability

FIRING ORDER

To avoid confusion, replace spark plug wires one at a time.

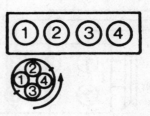

Firing order: 1-3-4-2
Distributor rotation: counterclockwise 1973 L18

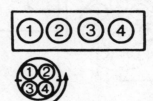

Firing order: 1-3-4-2
Distributor rotation: counterclockwise 1974 L18

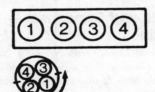

Firing order: 1-3-4-2
Distributor rotation: counterclockwise L20B

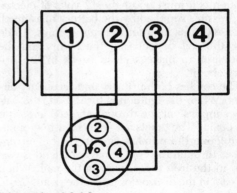

Firing order: 1-3-4-2
Distributor rotation: counterclockwise
1980 Z20 (49 states)

Firing order: 1-5-3-6-2-4
Distributor rotation: counterclockwise L24B

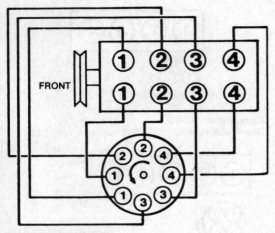

FRONT

Firing order: 1-3-4-2
Distributor rotation: counterclockwise
1980 Z20 (Calif.), 1981 and later (all)

Breaker Points and Condenser— Gasoline Engines

NOTE: *Certain 1975–77 and virtually all 1978 and later Datsuns are equipped with electronic, breakerless ignition systems. See the following section for maintenance procedures.*

The points function as a circuit breaker for the primary circuit of the ignition system. The ignition coil must boost the 12 volts of electrical pressure supplied by the battery to as much as 25,000 volts in order to fire the plugs. To do this, the coil depends on the points and the condenser to make a clean break in the primary circuit.

The coil has both primary and secondary circuits. When the ignition is turned on, the battery supplies voltage through the coil and onto the points. The points are connected to ground, completing the primary circuit. As the current passes through the coil, a magnetic field is created in the iron center core of the coil. When the cam in the distributor turns, the points open, breaking the primary circuit. The magnetic field in the primary circuit of the coil then collapses and cuts through the secondary circuit windings around the iron core. Because of the physical principle called "electromagnetic induction," the battery voltage is increased to a level sufficient to fire the spark plugs.

When the points open, the electrical charge in the primary circuit tries to jump the gap created between the two open contacts of the points. If this electrical charge were not transferred elsewhere, the metal contacts of the points would start to change rapidly.

The function of the condenser is to absorb excessive voltage from the points when they

open and thus prevent the points from becoming pitted or burned.

If you have ever wondered why it is necessary to tune-up your engine occasionally, consider the fact that the ignition system must complete the above cycle each time a spark plug fires. On a four-cylinder, four-cycle engine, two of the four plugs must fire once for every engine revolution. If the idle speed of your engine is 800 revolutions per minute (800 rpm), the breaker points open and close two times for ecah revolution. For every minute your engine idles, your points open and close 1,600 times ($2 \times 800 = 1,600$). And that is just at idle. What about at 60 mph?

There are two ways to check breaker point gap: with a feeler gauge or with a dwell meter. Either way you set the points, you are adjusting the amount of time (in degrees of distributor rotation) that the points will remain open. If you adjust the points with a feeler gauge, you are setting the maximum amount the points will open when the rubbing block on the points is on a high point of the distributor cam. When you adjust the points with a dwell meter, you are measuring the number of degrees (of distributor cam rotation) that the points will remain closed before they start to open as a high point of the distributor cam approaches the rubbing block of the points.

If you still do not understand how the points function, take a friend, go outside, and remove the distributor cap from your engine. Have your friend operate the starter (make sure that the transmission is not in gear) as you look at the exposed parts of the distributor.

There are two rules that should always be followed when adjusting or replacing points. *The points and condenser are a matched set; never replace one without replacing the other. If you change the point gap or dwell of the engine, you also change the ignition timing. Therefore, if you adjust the points, you must also adjust the timing.*

INSPECTION OF THE POINTS

A dual breaker point distributor was used on the 610 in 1973 as part of the emissions control system. The point sets are wired parallel in the primary ignition circuit. The two sets have a phase difference of 7°, making one a retard set and the other an advance. Ignition timing is advanced or retarded depending on which set is switching. Which set the engine operates on is controlled by a relay which in turn is connected to throttle position, temperature, and transmission switches. The dual points are adjusted with a feeler gauge in the same manner as the single point distributor.

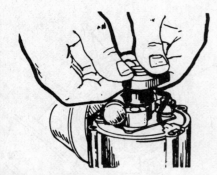

Pull the rotor straight up to remove it

1. Disconnect the high-tension wire from the top of the distributor and the coil.

2. Remove the distributor cap by prying off the spring clips on the sides of the cap.

3. Remove the rotor from the distributor shaft by pulling it straight up. Examine the condition of the rotor. If it is cracked or the metal tip is excessively worn or burned, it should be replaced. Clean the tip with fine emery paper.

4. Pry open the contacts of the points with a screwdriver and check the condition of the contacts. If they are excessively worn, burned or pitted, they should be replaced.

5. If the points are in good condition, adjust them and replace the rotor and the distributor cap. If the points need to be replaced, follow the replacement procedure given below.

REPLACEMENT OF THE BREAKER POINTS AND CONDENSER

1. Remove the coil high-tension wire from the top of the distributor cap. Remove the distributor cap and place it out of the way. Remove the rotor from the distributor shaft by pulling up.

2. On single point distributors, remove the condenser from the distributor body. On early

On dual point distributors, #1 and #2 are the mounting screws. Do not loosen #3, the phase adjusting screw

dual-point distributors, you will find that one condenser is virtually impossible to reach without removing the distributor from the engine. To do this, first note and mark the position of the distributor on the small timing scale on the front of the distributor. Then mark the position of the rotor in relation to the distributor body. Do this by simply replacing the rotor on the distributor shaft and marking the spot on the distributor body where the rotor is pointing. Be careful not to turn the engine over while performing this operation.

3. Remove the distributor on dual point models by removing the small bolt at the rear of the distributor. Lift the distributor out of the block. It is now possible to remove the rear condenser. Do not crank the engine with the distributor removed.

4. On single point distributors, remove the points assembly attaching screws and then remove the points. A magnetic screwdriver or one with a holding mechanism will come in handy here, so that you don't drop a screw into the distributor and have to remove the entire distributor to retrieve it. After the points are removed, wipe off the cam and apply new cam lubricant. If you don't, the points will wear out in a few thousand miles.

5. On dual point distributors, you will probably find it easier to simply remove the points assemblies while the distributor is out of the engine. Install the new points and condensers. You can either set the point gap now or later after you have reinstalled the distributor.

6. On dual point models, install the distributor, making sure the marks made earlier are lined up. Note that the slot for the oil pump drive is tapered and will only fit one way.

7. On single point distributors, slip the new set of points onto the locating dowel and install the screws that hold the assembly onto the plate. Don't tighten them all the way yet, since you'll only have to loosen them to set the point gap.

8. Install the new condenser on single point models and attach the condenser lead to the points.

9. Set the point gap and dwell (see the following sections).

ADJUSTMENT OF THE BREAKER POINTS WITH A FEELER GAUGE

Single Point Distributor

1. If the contact points of the assembly are not parallel, bend the stationary contact so that they make contact across the entire surface of the contacts. Bend only the stationary bracket part of the point assembly; not the movable contact.

2. Turn the engine until the rubbing block

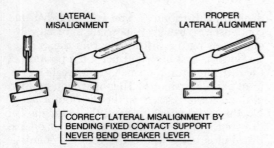

LATERAL MISALIGNMENT

PROPER LATERAL ALIGNMENT

CORRECT LATERAL MISALIGNMENT BY BENDING FIXED CONTACT SUPPORT NEVER BEND BREAKER LEVER

Check the points for proper alignment after installation

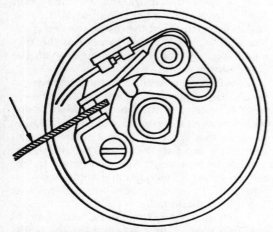

The arrow indicates the feeler gauge used to check the point gap

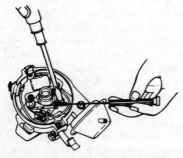

All single point distributor gaps are adjusted with the eccentric screw

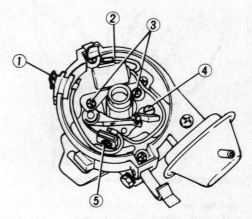

1. Primary lead terminal
2. Ground lead wire
3. Set screw
4. Adjuster
5. Screw

Single point distributor

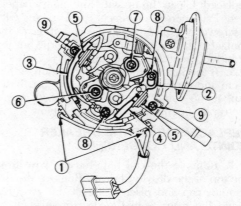

1. Lead wire terminal set screws
2. Adjuster plate
3. Primary lead wire—advanced points
4. Primary lead wire—retarded points
5. Primary lead wire set screw
6. Set screw—advanced points
7. Set screw—retarded points
8. Adjuster plate set screws
9. Breaker plate set screws

Dual point distributor. This view shows two screws (8) which must not be disturbed when adjusting or replacing points

of the points is on one of the high points of the distributor cam. You can do this by either turning the ignition switch to the start position and releasing it quickly ("bumping" the engine) or by using a wrench on the bolt which holds the crankshaft pulley to the crankshaft.

3. Place the correct size feeler gauge between the contacts (see the "Tune-Up" chart). Make sure that it is parallel with the contact surfaces.

4. With your free hand, insert a screwdriver into the eccentric adjusting screw, then twist the screwdriver to either increase or decrease the gap to the proper setting.

5. Tighten the adjustment lockscrew and recheck the contact gap to make sure that it didn't change when the lockscrew was tightened.

6. Replace the rotor and distributor cap, and the high-tension wire which connects the top of the distributor and the oil. Make sure that the rotor is firmly seated all the way onto the

distributor shaft and that the tab of the rotor is aligned with notch in the shaft. Align the tab in the base of the distributor cap with the notch in the distributor body. Make sure that the cap is firmly seated on the distributor and that the retainer clips are in place. Make sure that the end of the high-tension wire is firmly placed in the top of the distributor and the coil.

Dual Point Distributor

The two sets of breaker points are adjusted with a feeler gauge in the same manner as those in a single point distributor, except that you do the actual adjusting by twisting a screwdriver in the point set notch. Check the "Tune-Up Specifications" chart for the correct setting; both are set to the same opening.

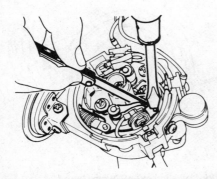

Point gap on the dual point distributor is adjusted by twisting a screwdriver in the notch

Dwell Angle—Gasoline Engines

The dwell angle or cam angle is the number of degrees that the distributor cam rotates while the points are closed. There is an inverse relationship between dwell angle and point gap. Increasing the point gap will decrease the dwell angle and vice versa. Checking the dwell angle with a meter is a far more accurate method of measuring point opening than the feeler gauge method.

After setting the point gap to specification with a feeler gauge as described above, check the dwell angle with a meter. Attach the dwell meter according to the manufacturer's instruction sheet. The negative lead is grounded and the positive lead is connected to the primary wire terminal which runs from the coil to the distributor. Start the engine, let it idle and reach operating temperature, and observe the dwell on the meter. The reading should fall within the allowable range. If it does not, the gap will have to be reset or the breaker points will have to be replaced.

ADJUSTMENT OF THE BREAKER POINTS WITH A DWELL METER

Dwell can be checked with the engine running or cranking. Decrease dwell by increasing the point gap; increase by decreasing the gap. Dwell angle is simply the number of degrees of distributor shaft rotation during which the points stay closed. Theoretically, if the point gap is correct, the dwell should also be correct or nearly so. Adjustment with a dwell meter produces more exact, consistent results since it is a dynamic adjustment. If dwell varies more than 3 degrees from idle speed to 1,750 engine rpm, the distributor is worn.

Single Point Distributor

1. Adjust the points with a feeler gauge as previously described.
2. Connect the dwell meter to the ignition circuit as according to the manufacturer's instructions. One lead of the meter is connected to a ground and the other lead is connected to the distributor post on the coil. An adapter is usually provided for this purpose.
3. If the dwell meter has a set line on it, adjust the meter to zero the indicator.
4. Start the engine.
NOTE: *Be careful when working on any vehicle while the engine is running. Make sure that the transmission is in Neutral and that the parking brake is applied. Keep hands, clothing, tools and the wires of the test instruments clear of the rotating fan blades.*
5. Observe the reading on the dwell meter. If the reading is within the specified range, turn off the engine and remove the dwell meter.
NOTE: *If the meter does not have a scale for 4 cylinder engines, multiply the 8 cylinder reading by two.*
6. If the reading is above the specified range, the breaker point gap is too small. If the reading is below the specified range, the gap is too large. In either case, the engine must be stopped and the gap adjusted in the manner previously covered.
After making the adjustment, start the engine and check the reading on the dwell meter. When the correct reading is obtained, disconnect the dwell meter.
7. Check the adjustment of the ignition timing.

Dual Point Distributor

Adjust the point gap of a dual point distributor with a dwell meter as follows:
1. Disconnect the wiring harness of the distributor from the engine wiring harness.
2. Using a jumper wire, connect the black wire of the engine side of the harness to the

Use the terminals provided (arrows) for jumper wire connections

black wire of the distributor side of the harness (advance points).

3. Start the engine and observe the reading on the dwell meter. Shut the engine off and adjust the points accordingly as previously outlined for single point distributors.

4. Disconnect the jumper wire from the black wire of the distributor side of the wiring harness and connect it to the yellow wire (retard points).

5. Adjust the point gap as necessary.

6. After the dwell of both sets of points is correct, remove the jumper wire and connect the engine-to-distributor wiring harness securely.

Datsun Electronic Ignition—Gasoline Engines

In 1975, in order to comply with California's tougher emission laws, Datsun introduced electronic ignition systems for all models sold in that state. Since that time, the Datsun electronic ignition system has undergone a metamorphosis from a standard transistorized circuit (1975–78) to an Integrated Circuit system (IC), 1979 and later, to the special dual spark plug system used in 1980 and later 510 and 200SX models with the Z20 engine.

The electronic ignition systmem differs from the conventional breaker points system in form only; its function is exactly the same—to supply a spark to the spark plugs at precisely the right moment to ignite the compressed gas in the cylinders and create mechanical movement.

Located in the distributor, in addition to the normal rotor cap, is a spoked rotor (reluctor) which fits on the distributor shaft where the breaker points cam is found on nonelectronic ignitions. The rotor (reluctor) revolves with the top rotor cap and, as it passes a pickup coil in-

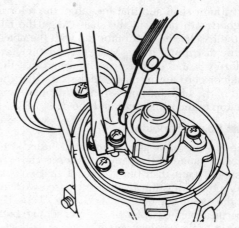

Checking the air gap—1975–78

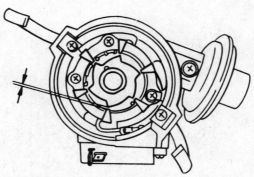

Checking the air gap—1979 and later

side the distributor body, breaks a high flux phase which occurs while the space between the reluctor spokes passes the pickup coil. This allows current to flow to the pickup coil. Primary ignition current is then cut off by the electronic ignition unit, allowing the magnetic field in the ignition coil to collapse, creating the spark which the distributor passes on to the spark plug.

The 1979 and later IC ignition system uses a ring type pickup coil which surrounds the reluctor instead of the single post type pickup coil on earlier models.

The dual spark plug ignition system used on some 1980 uses two ignition coils and each cylinder has two spark plugs which fire simultaneously. In this manner the engine is able to consume large quantities of recirculated exhaust gas which would cause a single spark plug cylinder to misfire and idle roughly.

Because no points or condenser are used, and because dwell is determined by the electronic unit, no adjustments are necessary. Ignition timing is checked in the usual way, but unless the distributor is disturbed it is not likely to ever change very much.

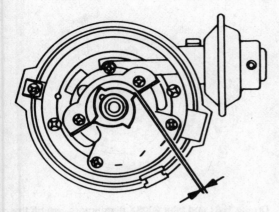

Checking the air gap—1980 and later models with the Z20 engine

Service consists of inspection of the distributor cap, rotor, and ignition wires, replacing when necessary. These parts can be expected to last for at least 40,000 miles. In addition, the reluctor air gap should be checked periodically.

1. The distributor cap is held on by two clips. Release them with a screwdriver and lift the cap straight up and off, with the wires attached. Inspect the cap for cracks, carbon tracks, or a worn center contact. Replace it if necessary, transferring the wires one at a time from the old cap to the new.

2. Pull the ignition rotor (not the spoked reluctor) straight up to remove. Replace it if its contacts are worn, burned, or pitted. Do not file the contacts. To replace, press it firmly onto the shaft. It only goes on one way, so be sure it is fully seated.

3. Before replacing the ignition rotor, check the reluctor air gap. *Use a non-magnetic feeler gauge.* Rotate the engine until a reluctor spoke is aligned with the pick-up coil (either bump the engine around with the starter, or turn it with a wrench on the crankshaft pulley bolt). The gap should measure 0.008–0.016 in. through 1978, or 0.012–0.020 in. for 1979 and later. Adjustment, if necessary, is made by loosening the pickup coil mounting screws and shifting the coil either closer to or farther from the reluctor. On 1979 and later models, center the pickup coil (ring) around the reluctor. Tighten the screws and recheck the gap.

4. Inspect the wires for cracks or brittleness. Replace them one at a time to prevent crosswiring, carefully pressing the replacement wires into place. The cores of electronic wires are more susceptible to breakage than those of standard wires, so treat them gently.

PICK-UP COIL AND RELUCTOR REPLACEMENT

1975–78

The reluctor cannot be removed on some early models—it is an integral part of the distributor shaft. Non-removable reluctors can be distinguished by the absence of a "roll pin" (retaining pin) which locks the reluctor in place on the shaft.

To replace the pick-up coil on all 1975–78 models:

1. Remove the distributor cap by releasing the two spring clips. Remove the ignition rotor by pulling it straight up and off the shaft.

2. Disconnect the distributor wiring harness at the terminal block.

3. Remove the two pick-up coil mounting screws. Remove the screws retaining the wiring harness to the distributor.

4. Remove the pick-up coil.

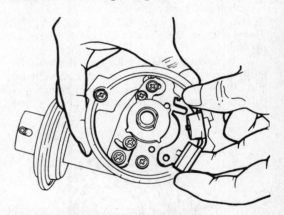

Removing the pick up coil—1975–78

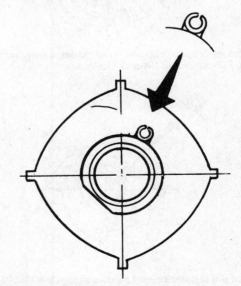

Roll pin installation—1975–80

To replace the pick-up coil, reverse the removal procedure, but leave the mounting screws slightly loose to facilitate air gap adjustment.

To replace the reluctor on models with a roll pin:

1. Remove the distributor cap, ignition rotor and the pick-up coil.

2. Use two screwdrivers or pry bars to pry the reluctor from the distributor shaft. Be extremely careful not to damage the reluctor teeth. Remove the roll pin.

3. To replace, press the reluctor firmly onto the shaft. Install a new roll pin with the slit facing away from the distributor shaft. Do not re-use the old roll pin.

1979 and Later

NOTE: *1980 200SX and 510 models (Calif. only) and 1981 200SX and 510 models (ex. Canada) use the Z20 engine. This engine is equipped with a slightly different ignition system and does not utilize a pick-up coil.*

The 1984 and later CA20E and CA18ET Turbo engines (200SX) also do not utilize a pick-up coil.

1. Remove the distributor cap. Remove the ignition rotor by pulling the rotor straight up and off the shaft. On 1984 and later 200SX distributors, remove the round rotor head by first

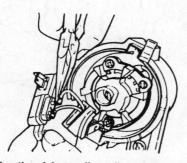

Removing the pickup coil on all models except twin-plug (Z-series and CA-series) engines

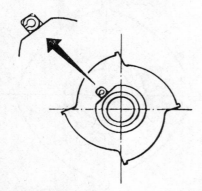

Roll pin installation—all models except the 1980–84 810 and Maxima and the 1984 and later 200SX

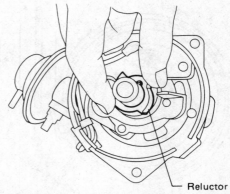

On the 1984 and later 200SX distributors, pry off the reluctor after first removing the distributor cap and rotor head

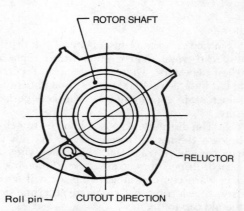

Roll pin installation, 1984 and later CA20E engines (200SX)

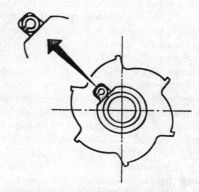

Roll pin installation—1980 and later 810 and Maxima

removing the set screw, then carefully pry off the rotor (see the exploded view of this distributor in this chapter for more detail).

2. On all models except the 1984 and later 200SX, use a pair of needle nose pliers to disconnect the pick-up coil spade connectors from the ignition unit. Do not pull on the pick-up coil wires themselves.

3. Remove the toothed stator and the ring magnet underneath it by removing the three mounting screws.

4. Remove the reluctor by prying it from the distributor shaft with two small pry bars or a small puller. Be careful not to damage any of the reluctor teeth. Remove the roll pin.

5. On all models except the 1984 and later 200SX, remove the screw retaining the pick-up coil wiring harness to the distributor. Remove the pick-up coil.

6. On all models except the 1984 and later 200SX, install the pick-up coil into place in the distributor body. Replace the wiring harness retainer.

7. Press the reluctor firmly into place on the shaft. Install a new roll pin with the slit in the pin parallel to the flat on the shaft.

8. Install the magnet and stator, and center the stator around the reluctor. Air gap is 0.3–0.4 mm (0.012–0.020 in.).

9. Press the pick-up coil spade connectors onto the ignition unit terminals with your fingers. The proper connections can be determined from the color code marked on the grommet. Replace the ignition rotor and the distributor cap.

Ignition Timing

GASOLINE ENGINES

Ignition timing is the measurement, in degrees of crankshaft rotation, of the point at which the spark plugs fire in each of the cylinders. It is measured in degrees before or after Top Dead Center (TDC) of the compression stroke.

Because it takes a fraction of a second for the spark plug to ignite the mixture in the cylinder, the spark plug must fire a little before the piston reaches TDC. Otherwise, the mixture will not be completely ignited as the piston passes TDC and the full power of the explosion will not be used by the engine.

The timing measurement is given in degrees of crankshaft rotation before the piston reaches TDC (BTDC). If the setting for the ignition timing is 5° BTDC, the spark plug must fire 5° before each piston reaches TDC. This only holds true, however, when the engine is at idle speed.

As the engine speed increases, the pistons go faster. The spark plugs have to ignite the fuel even sooner if it is to be completely ignited when the piston reaches TDC. To do this, the distributor has two means to advance the timing of the spark as the engine speed increases: a set of centrifugal weights within the distributor, and a vacuum diaphragm, mounted on the side of the distributor.

If the ignition is set too far advanced (BTDC), the ignition and expansion of the fuel in the cylinder will occur too soon and tend to force the piston down while it is still traveling up. This causes engine ping. If the ignition spark is set too far retarded, after TDC (ATDC), the piston will have already passed TDC and started on its way down when the fuel is ignited. This will cause the piston to be forced down for only a portion of its travel. This will result in poor engine performance and lack of power.

Timing marks consist of a notch on the rim of the crankshaft pulley and a scale of degrees attached to the front of the engine. The notch corresponds to the position of the piston in the number 1 cylinder. A stroboscopic (dynamic) timing light is used, which is hooked into the circuit of the No. 1 cylinder spark plug. Every time the spark plug fires, the timing light flashes. By aiming the timing light at the timing marks, the exact position of the piston within the cylinder can be read, since the stroboscopic flash makes the mark on the pulley appear to be standing still. Proper timing is indicated when the notch is aligned with the correct number on the scale.

There are three basic types of timing light available. The first is a simple neon bulb with two wire connections (one for the spark plug and one for the plug wire, connecting the light in series). This type of light is quite dim, and must be held closely to the marks to be seen, but it is inexpensive. The second type of light operates from the car battery. Two alligator clips connect to the battery terminals, while a third wire connects to the spark plug with an adapter. This type of light is more expensive, but the

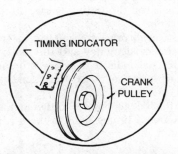

Typical timing indicator-to-pulley relationship

Typical Datsun timing marks

xenon bulb provides a nice bright flash which can even be seen in sunlight. The third type replaces the battery source with 110 volt house current. Some timing lights have other functions built into them, such as dwell meters, tachometers, or remote starting switches. These are convenient, in that they reduce the tangle of wires under the hood, but may duplicate the functions of tools you already have.

If your Datsun has electronic ignition, you should use a timing light with an inductive pickup. This pickup simply clamps onto the No. 1 plug wire, eliminating the adapter. It is not prone to crossfiring or false triggering, which may occur with a conventional light, due to the greater voltages produced by electronic ignition.

Ignition Timing Adjustment
EXCEPT 1983 AND LATER 200SX

Refer to Chapter 4, "Emission Controls and Fuel System," for the procedure to check and adjust the phase timing of the dual points or dual pickups in 1973 models.

NOTE: *Datsun does not give ignition timing adjustments for 1980 California models or for any 1981–82 200SXs and for 1981 and later 810s and Maxima models. These models are not covered in this section. If the ignition timing requires adjustment, please refer to the underhood specifications sticker for applicable procedures.*

1. Set the dwell of the breaker points to the proper specification.
2. Locate the timing marks on the crankshaft pulley and the front of the engine.
3. Clean off the timing marks, so that you can see them.
4. Use chalk or white paint to color the mark on the crankshaft pulley and the mark on the scale which will indicate the correct timing when aligned with the notch on the crankshaft pulley.
5. Attach a tachometer to the engine.
6. Attach a timing light to the engine, ac-

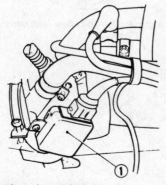

1980 throttle valve switch (1)

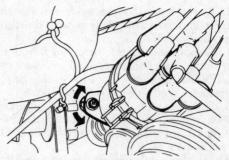

Loosen the distributor lockbolt and turn the distributor slightly to advance (upper arrow) or retard (lower arrow) the timing

cording to the manufacturer's instructions. If the timing light has three wires, one, usually green or blue, is attached to the No. 1 spark plug with an adapter. The other wires are connected to the battery. The red wire goes to the positive side of the battery and the black wire is connected to the negative terminal of the battery.

7. Leave the vacuum hose connected to the distributor advance vacuum diaphragm on all models through 1979.

On 1980 models: disconnect the throttle valve switch harness connector (810 only). Disconnect and plug the canister purge hose from the intake manifold (810 only). Plug the opening in the intake manifold. On 1980 49 States models, also disconnect the hose from the air induction pipe and cap the pipe, and disconnect and plug the vacuum advance hose at the distributor. *Note that the disconnect and plug instructions for the air induction pipe and the distributor vacuum advance do not apply to 1980 models sold in Canada.*

8. Check that all of the wires clear the fan, pulleys, and belts, and then start the engine. Allow the engine to reach normal operating temperature.

CAUTION: *Block the front wheels and set the parking brake. Shift the manual transmission to Neutral or the automatic transmission to Drive. Do not stand in front of the car when making adjustments!*

9. Adjust the idle to the correct setting. See the "Idle Speed and Mixture" section later in this chapter.

10. Aim the timing light at the timing marks. If the marks which you put on the pulley and the engine are aligned when the light flashes, the timing is correct. Turn off the engine and remove the tachometer and the timing light. If the marks are not in alighnemt, proceed with the following steps.

11. Turn off the engine.

12. Loosen the distributor lockbolt just

enough so that the distributor can be turned with a little effort.

13. Start the engine. Keep the wires of the timing light clear of the fan.

14. With the timing light aimed at the pulley and the marks on the engine, turn the distributor in the direction of rotor rotation to retard the spark, and in the opposite direction of rotor rotation to advance the spark. Align the marks on the pulley and the engine with the flashes of the timing light.

15. Tighten the distributor lockbolt and recheck the timing.

1983 AND LATER 200SX

NOTE: *When checking ignition timing on air conditioner-equipped cars, make sure that the air conditioner is "off" when proceding with the check.*

CAUTION: *Automatic transmission-equipped models should be shifted into "D" for idle speed checks. When in "Drive", the parking brake must be fully applied and both front and rear wheels chocked. When racing the engine on automatic transmission-equipped models, make sure that the shift lever is in the "N" or "P" position, and always have an assistant in the driver's seat with his or her foot on the brake pedal. After all adjustments are made, shift the car to the "P" position and remove the wheel chocks.*

1. Run the engine up to normal operating temperature.

2. Open the hood, and run the engine up to 2,000 rpm for about 2 minutes under no-load (all accessories "off").

3. Run the engine at idle speed. Disconnect the hose from the air induction pipe, and cap the pipe.

4. Race the engine two or three times under no-load, then run the engine for one minute at idle.

5. Check idle speed. Manual transmission cars should be idling at 750 rpm (plus 50 rpm, or minus 150). Automatic transmission cars should be idling in the "D" position at 750 rpm plus 50 rpm, or minus 150 rpm). Adjust the

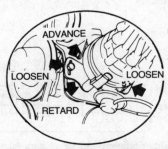

Ignition timing adjustments on 1983 and later 200SX

idle speed by turning the idle speed adjusting screw.

6. Connect a timing light according to the light's manufacturer's instructions. Ignition timing should be 8° plus or minus 2° BTDC. Adjust the timing by loosening the distributor hold-down bolts and turning the distributor clockwise to advance and counter-clockwise to retard.

7. Reconnect the air induction pipe hose.

Injection Pump Timing
DIESEL ENGINES

For information and procedures regarding injection pump timing, please refer to Chapter 4.

Valve Lash

Valve adjustment determines how far the valves enter the cylinder and how long they stay open and closed.

If the valve clearance is too large, part of the lift of the camshaft will be used in removing the excessive clearance. Consequently, the valve will not be opening for as long as it should. This condition has two effects: the valve train components will emit a tapping sound as they take up the excessive clearance and the engine will perform poorly because the valves don't open fully and allow the proper amount of gases to flow into and out of the engine.

If the valve clearance is too small, the intake valves and the exhaust valves will open too far and they will not fully seat on the cylinder head when they close. When a valve seats itself on the cylinder head, it does two things: it seals the combustion chamber so that none of the gases in the cylinder escape and it cools itself by transferring some of the heat it absorbs from the combustion in the cylinder to the cylinder head and to the engine's cooling system. If the valve clearance is too small, the engine will run poorly because of the gases escaping from the combustion chamber. The valves will also become overheated and will warp, since they cannot transfer heat unless they are touching the valve seat in the cylinder head.

NOTE: *While all valve adjustments must be made as accurately as possible, it is better to have the valve adjustment slightly loose than slightly tight, as a burned valve may result from overly tight adjustments.*

ADJUSTMENT
610, 710 and 1977–80 510, 200SX (Single Plug Engine)

1. The valves are adjusted with the engine at normal operating temperature. Oil temper-

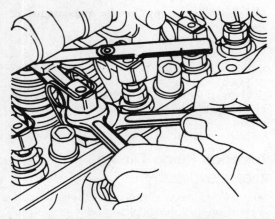

Loosen the locknut and turn the pivot adjuster to adjust the valve clearance—all models except those with twin-plug engines

ature, and the resultant parts expansion, is much more important than water temperature. Run the engine for at least fifteen minutes to ensure that all the parts have reached their full expansion. After the engine is warmed up, shut it off.

2. Purchase either a new gasket or some silicone gasket seal before removing the camshaft cover. Note the location of any wires and hoses which may interfere with cam cover removal, disconnect them and move them aside. Then remove the bolts which hold the cam cover in place and remove the cam cover.

3. Place a wrench on the crankshaft pulley bolt and turn the engine over until the valves for No. 1 cylinder are closed. When both cam lobes are pointing up, the valves are closed. If you have not done this before, it is a good idea to turn the engine over slowly several times and watch the valve action until you have a clear idea of just when the valve is closed.

4. Check the clearance of the intake and exhaust valves. You can differentiate between

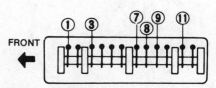

Checking the valve clearance with a flat feeler gauge— all models except those with twin-plug engines

them by lining them up with the tubes of the intake and exhaust manifolds. The correct size feeler gauge should pass between and the base circle of the cam and the rocker arm with just a slight drag. Be sure the feeler gauge is inserted *straight* and not on an angle.

5. If the valves need adjustment, loosen the locking nut and then adjust the clearance with the adjusting screw. You will probably find it necessary to hold the locking nut while you turn the adjuster. After you have the correct clearance, tighten the locking nut and recheck the clearance. Remember, it's better to have them too loose than too tight, especially exhaust valves.

6. Repeat this procedure (Steps 3–5) until you have checked and/or adjusted all the valves. (Be sure to adjust in the firing order.) Keep in mind that all that is necessary is to have the valves closed and the camshaft lobes pointing up. It is not particularly important what stroke the engine is on.

7. Install the cam cover gasket, the cam cover, and any wires and hoses which were removed.

810 and Maxima

1977 810 engines must be "overnight" cold before the valves can be adjusted. They must not be operated for about eight hours before adjustment. 1978 and later 810 and Maxima engines are adjusted hot.

NOTE: *Skip steps 7 and 8 if you have a 1978-and later 810 or Maxima; complete Steps 7 and 8 if you have a 1977 810.*

1. Note the locations of all hoses or wires that would interfere with valve cover removal, disconnect them and move them aside. Then, remove the six bolts which hold the valve cover in place.

2. Bump one end of the cover sharply to loosen the gasket and then pull the valve cover off the engine vertically.

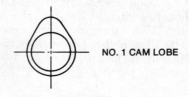

Primary valve adjustment, No. 1 cam lobe pointing up—810 and Maxima

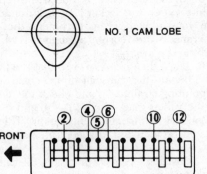

Secondary valve adjustment, No. 1 cam lobe pointing down—810 and Maxima

3. Place a wrench on the crankshaft pulley bolt and turn the engine over until the first cam lobe is pointing straight up. The timing marks on the crankshaft pulley should be lined up approximately where they would be when the No. 1 spark plug fires.

NOTE: *If you decide to turn the engine by "bumping" it with the starter, be sure to disconnect the high tension wire from the coil to prevent the engine from accidentally starting and spewing oil all over the engine compartment.*

CAUTION: *Never attempt to turn the engine by using a wrench on the camshaft sprocket bolt; this would put a tremendous strain on the timing chain.*

4. See the illustration for primary adjustment and check the clearance for valves (1), (3), (7), (8), (9) and (11) using a flat-bladed feeler gauge. The feeler gauge should pass between the cam and the cam follower with a very slight drag. Insert the feeler gauge *straight*, not at an angle.

5. If the clearance is not within the specified limits, loosen the pivot locking nut and then insert the feeler gauge between the cam and the cam follower. Adjust the pivot screw until there is a very slight drag on the gauge, tighten the locking nut, recheck the adjustment and correct as necessary.

6. Turn the engine over so that the first cam lobe is pointing straight down. See the illustration for secondary adjustment and then check the clearance on valves (2), (4), (5), (6), (10) and (12). If clearance is not within specifications, adjust as detailed in Step 5.

7. Reinstall the valve cover gasket and hoses, start the engine, and operate it until it is fully warmed up (1977 only).

8. Repeat the entire valve adjustment procedure using the gauges specified in the "Tune-Up" chart, but do not loosen the locking nuts

unless the gauge indicates that adjustment is required (1977 only).

9. When all valves are at hot specifications, clean all traces of old gasket material from the valve cover and the head. Install the new gasket in the valve cover with sealer and install the valve cover. Tighten the valve cover bolts evenly in several stages going around the cover to ensure a good seal. Reconnect all hoses and wires securely and operate the engine to check for leaks.

1980–83 510 and 200SX (Twin-plug Engines)

1. The valves must be adjusted with the engine warm, so start the car and run the engine until the needle on the temperature gauge reaches the middle of the gauge. After the engine is warm, shut it off.

2. Purchase either a new gasket or some silicone gasket sealer before removing the camshaft cover. Counting on the old gasket to be in good shape is a losing proposition; always use new gaskets. Note the location of any wires and hoses which may interfere with cam cover removal, disconnect them and move them to one side. Remove the bolts holding the cover in place and remove the cover. Remember, the engine will be hot, so be careful.

3. Place a wrench on the crankshaft pulley bolt and turn the engine over until the first cam lobe behind the camshaft timing chain sprocket is pointing straight down.

NOTE: *If you decide to turn the engine by "bumping" it with the starter, be sure to disconnect the high tension wire from the coil(s) to prevent the engine from accidentally starting and spewing oil all over the engine compartment.*

CAUTION: *Never attempt to turn the engine by using a wrench on the camshaft sprocket bolt; there is a one to two turning ratio between the camshaft and the crankshaft which will put a tremendous strain on the timing chain.*

4. See the illustration for primary adjust-

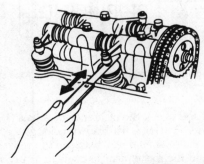

Checking the valve clearance with a flat feeler gauge— Z20 and Z22 (twin-plug) series engines

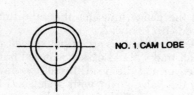

NO. 1 CAM LOBE

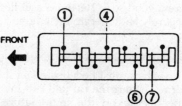

FRONT

Primary valve adjustment, No. 1 cam lobe pointing down—Z20 and Z22 series engines

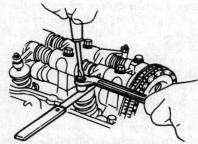

Loosen the locknut and turn the adjusting screw to adjust the valve clearance—Z20 and Z22 series engines

NO. 1 CAM LOBE

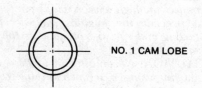

FRONT

Secondary valve adjustment, No. 1 cam lobe pointing up—Z20 and Z22 series engines

ment and check the clearance of valves (1), (4), (6), and (7) using a flat-bladed feeler gauge. The feeler gauge should pass between the valve stem end and the rocker arm screw with a very slight drag. Insert the feeler gauge *straight*, not at an angle.

5. If the clearance is not within specified value, loosen the rocker arm lock nut and turn the rocker arm screw to obtain the proper clearance. After correct clearance is obtained, tighten the lock nut.

6. Turn the engine over so that the first cam lobe behind the camshaft timing chain sprocket is pointing straight up and check the clearance of the valves marked (2), (3), (5), and (8) in the secondary adjustment illustration. They, too, should be adjusted to specifications as in Step 5.

7. Install the cam cover gasket, the cam cover and any wires and hoses which were removed.

1984 and Later 200SX

Follow the procedure above for 1980–83 models, with the following exceptions: on step 4, check and adjust the clearance valves 1, 2, 4 and 6 as shown in the accompanying illustration. This is with No. 1 cylinder at TDC on compression. On step 6, check and adjust the clearance on valves 3, 5, 7 and 8 with the No. 4 cylinder at TDC on compression.

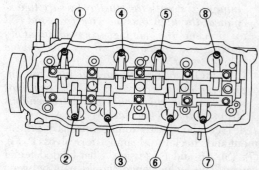

Valve location, 1984 and later 200SX (CA20E and CA18ET engines). See text for sequence

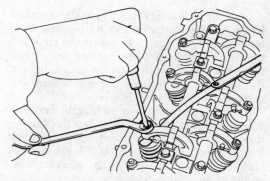

Adjusting the CA20E and CA18ET valves. Clearance is 0.012 in.

Carburetor

This section contains only tune-up adjustment procedures for carburetors. Descriptions, ad-

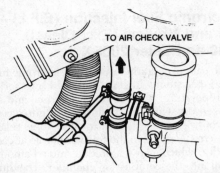

Disconnecting air hose between three way connector and check valve, 1978 510 shown

Mixture screw (arrow). Note limiter tab

justments, and overhaul procedures for carburetors can be found in Chapter 4.

When the engine in your Datsun is running, the air-fuel mixture from the carburetor is being drawn into the engine by a partial vacuum which is created by the movement of the pistons downward on the intake stroke. The amount of air-fuel mixture that enters into the engine is controlled by the throttle plate(s) in the bottom of the carburetor. When the engine is not running the throttle plate(s) is closed, completely blocking off the bottom of the carburetor from the inside of the engine. The throttle plates are connected by the throttle linkage to the accelerator pedal in the passenger compartment of the Datsun. When you depress the pedal, you open the throttle plates in the carburetor to admit more air-fuel mixture to the engine.

When the engine is not running, the throttle plates are closed. When the engine is idling, it is necessary to have the throttle plates open

slightly. To prevent having to hold your foot on the pedal when the engine is idling, an idle speed adjusting screw was added to the carburetor linkage.

The idle adjusting screw contacts a lever (throttle lever) on the outside of the carburetor. When the screw is turned, it either opens or closes the throttle plates of the carburetor, raising or lowering the idle speed of the engine. This screw is called the curb idle adjusting screw.

IDLE SPEED AND MIXTURE ADJUSTMENT

Note: *1980 model Datsuns require a CO meter to adjust their mixture ratios, therefore, no procedures concerning this adjustment are given. Also, many California model Datsuns have a plug over their mixture control screw. It is suggested that in both of these cases, mixture adjustment be left to a qualified technician.*

1. Start the engine and allow it to run until it reaches normal operating temperature.

2. Allow the engine idle speed to stabilize by running the engine at idle for at least two minutes.

3. If you have not done so already, check and adjust the ignition timing to the proper setting.

4. Shut off the engine and connect a tachometer as per the manufacturer's instructions.

5. Disconnect and plug the air hose between the three way connector and the check valve, if equipped. On 1980 models with the Z20S engine, disconnect the air induction hose and plug the pipe, also disconnect and plug the vacuum hose at the distributor. With the transmission in Neutral, check the idle speed on the tachometer. If the reading is correct, continue on to Step 6 for 1973–79 models. For 1980 and later, and certain California models, proceed to step 10 below if the idle is correct. If the idle is not correct, for all models, turn the idle speed adjusting screw clockwise with a screwdriver to increase idle speed or counterclockwise to decrease it.

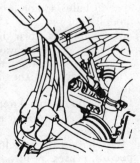

810 idle speed screw

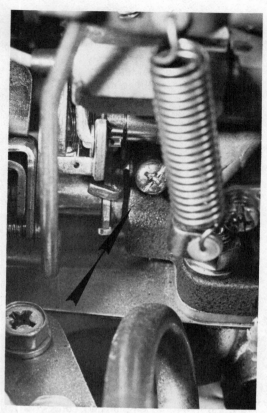

Idle speed screw (arrow)

6. With the automatic transmission in Drive (wheels blocked and parking brake on) or the manual transmission in Neutral, turn the mixture screw out until the engine rpm starts to drop due to an overly rich mixture.

7. Turn the screw until just before the rpm starts to drop due to an overly lean mixture. Turn the mixture screw in until the idle speed drops 60–70 rpm with manual transmission, or 15–25 rpm with automatic transmission (in Drive) for 1975–76 610 and 710 models; 45–55 rpm for all 1977 710's, and 1978–79 510's and 200SX's. If the mixture limiter cap will not allow this adjustment, remove it, make the adjustment, and re-install it. Go on to Step 10 for all 1975–79 models.

8. On 1973–74 models, turn the mixture screw back out to the point midway between the two extreme positions where the engine began losing rpm to achieve the fastest and smoothest idle.

9. Adjust the curb idle speed to the proper specification, on 1973–74 models, with the idle speed adjusting screw.

10. Install the air hose (if so equipped). If the engine speed increases, reduce it with the idle speed screw.

Electronic Fuel Injection (E.F.I.)— 810 and Maxima (Exc. Diesel), 1980 and Later 200SX

These cars use a rather complex electronic fuel injection system which is controlled by a series of temperature, altitude (for California) and air flow sensors which feed information into a central control unit. The control unit then relays an electronic signal to the injector nozzle at each cylinder, which allows a predetermined amount of fuel into the combustion chamber. To adjust the mixture controls on these units requires a CO meter and several special Datsun tools; therefore we will confine ourselves to idle speed adjustment.

IDLE SPEED ADJUSTMENT

1. Start the engine and run it until the water temperature indicator points to the middle of the temperature gague. It might be quicker to take a short spin down the road and back.

2. Open the engine hood. Run the engine at about 2,000 rpm for a few minutes with the transmission in Neutral and all accessories off. If you have not already done so, check the ignition timing and make sure it is correct. Hook

Idle speed adjusting screw—200SX

Idle speed adjusting screw—1977–80 810

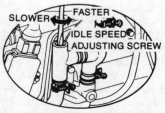

Idle speed adjusting screw—1981 and later 810 and Maxima

up a tachometer as per the manufacturer's instructions. For automatic transmission, set the parking brake, block the wheels and set the shift selector in the Drive position.

3. Run the engine at idle speed and disconnect the hose from the air induction pipe, then plug the pipe. Allow the engine to run for about a minute at idle speed.

4. Check the idle against the specifications given earlier in this chapter. Adjust the idle speed by turning the idle speed adjusting screw, located near the air cleaner on the 200SX and the throttle chamber on the 810. Turn the screw clockwise for slower idle speed and counterclockwise for faster idle speed.

5. Connect the hose and disconnect the tachometer. If idle speed increases, adjustg it with the idle speed adjusting screw.

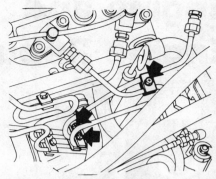

You may wish to remove all the clamps on the No. 1 injection tube to obtain a more accurate rpm reading

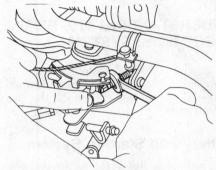

Loosen the idle screw locknut while holding the control lever

Diesel Fuel Injection

IDLE SPEED ADJUSTMENT

NOTE: *A special diesel tachometer will be required for this procedure. A normal tachometer will not work.*

1. Make sure all electrical accessories are turned off.

2. The automatic transmission (if so equipped) should be in 'D' with the parking brake on and the wheels blocked.

3. Start the engine and run it until it reaches the normal operating temperature.

4. Attach the diesel tachometer's pick-up to the No. 1 injection tube.

NOTE: *In order to obtain a more accurate reading of the idle speed, you may wish to remove all the clamps on the No. 1 injection tube.*

5. Run the engine at about 2,000 rpm for two minutes under no-load conditions.

6. Slow the engine down to idle speed for about 1 min. and then check the idle.

7. If the engine is not idling at the proper speed, turn it off and disconnect the accelerator wire from the injection pump control lever.

8. Move the control lever to the full acceleration side, and then loosen the idle screw lock nut while still holding the control lever.

9. Start the engine again and turn the adjusting screw until the proper idle is obtained. Stop the engine.

10. Tighten the idle adjusting screw lock nut while still holding the control level to the full acceleration side and then connect the accelerator wire.

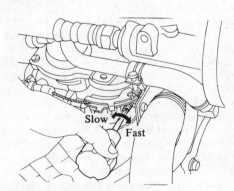

Idle speed adjusting screw—diesel

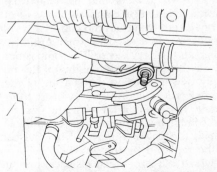

Tighten the idle adjusting screw lock nut when the adjustment is completed

Engine and Engine Rebuilding

3

UNDERSTANDING THE ENGINE ELECTRICAL SYSTEM

The engine electrical system can be broken down into three separate and distinct systems—(1) the starting system; (2) the charging system; and (3) the ignition system.

Battery and Starting System

The battery is the first link in the chain of mechanisms which work together to provide cranking of the automobile engine. In most modern cars, the battery is a lead-acid electrochemical device consisting of six two-volt (2 V) subsections connected in series so the unit is capable of producing approximately 12 V of electrical pressure. Each subsection, or cell, consists of a series of positive and negative plates held a short distance apart in a solution of sulfuric acid and water. The two types of plates are of dissimilar metals. This causes a chemical reaction to be set up, and it is this reaction which produces current flow from the battery when its positive and negative terminals are connected to an electrical appliance such as a lamp or motor. The continued transfer of electrons would eventually convert the sulfuric acid in the electrolyte to water, and make the two plates identical in chemical composition. As electrical energy is removed from the battery, its voltage output tends to drop. Thus, measuring battery voltage and battery electrolyte composition are two ways of checking the ability of the unit to supply power. During the starting of the engine, electrical energy is removed from the battery. However, if the charging circuit is in good condition and the operating conditions are normal, the power removed from the battery will be replaced by the generator (or alternator) which will force electrons back through the battery, reversing the normal flow, and restoring the battery to its original chemical state.

The battery and starting motor are linked by very heavy electrical cables designed to minimize resistance to the flow of current. Generally, the major power supply cable that leaves the battery goes directly to the starter, while other electrical system needs are supplied by a smaller cable. During the starter operation, power flows from the battery to the starter and is grounded through the car's frame and the battery's negative ground strap.

The starting motor is a specially designed, direct current electric motor capable of producing a very great amount of power for its size. One thing that allows the motor to produce a great deal of power is its tremendous rotating speed. It drives the engine through a tiny pinion gear (attached to the starter's armature), which drives the very large flywheel ring gear at a greatly reduced speed. Another factor allowing it to produce so much power is that only intermittent operation is required of it. Thus, little allowance for air circulation is required, and the windings can be built into a very small space.

The starter solenoid is a magnetic device which employs the small current supplied by the starting switch circuit of the ignition switch. This magnetic action moves a plunger which mechanically engages the starter and electrically closes the heavy switch which connects it to the battery. The starting switch circuit consists of the starting switch contained within the ignition switch, a transmission neutral safety switch or clutch pedal switch, and the wiring necessary to connect these with the starter solenoid or relay.

A pinion, which is a small gear, is mounted to a one-way drive clutch. This clutch is splined to the starter armature shaft. When the ignition switch is moved to the "start" position, the solenoid plunger slides the pinion toward the flywheel ring gear via a collar and spring. If the teeth on the pinion and flywheel match properly, the pinion will engage the flywheel immediately. If the gear teeth butt one another, the spring will be compressed and will force the gears to mesh as soon as the starter turns far enough to allow them to do so. As the solenoid plunger reaches the end of its travel, it closes the contacts that connect the battery and starter and then the engine is cranked.

As soon as the engine starts, the flywheel ring gear begins turning fast enough to drive the pinion at an extremely high rate of speed. At this point, the one-way clutch begins allowing the pinion to spin faster than the starter shaft so that the starter will not operate at excessive speed. When the ignition switch is released from the starter position, the solenoid is de-energized, and a spring contained within the solenoid assembly pulls the gear out of mesh and interrupts the current flow to the starter.

Some starters employ a separate relay, mounted away from the starter, to switch the motor and solenoid current on and off. The relay thus replaces the solenoid electrical switch, but does not eliminate the need for a solenoid mounted on the starter used to mechanically engage the starter drive gears. The relay is used to reduce the amount of current the starting switch must carry.

The Charging System

The automobile charging system provides electrical power for operation of the vehicle's ignition and starting systems and all the electrical accessories. The battery serves as an electrical surge or storage tank, storing (in chemical form) the energy originally produced by the engine-driven generator. The system also provides a means of regulating generator output to protect the battery from being overcharged and to avoid excessive voltage to the accessories.

The storage battery is a chemical device incorporating parallel lead plates in a tank containing a sulfuric acid-water solution. Adjacent plates are slightly dissimilar, and the chemical reaction of the two dissimilar plates produces electrical energy when the battery is connected to a load such as the starter motor. The chemical reaction is reversible, so that when the generator is producing a voltage (electrical pressure) greater than that produced by the battery, electricity is forced into the battery, and the battery is returned to its fully charged state.

The vehicle's generator is driven mechanically, through V belts, by the engine crankshaft. It consists of two coils of fine wire, one stationary (the "stator"), and one movable (the "rotor"). The rotor may also be known as the "armature," and consists of fine wire wrapped around an iron core which is mounted on a shaft. The electricity which flows through the two coils of wire (provided initially by the battery in some cases) creates an intense magnetic field around both rotor and stator, and the interaction between the two fields creates voltage, allowing the generator to power the accessories and charge the battery.

There are two types of generators; the earlier is the direct current (DC) type. The curent produced by the DC generator is generated in the armature and carried off the spinning armature by stationary brushes contacting the commutator. The commutator is a series of smooth metal contact plates on the end of the armature. The commutator plates, which are separated from one another by a very short gap, are connected to the armature circuits so that current will flow in one direction only in the wires carrying the generator output. The generator stator consists of two stationary coils of wire which draw some of the output current of the generator to form a powerful magnetic field and create the interaction of fields which generates the voltage. The generator field is wired in series with the regulator.

Newer automobiles use alternating current generators or "alternators" because they are more efficient, can be rotated at higher speeds, and have fewer brush problems. In an alternator, the field rotates while all the current produced passes only through the stator windings. The brushes bear against continuous slip rings rather than a commutator. This causes the current produced to periodically reverse the direction of its flow. Diodes (electrical one-way switches) block the flow of curent from traveling in the wrong direction. A series of diodes is wired together to permit the alternating flow of the stator to be converted to a pulsating, but uni-directional flow at the alternator output. The alternator's field is wired in series with the voltage regulator.

The regulator consists of several circuits. Each circuit had a core, or magnetic coil of wire, which operates a switch. Each switch is connected to ground through one or more resistors. The coil of wire responds directly to system voltage. When the voltage reaches the required level, the magnetic field created by the winding of wire closes the switch and inserts a resistance into the generator field circuit, thus reducing the output. The contacts of the switch cycle open and close many times each second to precisely control voltage.

While alternators are self-limiting as far as maximum current is concerned, DC generators employ a current regulating circuit which responds directly to the total amount of current flowing through the generator circuit rather than to the output voltage. The curent regulator is similar to the voltage regulator except that all system current must flow through the energizing coil on its way to the various accessories.

SAFETY PRECAUTIONS

Observing these precautions will ensure safe handling of the electrical system components, and will avoid damage to the vehicle's electrical system:

A. Be *absolutely* sure of the polarity of a booster battery before making connections. Connect the cables positive to positive, and negative to negative. Connect positive cables first and then make the last connection to a ground on the body of the booster vehicle so that arcing cannot ignite hydrogen gas that may have accumulated near the battery. Even momentary connection of a booster battery with the polarity reversed will damage alternator diodes.

B. Disconnect both vehicle battery cables before attempting to charge a battery.

C. Never ground the alternator or generator output or battery terminal. Be cautious when using metal tools around a battery to avoid creating a short circuit between the terminals.

D. Never ground the field circuit between the alternator and regulator.

E. Never run an alternator or generator without load unless the field circuit is disconnected.

F. Never attempt to polarize an alternator.

G. Keep the regulator cover in place when taking voltage and current limiter readings.

H. Use insulated tools when adjusting the regulator.

I. Whenever DC generator-to-regulator wires have been disconnected, the generator *must* be repolarized. To do this with an externally grounded, light duty generator, momentarily place a jumper wire between the battery terminal and the generator terminal of the regulator. With an internally grounded heavy duty unit, disconnect the wire to the regulator field terminal and touch the regulator battery terminal with it.

Troubleshooting the Datsun Electronic Ignition System

1975–78

The main differences between the 1975–77 and 1978 systems are: (1) the 1975–77 system uses an external ballast resistor located next to the ignition coil, and (2) the earlier system uses a wiring harness with individual eyelet connectors to the electronic unit, while the later system uses a multiple plug connector. You will need an accurate voltmeter and ohmmeter for these tests, which must be performed in the order given.

1. Check all connections for corrosion, looseness, breaks, etc., and correct if necessary. Clean and gap the spark plugs.

2a. Disconnect the harness (connector of plug) from the electronic unit. Turn the igniton switch On. Set the voltmeter to the DC 50v range. Connect the positive (+) voltmeter lead to the black/white wire terminal, and the negative (−) lead to the black wire terminal. Battery voltage should be obtained. If not, check the black/white and black wires for continuity; check the battery terminals for corrosion; check the battery state of charge.

2b. Next, connect the voltmeter + lead to the blue wire and the − lead to the black wire. Battery voltage should be obtained. If not check the blue wire for continuity; check the ignition coil terminals for corrosion or looseness; check the coil for continuity. On 1975–77 models, also check the external ballast resistor.

3. Disconnect the distributor harness wires from the ignition coil ballast resistor on 1975–77 models, leaving the ballast resistor-to-coil wires attached. On 1978 models, disconnect the ignition coil wires. Connect the leads of an ohmmeter to the ballast resistor outside terminals (at each end) for 1975–77, and to the two coil terminals for 1978. With the ohmmeter set in the X1 range, the following model years should show a reading of 1.6–2.0 ohms: 1976 710, 610; 1977 810, 710.

The following models should show a reading of approximately 0 ohms: 1975 710; 1978 810, 200SX. The maximum allowable limit for the 1.6–2.0 ohm range models is 2.0 ohms. The limit for the 0 ohm models is 1.8 ohms. If a reading higher than the limit is received, replace the ignition coil assembly.

4. Disconnect the harness from the electronic control unit. Connect an ohmmeter to the red and the green wire terminals. Resistance should be 720 ohms. If far more or far less, replace the distributor pick-up coil.

5. Disconnect the anti-dieseling solenoid connector (see Chapter 4). Connect a voltmeter to the red and green terminals of the electronic control harness. When the starter is cranked, the needle should deflect slightly. If not, replace the distributor pick-up coil.

6. Reconnect the ignition coil and the electronic control unit. Leave the anti-dieseling solenoid wire disconnected. Unplug the high tension lead (coil to distributor) from the distributor and hold it ⅛–¼ in. from the cylinder head with a pair of insulated pliers and a heavy glove. When the engine is cranked, a spark

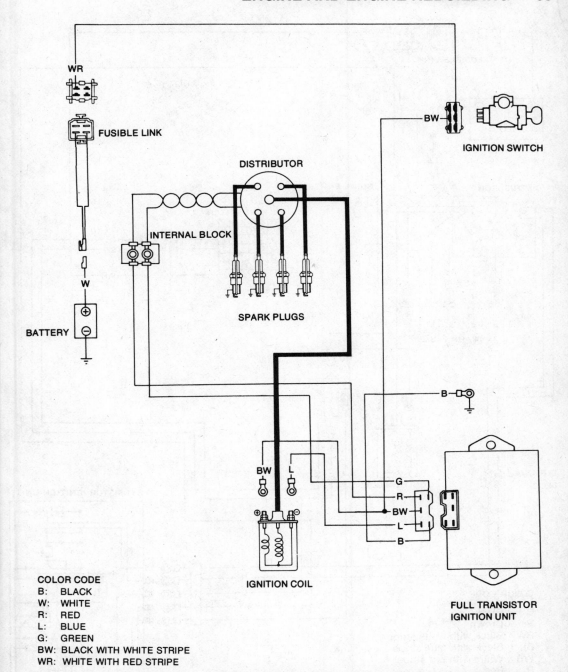

WR

FUSIBLE LINK

BATTERY

W

DISTRIBUTOR

INTERNAL BLOCK

SPARK PLUGS

BW

IGNITION SWITCH

B

BW   L

G
R
BW
L
B

IGNITION COIL

FULL TRANSISTOR
IGNITION UNIT

COLOR CODE
B: BLACK
W: WHITE
R: RED
L: BLUE
G: GREEN
BW: BLACK WITH WHITE STRIPE
WR: WHITE WITH RED STRIPE

Electronic ignition schematic—1975–78 4 cylinder models (510 shown, other models similar)

should be observed. If not, check the lead, and replace if necessary. If still no spark, replace the electronic control unit.

7. Reconnect all wires.

1976–77: connect the voltmeter + lead to the blue electronic control harness connector and the − lead to the black wire. The harness should be attached to the control unit.

1978: connect the voltmeter + lead to the − terminal of the ignition coil coil and the − lead to ground.

As soon as the ignition switch is turned On, the meter should indicate battery voltage. If not, replace the electronic control unit.

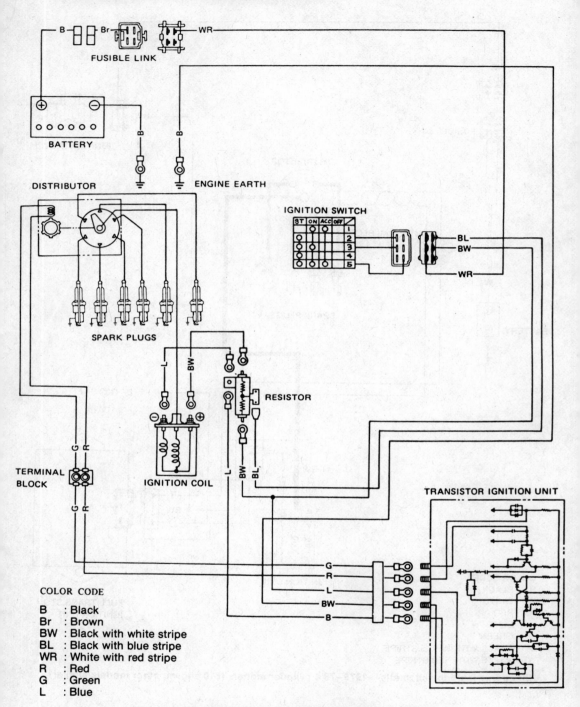

FUSIBLE LINK

BATTERY

DISTRIBUTOR

ENGINE EARTH

IGNITION SWITCH

	ST	ON	ACC	OFF	
	○	○	○		1
					2
	○	○			3
					4
	○	○	○		5

BL
BW
WR

SPARK PLUGS

BW

RESISTOR

TERMINAL BLOCK

IGNITION COIL

BW
BL

TRANSISTOR IGNITION UNIT

G
R
L
BW
B

COLOR CODE

B : Black
Br : Brown
BW : Black with white stripe
BL : Black with blue stripe
WR : White with red stripe
R : Red
G : Green
L : Blue

Electronic ignition schematic—1975–78 6 cylinder models

1979– and later

810 and Maxima; 1979–80 510; 200SX (Single Plug Engine)

1. Make a check of the power supply circuit. Turn the ignition OFF. Disconnect the connector from the top of the IC unit. Turn the ignition ON. Measure the voltage at each terminal of the connector in turn by touching the probe of the positive lead of the voltmeter to one of the terminals, and touching the probe of the negative lead of the voltmeter to a ground, such as the engine. In each case, battery voltage should be indicated. If not, check all wir-

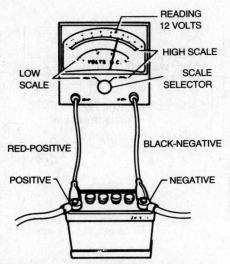

Testing battery voltage with a D.C. voltmeter

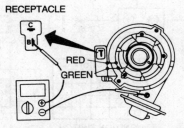

Testing the power supply circuit, 1983 200SX

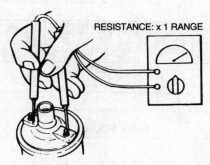

Checking the ignition coil primary circuit

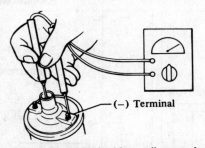

Testing the 1983 200SX ignition coil secondary circuit

ing, the ignition switch, and all connectors for breaks, corrosion, discontinuity, etc., and repair as necessary.

2. Check the primary windings of the ignition coil. Turn the ignition OFF. Disconnect the harness connector from the negative coil terminal. Use an ohmmeter to measure the re-

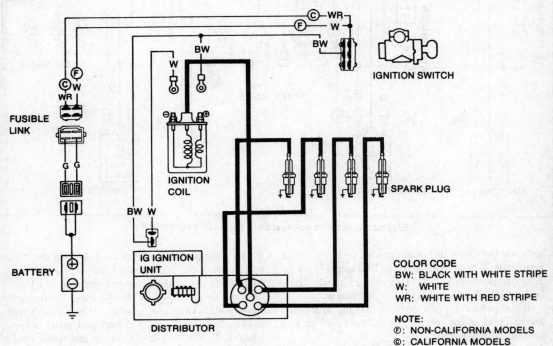

Electronic ignition schematic—1979 510 (200SX similar)

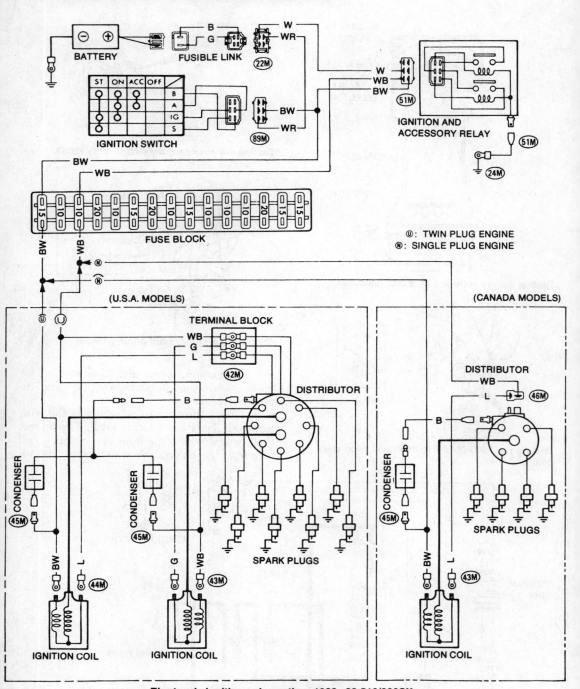

Electronic ignition schematic—1980–82 510/200SX

sistance between the positive and negative coil terminals. If resistance is 0.84–1.02 ohms (1.04–1.27 ohms, 200SX, 510–Twin Plug Engine) the coil is OK. Replace if far from this range.

If the power supply, circuits, wiring, and coil are in good shape, check the IC unit and pick-up coil, as follows:

3. Turn the ignition OFF. Remove the distributor cap and ignition rotor. Use an ohmme-

ter to measure the resistance between the two terminals of the pick-up coil, where they attach to the IC unit. Measure the resistance by reversing the polarity of the probes. If approximately 400 ohms are indicated, the pick-up coil is OK, but the IC unit is bad and must be replaced. If other than 400 ohms are measured, go to the next step.

4. Be certain the two pin connector to the

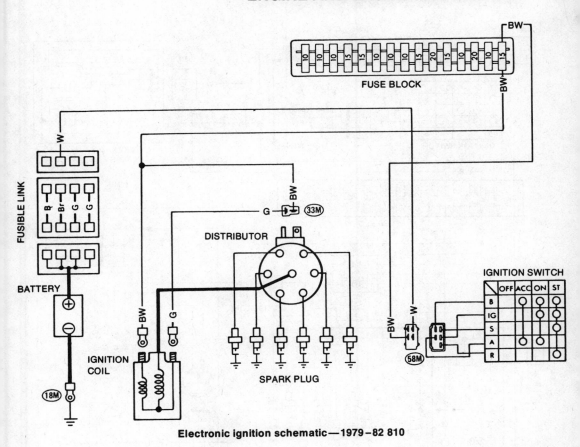

Electronic ignition schematic—1979-82 810

IC unit is secure. Turn the ignition ON. Measure the voltage at the ignition coil negative terminal. Turn the ignition OFF.

CAUTION: *Remove the tester probe from the coil negative terminal before switching the ignition OFF, to prevent burning out the tester.*

If zero voltage is indicated, the IC unit is bad and must be replaced. If battery voltage is indicated, proceed.

5. Remove the IC unit from the distributor:

a. Disconnect the battery ground (negative) cable.

b. Remove the distributor cap and ignition rotor.

c. Disconnect the harness connector at the top of the IC unit.

d. Remove the two screws securing the IC unit to the distributor.

e. Disconnect the two pick-up coil wires from the IC unit.

CAUTION: *Pull the connectors free with a pair of needlenosed pliers. Do not pull on the wires to detach the connectors.*

f. Remove the IC unit.

6. Measure the resistance between the terminals of the pick-up coil. It should be approximately 400 ohms. If so, the pick-up coil is OK, and the IC unit is bad. If not approximately 400 ohms, the pick-up coil is bad and must be replaced.

7. With a new pick-up coil installed, install the IC unit. Check for a spark at one of the spark plugs (see Step 4.1 in the Troubleshooting Section at the end of this Chapter). If a good spark is obtained, the IC unit is OK. If not, replace the IC unit.

1980 AND LATER, 510, 200SX (TWIN-PLUG ENGINE)

Complete Step 1-2 of the previous procedure; the resistance should be between 1.04-1.27 ohms. If not, replace ignition coil(s).

NOTE: *The manufacturer does not give a complete system of tests for the 1980 200SX/510 California ignition system. Therefore, before attempting anything else, try this spark performance test:*

1. Turn the ignition switch to the "OFF" position.

2. On the 510, disconnect the antidieseling solenoid valve connector to cut off the fuel supply to the engine. On the 200SX, disconnect the electronic fuel injection (EFI) fusible link (see Chapter 4).

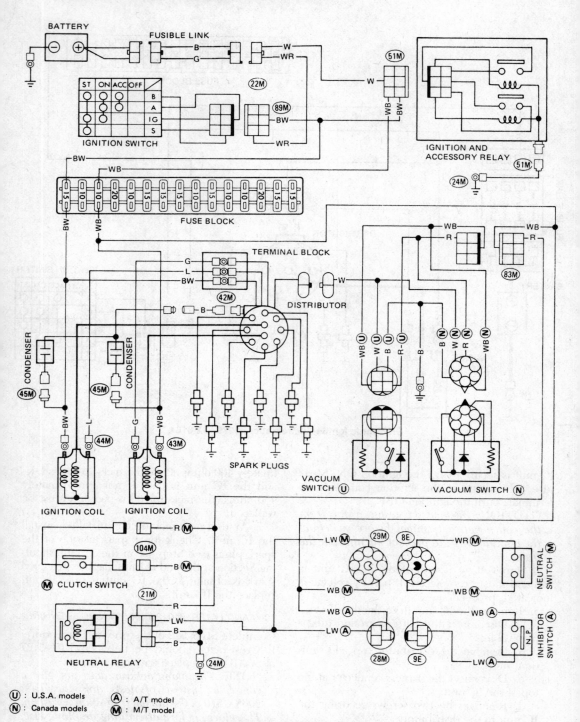

1983–84 200SX ignition wiring diagram

3. Disconnect the high tension cable from the distributor. Hold the cable with insulated pliers to avoid getting shocked. Position the wire about a ¼ of an inch from the engine block and have an assistant turn over the engine using the starter. A spark should jump from the cable to the engine block. If not, there is probably something amiss with the ignition system. Fur-

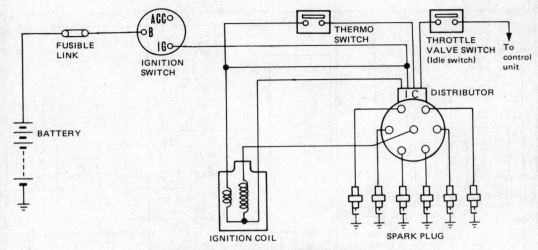

1983–84 810 and Maxima ignition schematic

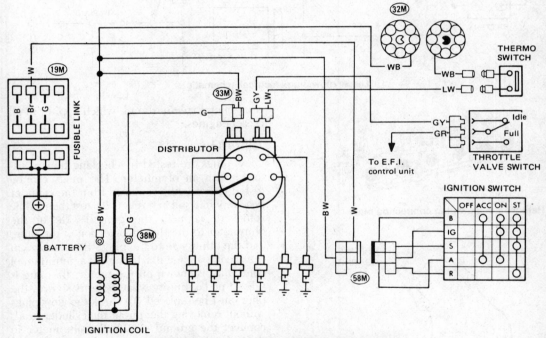

1983–84 810 and Maxima ignition wiring diagram

ther testing should be left to an authorized service technician with the proper test equipment.

Diesel Engine Auto-Glow System

The glow plug circuit is used on diesel engines to initially start the engine from cold. The glow plugs heat up the combustion chambers prior to cranking the engine. This heat, combined with the first "squirt" of fuel from the injectors and the extremely high cylinder pressures, fires the engine during cold starts. After normal operating temperature is reached, the water temperature sensor wired in the glow plug system changes the system's electrical resistance and cancels glow plug operation during hot starting.

GLOW PLUG REMOVAL
LD28 DIESEL

1. Disconnect the glow plug electrical leads. Remove the glow plug connecting plate.

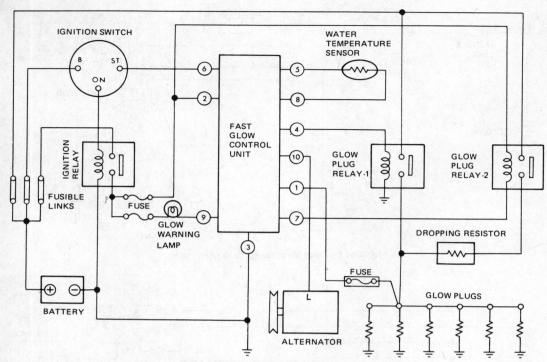

Diesel glow plug electrical schematic

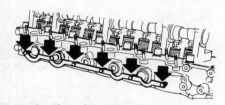

Remove the glow plug connecting plate

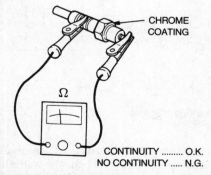

Check glow plug continuity with an ohmmeter (glow plug removed here; connect the ground wire to the threaded portion)

2. Remove the glow plugs by unscrewing them from the cylinder head.

3. Inspect the tips of the plugs for any evidence of melting. If even one glow plug tip looks bad, all the glow plugs must be replaced. This is a general rule-of-thumb which applies to all diesel engines.

TESTING

Glow plugs are tested by checking their resistance with an ohmmeter. The plugs can be tested either while removed from the cylinder head or while still in position. To test them while removed, connect the ground side of the ohmmeter to the threaded section of the plug, and the other side to the plug's tip as shown in the accompanying illustration. If a minimum of continuity is shown on the meter, the plug is OK. If no continuity whatsoever is shown, the plug must be replaced. To check the glow plugs without removing them from the cylinder head, connect the ground side of the ohmmeter to the engine block (or any other convenient ground) and the other end to the glow plug tip. Likewise, a minimum of continuity shown signifies that the plug is OK; a lack of continuity and the plug must be replaced.

INSTALLATION

To install the glow plugs, reverse the removal procedure. Torque the glow plugs to 14–18 ft. lbs., and the glow plug connecting plate bolts to 1 ft. lb.

CHECKING GLOW PLUG CONNECTIONS

A diesel engine's reluctance to start can often be traced to the glow plug busbar (the wire connections to the plugs.). Because diesel engines have a certain degree of vibration when running, they tend to loosen the glow plug busbars. This causes hard starting, as the plugs are not receiving their full current. Periodically tighten the wire connection to all glow plugs.

CAUTION: *The Datsun/Nissan glow plug system is a 12 volt system equipped with a dropping resistor and fast glow control unit. The resistor reduces the amount of current flowing through the plugs during the after-glow period, and the glow plug control unit stops the after-glow when more than 7 volts is detected flowing through the glow plugs. Never apply a full 12 volts directly to any part of the glow plug system, especially the glow plugs themselves.*

FAST GLOW CONTROL UNIT OPERATION

The fast glow control unit on 810 and Maxima diesels has multiple functions, controlling various components of the glow plug system. It has a total often terminals:

① Terminal:
A terminal at which voltage being applied to the glow plug is measured. It serves two functions:
(1) Determines the pre-glow time (approx. 4 to 12 seconds)
(2) Stops after-glow operations when a voltage of more than 7 volts is detected after pre-glow operation
② Terminal:
Control unit's power source terminal
③ Terminal:
Control unit's ground terminal
④ Terminal:
A terminal that controls the ON-OFF operation of glow plug relay-1.
⑤ Terminal:
A terminal connected to the water temperature sensor to serve three functions:
(1) Determines the period that the warning lamp remains illuminated (approx. 1 to 9 seconds)
(2) Determines the after-glow time (approx. 5 to 32 seconds)
(3) Stops pre-glow operation when coolant temperature is higher than 50°C (122°F)

⑥ Terminal:
A terminal connected to the "START" position of the ignition swich (When the ignition key is returned from "START" to "ON", after-glow operation begins.)
⑦ Terminal:
Controls the ON-OFF operation of glow plug relay-2.
⑧ Terminal:
A grounding terminal for the water temperature sensor
⑨ Terminal:
A terminal for the glow/fuel filter warning lamp
⑩ Terminal:
A terminal used to determine whether the engine has started or not (Glow plug relay is turned "OFF" by means of terminal ④ immediately after the engine has started.)

CHECKING PRE-GLOW SYSTEM

1. Connect a test light to the blue/yellow wire leading to the glow control unit. Measure the length of time that the test light is lighted.

Standard operation (except re-start operation within 60 seconds):

Engine Coolant Temperature °C (°F)	Glow Plug Terminal Voltage	Time (sec.)
Below 50 (122)	8V	Approx. 13
	10.5V	Approx. 6
Above 50 (122)	—	Approx. 0

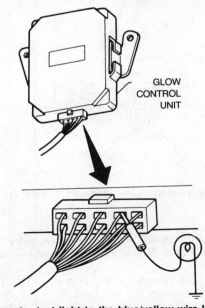

GLOW CONTROL UNIT

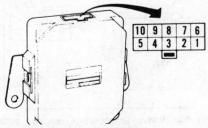

Fast glow control unit connections

Connect a test light to the blue/yellow wire leading into the fast glow control unit

Re-start operation (within 80 seconds): The length of time the light is "ON" should be less than 6.5 seconds. For example, when re-starting the engine 5 seconds after the ignition switch is turned off, the lamp should be "ON" for 1.5 seconds (with engine coolant temperature below 122°F and glow plug voltage 10.5 volts).

AFTER-GLOW OPERATION

1. Connect a test light to the blue/red wire leading to the glow control unit. Measure the length of time that the light is lighted.

Normal condition, when the ignition switch is turned "ON" from "ST" or "OFF":

Engine Coolant Temperature °C (°F)	Time (sec.)
Below −25 (−13) (approx.)	Approx. 31
Approx. 20 (68)	Approx. 17
Approx. 40 (104)	Approx. 9
Above 50 (122) (approx.)	0

Glow Plug Terminal Voltage	Test Lamp ②
Above 7V	OFF
Below 7V	ON

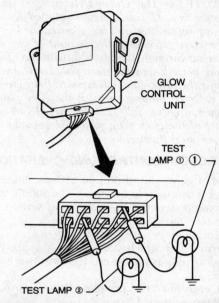

Testing the on/off operation of the glow plug relays 1 and 2

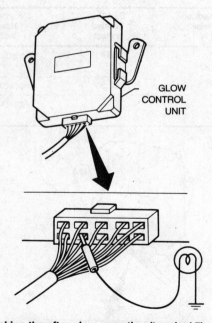

Checking the after-glow operation (terminal 7)

TEMPERATURE °C (°F)	RESISTANCE kΩ
10(50)	3.25 − 4.15
20(68)	2.25 − 2.75
50(122)	0.74 − 0.94
80(176)	0.29 − 0.36

Ignition switch in "ST", the test light is on continuously. Refer to the accompanying illustration.

2. After the pre-glow system turns off, check the operation of the test light ② in the accompanying illustration; (test light no. ① in the illustration is OFF).

Testing the water temperature sensor with an ohmmeter

WATER TEMPERATURE SENSOR OPERATION

The water temperature sensor is connected to the fast glow control unit. Sensor resistance varies with changes in the temperature of the engine coolant.

TESTING

The sensor is tested by measuring resistance while removed from the engine and inserted in a vessel of water as shown in the illustration. Replace the sensor if resistance figures vary greatly from those shown.

Distributor

REMOVAL

1. Unfasten the retaining clips and lift the distributor cap straight up. It will be easier to install the distributor if the wiring is not disconnected from the cap. If the wires must be removed from the cap, mark their positions to aid in installation.

2. Disconnect the distributor wiring harness.

3. Disconnect the vacuum lines.

4. Note the position of the rotor in relation

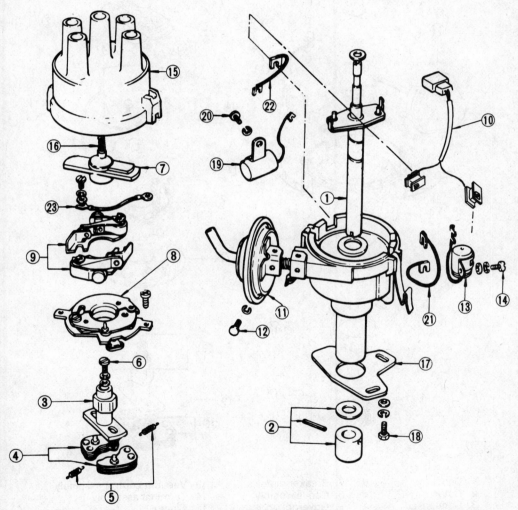

1. Shaft assembly	9. Breaker points	17. Retaining plate
2. Collar set assembly	10. Connector assembly	18. Bolt
3. Cam assembly	11. Vacuum control assembly	19. Condenser
4. Governor weight assembly	12. Screw	20. Screw
5. Governor spring set	13. Condenser	21. Lead wire
6. Screw	14. Screw	22. Lead wire
7. Rotor	15. Distributor cap	23. Ground wire
8. Breaker plate	16. Carbon point assembly	

Exploded view of the dual point distributor

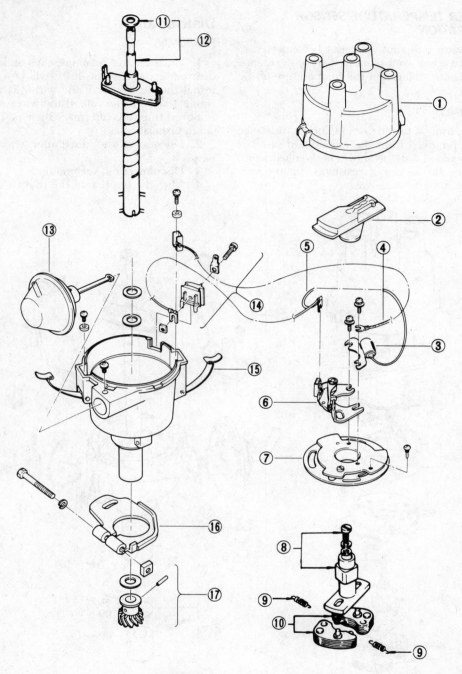

1. Cap	7. Breaker plate	13. Vacuum control assembly
2. Rotor	8. Cam assembly	14. Terminal assembly
3. Condenser	9. Governor spring	15. Clamp
4. Ground wire	10. Governor weight	16. Retaining plate
5. Lead wire	11. Thrust washer	17. Gear set
6. Breaker points	12. Shaft assembly	

Exploded view of the single point distributor

to the base. Scribe a mark on the base of the distributor and on the engine block to facilitate reinstallation. Align the marks with the direction the metal tip of the rotor is pointing.

5. Remove the bolt(s) which holds the distributor to the engine.

6. Lift the distributor assembly from the engine.

INSTALLATION

1. Insert the distributor shaft and assembly into the engine. Line up the mark on the distributor and the one on the engine with the metal tip of the rotor. Make sure that the vacuum advance diaphragm is pointed in the same direction as it was pointed originally. This will be done automatically if the marks on the engine and the distributor are lined up with the rotor.

2. Install the distirbutor hold-down bolt and clamp. Leave the screw loose enough so that you can move the distributor with heavy hand pressure.

3. Connect the primary wire to the coil. Install the distributor cap on the distributor housing. Secure the distributor cap with the spring clips.

4. Install the spark plug wires if removed.

Make sure that the wires are pressed all the way into the top of the distributor cap and firmly onto the spark plug.

5. Adjust the point dwell and set the ignition timing.

NOTE: *If the crankshaft has been turned or the engine disturbed in any manner (i.e., disassembled and rebuilt) while the distributor was removed, or if the marks were not drawn, it will be necessary to initially time the engine. Follow the procedure given below.*

INSTALLATION—ENGINE DISTURBED

1. It is necessary to place the No. 1 cylinder in the firing position to correctly install the distributor. To locate this position, the ignition timing marks on the crankshaft front pulley are used.

2. Remove the No. 1 cylinder spark plug. Turn the crankshaft until the piston in the No. 1 cylinder is moving up on the compression stroke. This can be determined by placing your thumb over the spark plug hole and feeling the air being forced out of the cylinder. Stop turning the crankshaft when the timing marks that are used to time the engine are aligned.

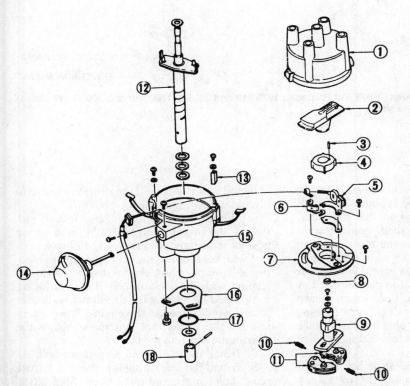

1. Cap assembly
2. Rotor head assembly
3. Roll pin
4. Reluctor
5. Pick-up coil
6. Contactor
7. Breaker plate assembly
8. Packing
9. Rotor shaft
10. Governor spring
11. Governor weight
12. Shaft assembly
13. Cap setter
14. Vacuum controller
15. Housing
16. Fixing plate
17. O-ring
18. Collar

Exploded view of the distributor—1975–77 California models, 610, 710 and 200SX; 1977–78 510, 200SX and 810

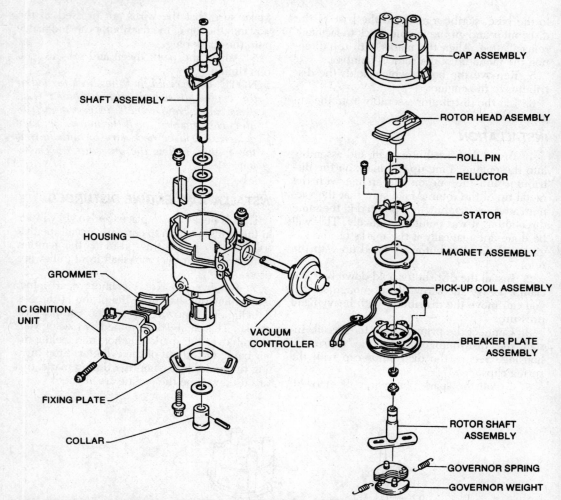

SHAFT ASSEMBLY

HOUSING

GROMMET

IC IGNITION UNIT

FIXING PLATE

COLLAR

VACUUM CONTROLLER

CAP ASSEMBLY

ROTOR HEAD ASEMBLY

ROLL PIN

RELUCTOR

STATOR

MAGNET ASSEMBLY

PICK-UP COIL ASSEMBLY

BREAKER PLATE ASSEMBLY

ROTOR SHAFT ASSEMBLY

GOVERNOR SPRING

GOVERNOR WEIGHT

Exploded view of the distributor—1979 510 (Canada); 1979 510 and 200SX; 1980 510 and 200SX (49-states). 1979 and later 810 and Maxima similar

3. Oil the distributor housing lightly where the distributor bears on the cylinder block.

4. Install the distributor so that the rotor, which is mounted on the shaft, points toward the No. 1 spark plug terminal tower position when the cap is installed. Of course you won't be able to see the direction in which the rotor is pointing if the cap is on the distributor. Lay the cap on the top of the distributor and make a mark on the side of the distributor housing just below the No. 1 spark plug terminal. Make sure that the rotor points toward that mark when you install the distributor.

5. When the distributor shaft has reached the bottom of the hole, move the rotor back and forth slightly until the driving lug on the end of the shaft enters the slots cut in the end

of the oil pump shaft and the distributor assembly slides down into place.

6. When the distributor is correctly installed, the breaker points should be in such a position that they are just ready to break contact with each other; or, on engines with electronic ignition, the reluctor teeth should be aligned with the pick-up coil. This can be accomplished by rotating the distributor body after it has been installed in the engine. Once again, line up the marks that you made before the distributor was removed.

7. Install the distributor hold-down bolt.

8. Install the spark plug into the No. 1 spark plug hole and continue from Step 3 of the preceding distributor installation procedure.

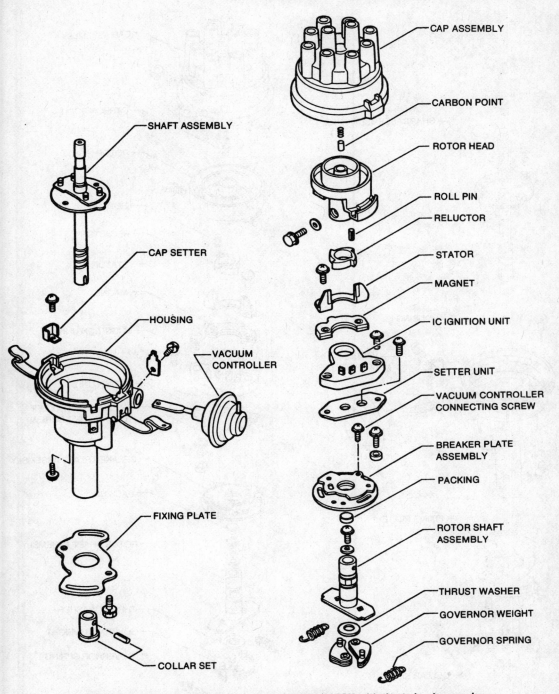

- SHAFT ASSEMBLY
- CAP SETTER
- HOUSING
- VACUUM CONTROLLER
- FIXING PLATE
- COLLAR SET
- CAP ASSEMBLY
- CARBON POINT
- ROTOR HEAD
- ROLL PIN
- RELUCTOR
- STATOR
- MAGNET
- IC IGNITION UNIT
- SETTER UNIT
- VACUUM CONTROLLER CONNECTING SCREW
- BREAKER PLATE ASSEMBLY
- PACKING
- ROTOR SHAFT ASSEMBLY
- THRUST WASHER
- GOVERNOR WEIGHT
- GOVERNOR SPRING

Exploded view of the distributor—1980–82 510/200SX with the twin plug engine

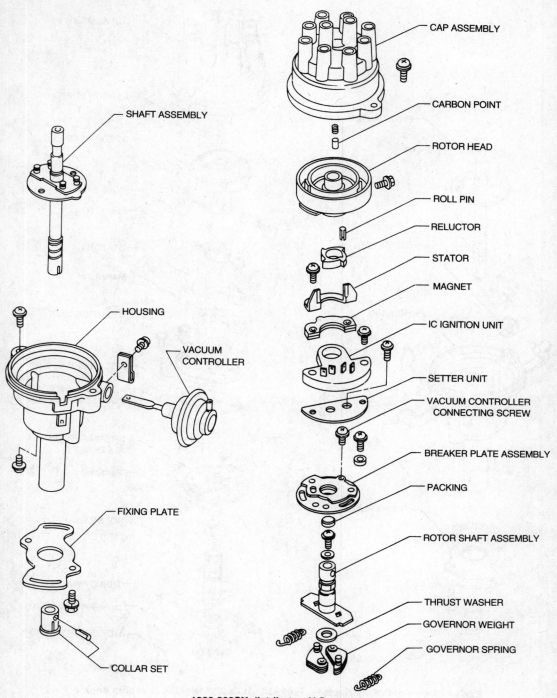

CAP ASSEMBLY

CARBON POINT

ROTOR HEAD

ROLL PIN

RELUCTOR

STATOR

MAGNET

IC IGNITION UNIT

SETTER UNIT

VACUUM CONTROLLER
CONNECTING SCREW

BREAKER PLATE ASSEMBLY

PACKING

ROTOR SHAFT ASSEMBLY

THRUST WASHER

GOVERNOR WEIGHT

GOVERNOR SPRING

SHAFT ASSEMBLY

HOUSING

VACUUM
CONTROLLER

FIXING PLATE

COLLAR SET

1983 200SX distributor, U.S. models

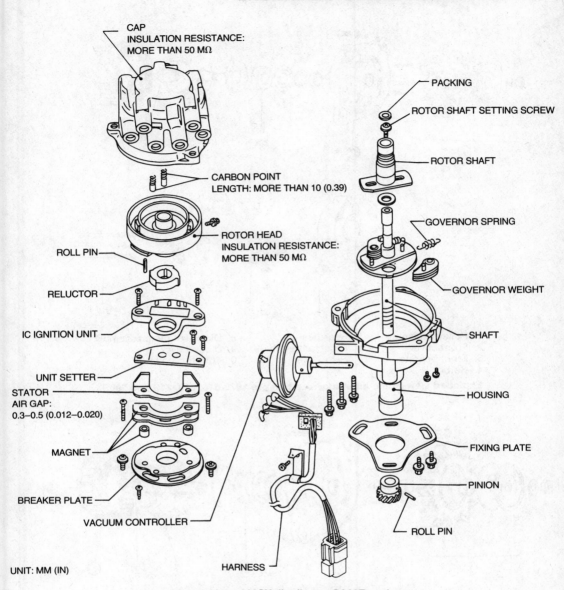

CAP
INSULATION RESISTANCE:
MORE THAN 50 MΩ

PACKING

ROTOR SHAFT SETTING SCREW

ROTOR SHAFT

CARBON POINT
LENGTH: MORE THAN 10 (0.39)

GOVERNOR SPRING

ROTOR HEAD
INSULATION RESISTANCE:
MORE THAN 50 MΩ

ROLL PIN

RELUCTOR

GOVERNOR WEIGHT

IC IGNITION UNIT

SHAFT

UNIT SETTER

STATOR
AIR GAP:
0.3–0.5 (0.012–0.020)

HOUSING

FIXING PLATE

MAGNET

PINION

BREAKER PLATE

ROLL PIN

VACUUM CONTROLLER

UNIT: MM (IN)

HARNESS

1984 and later 200SX distributor, CA20E engines

Regulator

REMOVAL AND INSTALLATION

NOTE: *1978 and later models are equipped with integral regulator alternators. Since the regulator is part of the alternator no adjustments are possible or necessary.*

1. Disconnect the negative battery terminal.

2. Disconnect the electrical lead connector of the regulator.

3. Remove the two mounting screws and remove the regulator from the vehicle.

4. Install the regulator in the reverse order of removal.

ADJUSTMENT

1. Adjust the voltage regulator core gap on regulators that are adjustable by loosening the screw which is used to secure the contact set on the yoke, and move the contact up or down as necessary. Retighten the screw. The gap should be 0.024–0.039 in.

2. Adjust the point gap of the voltage regulator coil by loosening the screw used to secure the upper contact and move the upper contact up or down. The gap for 1973–75 models is 0.012–0.016 in. The point gap for all other models is 0.014–0.018 in.

3. The core gap and point gap on the charge relay coil is or are adjusted in the same manner

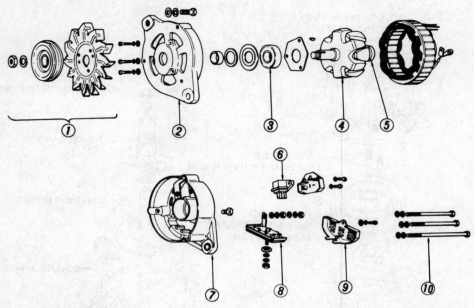

1. Pulley assembly
2. Front cover
3. Front bearing
4. Rotor
5. Rear bearing
6. Brush assembly
7. Rear cover
8. Diode set plate assembly
9. Diode cover
10. Through-bolts

Exploded view of the alternator used on pre-1978 510, 610, 710 and 200SX

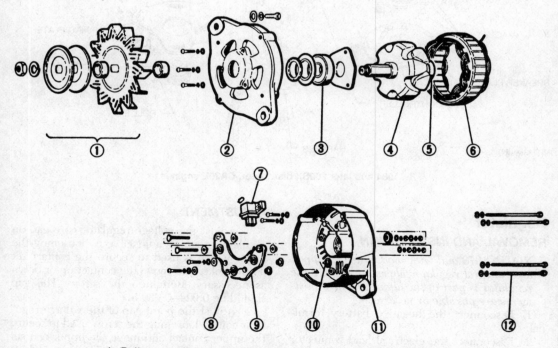

1. Pulley assembly
2. Front cover
3. Front bearing
4. Rotor
5. Rear bearing
6. Stator assembly
7. Brush assembly
8. Diode
9. SR holder
10. Diode
11. Rear cover
12. Through bolts

Exploded view of 1977 810 alternator

as previously outlined for the voltage regulator coil. The core gap is to be set at 0.032–0.039 in. and the point gap adjusted to 0.016–0.024 in.

4. The regulated voltage is adjusted by loosening the locknut and turning the adjusting screw clockwise to increase, or counterclockwise to decrease the regulated voltage. The voltage should be between 14.3–15.3 volts at 68°F.

Alternator

ALTERNATOR PRECAUTIONS

To prevent damage to the alternator and regulator, the following precautionary measures must be taken when working with the electrical system.

1. Never reverse battery connections.

2. Booster batteries for starting must be connected properly. Make sure that the positive cable of the booster battery is connected to the positive terminal of the battery that is getting the boost. This applies to both negative and ground cables.

3. Disconnect the battery cables before using a fast charger; the charger has a tendency to force current through the diodes in the opposite direction for which they are designed. This burns out the diodes.

4. Never use a fast charger as a booster for starting the vehicle.

5. Never disconnect the voltage regulator while the engine is running.

6. Do not ground the alternator output terminal.

7. Do not operate the alternator on an open circuit with the field energized.

8. Do not attempt to polarize an alterntor.

REMOVAL

1. Disconnect the negative battery terminal.

2. Disconnect the two lead wires and connector from the alternator.

3. Loosen the drive belt adjusting bolt and remove the belt.

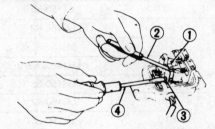

1. Contacts
2. Feeler gauge
3. Adjusting screw
4. Phillips screwdriver

Adjusting the core gap

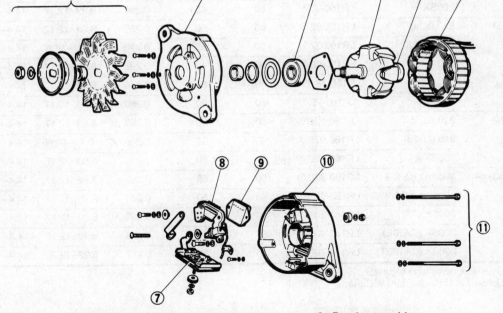

1. Pulley assembly
2. Front cover
3. Front bearing
4. Rotor
5. Rear bearing
6. Stator
7. Diode (Set plate) assembly
8. Brush assembly
9. IC voltage regulator
10. Rear cover
11. Through bolt

Integral regulator-type alternator—most models similar

Alternator and Regulator Specifications

Year	Model	Alternator Identification Number	Rated Output @ 5000 RPM	Output @ 2500 RPM (not less than)	Brush Length (in.)	Brush Spring Tension (oz)	Regulated Voltage
1973	610	LT150-05B	50	37.5	0.571	8.8–12.32	14.3–15.3
1974	610	LT150-05B	50	37.5	0.571	8.8–12.32	14.3–15.3
	710	LT150-13	50	37.5	0.571	8.80	14.3–15.3
1975	610	LT150-13	50	37.5	0.310	9.0–12.2	14.3–15.3
	710	LT150-13	50	37.5	0.571	8.80	14.3–15.3
1976	610	LT150-13	50	37.5	0.310	9.0–12.2	14.3–15.3
	710	LT150-13	50	37.5	0.295	9.0–12.2	14.3–15.3
1977	710	LT150-25	50	37.5	0.295	9.0–12.2	14.3–15.3
	810	LT160-39	60	40	0.310	9.0–12.2	14.3–15.3
	200SX	LT150-35 ①	50	40	0.295	8.99–12.17	14.4–15.0
1978	810	LR160-42 ①	60	40	0.280	8.99–12.17	14.4–15.0
	510	LR150-35 ①	50	40	0.295	8.99–12.17	14.4–15.0
		LR160-47 ①②	60	41	0.295	8.99–12.17	14.4–15.0
	200SX	LR150-35 ①	50	40	0.295	8.99–12.17	14.4–15.0
1979	810	LR160-42 ①	60	40	0.280	8.99–12.17	14.4–15.0
	510	LR150-35 ①	50	40	0.295	8.99–12.17	14.4–15.0
		LR160-47 ①②	60	41	0.295	8.99–12.17	14.4–15.0
	200SX	LR150-35 ①	50	40	0.295	8.99–12.17	14.4–15.0
1980	810	LR160-42B ①	60	50	0.295	8.99–12.17	14.4–15.0
	510	LR150-52 ①	50	40	0.295	8.99–12.17	14.4–15.0
	200SX	LR160-47 ①	60	45	0.295	8.99–12.17	14.4–15.0
1981	810 (L24)	LR160-82 ①	60	50	0.280	8.99–12.17	14.4–15.0
	810 (LD28)	LR160-97 ①	60	52	0.240	10.79–14.60	14.4–15.0
	510	LR150-98 ①	50	40	0.295	8.99–12.17	14.4–15.0
		LR160-78 ①②	60	50	0.276	8.99–12.17	14.4–15.0
	200SX	LR160-78 ①	60	50	0.280	8.99–12.17	14.4–15.0
1982	810 (L24)	LR160-82B ①	60	50	0.280	8.99–12.17	14.4–15.0
	810 (LD28)	LR160-97B ①	60	52	0.240	10.79–14.60	14.4–15.0
	200SX	LR160-78B ①	60	50	0.280	8.99–12.17	14.4–15.0
1983–84	Maxima (L24E)	LR160-82B ①	60	50	0.280	8.99–12.17	14.4–15.0
	Maxima (LD28)	LR160-97C ①	60	50	0.280	8.99–12.17	14.4–15.0
	200SX (Z22E)	LR160-109 ①	60	50	0.280	8.99–12.17	14.4–15.0
	200SX (CA20E)	LR160-104 ①	60	50	0.276	8.99–12.17	14.4–15.1
	200SX (CA18ET)	LR170-706 ①	70	50	0.217	5.29–12.70	14.4–15.0

① Uses integral voltage regulator
② Optional in U.S., standard in Canada

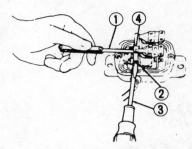

1. Feeler gauge
2. Screw
3. Phillips screwdriver
4. Upper contact

Adjust the point gap

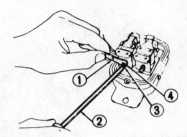

1. Wrench
2. Phillips screwdriver
3. Adjusting screw
4. Locknut

Adjust the regulated voltage

4. Unscrew the alternator attaching bolts and remove the alternator from the vehicle.

INSTALLATION AND BELT ADJUSTMENT

To install, reverse the above removal procedure. Alternator belt tension is quite critical. A belt that is too tight may cause alternator bearing failure; one that is too loose will cause a gradual battery discharge. For details on correct belt adjustment, see "Drive Belts" in Chapter one.

Starter

Datsun began using a reduction gear starter in 1978 on the 810 and in the Canadian versions of the 510 and 200SX. They were also available as an option on the U.S. 510 and 200SX. The differences between the gear reduction and conventional starters are: the gear reduction starter has a set of ratio reduction gears while the conventional starter does not; the brushes on the gear reduction starter are located on a plate behind the starter drive housing, while the conventional starter's brushes are located in its rear cover. The extra gears on the gear reduction starter make the starter pinion gear turn at about half the speed of the starter, giving the starter twice the turning powr of a conventional starter.

Note the wire locations before removing the starter

REMOVAL AND INSTALLATION

1. Disconnect the negative battery cable from the battery.

2. Disconnect the starter wiring at the starter, taking note of the positions for correct installation.

3. Remove the bolts attaching the starter to the engine and remove the starter from the vehicle.

4. Install the starter in the reverse order of removal.

BRUSH REPLACEMENT

Non-Reduction Gear Type

1. With the starter out of the vehicle, remove the bolts holding the solenoid to the top of the starter and remove the solenoid.

2. To remove the brushes, remove the two thru-bolts, and the two rear cover attaching screws and remove the rear cover.

3. Disconnect the electrical leads and remove the brushes.

4. Install the brushes in the reverse order of removal.

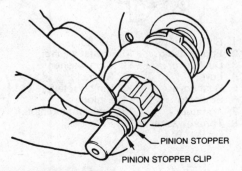

PINION STOPPER
PINION STOPPER CLIP

Pinion stopper removal

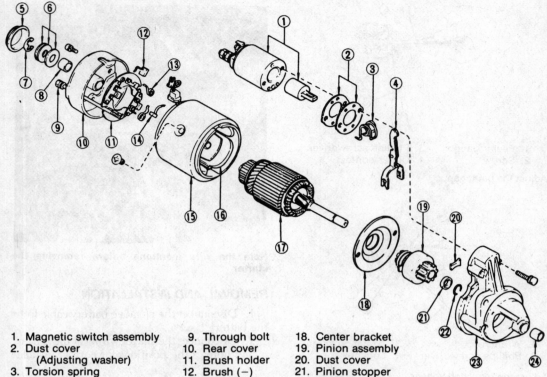

1. Magnetic switch assembly
2. Dust cover
   (Adjusting washer)
3. Torsion spring
4. Shift lever
5. Dust cover
6. Thrust washer
7. E-ring
8. Rear cover metal
9. Through bolt
10. Rear cover
11. Brush holder
12. Brush (−)
13. Brush spring
14. Brush (+)
15. Yoke
16. Field coil
17. Armature
18. Center bracket
19. Pinion assembly
20. Dust cover
21. Pinion stopper
22. Stopper clip
23. Gear case
24. Gear case metal

Exploded view of non-reduction gear starter

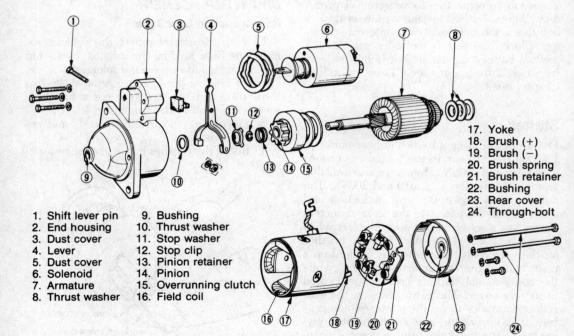

1. Shift lever pin
2. End housing
3. Dust cover
4. Lever
5. Dust cover
6. Solenoid
7. Armature
8. Thrust washer
9. Bushing
10. Thrust washer
11. Stop washer
12. Stop clip
13. Pinion retainer
14. Pinion
15. Overrunning clutch
16. Field coil
17. Yoke
18. Brush (+)
19. Brush (−)
20. Brush spring
21. Brush retainer
22. Bushing
23. Rear cover
24. Through-bolt

Exploded view of the reduction gear starter motor

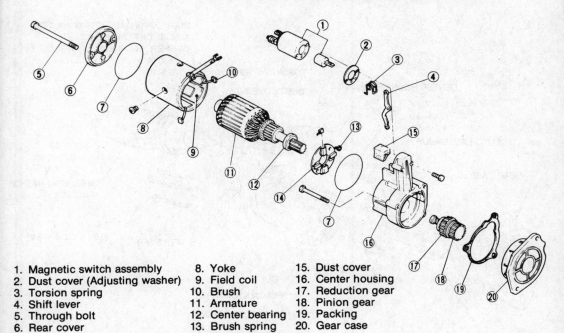

1. Magnetic switch assembly
2. Dust cover (Adjusting washer)
3. Torsion spring
4. Shift lever
5. Through bolt
6. Rear cover
7. O-ring
8. Yoke
9. Field coil
10. Brush
11. Armature
12. Center bearing
13. Brush spring
14. Brush holder
15. Dust cover
16. Center housing
17. Reduction gear
18. Pinion gear
19. Packing
20. Gear case

Gear reduction starter

Battery and Starter Specifications

All cars use 12 volt, negative ground electrical systems

| Year | Model | Battery Amp Hour Capacity | Starter | | | | | | Brush Spring Tension (oz) | Min Brush Length (in.) |
| | | | Lock Test | | | No Load Test | | | | |
			Amps	Volts	Torque (ft. lbs.)	Amps	Volts	RPM		
1973–77	610, 710	50, 60	430 MT	6.0	6.3	60	12	7,000	49–64	0.47
			540 AT	5.0	6.0	60	12	6,000	49–64	0.47
1977–78	200SX, 510	60	—	—	—	60 MT	12	7,000	49–64	0.47
						60 AT	12	6,000	49–64	0.47
						100 RG	12	4,300	56–70	0.43
1979–82	200SX, 510	60 ①	—	—	—	60 MT	11.5	7,000	49–64	0.47
						60 AT	11.5	6,000	49–64	0.47
						100RG	11.0	3,900	56–70	0.43
1977–79	810	60 ②	—	—	—	100 RG	12	4,300	56–70	0.43
1980–82	810 (L24)	60 ②	—	—	—	100 RG	11	3,900	56–70	0.43
	810 (LD28)	80	—	—	—	100 RG	11	3,900	96–116.8	0.35
1983–84	Maxima (L24E)	60 ②	—	—	—	100 RG	11	3,900	56–70	0.43
	Maxima (LD28)	80	—	—	—	140 RG	11	3,900	96–116.8	0.35
	200SX (Z22E)	60	—	—	—	60 AT	11.5	6,000	64–78.4	0.47
	200SX (Z22E)	60	—	—	—	60 MT	11.5	7,000	64–78.4	0.47
	200SX (Z22E) ③	70	—	—	—	100 RG	11	3,900	56–70	0.43
	200SX ④	60 ②	—	—	—	60	11.5	7,000	64–78.4	0.43
	200SX ④	60 ②	—	—	—	100 RG	11	3,900	56–70	0.43

MT: Manual Transmission
AT: Automatic Transmission
RG: Reduction Gear Starter
—: Not Recommended
① Canada—65
② Canada, optional U.S.—70
③ Canada
④ 1984 and later

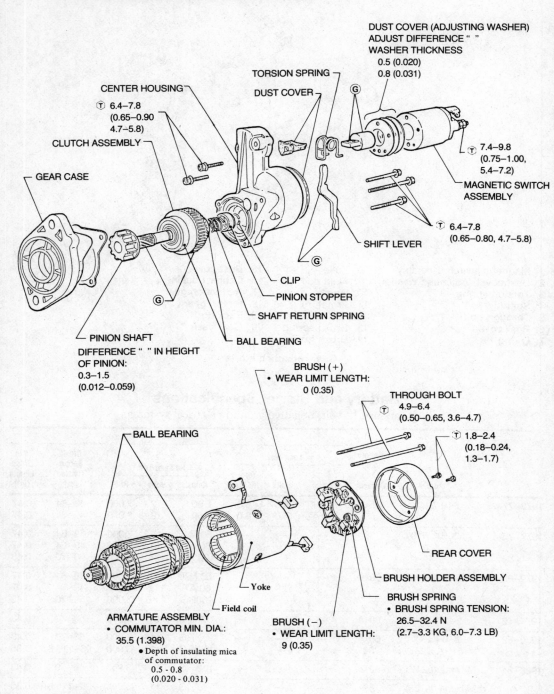

DUST COVER (ADJUSTING WASHER)
ADJUST DIFFERENCE " "
WASHER THICKNESS
0.5 (0.020)
0.8 (0.031)

TORSION SPRING

CENTER HOUSING

DUST COVER

Ⓣ 6.4–7.8
(0.65–0.90
4.7–5.8)

CLUTCH ASSEMBLY

Ⓖ

Ⓣ 7.4–9.8
(0.75–1.00,
5.4–7.2)

MAGNETIC SWITCH
ASSEMBLY

GEAR CASE

Ⓣ 6.4–7.8
(0.65–0.80, 4.7–5.8)

SHIFT LEVER

Ⓖ

CLIP

PINION STOPPER

SHAFT RETURN SPRING

Ⓖ

PINION SHAFT
DIFFERENCE " " IN HEIGHT
OF PINION:
0.3–1.5
(0.012–0.059)

BALL BEARING

BRUSH (+)
• WEAR LIMIT LENGTH:
0 (0.35)

THROUGH BOLT
4.9–6.4
(0.50–0.65, 3.6–4.7)

Ⓣ 1.8–2.4
(0.18–0.24,
1.3–1.7)

BALL BEARING

REAR COVER

BRUSH HOLDER ASSEMBLY

BRUSH SPRING
• BRUSH SPRING TENSION:
26.5–32.4 N
(2.7–3.3 KG, 6.0–7.3 LB)

Yoke

Field coil

ARMATURE ASSEMBLY
• COMMUTATOR MIN. DIA.:
35.5 (1.398)
  • Depth of insulating mica
    of commutator:
    0.5 - 0.8
    (0.020 - 0.031)

BRUSH (−)
• WEAR LIMIT LENGTH:
9 (0.35)

Ⓖ : HIGH-TEMPERATURE GREASE POINTS
Ⓣ : N·M (KG-M, FT-LB)
UNIT: MM (IN)

LD28 diesel gear reduction starter

Reduction Gear Type

1. Remove the starter. Remove the solenoid.

2. Remove the through bolts and the rear cover. The rear cover can be pried off with a screwdriver, but be careful not to damage the O-ring.

3. Remove the starter housing, armature, and brush holder from the center housing. They can be removed as an assembly.

4. Remove the positive side brush from its holder. The positive brush is insulated from the brush holder, and its lead wire is connected to the field coil.

5. Carefully lift the negative brush from the commutator and remove it from the holder.

6. Installation is the reverse.

STARTER DRIVE REPLACEMENT

Non-Reduction Gear Type

1. With the starter motor removed from the vehicle, remove the solenoid from the starter.

2. Remove the two thru-bolts and separate the gear case from the yoke housing.

3. Remove the pinion stopper clip and the pinion stopper.

4. Slide the starter drive off the armature shaft.

5. Install the starter drive and reassemble the starter in the reverse order of removal.

Reduction Gear Type

1. Remove the starter.

2. Remove the solenoid and the shift lever.

3. Remove the bolts securing the center housing to the front cover and separate the parts.

4. Remove the gears and starter drive.

5. Installation is the reverse.

Battery

Refer to Chapter One for details on battery maintenance.

REMOVAL AND INSTALLATION

1. Disconnect the negative (ground) cable from the terminal, and then the positive cable. Special pullers are available to remove the cable clamps.

NOTE: *To avoid sparks, always disconnect the ground cable first, and connect it last.*

2. Remove the battery hold-down clamp.

3. Remove the battery, being careful not to spill the acid.

NOTE: *Spilled acid can be neutralized with a baking soda/water solution. If you somehow get acid into your eyes, flush it out with lots of water and get to a doctor.*

4. Clean the battery posts thoroughly before reinstalling, or when installing a new battery.

5. Clean the cable clamps, using a wire brush, both inside and out.

6. Install the battery and the hold-down clamp or strap. Connect the positive, and then the negative cable. Do not hammer them in place. The terminals should be coated lightly (externally) with grease to prevent corrosion. There are also felt washers impregnated with an anti-corrosion substance which are slipped over the battery posts before installing the cables; these are available in auto parts stores.

CAUTION: *Make absolutely sure that the battery is connected properly before you turn on the ignition switch. Reversed polarity can burn out your alternator and regulator within a matter of seconds.*

Cylinder Compression

CHECKING

Use the "Checking Engine Compression" page in this chapter when doing a compression check of the engine's cylinders. Maximum cylinder compression for all Datsun/Nissan gasoline engines covered in this guide (except the L24 engine in the 1977–78 810) is 171 psi at 350 rpm. Minimum cylinder compression is 128 psi at 350 rpm. Maximum compression pressure for the 1977–78 810 L24 is 185 psi at 350 rpm. Compression pressures for the LD28 diesel are 455 psi maximum, 356 psi minimum, at 200 rpm.

1984 and Later 200SX

When checking cylinder compression on both the CA20E and CA18ET engines, be sure to disconnect the distributor harness connector prior to doing the compression check.

LD28 Diesel

Checking compression on the Datsun/Nissan LD28 diesel engine is the same procedure as on the gasoline engines, except for the following:

1. A special compression gauge adaptor suitable for diesel engines *must* be used.

2. Begin the procedure by removing the spill tube assembly, the injection tubes on the nozzle side, and the nozzle assemblies.

CAUTION: *Remove the nozzle washer with a pair of tweezers. Don't forget to remove this washer; otherwise, it may get lost when the engine is cranked.*

3. When fitting the compression gauge adaptor to the cylinder head, make sure the bleeder of the gauge is closed.

ENGINE OVERHAUL

Most engine overhaul procedures are fairly standard. In addition to specific parts replacement procedures and complete specifications for your individual engine, this chapter also is a guide to accepted rebuilding procedures. Examples of standard rebuilding practice are shown and should be used along with specific details concerning your particular engine.

Competent and accurate machine shop services will ensure maximum performance, reliability and engine life. Procedures marked with the symbol shown above should be performed by a competent machine shop, and are provided so that you will be familiar with the procedures necessary to a successful overhaul.

In most instances it is more profitable for the do-it-yourself mechanic to remove, clean and inspect the component, buy the necessary parts and deliver these to a shop for actual machine work.

On the other hand, much of the rebuilding work (crankshaft, block, bearings, pistons, rods, and other components) is well within the scope of the do-it-yourself mechanic.

Tools

The tools required for an engine overhaul or parts replacement will depend on the depth of your involvement. With a few exceptions, they will be the tools found in a mechanic's tool kit (see Chapter 1). More in-depth work will require any or all of the following:
• a dial indicator (reading in thousandths) mounted on a universal base
• micrometers and telescope gauges
• jaw and screw-type pullers
• scraper
• valve spring compressor
• ring groove cleaner
• piston ring expander and compressor
• ridge reamer
• cylinder hone or glaze breaker

• Plastigage®
• engine stand

Use of most of these tools is illustrated in this chapter. Many can be rented for a one-time use from a local parts jobber or tool supply house specializing in automotive work.

Occasionally, the use of special tools is called for. See the information on Special Tools and the Safety Notice in the front of this book before substituting another tool.

Inspection Techniques

Procedures and specifications are given in this chapter for inspecting, cleaning and assessing the wear limits of most major components. Other procedures such as Magnaflux and Zyglo can be used to locate material flaws and stress cracks. Magnaflux is a magnetic process applicable only to ferrous materials. The Zyglo process coats the material with a flourescent dye penetrant and can be used on any material. Check for suspected surface cracks can be more readily made using spot check dye. The dye is sprayed onto the suspected area, wiped off and the area sprayed with a developer. Cracks will show up brightly.

Overhaul Tips

Aluminum has become extremely popular for use in engines, due to its low weight. Observe the following precautions when handling aluminum parts:
• Never hot tank aluminum parts (the caustic hot-tank solution will eat the aluminum)
• Remove all aluminum parts (identification tag, etc.) from engine parts prior to hot-tanking.
• Always coat threads lightly with engine oil or anti-seize compounds before installation, to prevent seizure.
• Never over-torque bolts or spark plugs, especially in aluminum threads.

Stripped threads in any component can be repaired using any of several commercial repair kits (Heli-Coil, Microdot, Keen-serts, etc.)

When assembling the engine, any parts that will be in frictional contact must be pre-lubed to provide lubrication at initial start-up. Any product specifically formulated for this purpose can be used, but engine oil is not recommended as a pre-lube.

When semi-permanent (locked, but removable) installation of bolts or nuts is desired, threads should be cleaned and coated with Loctite® or other similar, commercial non-hardening sealant.

Repairing Damaged Threads

Several methods of repairing damaged threads are available. Heli-Coil® (shown here), Keenserts® and Microdot® are among the most widely used. All involve basically the same principle—drilling out stripped threads, tapping the hole and installing a pre-wound insert—making welding, plugging and oversize fasteners unnecessary.

Two types of thread repair inserts are usually supplied—a standard type for most Inch Coarse, Inch Fine, Metric Coarse and Metric Fine thread sizes and a spark plug type to fit most spark plug port sizes. Consult the individual manufacturer's catalog to determine exact applications. Typical thread repair kits will contain a selection of pre-wound threaded inserts, a tap (corresponding to the outside diameter threads of the insert) and an installation tool. Spark plug inserts usually differ because they require a tap equipped with pilot threads and a combined reamer/tap section. Most manufacturers also supply blister-packed thread repair inserts separately in addition to a master kit containing a variety of taps and inserts plus installation tools.

Before effecting a repair to a threaded hole, remove any snapped, broken or damaged bolts or studs. Penetrating oil can be used to free frozen threads; the offending item can be removed with locking pliers or with a screw or stud extractor. After the hole is clear, the thread can be repaired, as follows:

Drill out the damaged threads with specified drill. Drill completely through the hole or to the bottom of a blind hole

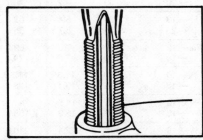

With the tap supplied, tap the hole to receive the thread insert. Keep the tap well oiled and back it out frequently to avoid clogging the threads

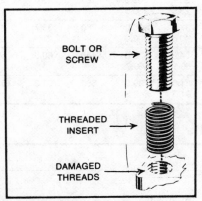

BOLT OR SCREW

THREADED INSERT

DAMAGED THREADS

Damaged bolt holes can be repaired with thread repair inserts

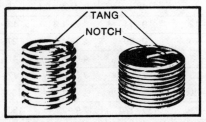

TANG

NOTCH

Standard thread repair insert (left) and spark plug thread insert (right)

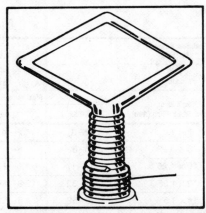

Screw the threaded insert onto the installation tool until the tang engages the slot. Screw the insert into the tapped hole until it is ¼–½ turn below the top surface. After installation break off the tang with a hammer and punch

Standard Torque Specifications and Fastener Markings

In the absence of specific torques, the following chart can be used as a guide to the maximum safe torque of a particular size/grade of fastener.

- There is no torque difference for fine or coarse threads.
- Torque values are based on clean, dry threads. Reduce the value by 10% if threads are oiled prior to assembly.
- The torque required for aluminum components or fasteners is considerably less.

U.S. Bolts

SAE Grade Number	1 or 2			5			6 or 7		
Number of lines always 2 less than the grade number.									
	Maximum Torque			Maximum Torque			Maximum Torque		
Bolt Size (Inches)—(Thread)	Ft./Lbs.	Kgm	Nm	Ft./Lbs.	Kgm	Nm	Ft./Lbs.	Kgm	Nm
¼—20	5	0.7	6.8	8	1.1	10.8	10	1.4	13.5
—28	6	0.8	8.1	10	1.4	13.6			
5/16—18	11	1.5	14.9	17	2.3	23.0	19	2.6	25.8
—24	13	1.8	17.6	19	2.6	25.7			
⅜—16	18	2.5	24.4	31	4.3	42.0	34	4.7	46.0
—24	20	2.75	27.1	35	4.8	47.5			
7/16—14	28	3.8	37.0	49	6.8	66.4	55	7.6	74.5
—20	30	4.2	40.7	55	7.6	74.5			
½—13	39	5.4	52.8	75	10.4	101.7	85	11.75	115.2
—20	41	5.7	55.6	85	11.7	115.2			
9/16—12	51	7.0	69.2	110	15.2	149.1	120	16.6	162.7
—18	55	7.6	74.5	120	16.6	162.7			
⅝—11	83	11.5	112.5	150	20.7	203.3	167	23.0	226.5
—18	95	13.1	128.8	170	23.5	230.5			
¾—10	105	14.5	142.3	270	37.3	366.0	280	38.7	379.6
—16	115	15.9	155.9	295	40.8	400.0			
⅞— 9	160	22.1	216.9	395	54.6	535.5	440	60.9	596.5
—14	175	24.2	237.2	435	60.1	589.7			
1— 8	236	32.5	318.6	590	81.6	799.9	660	91.3	894.8
—14	250	34.6	338.9	660	91.3	849.8			

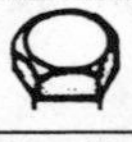

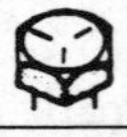

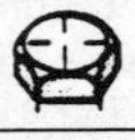

Metric Bolts

Relative Strength Marking	4.6, 4.8			8.8		
Bolt Markings						
	Maximum Torque			Maximum Torque		
Bolt Size Thread Size x Pitch (mm)	Ft./Lbs.	Kgm	Nm	Ft./Lbs.	Kgm	Nm
6 x 1.0	2–3	.2–.4	3–4	3–6	.4–.8	5–8
8 x 1.25	6–8	.8–1	8–12	9–14	1.2–1.9	13–19
10 x 1.25	12–17	1.5–2.3	16–23	20–29	2.7–4.0	27–39
12 x 1.25	21–32	2.9–4.4	29–43	35–53	4.8–7.3	47–72
14 x 1.5	35–52	4.8–7.1	48–70	57–85	7.8–11.7	77–110
16 x 1.5	51–77	7.0–10.6	67–100	90–120	12.4–16.5	130–160
18 x 1.5	74–110	10.2–15.1	100–150	130–170	17.9–23.4	180–230
20 x 1.5	110–140	15.1–19.3	150–190	190–240	26.2–46.9	160–320
22 x 1.5	150–190	22.0–26.2	200–260	250–320	34.5–44.1	340–430
24 x 1.5	190–240	26.2–46.9	260–320	310–410	42.7–56.5	420–550

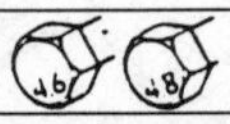

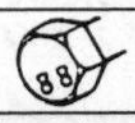

CHECKING ENGINE COMPRESSION

A noticeable lack of engine power, excessive oil consumption and/or poor fuel mileage measured over an extended period are all indicators of internal engine wear. Worn piston rings, scored or worn cylinder bores, blown head gaskets, sticking or burnt valves and worn valve seats are all possible culprits here. A check of each cylinder's compression will help you locate the problems.

As mentioned in the "Tools and Equipment" section of Chapter 1, a screw-in type compression gauge is more accurate than the type you simply hold against the spark plug hole, although it takes slightly longer to use. It's worth it to obtain a more accurate reading. Follow the procedures below for gasoline and diesel-engined cars.

Gasoline Engines

1. Warm up the engine to normal operating temperature.
2. Remove all spark plugs.

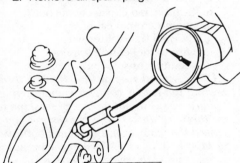

The screw-in type compression gauge is more accurate

3. Disconnect the high-tension lead from the ignition coil.
4. On carbureted cars, fully open the throttle either by operating the carburetor throttle linkage by hand or by having an assistant "floor" the accelerator pedal. On fuel-injected cars, disconnect the cold start valve and all injector connections.
5. Screw the compression gauge into the No. 1 spark plug hole until the fitting is snug.
   NOTE: *Be careful not to crossthread the plug hole. On aluminum cylinder heads use extra care, as the threads in these heads are easily ruined.*
6. Ask an assistant to depress the accelerator pedal fully on both carbureted and fuel-injected cars. Then, while you read the compression gauge, ask the assistant to crank the engine two or three times in short bursts using the ignition switch.

7. Read the compression gauge at the end of each series of cranks, and record the highest of these readings. Repeat this procedure for each of the engine's cylinders. Compare the highest reading of each cylinder to the compression pressure specifications in the "Tune-Up Specifications" chart in Chapter 2. The specs in this chart are maximum values.

A cylinder's compression pressure is usually acceptable if it is not less than 80% of maximum. The difference between each cylinder should be no more than 12–14 pounds.

8. If a cylinder is unusually low, pour a tablespoon of clean engine oil into the cylinder through the spark plug hole and repeat the compression test. If the compression comes up after adding the oil, it appears that that cylinder's piston rings or bore are damaged or worn. If the pressure remains low, the valves may not be seating properly (a valve job is needed), or the head gasket may be blown near that cylinder. If compression in any two adjacent cylinders is low, and if the addition of oil doesn't help the compression, there is leakage past the head gasket. Oil and coolant water in the combustion chamber can result from this problem. There may be evidence of water droplets on the engine dipstick when a head gasket has blown.

Diesel Engines

Checking cylinder compression on diesel engines is basically the same procedure as on gasoline engines except for the following:

1. A special compression gauge adaptor suitable for diesel engines (because these engines have much greater compression pressures) must be used.
2. Remove the injector tubes and remove the injectors from each cylinder.
   NOTE: *Don't forget to remove the washer underneath each injector; otherwise, it may get lost when the engine is cranked.*

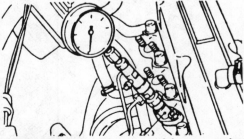

Diesel engines require a special compression gauge adaptor

3. When fitting the compression gauge adaptor to the cylinder head, make sure the bleeder of the gauge (if equipped) is closed.
4. When reinstalling the injector assemblies, install new washers underneath each injector.

CA20E ENGINE

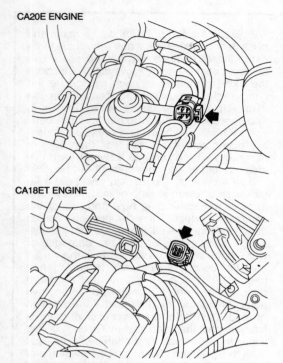

CA18ET ENGINE

Distributor harness connector locations, 1984 and later 200SX engines

4. When reinstalling the injector assemblies, install new nozzle washers.

ENGINE MECHANICAL

Engine Removal and Installation

The engine and transmission are removed together and then separated when out of the car.

1. Mark the location of the hinges on the hood. Unbolt and remove the hood.

2. Disconnect the battery cables. Remove the battery from the models with the L16 engine and Z20E models with air conditioning.

3. Drain the coolant and automatic transmission fluid.

4. Remove the grille on the 510, 610, and 710 models. Remove the radiator and radiator shroud after disconnecting the automatic transmission coolant tubes.

5. Remove the air cleaner.

6. Remove the fan and pulley.

7. Disconnect:
   a. water temperature gauge wire;
   b. oil pressure sending unit wire;
   c. ignition distributor primary wire;
   d. starter motor connections;
   e. fuel hose;

CAUTION: *On all fuel injected models, the fuel pressure must be released before the fuel lines can be disconnected. See the pressure releasing procedure under "Gasoline Engine Fuel Filter" in Chapter 1.*

   f. alternator leads;
   g. heater hoses;
   h. throttle and choke connections;
   i. engine ground cable;
   j. thermal transmitter wire;
   k. wire to fuel cut-off solenoid;
   l. vacuum cut solenoid wire.

NOTE: *A good rule of thumb when disconnecting the rather complex engine wiring of today's cars is to put a piece of masking tape on the wire and on the connection you removed the wire from, then mark both pieces of tape 1, 2, 3, etc. When replacing wiring, simply match the pieces of tape.*

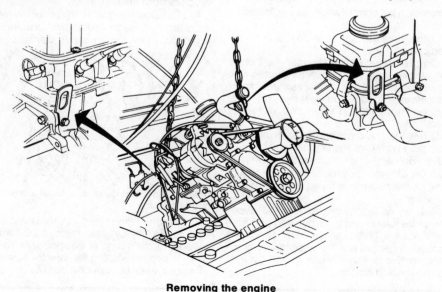

Removing the engine

CAUTION: *On models with air conditioning, it is necessary to remove the compressor and the condenser from their mounts. DO NOT ATTEMPT TO UNFASTEN ANY OF THE AIR CONDITIONER HOSES. See Chapter One for additional warnings.*

8. Disconnect the power brake booster hose from the engine.

9. Remove the clutch operating cylinder and return spring.

10. Disconnect the speedometer cable from the transmission. Disconnect the backup light switch and any other wiring or attachments to the transmission. On cars with the L18 and L20B engine, disconnect the parking brake cable at the rear adjuster.

11. Disconnect the column shift linkage. Remove the floorshift lever. On Z20 models, remove the boot, withdraw the lock pin, and remove the lever from inside the car.

12. Detach the exhaust pipe from the exhaust manifold. Remove the front section of the exhaust system.

13. Mark the relationship of the driveshaft flanges and remove the driveshaft.

14. Place a jack under the transmission. Remove the rear crossmember.

Gearshift lever removal—1980 and later 510 and 200SX

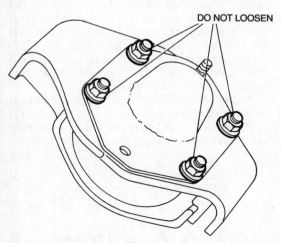

On 1984 and late 200SXs, do not loosen the front engine mounting insulation cover securing bolts

15. Attach a hoist to the lifting hooks on the engine (at either end of the cylinder head). Support the engine.

CAUTION: *On 1984 and later 200SX models, do not loosen the front engine mounting insulator cover securing nuts. When the cover is removed, the damper oil will flow out and the mounting insulator will not function.*

16. Unbolt the front engine mounts. Tilt the engine by lowering the jack under the transmission and raising the hoist.

17. Reverse the procedure to install the engine.

NOTE: *When installing the CA20E and CA18ET engines into 1984 and later 200SXs, the rear engine mounting bracket must be adjusted. Using the accompanying illustration as a guide, adjust the rear mounting stopper clearance ("X" in the illustration) to 0.51 in.*

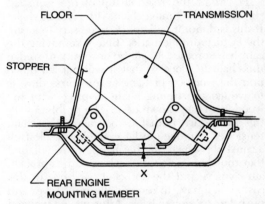

When installing the 1984 and later 200SX engine, adjust the rear mounting stopper clearance ("x") to 0.51 in.

Cylinder Head
REMOVAL AND INSTALLATION

NOTE: *To prevent distortion or warping of the cylinder head, allow the engine to cool completely before removing the head bolts.*

L18 and L20B

1. Crank the engine until the No. 1 piston is TDC of the compression stroke and disconnect the negative battery cable, drain the cooling system and remove the air cleaner and attending hoses.

2. Remove the alternator.

3. Disconnect the carburetor throttle linkage, the fuel line and any other vacuum lines or electrical leads, and remove the carburetor.

4. Disconnect the exhaust pipe from the exhaust manifold.

5. Remove the fan and fan pulley.

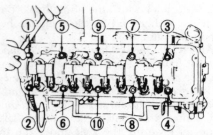

Cylinder head bolt loosening sequence, L18 and L20 4-cylinder engines

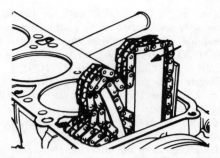

Wedge the chain with a wooden block (arrow). If you don't you'll be fishing for the chain in the crankcase (overhead cam engines)

6. Remove the spark plugs to protect them from damage. Lay the spark plugs aside and out of the way.

7. Remove the rocker cover.

8. Remove the water pump.

9. Remove the fuel pump.

10. Remove the fuel pump drive cam.

11. Mark the relationship of the camshaft sprocket to the timing chain with paint or chalk. If this is done, it will not be necessary to locate the factory timing marks. Before removing the camshaft sprocket, it will be necessary to wedge the chain in place so that it will not fall down into the front cover. The factory procedure is to wedge the timing chain in place with the wooden wedge shown here. The problem with this procedure is that it may allow the chain tensioner to move out far enough to cock itself against the chain. If this happens, you'll find that the chain won't go back over the sprocket after you've put the sprocket back on. In this case, you'll have to remove the front cover and push the tensioner back. After you've wedged the chain, unbolt the camshaft sprocket and remove it.

12. Loosen and remove the cylinder head bolts. You will need a 10 mm Allen wrench to remove the head bolts. Keep the bolts in order since they are different sizes. Lift the cylinder head assembly from the engine. Remove the intake and exhaust manifolds as necessary.

13. Thoroughly clean the cylinder block and head mating surfaces and install a new cylinder head gasket. Check for head and block war-

page; see "Cleaning and Inspection" and "Resurfacing" below. Do not use sealer on the cylinder head gasket.

14. With the crankshaft turned so that the No. 1 piston is at TDC of the compression stroke (if not already done so as mentioned in Step 1), make sure that the camshaft sprocket timing mark and the oblong groove in the plate are aligned.

15. Place the cylinder head in position on the cylinder block, being careful not to allow any of the valves to come in contact with any of the pistons. Do not rotate the crankshaft or camshaft separately because of possible damage which might occur to the valves.

16. Temporarily tighten the two center right and left cylinder head bolts to 14.5 ft. lbs.

17. Install the camshaft sprocket together with the timing chain to the camshaft. Make sure the marks you made earlier line up with each other. If you get into trouble, see "Timing Chain Removal and Installation" for timing procedures.

18. Install the cylinder head bolts. Note that there are two sizes of bolts used; the longer bolts are installed on the driver's side of the engine with a smaller bolt in the center position. The remaining small bolts are installed on the opposite side of the cylinder head.

19. Tighten the cylinder head bolts in three stages: first to 29 ft. lbs., second to 43 ft. lbs., and lastly to 47–62 ft. lbs.

Tighten the cylinder head bolts on all models in the proper sequence.

20. Install and assemble the remaining components of the engine in the reverse order of removal. Adjust the valves. Fill the cooling

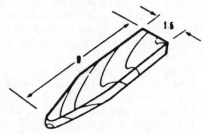

Wooden wedge dimensions (9 in. x 1.5 in.) used to hold cam chain in place

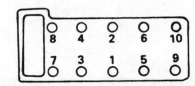

L-series four cylinder cylinder head torque sequence

system; start the engine and run it until normal operating temperature is reached. Retorque the cylinder head bolts to specifications, then readjust the valves. Retorque the head bolts again after 600 miles, and readjust the valves at that time.

L24 and LD28

1. Crank the engine until the No. 1 piston is at TDC of the compression stroke, disconnect the battery, and drain the cooling system.

NOTE: *To set the No. 1 piston at TDC of the compression stroke on the LD28 engine, remove the blind plug from the rear plate. Rotate the crankshaft until the marks on the flywheel and rear plate are in alignment. The No. 1 piston should now be at TDC.*

2. Remove the radiator hoses and the heater hoses. Unbolt the alternator mounting bracket and move the alternator to one side, if necessary.

3. If the car is equipped with air-conditioning, unbolt the compressor and place it to one side. *Do not disconnect the compressor lines. Severe injury could result.*

4. Remove the power steering pump.

5. Remove the spark plug leads from the spark plugs (gasoline engine only).

6. Remove the cold start valve and the fuel pipe as an assembly. Remove the throttle linkage.

7. Remove all lines and hoses from the intake manifold. Mark them first so you will know where they go.

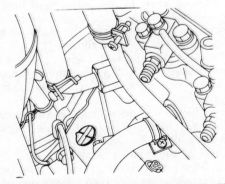

Remove the plug in the rear plate to set the No. 1 piston at TDC—diesel

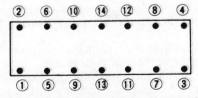

L24 series and LD28 cylinder head loosening sequence

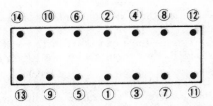

L24 series and LD28 cylinder head torque sequence

8. Unbolt the exhaust manifold from the exhaust pipe. The cylinder head can be removed with both the intake and exhaust manifolds in place.

9. Remove the camshaft cover.

10. Mark the relationship of the camshaft sprocket to the timing chain with paint. There are timing marks on the chain and the sprocket which should be visible when the No. 1 piston is at TDC, but the marks are quite small and not particularly useful.

11. Before removing the camshaft sprocket, it will be necessary to wedge the chain in place so that it will not fall down into the front cover. The factory procedure is to wedge the timing chain in place with the wooden wedge as detailed in the previous procedure. The problem with this procedure is that it may allow the chain tensioner to move out far enough to cock itself against the chain. If this happens, you'll find that the chain won't go back over the sprocket after you've put the sprocket back on. In this case, you'll have to remove the front cover and push the tensioner back. After you've wedged the chain, unbolt the camshaft sprocket and remove it.

12. Remove the cylinder head bolts. They require an Allen wrench type socket adapter. Keep the bolts in order as two different sizes are used.

13. Lift off the cylinder head. You may have to tap it *lightly* with a hammer.

To install the cylinder head:

14. Install a new head gasket and place the head in position on the block.

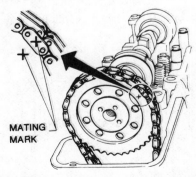

Matchmark the timing chain to the camshaft sprocket

15. Install the head bolts in their original locations.

16. Torque the head bolts in three stages: first to 29 ft. lbs., then to 43 ft. lbs., then to 61 ft. lbs.

17. Reinstall the camshaft sprocket in its original location. The chain is installed at the same time as the sprocket. Make sure the marks you made earlier line up. If the chain has slipped, or the engine has been disturbed, correct the timing as described under "Timing Chain Removal and Installation."

18. Reinstall all ancillary parts, coolant, etc.

19. Adjust the valves as described in Chapter 2.

20. After 600 miles of driving, retorque the head bolts and readjust the valves.

Z20E, Z20S and Z22

1. Complete Steps 1–5 under "L24". Observe the following note for Step 5.

NOTE: *The spark plug leads should be marked; however, it would be wise to mark them yourself, especially on the dual spark plug models.*

2. Disconnect the throttle linkage, the air cleaner or its intake hose assembly (fuel injection). Disconnect the fuel line, the return fuel line and any other vacuum lines or electrical leads. On the Z20S, remove the carburetor to avoid damaging it while removing the head.

NOTE: *A good rule of thumb when disconnecting the rather complex engine wiring of today's automobiles is to put a piece of masking tape on the wire or hose and on the connection you removed the wire or hose from, then mark both pieces of tape 1, 2, 3, etc. When replacing wiring, simply match the pieces of tape.*

3. Remove the E.G.R. tube from around the rear of the engine.

4. Remove the exhaust air induction tubes from around the front of the engine on Z20S engines and from the exhaust manifold on Z20E engines.

5. Unbolt the exhaust manifold from the

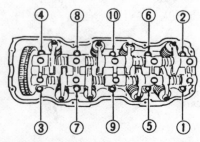

Z-series engine cylinder head bolt loosening sequence

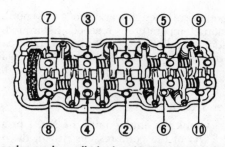

Z-series engine cylinder head bolt torque sequence

exhaust pipe. On the Z20S, remove the fuel pump.

6. On the Z20E, remove the intake manifold supports from under the manifold. Remove the P.C.V. valve from around the rear of the engine if necessary.

7. Remove the spark plugs to protect them from damage. Remove the valve cover.

8. Mark the relationship of the camshaft sprocket to the timing chain with paint or chalk. If this is done, it will not be necessary to locate the factory timing marks. Before removing the camshaft sprocket, it will be necessary to wedge the chain in place so that it will not fall down into the front cover. The factory procedure is to wedge the timing chain in place with the wooden wedge as detailed in the previous procedure. The problem with this procedure is that it may allow the chain tensioner to move out far enough to cock itself against the chain. If this happens, you'll find that the chain won't go back over the sprocket after you've put the sprocket back on. In this case, you'll have to remove the front cover and push the tensioner back. After you've wedged the chain, unbolt the camshaft sprocket and remove it.

9. Working from both ends in, loosen the cylinder head bolts and remove them. Remove the bolts securing the cylinder head to the front cover assembly.

10. Lift the cylinder head off the engine block. It may be necessary to tap the head *lightly* with a copper or brass mallet to loosen it.

To install the cylinder head:

11. Thoroughly clean the cylinder block and head surfaces and check both for warpage.

12. Fit the new head gasket. Don't use sealant. Make sure that no open valves are in the way of raised pistons, and do not rotate the crankshaft or camshaft separately because of possible damage which might occur to the valves.

13. Temporarily tighten the two center right and left cylinder head bolts to 14 ft. lbs.

14. Install the camshaft sprocket together with the timing chain to the camshaft. Make sure the marks you made earlier line up with each other. If you get into trouble, see "Timing

Chain Removal and Installation" for timing procedures.

15. Install the cylinder head bolts and torque them to 20 ft. lbs., then 40 ft. lbs., then 58 ft. lbs. in the order shown in the illustration.

16. Assemble the rest of the components in the reverse order of dissassembly.

NOTE: *It is always wise to drain the crankcase oil after the cylinder head has been installed to avoid coolant contamination.*

CA20E and CA18ET

1. Drain the cooling system.
2. Turn the crankshaft so that the No. 1 cylinder is at TDC on the compression stroke.
3. Remove the drive belts.

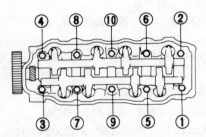

CA20E/CA18ET cylinder head bolt loosening sequence

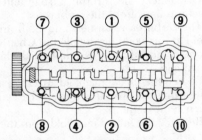

CA20E/CA18ET cylinder head bolt torque sequence. Bolt No. 8 is the longest

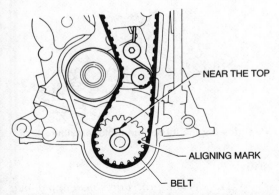

Set the CA20E and CA18ET No. 1 cylinder at TDC on the compression stroke. The keyway on the crankshaft sprocket will be almost at 12:00.

CA20E, CA18ET camshaft knock pin position for cylinder head assembly

4. Remove the water pump pulley and crankshaft pulley.
5. On CA18ET engines, remove the air intake pipe.
6. Remove the timing belt.
7. Remove the distributor-to-canister vacuum tube.
8. Remove the alternator adjusting bracket.

CAUTION: *After removing the timing belt, do not rotate the crankshaft and camshaft separately, as there is now no timing and the valves will hit the piston heads.*

9. Loosen the cylinder head bolts in two or three stages in the sequence shown.
10. With the cylinder head removed, see the "Cleaning and Inspection" and "Resurfacing" procedures below for cylinder head service.
11. To install the head, first set the No. 1 cylinder to TDC on the compression stroke. Make sure the crankshaft keyway is near the 12:00 position as shown in the accompanying illustration.
12. Set the camshaft pin on the top as shown.
13. Install the cylinder head on the clean top of the cylinder block, using a new head gasket.
14. Make sure all cylinder head bolts have washers. Tighten all bolts in the order shown, using the following procedure:

    a. Torque all bolts to 22 ft. lbs.
    b. Torque all bolts to 58 ft. lbs.
    c. Loosen all bolts completely.
    d. Torque all bolts to 22 ft. lbs.
    e. Torque all bolts to 54–61 ft. lbs., or if you are using an angle wrench, turn all bolts 90 to 95 degrees clockwise.

CLEANING AND INSPECTION

All Cylinder Heads

1. With the valves installed to protect the valve seats, remove deposits from the combustion chambers and valve heads with a scraper and a wire brush. Be careful not to damage the cylinder head gasket surface. After the valves are removed, clean the valve guide bores with a valve guide cleaning tool. Using cleaning solvent to remove dirt, grease and other deposits,

MEASURING POINTS

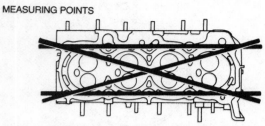

Use a straightedge to measure cylinder head flatness at these points

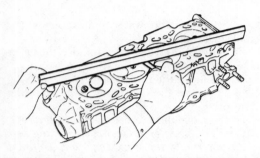

Check cylinder head flatness and warpage with a straightedge and feeler gauge. Warpage should not exceed 0.004 in.

clean all bolt holes; be sure the oil passages are clean.

2. Remove all deposits from the valves with a fine wire brush or buffing wheel.

3. Inspect the cylinder head for cracks or excessively burned areas in the exhaust outlet ports.

4. Check the cylinder head for cracks and inspect the gasket surface for burrs and nicks. Replace the head if it is cracked.

5. On cylinder heads that incorporate valve seat inserts, check the inserts for excessive wear, cracks or looseness.

RESURFACING

Cylinder Head Flatness

When a cylinder head is removed, check the flatness of the cylinder head gasket surface.

1. Place a straight-edge across the gasket surface of the cylinder head. Using feeler gauges, determine the clearance at the center of the straight-edge.

2. If warpage exceeds .004 in. over the total length, the cylinder head must be resurfaced. Cylinder head height after resurfacing must not exceed 4.61 in.

3. If necessary to refinish the cylinder head gasket surface, do not plane or grind off more than 0.2 mm (0.008 in.) from the original gasket surface.

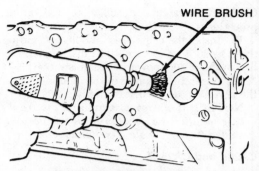

WIRE BRUSH

Clean the combustion chambers with a wire brush. Make sure you remove the deposits and do not scratch the head

Rocker Shaft

REMOVAL AND INSTALLATION

Rocker shaft removal and installation procedures are included in the "Camshaft Removal and Installation" section later in this chapter.

Intake Manifold

REMOVAL AND INSTALLATION

All Except 810 and 1980–84 200SX/510

1. Remove the air cleaner assembly together with all of the attending hoses.

2. Disconnect the throttle linkage and fuel and vacuum lines from the carburetor.

3. The carburetor can be removed from the manifold at this point (as detailed in Chapter 4) or can be removed as an assembly with the intake manifold.

4. Loosen the intake manifold attaching nuts, working from the two ends toward the center, and then remove them.

5. Remove the intake manifold from the engine.

6. Install the intake manifold in the reverse order of removal.

L-series engine intake manifold (4 cylinder)

810

NOTE: *Certain procedures may apply only to the gasoline engine.*

1. Disconnect all hoses to the air cleaner and remove the air cleaner.

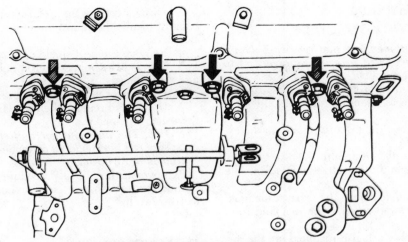

810 intake manifold mounting bolt locations—gasoline engine

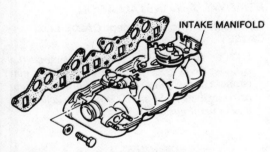

810 intake manifold—diesel engine

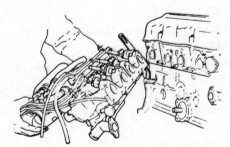

Z20E: remove the manifold with injectors, etc., still attached

2. Disconnect all air, water vacuum and fuel hoses to the intake manifold. Remove the cold start valve and fuel pipe as an assembly. Remove the throttle linkage.

3. Remove the B.P.T. valve control tube from the intake manifold. Remove the EGR hoses.

4. Disconnect all electrical wiring to the fuel injection unit. Note the location of the wires and mark them in some manner to facilitate reinstallation.

5. Make sure all wires, hoses, lines, etc. are removed. Unscrew the intake manifold bolts. Keep the bolts in order since they are of two different sizes. Remove the manifold.

6. Installation is the reverse of removal. Use a new gasket, clean both sealing surfaces, and torque the bolts in several stages, working from the center outward.

1980–84 200SX/510

1. Drain the coolant.

2. On the fuel injected engine, remove the air cleaner hoses. On the carbureted engine, remove the air cleaner.

3. Remove the radiator hoses from the manifold.

4. For the carbureted engine, remove the fuel, air and vacuum hoses from the carburetor. Remove the throttle linkage and remove the carburetor.

5. Remove the throttle cable and disconnect the fuel pipe and the return fuel line on fuel injection engines. Plug the fuel pipe to prevent spilling fuel.

NOTE: *When unplugging wires and hoses, mark each hose and its connection with a piece of masking tape, then match-code the two pieces of tape with the numbers 1,2,3, etc. When assembling, simply match the pieces of tape.*

6. Remove all remaining wires, tubes, the air cleaner bracket (carbureted engines) and the E.G.R. and P.C.V. tubes from the rear of the intake manifold. Remove the air induction pipe from the front of the carbureted engine. Remove the manifold supports on the fuel injected engine.

7. Unbolt and remove the intake manifold. On fuel injected engines, remove the manifold with injectors, E.G.R. valve, fuel tubes, etc., still attached.

8. Installation is the reverse of removal. Use a new intake manifold gasket.

Exhaust Manifold
REMOVAL AND INSTALLATION

NOTE: *You may find that removing the intake manifold will provide better access to the exhaust manifold.*

1. Remove the air cleaner assembly, if necessary for access. Remove the heat shield, if present.

2. Disconnect the exhaust pipe from the exhaust manifold.

3. Remove all temperature sensors, air induction pipes and other attachments from the manifold.

4. Loosen and remove the exhaust manifold attaching nuts and remove the manifold from the engine.

5. Install the exhaust manifold in the reverse order of removal.

Turbocharger
REMOVAL AND INSTALLATION
CA18ET Engine
1984 AND LATER 200SX

1. Drain the engine coolant.

2. Remove the air duct and hoses, and the air intake pipe.

3. Disconnect the front exhaust pipe at the exhaust manifold (exhaust outlet in the illustration).

4. Remove the heat shield plates.

5. Tag and disconnect the oil delivery tube and return hose.

6. Disconnect the water inlet tube.

7. Unbolt and remove the turbocharger from the exhaust manifold.

NOTE: *The turbocharger unit should only be serviced internally by an engine specialist trained in turbocharger repair.*

8. Reverse the above procedure to install. Torque the turbocharger outlet-to-housing bolts to 16–22 ft. lbs.

Timing Chain Cover

REMOVAL AND INSTALLATION
All Gasoline Engines Except CA20E and CA18ET

NOTE: *It may be necessary to remove the cylinder head to perform this operation if you cannot cut the front of the head gasket cleanly as described in Step 10. If so, you will need a new head gasket.*

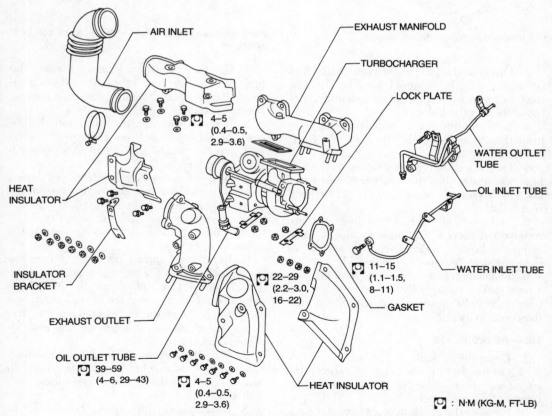

1984 and later 200SX (CA18ET engine) turbocharger assembly

1. Disconnect the negative battery cable from the battery, drain the cooling system, and remove the radiator together with the upper and lower radiator hoses.

2. Loosen the alternator drive belt adjusting screw and remove the drive belt. Remove the bolts which attach the alternator bracket to the engine and set the alternator aside out of the way.

3. Remove the distributor.

4. Remove the oil pump attaching screws, and take out the pump and its drive spindle.

5. Remove the cooling fan and the fan pulley together with the drive belt.

6. Remove the water pump.

7. Remove the crankshaft pulley bolt and remove the crankshaft pulley.

8. Remove the bolts holding the front cover to the front of the cylinder block, the four bolts which retain the front of the oil pan to the bottom of the front cover, and the two bolts which are screwed down through the front of the cylinder head and into the top of the front cover.

9. Carefully pry the front cover off the front of the engine.

10. Cut the exposed front section of the oil pan gasket away from the oil pan. Do the same to the gasket at the top of the front cover. Remove the two side gaskets and clean all of the mating surfaces.

11. Cut the portions needed from a new oil pan gasket and top front cover gasket.

12. Apply sealer to all of the gaskets and position them on the engine in their proper places.

13. Apply a light coating of grease to the crankshaft oil seal and carefully mount the front cover to the front of the engine and install all of the mounting bolts.

Tighten the 8 mm bolts to 7–12 ft. lbs. and the 6 mm bolts to 3–6 ft. lbs. Tighten the oil pan attaching bolts to 4–7 ft. lbs.

14. Before installing the oil pump, place the gasket over the shaft and make sure that the mark on the drive spindle faces (aligned) with the oil pump hole.

Install the oil pump after priming it with oil. For oil pump installation procedures, see "Oil Pump Removal and Installation" in this chapter.

Diesel Engine

NOTE: *It may be necessary to remove the cylinder head to perform this procedure if you cannot cut the front of the head gasket cleanly as described in Step 16. If so, you will need a new head gasket.*

CAUTION: *This procedure requires the removal and subsequent installation of the fuel injection pump. It is a good idea to read through the "Diesel Fuel Injection" section in Chapter 4 before you continue with this procedure—you may decide that the job is better left to a qualified service technician.*

1. Disconnect the negative battery cable. Drain the cooling system and then remove the radiator together with the upper and lower radiator hoses.

2. Remove the fan, fan coupling and fan pulley.

3. Unscrew the retaining bolts on the crankshaft damper pulley. Use a plastic mallet and lightly tap around the outer edges of the pulley, this should loosen it enough so that you can pull it off. If not, use a two armed gear puller.

4. Remove the power steering pump, bracket and idler pulley (if so equipped).

5. Unscrew the five mounting bolts and remove the front dust cover.

6. Remove the thermostat housing and the bottom bypass inlet with the hose.

7. Remove the engine slinger.

8. Tag and disconnect all hoses and lines running from the injection pump. Make sure to plug any hoses or lines to prevent dust or dirt from entering.

9. Drain the engine oil.

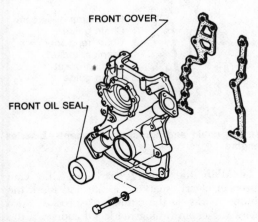

Timing chain front cover—gasoline engine

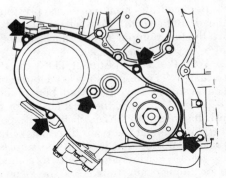

Remove the dust cover—diesel engine

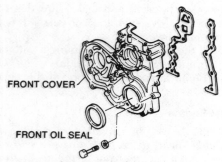

Front cover—Diesel Engine

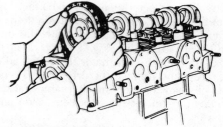

Removing the camshaft sprocket

10. Remove the oil cooled and coolant hose together with the oil filter.

11. Remove the water inlet, the oil dipstick and the right side engine mounting bracket.

12. Remove the oil pump.

13. Remove the injection pump as detailed in Chapter 4.

14. Remove the water pump.

15. Loosen the mounting bolt and remove the injection pump drive crank pulley. You will need a two armed gear puller.

16. Remove the bolts holding the front cover to the front of the cylinder block, the four bolts which retain the front of the oil pan to the bottom of the front cover, and the two bolts which are screwed down through the front of the cylinder head and into the top of the front cover.

17. Carefully pry the front cover off the front of the engine.

18. Follow Steps 10–14 of the previous "Gasoline Engine" procedure.

19. Installation of the remaining components is in the reverse order of removal.

Timing Chain and Tensioner
REMOVAL AND INSTALLATION
All Gasoline Engines Except CA20E and CA18ET

1. Before beginning any disassembly procedures, position the No. 1 piston at TDC on the compression stroke.

2. Remove the front cover as previously outlined. Remove the camshaft cover and remove the fuel pump if it runs off a cam lobe in front of the camshaft sprocket.

3. With the No. 1 piston at TDC, the timing marks n the camshaft sprocket and the timing chain should be visible. Mark both of them with paint. Also mark the relationship of the camshaft sprocket to the camshaft. At this point you will notice that there are three sets of timing marks and locating holes in the sprocket. They are for making adjustments to compensate for timing chain stretch. See the following "Timing Chain Adjustment" for more details.

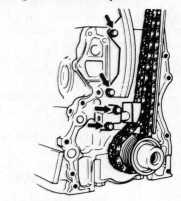

Tensioner and chain guide removal

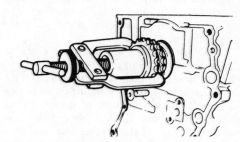

Crankshaft sprocket removal

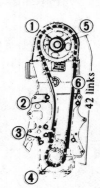

1. Fuel pump drive cam
2. Chain guide
3. Chain tensioner
4. Crank sprocket
5. Cam sprocket
6. Chain guide

Timing chain and sprocket alignment—L-series engine

4. With the timing marks on the cam sprocket clearly marked, locate and mark the timing marks on the crankshaft sprocket. Also mark the chain timing mark. Of course, if the chain is not to be re-used, marking it is useless.

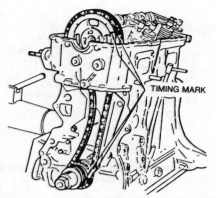

Timing chain and sprocket alignments—Z20 engines

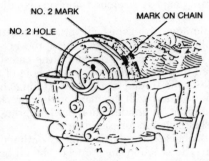

Use the No. 2 mark and hole to align camshaft—Z20 engines

5. Unbolt the camshaft sprocket and remove the sprocket along with the chain. As you remove the chain, hold it where the chain tensioner contacts it. When the chain is removed, the tensioner is going to come apart. Hold on to it and you won't lose any of the parts. There is no need to remove the chain guide unless it is being replaced.

6. Using a two-armed gear puller, remove the crankshaft sprocket.

7. Install the timing chain and the camshaft sprocket together after first positioning the chain over the crankshaft sprocket. Position the sprocket so that the marks made earlier line up. This is assuming that the engine has not been disturbed. The camshaft and crankshaft keys should both be pointed upward. If a new chain and/or gear is being installed, position the sprocket so that the timing marks on the chain align with the marks on the crankshaft sprocket and the camshaft sprocket (with both keys pointing up). The marks are on the right-hand side of the sprockets as you face the engine. The L18 has 42 pins between the mating marks of the chain and sprockets when the chain is installed correctly. The L20B has 44 pins. The 1977–78 L24 engine used in the 810 has 42 pins between timing marks. The L24 (1979–

84), Z20E and Z20S engines do not use the pin counting method for finding correct valve timing. Instead, position the key in the crankshaft sprocket so that it is pointing upward and install the camshaft sprocket on the camshaft with its dowel pin at the top using the No. 2 (No. 1 on the L24) mounting hole and timing mark. The painted links of the chain should be on the right hand side of the sprockets as you face the engine. See the illustration.

NOTE: *The factory manual refers to the pins you are to count in the L-series engines as links, but in America, this is not correct. Count the pins. There are two pins per link. This is an important step. If you do not get the exact number of pins between the timing marks, valve timing will be incorrect and the engine will either not run at all, in which case you may stand the chance of bending the valves, or the engine will run very feebly.*

8. Install the chain tensioner. Install the remaining components in the reverse order of disassembly.

Diesel Engine

1. Follow Steps 1–6 of the preceding "Gasoline Engine" procedure. You need not remove the fuel pump as detailed in Step 2.

2. Install the crankshaft sprocket. Make sure that the mating marks on the sprocket face the front of the car.

3. Install the timing chain and the camshaft sprocket together after first positioning the chain over the crankshaft sprocket. Position the cam sprocket so that the marks made earlier line up. This is assuming that the engine has not been disturbed. The camshaft and crankshaft keys should be pointing upward. If a new chain and/or gear is being installed, position the sprocket so that the timing marks on the chain align with the marks on the crankshaft and camshaft sprockets (with both keys pointing up). The marks are on the right-hand side of the sprockets as you face the engine. Insert the camshaft dowel pin into the No. 1 hole in the camshaft sprocket. Install and tighten the camshaft sprocket bolt.

4. Install the chain guide (if removed) and the chain tensioner. Tighten the slack side (left side when facing the engine) chain guide mounting bolt so that the protrusion of the chain tensioner spindle is 0 in.

5. Installation of the remaining components is in the reverse order of removal.

TIMING CHAIN ADJUSTMENT

When the timing chain stretches excessively, the valve timing will be adversely affected.

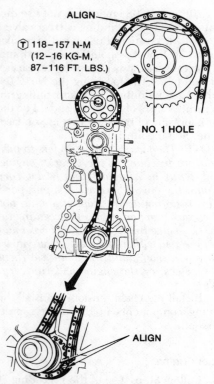

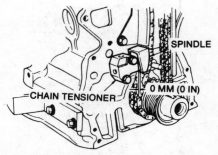

ALIGN

Ⓣ 118–157 N-M
(12–16 KG-M,
87–116 FT. LBS.)

NO. 1 HOLE

SPINDLE

CHAIN TENSIONER

0 MM (0 IN)

Chain tensioner mounting—1979 and later 810 and Maxima, gasoline and diesel engines

ALIGN

Timing chain and sprocket alignment—1979 and later 810 and Maxima, gasoline and diesel engines

There are three sets of holes and timing marks on the camshaft sprocket.

If the stretch of the chain roller links is excessive, adjust the camshaft sprocket location by transferring the set position of the camshaft sprocket from the factory position of No. 1 or No. 2 to one of the other positions as follows:

1. Turn the crankshaft until the No. 1 piston is at TDC on the compression stroke. Examine whether the camshaft sprocket location notch is to the left of the oblong groove on the cam-

shaft retaining plate. If the notch in the sprocket is to the left of the groove in the retaining plate, then the chain is stretched and needs adjusting.

2. Remove the camshaft sprocket together with the chain and reinstall the sprocket and chain with the locating dowel on the camshaft inserted into either the No. 2 or 3 hole of the sprocket. The timing mark on the timing chain must be aligned with the mark on the sprocket. The amount of modification is 4 degrees of crankshaft rotation for each mark.

3. Recheck the valve timing as outlined in Step 1. The notch in the sprocket should be to the right of the groove in the camshaft retaining plate.

4. If and when the notch cannot be brought to the right of the groove, the timing chain is worn beyond repair and must be replaced.

Timing Belt

REMOVAL AND INSTALLATION

CA20E and CA18ET Engines

1. Remove the battery ground cable.
2. On the CA20E engine, remove the air intake ducts.

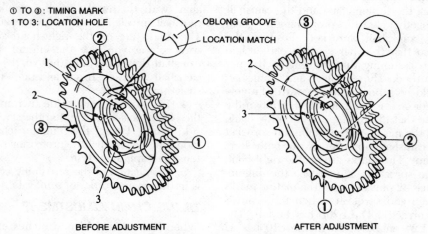

① TO ③: TIMING MARK
1 TO 3: LOCATION HOLE

OBLONG GROOVE

LOCATION MATCH

BEFORE ADJUSTMENT

AFTER ADJUSTMENT

Timing chain adjustment

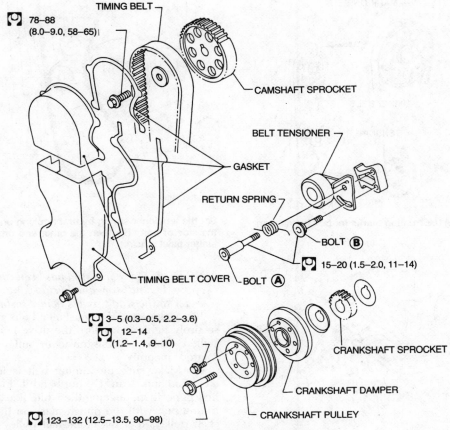

78–88
(8.0–9.0, 58–65)

TIMING BELT

CAMSHAFT SPROCKET

BELT TENSIONER

GASKET

RETURN SPRING

BOLT **B**

15–20 (1.5–2.0, 11–14)

TIMING BELT COVER — BOLT **A**

3–5 (0.3–0.5, 2.2–3.6)
12–14
(1.2–1.4, 9–10)

CRANKSHAFT SPROCKET

CRANKSHAFT DAMPER

CRANKSHAFT PULLEY

123–132 (12.5–13.5, 90–98)

CA20E, CA18ET timiig belt assembly

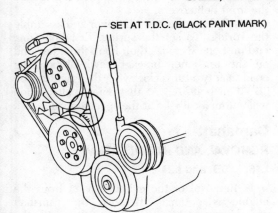

SET AT T.D.C. (BLACK PAINT MARK)

CA20E, CA18ET timing marks for finding TDC

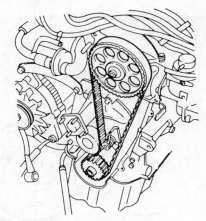

Timing belt with covers removed

3. Remove the cooling fan.

4. Remove the power steering, alternator, and air conditioner compressor belts.

5. Set the No. 1 cylinder at TDC on the compression stroke. The accompanying illustration shows the timing mark alignment for TDC.

6. Remove the front upper and lower timing belt covers.

7. Loosen the timing belt tensioner and return spring, then remove the timing belt.

8. Carefully inspect the condition of the timing belt. There should be no breaks or cracks anywhere on the belt. Especially check around the bottoms of the teeth, where they interesect the belt; cracks often show up here. Evidence

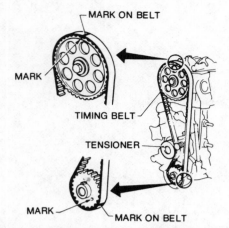

CA20E, CA18ET timing marks for belt installation

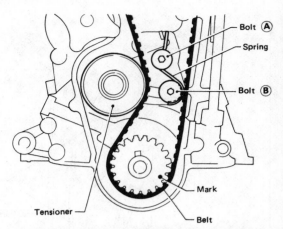

Set the tensioner spring by first hooking one end to the side of bolt "B", then the other end on the tensioner pawl bracket

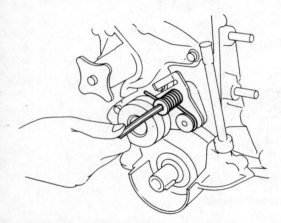

Installing the belt tensioner and return spring

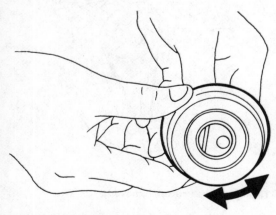

Spin the tensioner pulley to make sure it works smoothly

of any wear or damage on the belt means the belt should be replaced.

9. To install the belt, first make sure that No. 1 cylinder is set at TDC on compression. Install the belt tensioner and return spring.

NOTE: *If the coarse stud has been removed, apply Loctite® or another locking thread sealer to the stud threads before installing.*

10. Make sure the tensioner bolts are not securely tightened before the drive belt is installed. Make sure the tensioner pulley can be rotated smoothly.

11. Make sure the timing belt is in good condition and clean. Do not bend it. Place the belt in position, aligning the white lines on the timing belt with the punch mark on the camshaft pulleys and the crankshaft pulley. Make sure the arrow on the belt is pointing toward the front belt covers.

12. Tighten the belt tensioner and assemble the spring. To set the spring, first hook one end on bolt "B" side, then hook the other end on the tensioner bracket pawl. Rotate the crankshaft two turns clockwise, then tighten bolt "B" then bolt "A". At this point, belt tension will automatically be at the specified value.

Camshaft

REMOVAL AND INSTALLATION

L18, L20B, and L24

1. Removal of the cylinder head from the engine is optional. Remove the camshaft sprocket from the camshaft together with the timing chain.

2. Loosen the valve rocker pivot locknut and remove the rocker arm by pressing down on the valve spring.

3. Remove the two retaining nuts on the camshaft retainer plate at the front of the cylinder head and carefully slide the camshaft out of the camshaft carrier.

4. Check camshaft run-out, end-play, wear and journal clearance as described later in this chapter.

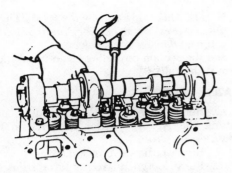

Remove the rocker arm by pressing down on the valve spring

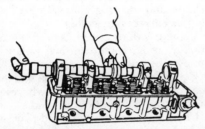

Carefully slide the camshaft out of the carrier

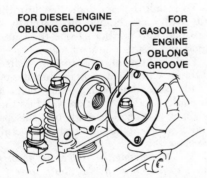

FOR DIESEL ENGINE OBLONG GROOVE

FOR GASOLINE ENGINE OBLONG GROOVE

When installing the retaining plate, make sure the oblong groove is facing the front of the engine

5. Lightly coat the camshaft bearings with clean motor oil and carefully slide the camshaft into place in the camshaft carrier.

6. Install the camshaft retainer plate with the oblong groove in the face of the plate facing toward the front of the engine.

7. Check the valve timing as outlined under "Timing Chain Removal and Installation" and install the timing sprocket on the camshaft, tightening the bolt together with the fuel pump cam (gasoline engines only) to 86–116 ft. lbs.

8. Install the rocker arms by pressing down the valve springs with a screwdriver and install the valve rocker springs.

9. Install the cylinder head, if it was removed, and assemble the rest of the engine in the reverse order of removal.

Z20E, Z20S, Z22

1. Removal of the cylinder head from the engine is optional. Remove the camshaft sprocket from the camshaft together with the timing chain, after setting the No. 1 piston at TDC on its compression stroke.

2. Loosen the bolts holding the rocker shaft assembly in place and remove the six center bolts. Do not pull the four end bolts out of the rocker assembly because they hold the unit together.

CAUTION: *When loosening the bolts, work from the ends in and loosen all of the bolts a little at a time so that you do not strain the camshaft or the rocker assembly. Remember, the camshaft is under pressure from the valve springs.*

3. After removing the rocker assembly, remove the camshaft.

NOTE: *Keep the disassembled parts in order.*

If you need to disassemble the rocker unit, assemble as follows.

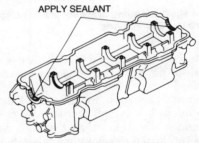

APPLY SEALANT

Apply sealant to these points on the Z-series cylinder head just before installing the camshaft

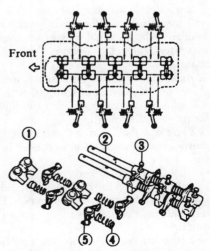

Front

1. Rocker bracket
2. Rocker shaft
3. Bolt
4. Spring
5. Rocker arm

Rocker shaft assembly—Z20 engines

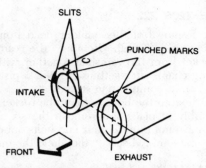

Note the difference in rocker shafts—Z20 engines

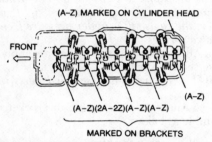

Rocker shaft mounting brackets are assembled in this order—Z20 engines

4. Install the mounting brackets, valve rockers and springs observing the following considerations.

The two rocker shafts are different. Both have punch marks in the ends that face the front of the engine. The rocker shaft that goes on the side of the intake manifold has two slits in its end just below the punch mark. The exhaust side rocker shaft does not have slits.

The rocker arms for the intake and exhaust valves are interchangeable between cylinders one and three and are identified by the mark "1". Similarly, the rockers for cylinders two and four are interchangeable and are identified by the mark "2".

The rocker shaft mounting brackets are also coded for correct placement with either an "A" or a "Z" plus a number code. See the illustration for proper placement.

5. Check camshaft run-out, end-play wear and journal clearance as described later in this chapter.

To install the camshaft and rocker assembly:

6. Apply sealant to the end camshaft saddles as shown in the accompanying illustration. Place the camshaft on the head with its dowel pin pointing up.

7. Fit the rocker assembly on the head, making sure you mount it on its knock pin.

8. Torque the bolts to 11–18 ft. lbs., in several stages working from the middle bolts and moving outwards on both sides.

NOTE: *Make sure the engine is on TDC of the compression stroke for No. 1 piston or you may damage some valves.*

See the section on timing chain installation. Adjust the valves.

CA20E, CA18ET

1. Remove the timing belt assembly, after setting the No. 1 cylinder to TDC on the compression stroke.

2. Remove the valve rocker cover.

3. Fully loosen all rocker arm adjusting screws (the valve adjustment screws). Loosen the rocker shaft securing bolts in two or three stages, and remove the rocker shafts with the rocker arms and securing bolts. *Keep all parts in order for correct reassembly.*

4. Using a tool designed to hold the camshaft pulley, remove the camshaft pulley bolt and remove the pulley.

5. Carefully pry the camshaft oil seal out of the front of the cylinder head. Slowly remove the camshaft out the front of the head.

6. Check camshaft run-out, end-play, wear and journal clearance as described later in this chapter.

7. To install the camshaft, first lubricate it liberally with clean engine oil. Carefully slide the camshaft into position. Lube the camshaft front end and install a new oil seal.

8. Lightly lubricate the rocker shafts and install them, with their rockers, into the cylinder head. Note that both of the shafts have punch marks on their front ends, while the intake shaft is also marked with two slits on its front end. All components must be assembled in the correct order.

NOTE: *To prevent the rocker shaft springs from slipping out of the shaft, insert the bracket bolts into the shaft.*

9. Tighten the rocker shaft bolts gradually, in two or three passes.

10. Install the camshaft pulley. Install the timing belt assembly.

11. Adjust the valve clearances. Install the rocker arm cover.

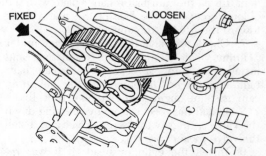

Use a sprocket holding tool when loosening the CA20E and CA18ET cam sprocket

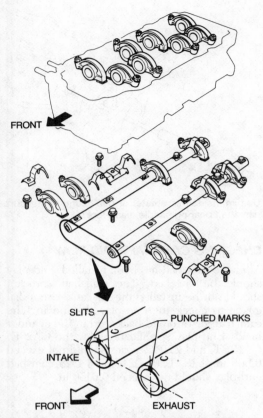

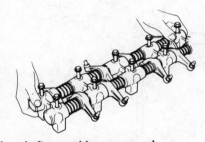

Rocker shaft assembly as removed

CA20E, CA18ET rocker shaft assembly. Note locating marks on the end of the shafts, slits on the intake shaft

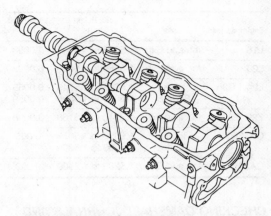

Carefully slide the camshaft into the camshaft saddles on the cylinder head

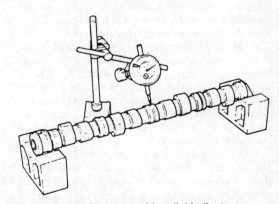

Check camshaft run-out with a dial indicator

CHECKING CAMSHAFT LOBE HEIGHT

Use a micrometer to check cam (lobe) height, making sure the anvil and the spindle of the micrometer are positioned directly on the heel and tip of the cam lobe as shown in the accompanying illustration. Use the specifications in the following chart to determine the lobe wear.

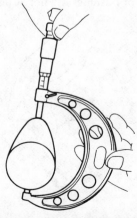

Use a micrometer to check camshaft cam lobe height

CHECKING CAMSHAFT RUN-OUT

Camshaft run-out should be checked when the camshaft has been removed from the cylinder head. An accurate dial indicator is needed for this procedure; engine specialists and most machine shops have this equipment. If you have access to a dial indicator, or can take your cam to someone who does, measure cam bearing journal run-out. The maximum (limit) run-out on the L18, L20, L24, LD28, CA20E and CA18ET camshafts is 0.008 in. (0.2 mm). The run-out limit on the Z20 and Z22 series camshafts is 0.0079 in. (0.20mm).

Engine Series	Lobe	Lobe Height (in.)	Wear Limit (in.)
L18	Int. and Exh.	1.5728 to 1.3748	0.0098
L20	Int. and Exh.	1.5866 to 1.5886	0.0098
L24, LD28	Intake	1.5728 to 1.5748	0.0059
	Exhaust	1.5866 to 1.5886	0.0059
Z20, Z22	Int. and Exh.	1.5148 to 1.5168	0.0098
CA18ET	Intake	1.5055 to 1.5075	0.008
	Exhaust	1.5289 to 1.5309	
CA20E	Int. and Exh.	1.5289 to 1.5309	0.008

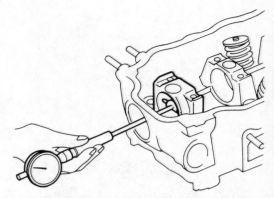

Use an inside micrometer or dial gauge to measure camshaft bearing saddle diameters

CHECKING CAMSHAFT JOURNALS AND CAMSHAFT BEARING SADDLES

While the camshaft is still removed from the cylinder head, the camshaft bearing journals should be measured with a micrometer. Compare the measurements with those listed in the "Camshaft Specifications" chart in this chapter. If the measurements are less than the limits listed in the chart, the camshaft will have to be replaced, since the camshafts in all of the engines covered in this guide run directly on the cylinder head surface; no actual bearings or bushings are used, so no oversize bearings or bushings are available.

Using an inside dial gauge or inside micrometer, measure the inside diameter of the camshaft saddles (the camshaft mounts that are either integrally-cast as part of the cylinder head, or are a bolted-on, one-piece unit. The Z-series engines use a saddle-and-cap arrangement. The inside diameter of the saddles on all engines except the CA20E/CA18ET is 1.8898 to 1.8904 in. The CA20E/CA18ET measurement is 1.8110 to 1.8116 in. Camshaft journal oil clearances are listed in the "Camshaft Specifications" chart in this chapter. If the saddle inside diameters exceed those listed above, the cylinder head must be replaced (again, because oversize bearings or bushings are not available).

CHECKING CAMSHAFT END-PLAY

After the camshaft has been installed, end-play should be checked. The camshaft sprocket should not be installed on the cam. Use a dial guage to check the end-play, by moving the camshaft forward and backward in the cylinder head. End-play specifications for the CA20E, CA18ET, and Z20/22 series should not exceed 0.008 in. L18, L20, L24 and LD28 camshaft end-play should not exceed 0.0150 in.

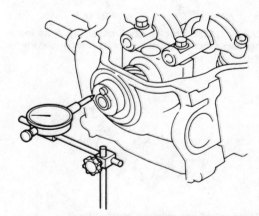

Checking camshaft end play with a dial gauge. Move the camshaft forward and backward

Valves and Guides

REMOVAL AND INSTALLATION

All Engines

The cylinder head must be removed on all engines before the valves can be removed.

A valve spring compressor is needed to remove the valves and springs; these are available at most auto parts and auto tool shops. A small magnet is very helpful for removing the keepers and spring seats.

Set the head on its side on the bench. Install

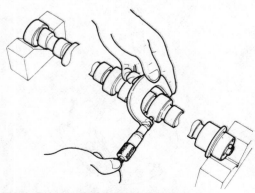

Measuring camshaft journal diameter

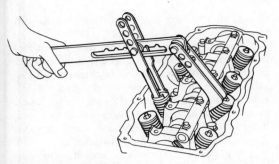

Compressing the valve springs using a valve spring compressor

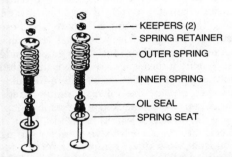

- KEEPERS (2)
- SPRING RETAINER
- OUTER SPRING
- INNER SPRING
- OIL SEAL
- SPRING SEAT

Typical valve components. Not all engines have double valve springs

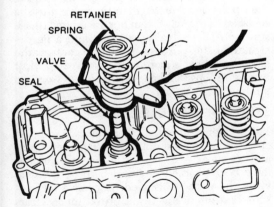

RETAINER

SPRING

VALVE

SEAL

Always install new valve stem seals

the spring compressor so that the fixed side of the tool is flat against the valve head in the combustion chamber, and the screw side is against the retainer. Slowly turn the screw in towards the head, compressing the spring. As the spring compresses, the keepers will be revealed; pick them off of the valve stem with the magnet as they are easily fumbled and lost. When the keepers are removed, back the screw out and remove the retainers and springs. Remove the compressor and pull the valves out of the head from the other side. Remove the valve seals by hand and remove the spring seats with the magnet.

Since it is very important that each valve

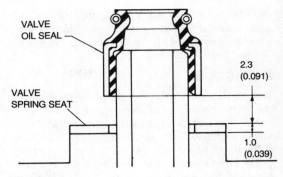

VALVE
OIL SEAL

VALVE
SPRING SEAT

2.3
(0.091)

1.0
(0.039)

UNIT: MM (IN)

Proper valve stem seal installation, CA20E and CA18ET

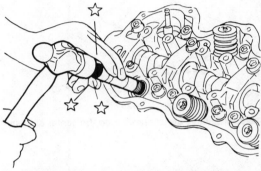

Valve spring seat installation, CA20E and CA18ET engines. Others similar

and its spring, retainer, spring seat and keepers is reassembled in its original location, you must keep these parts in order. The best way to do this is to cut either eight (four cylinder) or twelve (six cylinder) holes in a piece of heavy cardboard or wood. Label each hole with hte cylinder number and either "IN" or "EX", corresponding to the location of each valve in the head. As you remove each valve, insert it into the holder, and assemble the seats, springs, keepers and retainers to the stem on the labeled side of the holder. This way each valve and its attending parts are kept together, and can be put back into the head in their proper locations.

After lapping each valve into its seat (see "Valve Lapping" below), oil each valve stem, and install each valve into the head in the reverse order of removal, so that all parts except the keepers are assembled on the stem. *Always use new valve stem seals.* Install the spring compressor, and compress the retainer and spring until the keeper groove on the valve stem is fully revealed. Coat the groove with a wipe of grease (to hold the keepers until the retainer is released) and install both keepers, *wide end up.* Slowly back the screw of the compressor out until the spring retainer covers the keepers. Remove the tool. Lightly tap the end of each valve stem with a rubber hammer to ensure proper fit of the retainers and keepers. Adjust the valves.

INSPECTION

Before the valves can be properly inspected, the stem, lower end of the stem and the entire valve face and head must be cleaned. An old valve works well for clipping carbon from the valve head, and a wire brush, gasket scraper or putty knife can be used for cleaning the valve face and the area between the face and lower stem. Do not scratch the valve face during cleaning. Clean the entire stem with a rag

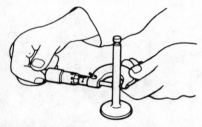

Measuring valve stem diameter on the center of stem

Use an inside dial indicator to measure valve guide inner diameter (I.D.)

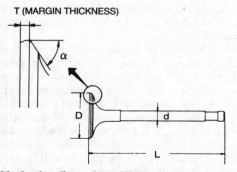

Critical valve dimensions. When the valve head has been worn down to 0.020 in. in margin thickness (T), replace the valve. Grinding allowance for the valve stem tip is 0.008 in. or less.

soaked in thinners to remove all varnish and gum.

Thorough inspection of the valves requires the use of a micrometer, and a dial indicator is needed to measure the inside diameter of the valve guides. If these instruments are not available to you, the valves and head can be taken to a reputable machine shop for inspection. Refer to the "Valve Specifications" chart for valve stem and stem-to-guide specifications.

If the above instruments are at your disposal, measure the diameter of each valve stem at the locations illustrated. Jot these measurements down. Using the dial indicator, measure the inside diameter of the valve guides at their bottom, top and midpoint 90° apart. Jot these measurements down also. Subtract the valve stem measurement from the valve guide inside measurement; if the clearance exceeds that listed in the specifications chart under "Stem-to-Guide Clearance", replace the valve(s). Stem-to-guide clearance can also be checked at a machine shop, where a dial indicator would be used.

Check the top of each valve stem for pitting and unusual wear due to improper rocker adjustment, etc. The stem tip can be ground flat if it is worn, but no more than 0.020 in. can be removed; if this limit must be exceeded to make the tip flat and square, then the valve must be replaced. If the valve stem tips are ground, make sure you fix the valve securely into a jig designed for this purpose, so the tip contacts the grinding wheel squarely at exactly 90°. Most machine shops that handle automotive work are equipped for this job.

STEM-TO-GUIDE CLEARANCE

Valve stem-to-guide clearance should be checked upon assembling the cylinder head, and is especially necessary if the valve guides have been reamed or knurled, or if oversize valves have been installed. Excessive oil consumption often is a result of too much clearance between the valve guide and valve stem.

Clean the valve stem with lacquer thinner or a similar solvent to remove all gum and var-

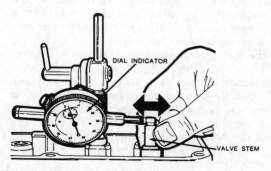

Measuring stem-to-guide clearance

nish. Clean the valve guides using solvent and an expanding wire-type valve guide cleaner (a rifle cleaning brush works well here).

2. Mount a dial indicator so that the stem is at 90° to the valve stem and as close to the valve guide as possible.

3. Move the valve off its seat, and measure the valve guide-to-stem clearance by rocking the stem back and forth to actuate the dial indicator. Measure the valve stems using a micrometer and compare to specifications, to determine whether stem or guide wear is responsible for excessive clearance.

VALUE GUIDE INSPECTION

Valve guides should be cleaned as outlined earlier, and checked when valve stem diameter and stem-to-guide clearance is checked. Generally, if the engine is using oil through the guides (assuming the valve seals are OK) and the valve stem diameter is within specification, it is the guides that are worn and need replacing.

VALVE GUIDE REMOVAL

The valve guides in all engines covered in this guide may be replaced. To remove the guide(s), heat the cylinder head to 302 to 320°F (150 to 160°C). Drive out the guides using a 2-ton press (many machine shops have this equipment) or a hammer and brass drift which has been modified with washers as in the accompanying illustration.

NOTE: *Some valve guides are retained by snap-rings, which must be removed prior to guide removal.*

With the guide(s) removed, the cylinder head valve guide holes should be reamed to accept the new guides. The head should then be heated again and the new guides pressed or driven into place. On engines which utilize valve guide snap-rings, install the snap-ring to the guide

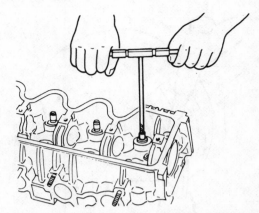

Always use two hands on the reamer handle when reaming valve guides

first, then install the guide into the head. Ream the new valve guide bores to 0.3150–0.3157 (all engines except CA20E/CA18ET); or 0.2756–0.2763 (CA20E/CA18ET).

KNURLING

Valve guides which are not excessively worn or distorted may, in some cases, be knurled rather than reamed. Knurling is a process in which metal inside the valve guide bore is displaced and raised (forming a very fine crosshatch pattern), thereby reducing clearance. Knurling also provides for excellent oil control. The possibility of knurling rather than reaming the guides should be discussed with a machinist.

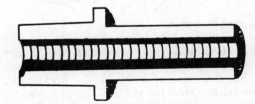

Cross-section of a knurled valve guide

REFACING

Valve refacing should only be handled by a reputable machine shop, as the experience and equipment needed to do the job are beyond that of the average owner/mechanic. During the course of a normal valve job, refacing is necessary when simply lapping the valves into their seats will not correct the seat and face wear. When the valves are reground (resurfaced), the valve seats must also be recut, again requiring special equipment and experience.

VALVE LAPPING

The valves must be lapped into their seats after resurfacing, to ensure proper sealing. Even if

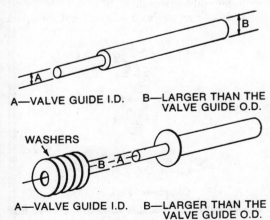

A—VALVE GUIDE I.D.   B—LARGER THAN THE VALVE GUIDE O.D.

WASHERS

A—VALVE GUIDE I.D.   B—LARGER THAN THE VALVE GUIDE O.D.

A brass drift can be modified for valve guide removal

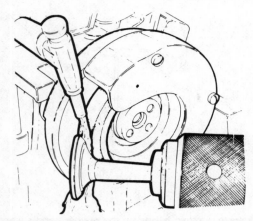

Valve refacing should be handled by an engine specialist or machinist

Lapping the valves

the valves have not been refaced, they should be lapped into the head before reassembly.

Set the cylinder head on the workbench, combustion chamber side up. Rest the head on wooden blocks on either end, so there are two or three inches between the tops of the valve guides and the bench.

1. Lightly lube the valve stem with clean engine oil. Coat the valve seat completely with valve grinding compound. Use just enough compound that the full width and circumference of the seat are covered.

2. Install the valve in its proper location in the head. Attach the suction cup end of the valve lapping tool to the valve head. It usually helps to put a small amount of saliva into the suction cup to aid it sticking to the valve.

3. Rotate the tool between the palms, changing position and lifting the tool often to prevent grooving. Lap the valve in until a smooth, evenly-polished seat and valve face are evident.

4. Remove the valve from the head. Wipe

away all traces of grinding compound from the valve face and seat. Wipe out the port with a solvent-soaked rag, and swab out the valve guide with a piece of solvent-soaked rag to make sure there are no traces of compound grit inside the guide. *This cleaning is very important, as the engine will ingest any grit remaining when started.*

5. Proceed through the remaining valves, one at a time. Make sure the valve faces, seats, cylinder ports and valve guides are clean before reassembling the valve train.

Valve Seats

REPLACEMENT

Check the valve seat inserts for any evidence of pitting or excessive wear at the valve contact surface. The valve seats in all engines covered here can be replaced. Because the cylinder head must be machined to accept the new seat inserts, consult an engine specialist or machinist about this work.

NOTE: *When repairing a valve seat, first check the valve and guide; if wear is evident here, replace the valve and/or guide, then correct the valve seat.*

Valve Springs

REMOVAL AND INSTALLATION

Z20, Z22, CA20E and CA18ET Engines

The valve springs in these engines can be removed without removing the camshaft, while the cylinder head is in place. Follow the "Valves Removal and Installation" procedure if the head has already been removed.

1. Remove the rocker cover. Set the cylinder on which you will be working to TDC on the compression stroke.

2. Remove the rocker shaft assembly.

3. Remove one spark plug on whichever cylinder you are working.

4. Install an air hose adaptor into the spark

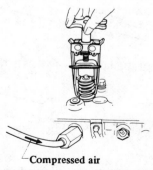

Compressed air

Use 71 psi of air pressure to keep the valve from dropping into the cylinder. Note the valve spring compressor

plug hole and apply about 71 psi of pressure into the cylinder. This will hold the valves in place, preventing them from dropping into the cylinder when the springs are removed.

5. Install a valve spring compressing tool similar to the one illustrated and remove the valve spring and valve steam seal. Use care not to lose the keepers.

NOTE: *Always install new oil seals during reassembly.*

6. Reassemble the components in the reverse order of disassembly, making sure the air pressure in the cylinder is at 71 psi while the springs are installed.

L18, L20, L24, LD28 Engines

The camshafts in these engines must be removed in order to remove the valve springs. Follow the "Camshaft Removal and Installation" procedure, then follow the valve spring removal procedure listed above for the Z-series and CA-series engines. If you are removing the valve springs with the cylinder head already removed from the engine, follow the procedure under "Valves Removal and Installation."

HEIGHT AND PRESSURE CHECK

1. Place the valve spring on a flat, clean surface next to a square.

2. Measure the height of the spring, and rotate it against the edge of the square to measure distortion (out-of-roundness). If spring height varies between springs by more than 1/16

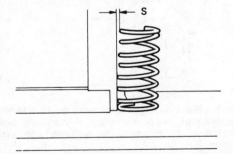

Measuring spring height and squareness. Make sure the closed coils face downward

Have the valve spring pressure tested

in. or if the distortion exceeds 1/16 in., replace the spring(s) in question. Outer valve spring squareness should not exceed 0.087 in. (2.2mm); inner spring squareness should not exceed 0.075 in. (1.9mm).

A valve spring tester is needed to test spring test pressure, so the valve springs usually must be taken to a machinest or engine specialist for this test. Compare the tested pressure with the pressures listed in the "Valve Specifications chart in this chapter.

Pistons and Connecting Rods
REMOVAL AND INSTALLATION
All Engines

1. Remove the cylinder head.
2. Remove the oil pan.
3. Remove any carbon buildup from the cylinder wall at the top end of the piston travel with a ridge reamer tool.
4. Position the piston to be removed at the bottom of its stroke so that the connecting rod bearing cap can be reached easily from under the engine.

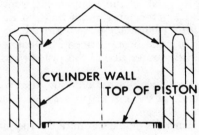

Ridge caused by cylinder wear

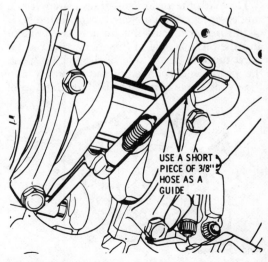

Install lengths of rubber tubing on the rod bolts before removing the piston assemblies. This will protect the cylinder walls from damage.

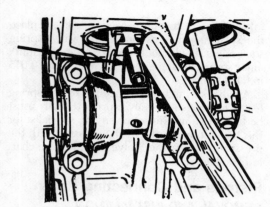

Tap out the piston assemblies with a wooden hammer handle. Note tubing covering rod bolts (arrow)

5. Unscrew the connecting rod bearing cap nuts and remove the cap and lower half of the beairng. Cover the rod bolts with lengths of rubber tubing to protect the cylinder walls when the rod and piston assembly is driven out.

6. Push the piston and connecting rod up and out of the cylinder block with a length of wood. Use care not to scratch the cylinder wall with the connecting rod or the wooden tool.

7. Keep all of the components from each cylinder together and install them in the cylinder from which they were removed.

8. Coat the bearing face of the connecting rod and the outer face of the pistons with engine oil.

9. See the illustrations for the correct placement of the piston rings for your model and your Datsun.

10. Turn the crankshaft until the rod journal of the particular cylinder you are working on is brought to the TDC position.

11. With the piston and rings clamped in a ring compressor, the notched mark on the head of the piston toward the front of the engine, and the oil hole side of the connecting rod toward the fuel pump side of the engine, push the piston and connecting rod assembly into the cylinder bore until the big bearing end of

the connecting rod contacts and is seated on the rod journal of the crankshaft. Use care not to scratch the cylinder wall with the connecting rod.

NOTE: *See "LD28 Diesel" below for piston installation details on that engine.*

12. Push down farther on the piston and turn the crankshaft while the connecting rod rides around on the crankshaft rod journal. Turn the crankshaft until the crankshaft rod journal is at BDC (bottom dead center).

13. Align the mark on the connecting rod bearing cap with that on the connecting rod and tighten the bearing cap bolts to the specified torque.

14. Install all of the piston/connecting rod assemblies in the manner outlined above and assemble the oil pan and cylinder head to the engine in the reverse order of removal.

LD28 Diesel

When replacing pistons in the LD28 diesel engine, the amount of projection of each piston crown above the deck of the block must be measured.

1. Clean the deck of the cylinder block completely.

2. Set a dial gauge, as shown on the cylinder block surface in the illustration, to zero.

3. For every cylinder, measure the piston projection and record the length.

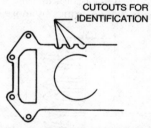

LD28 cylinder head gaskets have cutouts in them for identification purposes; when determining piston projection and selecting the suitable head gasket thickness

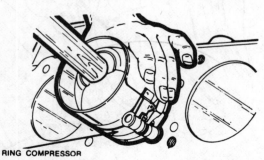

RING COMPRESSOR

Tap the piston assemblies down into the bores with a wooden hammer handle. Make sure the pistons and bores are well-lubed

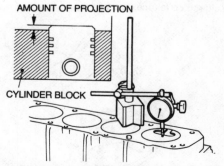

Set the dial gauge at zero, then measure and record the length of each piston projection in the LD28.

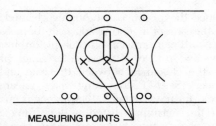

LD28 piston projection measuring points

NOTE: *Be sure to measure the length of piston projection at least three points for every cylinder.*

4. Determine the maximum length of piston projection and select the suitable head gasket according to the chart below.

Piston Projection mm (in)	Cylinder Head Gasket Thickness mm (in)	No. of Cutouts in Cylinder Head Gasket
Below 0.487 (0.0192)	1.12 (0.0441)	1
0.487–0.573 (0.0192–0.0226)	1.2 (0.047)	2
Above 0.573 (0.0226)	1.28 (0.0504)	3

NOTE: *The head gaskets have cutout(s) in them for identification purposes. When a head gasket needs to be replaced, always install a gasket of the same thickness.*

IDENTIFICATION AND POSITIONING

The pistons are marked with a number or "F" in the piston head. When installed in the engine the number or "F" markings are to be facing toward the front of the engine.

The connecting rods are installed in the engine with the oil hole facing toward the fuel pump side (right) of the engine.

NOTE: *It is advisable to number the pistons, connecting rods, and bearing caps in*

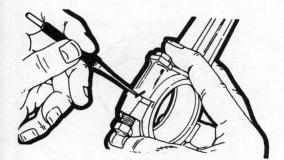

Matchmark each rod cap to its connecting rod

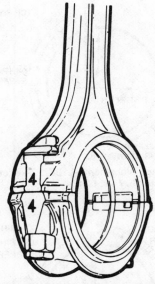

Number each rod and cap with its cylinder number for correct assembly

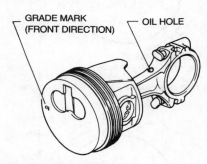

LD28 piston-to-rod relationship

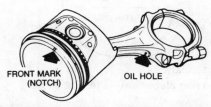

Piston and rod positioning—Z-series, L-series (except LD28) and CA20E, CA18ET engines

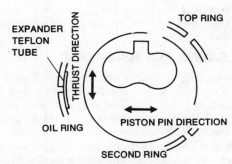

Piston ring placement—LD28 engine

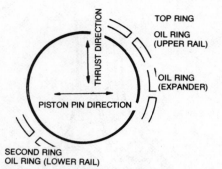

Piston ring placement—L20B, Z-series, CA20E, CA18ET and 1977–80 L24

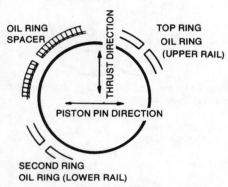

Piston ring placement—1981–84 L24 engines

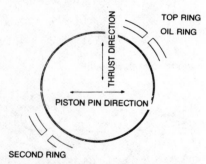

Piston ring placement—L16, L18 engines

some manner so that they can be reinstalled in the same cylinder, facing in the same direction from which they are removed. The CA-series rod and cap assemblies are factory-numbered.

CLEANING AND INSPECTION

Clean the piston after removing the rings (See "Piston Ring and Wrist Pin Removal and Installation below), by first scraping any carbon from the piston top. *Do not scratch the piston in any way during cleaning.* Use a broken piston ring or ring cleaning tool to clean out the ring grooves. Clean the entire piston with solvent and a brush (NOT a wire brush).

Once the piston is thoroughly cleaned, insert the side of a good piston ring (both No. 1 and No. 2 compression on each piston) into its respective groove. Using a feeler gauge, measure the clearance between the ring and its groove. (See "Piston Ring Side Clearance Check" for more details). If clearance is greater than the maximum listed under "Ring Side Clearance" in the "Piston and Ring" chart, replace the ring(s) and if necessary, the piston.

To check ring end-gap, insert a compression ring into the cylinder. Lightly oil the cylinder bore and push the ring down into the cylinder with a piston, to the bottom of its travel. Measure the ring end-gap with a feeler gauge. If the gap is not within specification, replace the ring; DO NOT file the ring ends.

CYLINDER BORE INSPECTION

Place a rag over the crankshaft journals. Wipe out each cylinder with a clean, solvent-soaked rag. Visually inspect the cylinder bores for roughness, scoring or scuffing; also check the bores by feel. Measure the cylinder bore diameter with an inside micrometer, or a telescope gauge and micrometer. Measure the bore at points parallel and perpendicular to the engine centerline at the top (below the ridge) and bottom of the bore. Subtract the bottom measurements from the top to determine cylinder taper.

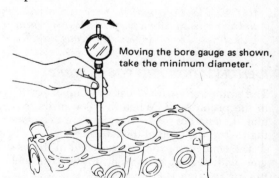

Moving the bore gauge as shown, take the minimum diameter.

Checking cylinder bore diameter with a telescope gauge

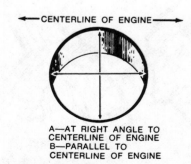

Cylinder bore measuring points

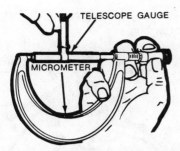

Measure the telescope gauge with a micrometer to determine cylinder bore diameter

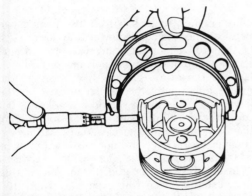

Measuring piston diameter. Check diameter on the wrist pin axis, and 90° away from the axis

Measure the piston diameter with a micrometer; since this micrometer may not be part of your tool kit as it is necessarily large, you may have to have the pistons miked at a machine shop. Take the measurements at right angles to the wrist pin center line, about an inch down the piston skirt from the top. Compare this measurement to the bore diameter of each cylinder—the difference is the piston clearance. If the clearance is greater than that specified in the "Piston and Ring Specifications" chart, have the cylinders honed or rebored and replace the pistons with an oversize set. Piston clearance can also be checked by inverting a piston into an oiled cylinder, and sliding in a feeler gauge between the two.

NOTE: *When any one cylinder needs boring, all cylinders must be bored.*

Piston Ring and Wrist Pin
REMOVAL

A piston ring expander is necessary for removing piston rings without damaging them; any other method (screwdriver blades, pliers, etc.) usually results in the rings being bent, scratched or distorted, or the piston itself being damaged. When the rings are removed, clean the ring grooves using an appropriate ring groove

Remove the piston rings with a ring expander

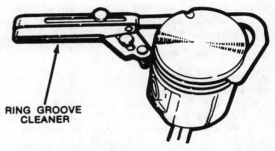

Use a ring groove cleaner to properly clean the ring groove

Wrist pin clips are removed with needle-nose or snap-ring pliers

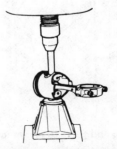

Wrist pins must be pressed in and out with a special press

cleaning tool, using care not to cut too deeply. Thoroughly clean all carbon and varnish from the piston with solvent.

All the Datsun/Nissan pistons covered in this

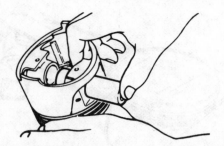

Wrist pin-to-piston fit should be such that the pin can be slid in smoothly by hand at room temperature

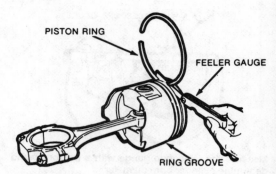

Measuring piston ring side clearance

guide have a pressed-in wrist pin, requiring a special press for removal. Take the piston and connecting rod assemblies to an engine specialist or machinist for wrist pin removal. The pins must also be pressed in during assembly.

PISTON RING END GAP

Piston ring end gap should be checked while the rings are removed from the pistons. Incorrect end gap indicates that the wrong size rings are being used; *ring breakage could occur.*

Compress the piston rings to be used in a cylinder, one at a time, into that cylinder. Squirt clean oil into the cylinder, so that the rings and the top 2 inches of cylinder wall are coated. Using an inverted piston, press the rings approximately 1 in. below the deck of the block. Measure the ring end gap with a feeler gauge, and compare to the "Ring Gap" chart in this chapter. Carefully pull the ring out of the cylinder and file the ends squarely with a fine file to obtain the proper clearance.

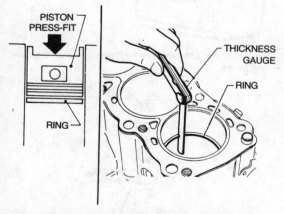

Checking ring end gap and piston-to-bore clearance

PISTON RING SIDE CLEARANCE CHECK AND INSTALLATION

Check the pistons to see that the ring grooves and oil return holes have been properly cleaned. Slide a piston ring into its groove, and check the side clearance with a feeler gauge. On gas-

oline engines, make sure you insert the gauge between the ring and its lower land (lower edge of the groove), because any wear that occurs forms a step at the inner portion of the lower land. If the piston grooves have worn to the extent that relatively high steps exist on the lower land, the piston should be replaced, because these will interfere with the operation of the new rings and ring clearances will be excessive. Piston rings are not furnished in oversize widths to compensate for ring groove wear.

Install the rings on the piston, *lowest ring* first, using a piston ring expander. There is a high risk of breaking or distorting the rings, or scratching the piston, if the rings are installed by hand or other means.

Position the rings on the piston as illustrated; *spacing of the various piston ring gaps is crucial to proper oil retention and even cylinder wear.* When installing new rings, refer to the installation diagram furnished with the new parts.

Connecting Rod

INSPECTION AND BEARING REPLACEMENT

Connecting rod side clearance and big-end bearing inspection and replacement should be performed while the rods are still installed in the engine. Determine the clearance between the connecting rod sides and the crankshaft us-

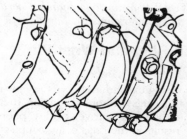

Checking con rod side clearance. Make sure the feeler gauge is between the shoulder of the crank journal and the side of the rod

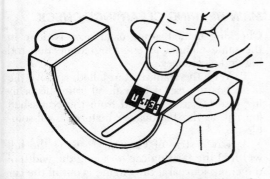

Check con rod bearing clearance with Plastigage®

ing a feeler gauge. If clearance is below the minimum tolerance, check with a machinist about machining the rod to provide adequate clearance. If clearance is excessive, substitute an unworn rod and recheck; if clearance is still outside specifications, the crankshaft must be welded and reground, or replaced.

To check connecting rod big-end bearing clearances, remove the rod bearing caps one at a time. Using a clean, dry shop rag, thoroughly clean all oil from the crank journal and bearing insert in the cap.

NOTE: *The Plastigage© gauging material you will be using to check clearances with is soluble in oil; therefore any oil on the journal or bearing could result in an incorrect reading.*

Lay a strip of Plastigage© along the full length of the bearing insert (along the crank journal if the engine is out of the car and inverted). Reinstall the cap and torque to specifications listed in the "Torque Specifications" chart.

3. Remove the rod cap and determine bearing clearance by comparing the width of the now flattened Plastigage© to the scale on the Plastigage© envelope. Journal taper is determined by comparing the width of the Plastigage© strip near its ends. Rotate the crankshaft 90° and retest, to determine journal eccentricity.

NOTE: *Do not rotate the crankshaft with the Plastigage© installed.*

If the bearing insert and crank journal ap-

pear intact and are within tolerances, no further service is required and the bearing caps can be reinstalled (remove Plastigage© before installation). If clearances are not within tolerances, the bearing inserts in both the connecting rod and rod cap must be replaced with undersize inserts, and/or the crankshaft must be reground. To install the bearing insert halves, press them into the bearing caps and connecting rods. Make sure the tab in each insert fits into the notch in each rod and cap. Lube the face of each insert with engine oil prior to installing each rod into the engine.

The connecting rods can be further inspected when they are removed from the engine and separated from their pistons. Rod alignment (straightness and squareness) must be checked by a machinist, as the rod must be set in a special fixture. Many machine shops also perform a Magnafluxing service, which is a process that shows up any tiny cracks that you may be unable to see.

Crankshaft and Main Bearings
REMOVAL AND INSTALLATION

NOTE: *Before removing the crankshaft, check main bearing clearances as described under "Main Bearing Clearance Check" below.*

1. Remove the piston and connecting rod assemblies following the procedure in this chapter.

2. Check crankshaft thrust clearance (end play) before removing the crank from the block. Using a pry bar, pry the crankshaft the extent of its travel forward, and measure thrust clearance at the center main bearing (No. 4 bearing on 6-cylinder engines, No. 3 on 4-cylinder engines) with a feeler gauge. Pry the crankshaft the extent of its rearward travel, and measure the other side of the bearing. If clearance is greater than that specified, the thrust washers must be replaced (see Main Bearing Replacement, below).

3. Using a punch, mark the corresponding main bearing caps and saddles according to po-

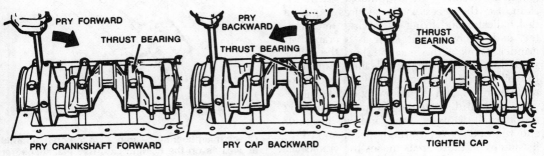

PRY FORWARD   THRUST BEARING   PRY BACKWARD   THRUST BEARING   THRUST BEARING

PRY CRANKSHAFT FORWARD   PRY CAP BACKWARD   TIGHTEN CAP

Checking crankshaft thrust

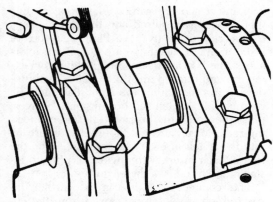

Check crankshaft end play with a feeler gauge

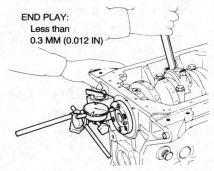

END PLAY:
Less than
0.3 MM (0.012 IN)

Crankshaft end-play can also be checked using a dial gauge

sition—one punch on the front main cap and saddle, two on the second, three on the third, etc. This ensures correct reassembly.

4. Remove the main bearing caps after they have been marked.

5. Remove the crankshaft from the block.

6. Follow the crankshaft inspection, main bearing clearance checking and replacement procedures below before reinstalling the crankshaft.

INSPECTION

Crankshaft inspection and servicing should be handled exclusively by a reputable machinist, as most of the necessary procedures require a dial indicator and fixing jig, a large micrometer, and machine tools such as a crankshaft grinder. While at the machine shop, the crankshaft should be thoroughly cleaned (especially the oil passages), Magnafluxed (to check for minute cracks) and the following checks made: Main journal diameter, crank pin (connecting rod journal) diameter, taper and out-of-round, and run-out. Wear, beyond specification limits, in any of these areas means the crankshaft must be reground or replaced.

MAIN BEARING CLEARANCE CHECK

Checking main bearing clearances is done in the same manner as checking connecting rod big-end clearances.

1. With the crankshaft installed, remove the main bearing cap. Clean all oil from the bearing insert in the cap and from the crankshaft journal, as the Plastigage© material is oil-soluble.

2. Lay a strip of Plastigage© along the full width of the bearing cap (or along the width of the crank journal if the engine is out of the car and inverted).

3. Install the bearing cap and torque to specification.

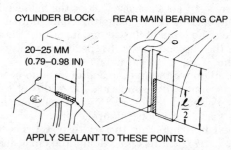

Checking main bearing clearance with Plastigage®

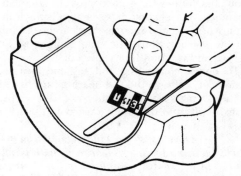

CYLINDER BLOCK   REAR MAIN BEARING CAP

20–25 MM
(0.79–0.98 IN)

APPLY SEALANT TO THESE POINTS.

On all L-series 4 and 6 cylinder engine main bearing caps, apply sealant here

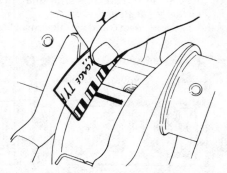

Check main bearing clearance on the crank journal as well as on the bearing cap. Use Plastigage® or equivalent

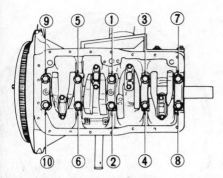

L18/L20 series main bearing cap bolt torque sequence

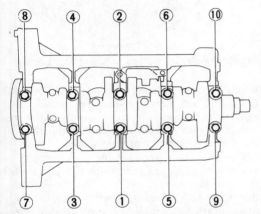

CA20E/CA18ET main bearing cap bolt torque sequence

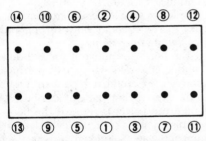

L24 and LD28 main bearing cap bolt torque sequence. Torque gradually in two or three stages, after installing the caps with the marks facing forward. Apply sealant as shown in the accompanying diagram

NOTE: *Do not rotate the crankshaft with the Plastigage© installed.*

4. Remove the bearing cap and determine bearing clearance by comparing the width of the now-flattened Plastigage© with the scale on the Plastigage© envelope. Journal taper is determined by comparing the width of the Plastigage© strip near its ends. Rotate the crankshaft 90° and retest, to determine journal eccentricity.

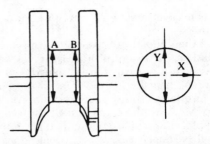

Check crankshaft journal eccentricity and taper with a micrometer at these points

5. Repeat the above for the remaining bearings. If the bearing journal and insert appear in good shape (with no unusual wear visible) and are within tolerances, no further main bearing service is required. If unusual wear is evident and/or the clearances are outside specifications, the bearings must be replaced and the cause of their wear found.

MAIN BEARING REPLACEMENT

Main bearings can be replaced with the crankshaft both in the engine (with the engine still in the car) and out of the engine (with the engine on a workstand or bench). Both procedures are covered here. The main bearings *must* be replaced if the crankshaft has been reground; the replacement bearings being available in various undersize increments from most auto parts jobbers or your local Datsun/Nissan dealer.

Engine Out of Car

1. Remove the crankshaft from the engine block.

2. Remove the main bearing inserts from the bearing caps and from the main bearing saddles. Remove the thrust washers from the No. 3 (4-cylinder) or No. 4 (6-cylinder) crank journal.

3. Thoroughly clean the saddles, bearing caps, and crankshaft.

4. *Make sure the crankshaft has been fully checked and is ready for reassembly.* Place the upper main bearings in the block saddles so that the oil grooves and/or oil holes are correctly aligned with their corresponding grooves or holes in the saddles.

5. Install the thrust washers on the center main bearing, with the oil grooves facing out.

6. Lubricate the faces of all bearings with clean engine oil, and place the crankshaft in the block.

7. Install the main bearing caps in numbered order with the arrows or any other orientation marks facing forward. Torque all bolts except the center cap bolts in sequence in two or three passes to the specified torque. Rotate

the crankshaft after each pass to ensure even tightness.

8. Align the thrust bearing by prying the crankshaft the extent of its axial travel several times with a pry bar. On last movement hold the crankshaft toward the front of the engine and torque the thrust bearing cap to specifications. Measure the crankshaft thrust clearance (end play) as previously described in this chapter. If clearance is outside specifications (too sloppy), install a new set of oversize thrust washers and check clearance again.

Engine and Crankshaft Installed

1. Remove the main bearing caps and keep them in order.

2. Make a bearing roll-out pin from a cotter pin as shown.

3. Carefully roll out the old inserts from the upper side of the crankshaft journal, noting the positions of the oil grooves and/or oil holes so the new inserts can be correctly installed.

4. Roll each new insert into its saddle after lightly oiling the crankshaft-side face of each. Make sure the notches and/or oil holes are correctly positioned.

5. Replace the bearing inserts in the caps with new inserts. Oil the face of each, and install the caps in numbered order with the arrows or other orientation marks facing forward. Torque the bolts to the specified torque in two or three passes in the sequence shown.

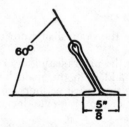

Make a bearing roll-out pin from a cotter pin

Cylinder Block

Most inspection and service work on the cylinder block should be handled by a machinist or professional engine rebuilding shop. Included in this work are bearing alignment checks, line boring, deck resurfacing, hot-tanking and cylinder honing or boring. A block that has been checked and properly serviced will last much longer than one which has not had the proper attention when the opportunity was there for it.

Cylinder de-glazing (honing) can, however, be performed by the owner/mechanic who is careful and takes his or her time. The cylinder

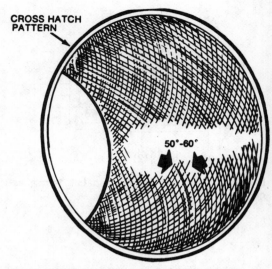

Proper cylinder bore cross-hatching after honing

bores become "glazed" during normal operation as the rings continually ride up and down against them. This shiny glaze must be removed in order for a new set of piston rings to be able to properly seat themselves.

Cylinder hones are available at most auto tool stores and parts jobbers. With the piston and rod assemblies removed from the block, cover the crankshaft completely with a rag or cover to keep grit from the hone and cylinder material off of it. Chuck a hone into a variable-speed power drill (preferable here to a constant-speed drill), and insert it into the cylinder.

NOTE: *Make sure the drill and hone are kept square to the cylinder bore throughout the entire honing operation.*

Start the hone and move it up and down in the cylinder at a rate which will produce approximately a 60° crosshatch pattern. DO NOT extend the hone below the cylinder bore! After developing the pattern, remove the hone and recheck piston fit. Wash the cylinders with a detergent and water solution to remove the hone and cylinder grit. Wipe the bores out several times with a clean rag soaked in clean engine oil. Remove the cover from the crankshaft, and check closely to see that no grit has found its way onto the crankshaft.

ENGINE LUBRICATION

Oil Pan
REMOVAL AND INSTALLATION
All Engines

To remove the oil pan it will be necessary to unbolt the motor mounts and jack the engine to gain clearance. Drain the oil, remove the

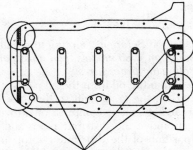

Apply sealant at these points

Z-series oil pan sealant points

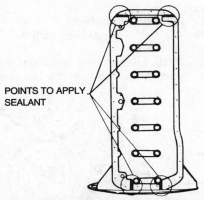

POINTS TO APPLY
SEALANT

**Apply sealant here when installing the oil pan on L24
and LD28 engines**

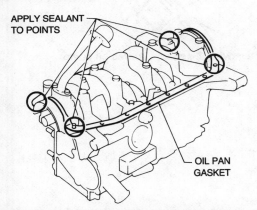

APPLY SEALANT
TO POINTS

OIL PAN
GASKET

**Apply sealant to the CA20E and CA18ET engine oil
pan mating surfaces here; also to the corresponding
points on the oil pan**

attaching screws, and remove the oil pan and
gasket. Install the oil pan in the reverse order
with a new gasket and sealant at the points indicated, tightening the screws to 4–7 ft. lbs.

Rear Main Oil Seal

REPLACEMENT

All Engines Except CA20E and CA18ET

In order to replace the rear main oil seal, the
rear main bearing cap must be removed. Re-

moval of the rear main bearing cap requires
the use of a special rear main bearing cap puller.
Also, the oil seal is installed with a special
crankshaft rear oil seal drift. Unless these or
similar tools are available to you, it is recommended that the oil seal be replaced by a Datsun service center.

1. Remove the engine and transmission assembly from the vehicle.

2. Remove the transmission from the engine. Remove the oil pan.

3. Remove the clutch from the flywheel.

4. Remove the flywheel from the crankshaft.

5. Remove the rear main bearing cap together with the bearing cap side seals.

6. Remove the rear main oil seal from
around the crankshaft.

7. Apply lithium grease around the sealing
lip of the oil seal and install the seal around the
crankshaft using a suitable tool.

8. Apply sealer to the rear main bearing
cap as indicated, install the rear main bearing
cap, and tighten the cap bolts to 33–40 ft. lbs.

9. Apply sealant to the rear main bearing
cap side seals and install the side seals, driving
the seals into place with a suitable drift.

10. Assemble the engine and install it in the
vehicle in the reverse order of removal.

CA20E and CA18ET

1. Remove the transmission.

2. Remove the flywheel.

3. Remove the rear oil seal retainer.

4. Using a pair of pliers, remove the oil seal
from the retainer.

5. Liberally apply clean engine oil to the new
oil seal and carefully install it into the retainer.

6. Install the rear oil seal retainer into the
engine, along with a new gasket. Torque the
bolts to 2.9–4.3 ft. lbs. Install the flywheel and
transmission in the reverse order of removal.

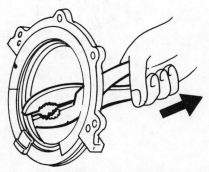

**Removing the CA20E and CA18ET rear oil seal from
the retainer**

Oil Pump

The oil pump is mounted externally on the engine, this eliminates the need to remove the oil pan in order to remove the oil pump on all engines except CA20E and CA18ET. The L-series and Z-series oil pumps are mounted in the timing chain cover.

REMOVAL AND INSTALLATION

1973–79

1. Remove the distributor on the L18, L20B and L24 engines.
2. Drain the engine oil.
3. Remove the front stabilizer bar if it is in the way of removing the oil pump.
4. Remove the splash shield.
5. Remove the oil pump body with the drive spindle assembly.
6. Turn the crankshaft so that the No. 1 piston is at TDC of the compression stroke.
7. Fill the pump housing with engine oil, then align the punch mark on the spindle with the hole in the oil pump.
8. With a new gasket placed over the drive spindle, install the oil pump and drive spindle assembly so that the projection on the top of the drive spindle is located in the 11:25 o'clock position.
9. Install the distributor with the metal tip of the rotor pointing toward the No. 1 spark plug tower of the distributor cap.
10. Assemble the remaining components in the reverse order of removal.

1980–84

EXCEPT CA20E, CA18ET

CAUTION: *Before attempting to remove the oil pump on 1980 models, you must perform the following procedures:*
    a. Drain the oil from the oil pan.
    b. Turn the crankshaft so that No. 1 piston is at TDC on its compression stroke.
    c. Remove the distributor cap and mark the position of the distributor rotor in relation to the distributor base with a piece of chalk (gasoline engine only).
1. Remove the front stabilizer bar, if so equipped.
2. Remove the splash shield.
3. Remove the oil pump body with the drive spindle assembly.
4. To install, fill the pump housing with engine oil, align the punch mark on the spindle

Removing Z-series, L-series oil pump

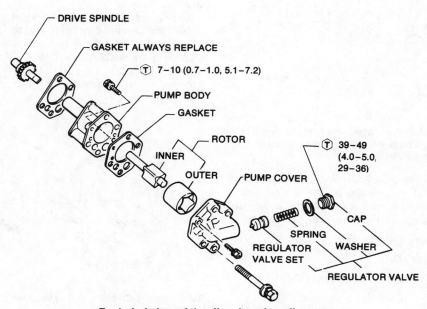

Exploded view of the diesel engine oil pump

1. Oil pump body
2. Inner rotor and shaft
3. Outer rotor
4. Oil pump cover
5. Regulator valve
6. Regulator spring
7. Washer
8. Regulator cap
9. Cover gasket

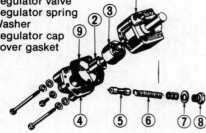

Exploded view of the Z-series, and gasoline engine L-series oil pump

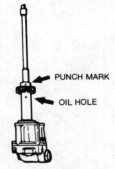

Z-series, L-series (gasoline) oil pump alignment

PUNCH MARK

OIL HOLE

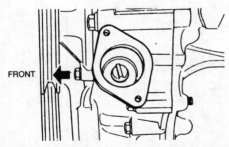

FRONT

Position of the distributor drive spindle—L-series gasoline engines

with the hole in the pump. No. 1 piston should be at TDC on its compression stroke.

5. With a new gasket placed over the drive spindle, install the oil pump and drive spindle assembly, on gasoline engines make sure the tip of the drive spindle fits into the distributor shaft notch securely. The distributor rotor should be pointing to the match mark you made earlier.

NOTE: *Great care must be taken not to disturb the distributor rotor while installing the oil pump, or the ignition timing will be wrong.*
Assemble the remaining components in the reverse order of removal.

CA20E, CA18ET 1984 and later

1. Remove all accessory drive belts and the alternator.
2. Remove the timing (cam) belt covers and remove the timing belt.
3. Unbolt the engine from its mounts and lift or jack the engine up from the unibody.
4. Remove the oil pan.
5. Remove the oil pump assembly along with the oil strainer.
6. If installing a new or rebuilt oil pump, first pack the pump full of petroleum jelly to prevent the pump from cavitating when the engine is started. Install the pump in the reverse order of removal, torquing the mounting bolts to 9–12 ft. lbs.

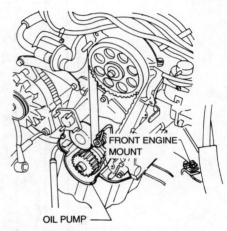

FRONT ENGINE MOUNT

OIL PUMP

CA20E, CA18ET oil pump location

ENGINE COOLING

Radiator

REMOVAL AND INSTALLATION

NOTE: *On some models it may be necessary to remove the front grille.*

1. Drain the engine coolant into a clean container. On fuel injected models, remove the air cleaner inlet pipe.
2. Disconnect the upper and lower radiator hoses and the expansion tank hose.
3. Disconnect the automatic transmission oil cooler lines after draining the transmission. Cap the lines to keep dirt out of them.
4. If the fan has a shroud, unbolt the shroud and move it back, hanging it over the fan.
5. Remove the radiator mounting bolts and the radiator.
6. Installation is the reverse of removal. Fill the automatic transmission to the proper level. Fill the cooling system.

General Engine Specifications

Year	Car Model	Engine Model	Engine Displacement Cu. In. (cc)	Carburetor Type	Horsepower (@ rpm)	Torque @ rpm (ft. lbs.)	Bore x Stroke (in.)	Compression Ratio	Oil Pressure @ rpm (psi)
1973	610	L18	108.0 (1770)	2 BBL	105 @ 6,000	108 @ 3,600	3.35 x 3.307	8.5:1	50–57
1974	610	L20B	119.1 (1952)	2 BBL	110 @ 3,500	112 @ 3,600	3.35 x 3.39	8.5:1	50–57
	710	L18	108.0 (1770)	2 BBL	105 @ 6,000	108 @ 3,600	3.35 x 3.307	8.5:1	50–57
1975	610	L20B	119.1 (1952)	2 BBL	110 @ 5,600	112 @ 3,600	3.35 x 3.39	8.5:1	50–57
	710	L20B	119.1 (1952)	2 BBL	100 @ 5,600	100 @ 3,600	3.35 x 3.39	8.5:1	50–57
1976	610	L20B	119.1 (1952)	2 BBL	112 @ 5,600	108 @ 3,600	3.35 x 3.39	8.5:1	50–57
	710	L20B	119.1 (1952)	2 BBL	110 @ 5,600	112 @ 5,600	3.35 x 3.39	8.5:1	50–57
1977	200SX	L20B	119.1 (1952)	2 BBL	97 @ 5,600	102 @ 3,200	3.35 x 3.39	8.5:1	50–57
	710	L20B	119.1 (1952)	2 BBL	110 @ 5,600	112 @ 5,600	3.35 x 3.39	8.5:1	50–57
	810	L24	146.0 (2393)	EFI	154 @ 5,600	155 @ 4,400	3.27 x 2.90	8.6:1	50–57
1978	200SX	L20B	119.1 (1952)	2 BBL	97 @ 5,600	102 @ 3,200	3.35 x 3.39	8.5:1	50–57
	510	L20B	119.1 (1952)	2 BBL	97 @ 5,600	102 @ 3,200	3.35 x 3.39	8.5:1	50–57
	810	L24	146.0 (2393)	EFI	154 @ 5,600	155 @ 4,400	3.27 x 2.90	8.6:1	50–57
1979	200SX	L20B	119.1 (1952)	2 BBL	92 @ 5,600	107 @ 3,200	3.35 x 3.39	8.5:1	50–57
	510	L20B	119.1 (1952)	2 BBL	92 @ 5,600	107 @ 3,200	3.35 x 3.39	8.5:1	50–57
	810	L24	146.0 (2393)	EFI	120 @ 5,200	125 @ 4,400	3.27 x 2.90	8.9:1	50–60

Year	Model	Engine	Displacement cu in (cc)	Fuel System	Horsepower @ rpm	Torque @ rpm	Bore x Stroke	Compression Ratio	Oil Pressure
1980	200SX	Z20E	119.1 (1952)	EFI	100 @ 5,200	112 @ 3,200	3.35 x 3.39	8.5:1	50–60
	510	L20B② Z20E③	119.1 (1952)	2 BBL	92 @ 5,200	112 @ 2,800	3.35 x 3.39	8.5:1	50–60
	810	L24	119.1 (1952)	EFI	120 @ 5,200	125 @ 4,400	3.27 x 2.90	8.9:1①	50–60
1981	200SX	Z20E	119.1 (1952)	EFI	100 @ 5,200	112 @ 3,200	3.35 x 3.39	8.5:1	50–60
	510	Z20S	119.1 (1952)	2 BBL	92 @ 5,200	112 @ 2,800	3.35 x 3.39	8.5:1	50–60
	810	L24E	146.0 (2393)	EFI	120 @ 5,200	134 @ 2,800	3.27 x 2.90	8.9:1	50–60
	810 Diesel	LD28	170.0 (2793)	DFI	80 @ 4,600	120 @ 2,400	3.33 x 3.27	22.7:1	NA
1982–83	200SX	Z22E	133.4 (2181)	EFI	102 @ 5,200	129 @ 2,800	3.43 x 3.62	8.5:1	50–60
	810 Maxima	L24E	146.0 (2393)	EFI	120 @ 5,200	134 @ 2,800	3.27 x 2.90	8.9:1	50–60
	810 Diesel	LD28	170.0 (2793)	DFI	80 @ 4,600	120 @ 2,400	3.33 x 3.27	22.7:1	NA
1984	200SX	CA20E	120.4 (1974)	EFI	102 @ 5,200	116 @ 3,200	3.33 x 3.46	8.5:1	57 @ 4,000
	200SX Turbo	CA18ET	110.3 (1809)	EFI	120 @ 5,200	134 @ 3,200	3.27 x 3.29	8.0:1	71 @ 4,000
	Maxima	L24E	146.0 (2393)	EFI	120 @ 5,200	134 @ 2,800	3.27 x 2.90	8.9:1	50–60

NA: Not Available
DFI: Diesel Fuel Injection
① 8.6 in California
② Canadian models
③ U.S. models

Valve Specifications

Model	Seat Angle (deg)	Face Angle (deg)	Spring Test Pressure (lbs. @ in.)		Spring Installed Height (in.)		Stem to Guide Clearance (in.)		Stem Diameter (in.)	
			Outer	Inner	Outer	Inner	Intake	Exhaust	Intake	Exhaust
L18, L20B	45	45	108 @ 1.161	56.2 @ 0.965	1.575	1.378	0.0008– 0.0021	0.0016– 0.0029	0.3136– 0.3142	0.3128– 0.3134
Z20E, Z20S	45	45	115.3 @ 1.18	57 @ 0.98	1.575	1.378	0.0008– 0.0021	0.0016– 0.0029	0.3136– 0.3142	0.3128– 0.3134
Z22E	45	45	115.3 @ 1.18	57 @ 0.98	1.575	1.378	0.0008– 0.0021	0.0016– 0.0029	0.3136– 0.3142	0.3128– 0.3134
CA20E, CA18ET	45	45	118.2 @ 1.00	66.6 @ 1.00	②	②	0.0008– 0.0021	0.0016– 0.0029	0.2742– 0.2748	0.2734– 0.2740
L24	45	45	108 @ 1.161 ①	56.2 @ 0.965 ①	1.575	1.378	0.0008– 0.0021	0.0016– 0.0029	0.3136– 0.3142	0.3128– 0.3134
LD28	45	45	115.3 @ 1.181	—	1.575	—	0.0008– 0.0021	0.0016– 0.0029	0.3136– 0.3142	0.3128– 0.3134

① Figure is for Exhaust; for Intake: Outer 105.2 @ 1.181
Inner 54.9 @ 0.984
② Free height: 1.967 Outer, 1.736 Inner

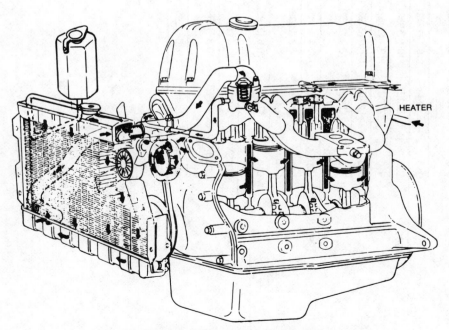

L-series engine cooling system (4 cylinder)

HEATER

Camshaft Specifications

(All measurements in inches)

Engine	Journal Diameter					Bearing Clearance	Lobe Lift		Camshaft End Play
	1	2	3	4	5		Intake	Exhaust	
L18, L20B	1.8878–1.8883	1.8878–1.8883	1.8878–1.8883	1.8878–1.8883	—	0.0015–0.0026	0.276	0.276	00031–0.0150
Z20E, Z20S, Z22E	1.2967–1.2974	1.2967–1.2974	1.2967–1.2974	1.2967–1.2974	—	0.0018–0.0035	NA	NA	0.008
L24, LD28	1.8878–1.8883	1.8878–1.8883	1.8878–1.8883	1.8878–1.8883	1.8878–1.8883	0.0015–0.0026	0.262	0.276	0.0031–0.0150
CA20E, CA18ET	1.8085–1.8092	1.8085–1.8092	1.8085–1.8092	1.8085–1.8092	1.8077–1.8085	0.004 ①	0.354	0.354	0.0028–0.0055

① Clearance limit

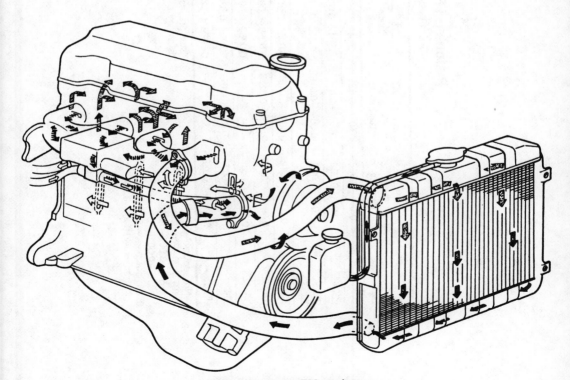

Cooling system—Z20 engines

Piston and Ring Specifications
All measurements in inches

Engine Model	Piston Clearance	Ring Gap			Ring Side Clearance		
		Top Compression	Bottom Compression	Oil Control	Top Compression	Bottom Compression	Oil Control
L18	0.001–0.002	0.014–0.022	0.012–0.020	0.012–0.035	0.002–0.003	0.002–0.003	—
L20B	0.001–0.002	0.010–0.016	0.012–0.020	0.012–0.035	0.002–0.003	0.001–0.003	—
Z20E, Z20S	0.001–0.002	0.0098–0.016	0.006–0.012	0.012–0.035	0.002–0.003	0.001–0.0025	—
Z22E	0.001–0.0018	0.0098–0.0157	0.0059–0.0118	0.0118–0.0354	0.0016–0.0029	0.0012–0.0025	—
CA20E	0.0010–0.0018	0.0098–0.0138	0.0059–0.0098	0.0079–0.0236	0.0016–0.0029	0.0012–0.0025	—
CA18ET	0.0010–0.0018	③	0.0059–0.0098	0.0079–0.0236	0.0016–0.0029	0.0012–0.0025	—
L24	0.001–0.002	0.010–0.016	0.006–0.012	0.012–0.035	0.002–0.003	0.001–0.003	①
LD28	0.0020–0.0028	②	0.0079–0.0138	0.0118–0.0177	0.0024–0.0039	0.0016–0.0031	0.0012–0.0028

— Not applicable
① 1977–80—combined
　1981—0.009–0.0028
　1982—0.0010
② Without mark—0.0079–0.0114
　With mark—0.0055–0.0087
③ Piston grades #1 and #2: 0.0098–0.0126 in.
　Piston grades #3, 4 and 5: 0.0075–0.0102 in.

Crankshaft and Connecting Rod Specifications
All measurements given in inches

Engine Model	Crankshaft					Connecting Rod Bearings		
	Main Brg Journal Dia	Main Brg Oil Clearance	Shaft End-Play	Thrust on No.		Journal Dia	Oil Clearance	Side Clearance
L18	2.1631–2.1636	0.001–0.002	0.002–0.007	3		1.9670–1.9675	0.001–0.002	0.008–0.012
L18 (710)	2.3599–2.360	0.0008–0.002	0.002–0.007	3		1.967–1.9675	0.001–0.002	0.008–0.012
L20B	2.3599–2.360	0.0008–0.0024	0.002–0.007	3		1.9660–1.9670	0.001–0.002	0.008–0.012
Z20S, Z20E, Z22E	2.1631–2.1636	0.0008–0.0024	0.002–0.0071	3		1.967–1.9675	0.001–0.0022	0.008–0.012
CA20E	2.0847–2.0852	0.0016–0.0024	0.012	3		1.8898–1.8903	0.0008–0.0024	0.0118
CA18ET	2.0847–2.0852	0.0016–0.0024	0.0020–0.0071	3		1.8898–1.8903	0.0008–0.0024	0.0118
L24	2.1631–2.1636	0.0008–0.0026	0.002–0.0071	Center		1.9670–1.9675	0.001–0.003	0.008–0.012
L24E	2.1631–2.1636	0.0008–0.0026	0.0020–0.0071	Center		1.7701–1.7706	0.0009–0.0024	0.008–0.012
LD28	2.1631–2.1636	0.0008–0.0024	0.0020–0.0071	Center		1.9670–1.9675	0.0008–0.0024	0.008–0.012

Torque Specifications
All readings in ft. lbs.

Engine Model	Cylinder Head Bolts	Main Bearing Bolts	Rod Bearing Bolts	Crankshaft Pulley Bolts	Flywheel to Crankshaft Bolts	Manifolds	
						Intake	Exhaust
L18	47–62	33–40	33–40	87–116	101–116	9–12	9–12
L20B	51–61	33–40	33–40	87–116	101–116	9–12	9–12
Z20E, Z20S, Z22E	51–58	33–40	33–40	87–116	101–116	12–15	12–15
CA20E	③	33–40	24–27	90–98	72–80	14–19	14–22
CA18ET	③	33–40	24–27	90–98	72–80	14–19	14–22
L24	51–61	33–40	33–40	101–116	94–108	①	
LD28	87–94	51–61	33–40	101–116	101–116	②	

① M10 bolt: 25–35 ft. lbs.
M8 bolt: 11–18 ft. lbs.
M8 nut: 9–12 ft. lbs.

② Upper bolt (M10): 24–27 ft. lbs.
Lower nut and bolt (M8): 12–18 ft. lbs.

③ Torque all bolts to 22 ft. lbs.; then to 58 ft. lbs. Loosen all bolts completely, then torque all bolts to 22 ft. lbs. Final torque all bolts to 54–61 ft. lbs. (if angle torquing, turn all bolts 90–95 degrees clockwise).

There maybe some Soft Plugs on th Sides of the Engir

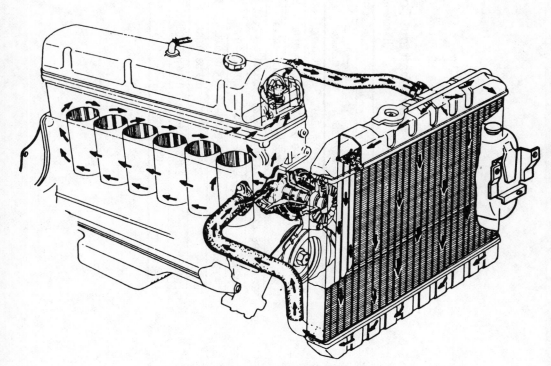

Cooling system—L24 engine (LD28 similiar)

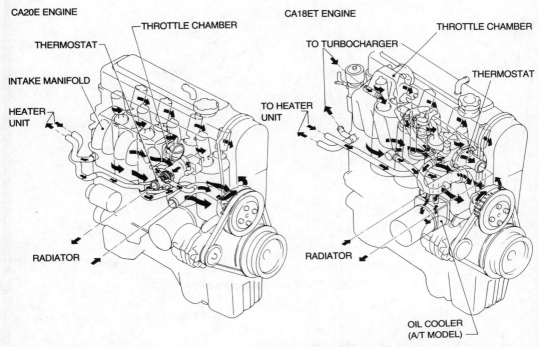

CA20E and CA18ET cooling system schematics showing thermostat and oil cooler (CA18ET) locations

Water Pump

REMOVAL AND INSTALLATION

1. Drain the engine coolant into a clean container.

2. Loosen the four bolts retaining the fan shroud to the radiator and remove the shroud.

3. Loosen the belt, then remove the fan and pulley from the water pump hub.

4. Remove the bolts retaining the pump and remove the pump together with the gasket from the front cover.

5. Remove all traces of gasket material and install the water pump in the reverse order with

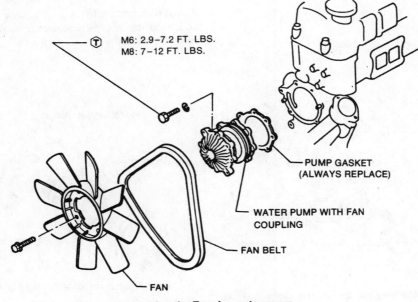

Removing the Z-series water pump

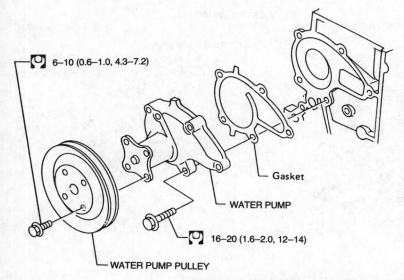

6–10 (0.6–1.0, 4.3–7.2)

Gasket

WATER PUMP

16–20 (1.6–2.0, 12–14)

WATER PUMP PULLEY

: N·M (KG-M, FT.LB.)

CA20E, CA18ET water pump installation

L-series water pump removal

a new gasket and sealer. Tighten the bolts uniformly.

Thermostat

REMOVAL AND INSTALLATION

1. Drain the engine coolant into a clean container so that the level is below the thermostat housing.

2. Disconnect the upper radiator hose at the water outlet.

3. Loosen the two securing nuts and remove the water outlet, gasket, and the thermostat from the thermostat housing.

4. Install the thermostat in the reverse order of removal, using a new gasket with sealer and with the thermostat spring toward the inside of the engine.

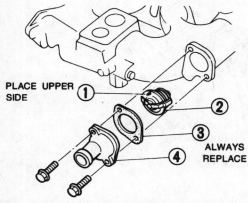

PLACE UPPER SIDE ①
②
③
④ ALWAYS REPLACE

Z20 engine (carbureted) thermostat location. Note jiggle valve (1)

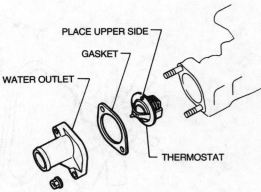

PLACE UPPER SIDE
GASKET
WATER OUTLET
THERMOSTAT

18–22 N·M (1.8–2.2 KG-M, 13–16 FT.LB.)

CA20E, CA18ET thermostat location

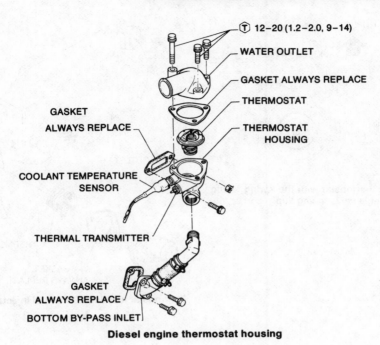

12–20 (1.2–2.0, 9–14)

WATER OUTLET

GASKET ALWAYS REPLACE

THERMOSTAT

GASKET ALWAYS REPLACE

THERMOSTAT HOUSING

COOLANT TEMPERATURE SENSOR

THERMAL TRANSMITTER

GASKET ALWAYS REPLACE

BOTTOM BY-PASS INLET

Diesel engine thermostat housing

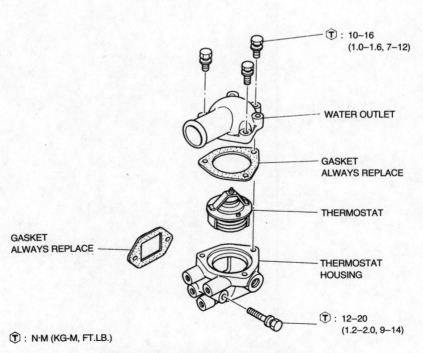

: 10–16 (1.0–1.6, 7–12)

WATER OUTLET

GASKET ALWAYS REPLACE

THERMOSTAT

GASKET ALWAYS REPLACE

THERMOSTAT HOUSING

: 12–20 (1.2–2.0, 9–14)

: N·M (KG-M, FT.LB.)

L24 thermostat installation and torque specs

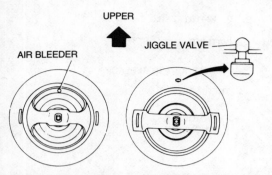

Always install the thermostat with the spring facing "down" and the jiggle valve facing "up"

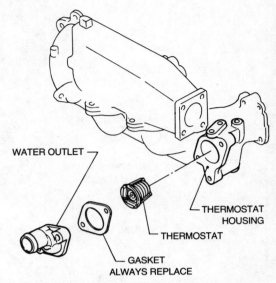

Thermostat location, Z22E (fuel injected) engines

Emission Controls and Fuel System

EMISSION CONTROLS

There are three sources of automotive pollutants: Crankcase fumes, exhaust gases and gasoline evaporation. The pollutants formed from these substances fall into three categories: unburnt hydrocarbons (HC), carbon monoxide (CO) and oxides of nitrogen (NO_x). The equipment that is used to limit these pollutants is commonly called emission control equipment.

Crankcase Emission Controls

The crankcase emission control equipment consists of a positive crankcase ventilation valve (PCV), a closed or open oil filler cap and hoses to connect this equipment.

NOTE: *The crankcase emission control system on the diesel engine is basically the same as that which is on the gasoline engine. Its*

major difference is the crankcase emission control valve; although its function is the same as the gasoline engine's PCV valve, it's shape and location are different.

When the engine is running, a small portion of the gases which are formed in the combustion chamber during combustion leak by the piston rings and enter the crankcase. Since these gases are under pressure they tend to escape from the crankcase and enter into the atmosphere. If these gases were allowed to remain in the crankcase for any length of time, they would contaminate the engine oil and cause sludge to build up. If the gases are allowed to escape into the atmosphere, they would pollute the air, as they contain unburned hydrocarbons. The crankcase emission control equipment recycles these gases back into the engine combustion chamber where they are burned.

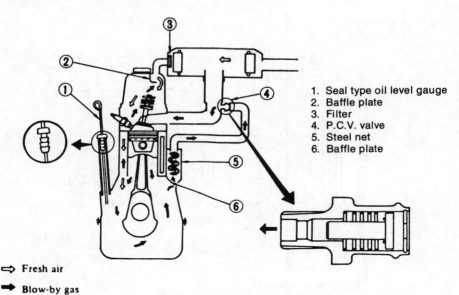

1. Seal type oil level gauge
2. Baffle plate
3. Filter
4. P.C.V. valve
5. Steel net
6. Baffle plate

⇨ Fresh air

➡ Blow-by gas

PCV system—L20B

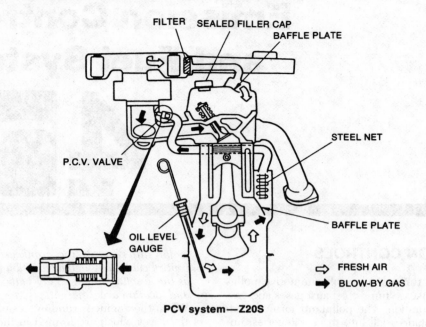

PCV system—Z20S

Crankcase gases are recycled in the following manner: while the engine is running, clean filtered air is drawn into the crankcase through the carburetor air filter and then through a hose leading to the rocket cover. As the air passes through the crankcase it picks up the combustion gases and carries them out of the crankcase, up through the PCV valve and into the intake manifold. After they enter the intake manifold they are drawn into the combustion chamber and burned.

The most critical component in the system is the PCV valve. This vacuum controlled valve regulates the amount of gases which are recycled into the combustion chamber. At low engine speeds the valve is partially closed, limiting the flow of gases into the intake manifold. As engine speed increases, the valve opens to admit greater quantities of the gases into the intake manifold. If the valve should become blocked or plugged, the gases will be prevented from escaping from the crankcase by the

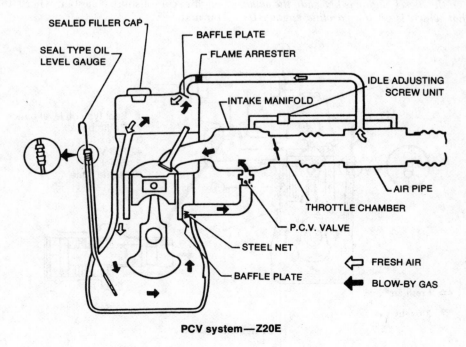

PCV system—Z20E

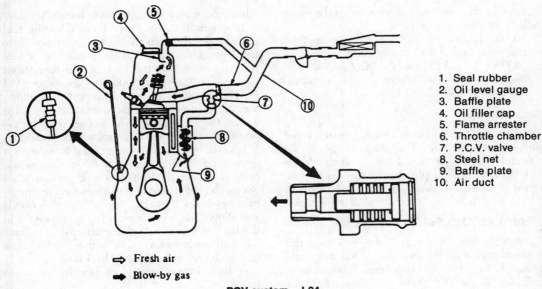

1. Seal rubber
2. Oil level gauge
3. Baffle plate
4. Oil filler cap
5. Flame arrester
6. Throttle chamber
7. P.C.V. valve
8. Steel net
9. Baffle plate
10. Air duct

⇨ Fresh air
➡ Blow-by gas

PCV system—L24

normal route. Since these gases are under pressure, they will find their own way out of the crankcase. This alternate route is usually a weak oil seal or gasket in the engine. As the gas escapes by the gasket it also creates an oil leak. Besides causing oil leaks, a clogged PCV valve also allows these gases to remain in the crankcase for an extended period of time, promoting the formation of sludge in the engine.

The above explanation and the troubleshooting procedure which follows applies to all engines with PCV systems.

TESTING

Check the PCV system hoses and connections, to see that there are no leaks; then replace or tighten, as necessary.

Gasoline Engine

To check the valve, remove it and blow through both of its ends. When blowing from the side which goes toward the intake manifold, very little air should pass through it. When blowing from the crankcase (valve cover) side, air should pass through freely.

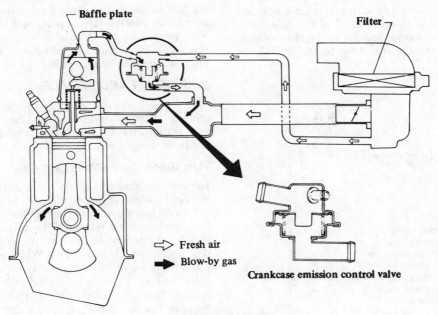

⇨ Fresh air
➡ Blow-by gas

Crankcase emission control valve

PCV system—LD28

Replace the valve with a new one, if the valve fails to function as outlined.

NOTE: *Do not attempt to clean or adjust the valve; replace it with a new one.*

NOTE: *For CA20E and CA18ET engine PCV diagrams and PCV valve locations, please refer to Chapter 1.*

Diesel Engine

Remove the crankcase emission control valve and suck on the pipe that leads to the intake manifold, air should flow freely. You should be able to hear the diaphragm in the valve click open while you are sucking. If the valve fails to function as detailed, replace it with a new one.

REMOVAL AND INSTALLATION

To remove the PCV valve, simply loosen the hose clamp and remove the valve from the manifold-to-crankcase hose and intake manifold. Install the PCV valve in the reverse order of removal.

Removal and installation procedures for the diesel crankcase emission control valve are detailed in Chapter 1.

Evaporative Emission Control System—Gasoline Engines Only

When raw fuel evaporates, the vapors contain hydrocarbons. To prevent these nasties from escaping into the atmosphere, the fuel evaporative emission control system was developed.

There are two different evaporative emission control systems used on Datsuns.

The system used through 1974 consists of a sealed fuel tank, a vapor-liquid separator, a flow guide (check) valve, and all of the hoses connecting these components, in the above order, leading from the fuel tank to the PCV hose,

which connects the crankcase to the PCV valve.

In operation, the vapor formed in the fuel tank passes through the vapor separator, onto the flow guide valve and the crankcase. When the engine is not running, if the fuel vapor pressure in the vapor separator goes above 0.4 in. Hg, the flow guide valve opens and allows the vapor to enter the engine crankcase. Otherwise the flow guide valve is closed to the vapor separator while the engine is not running. When the engine is running, and a vacuum is developed in the fuel tank or in the engine crankcase and the difference of pressure between the relief side and the fuel tank or crankcase becomes 2 in. Hg, the relief valve opens and allows ambient air from the air cleaner into the fuel tank or the engine crankcase. This ambient air replaces the vapor within the fuel tank or crankcase, bringing the fuel tank or crankcase back into a neutral or positive pressure range.

The system used on 1975 and later models consists of a sealed fuel tank, a vapor-liquid separator (certain models only), a vapor vent line, a carbon canister, a vacuum signal line and a canister purge line.

In operation, fuel vapors and/or liquid are routed to the liquid/vapor separator or check valve where liquid fuel is directed back into the fuel tank as fuel vapors flow into the charcoal filled canister. The charcoal absorbs and stores the fuel vapors when the engine is not running or is at idle. When the throttle valves in the carburetor (or air intakes for fuel injection) are opened, vacuum from above the throttle valves is routed through a vacuum signal line to the purge control valve on the canister. The control valve opens and allows the fuel vapors to be drawn from the canister through a purge line and into the intake manifold and the combustion chambers.

INSPECTION AND SERVICE

Check the hoses for proper connections and damage. Replace as necessary. Check the vapor separator tank for fuel leaks, distortion and dents, and replace as necessary.

Flow Guide Valve—Through 1974

Remove the flow guide valve and inspect it for leakage by blowing air into the ports in the valve. When air is applied from the fuel tank side, the flow guide valve is normal if the air passes into the check side (crankcase side), but not into the relief side (air cleaner side). When air is applied from the check side, the valve is normal if the passage of air is restricted. When air is applied from the relief side (air cleaner side), the valve is normal if air passes into the fuel tank side or into the check side.

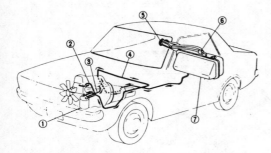

1. Carbon canister
2. Vacuum signal line
3. Canister vent line
4. Vapor vent line
5. Fuel filler cap with vacuum relief valve
6. Fuel check valve
7. Fuel tank

Evaporative emission control system schematic

When checking the purge control valve, apply vacuum (inhale) to the hose

Carbon Canister and Purge Control Valve—1975 and Later

To check the operation of the carbon canister purge control valve, disconnect the rubber hose between the canister control valve and the T-fitting, at the T-fitting. Apply vacuum to the hose leading to the control valve. The vacuum condition should be maintained indefinitely. If the control valve leaks, remove the top cover of the valve and check for a dislocated or cracked diaphragm. If the diaphragm is damaged, a repair kit containing a new diaphragm, retainer, and spring is available and should be installed.

The carbon canister has an air filter in the bottom of the canister. The filter element should be checked once a year or every 12,000 miles; more frequently if the car is operated in dusty areas. Replace the filter by pulling it out of the bottom of the canister and installing a new one.

REMOVAL AND INSTALLATION

Removal and installation of the various evaporative emission control system components consists of disconnecting the hoses, loosening retaining screws, and remove the part which is to be replaced or checked. Install in the reverse order. When replacing hose, make sure that it is fuel and vapor resistant.

Spark Timing Control System

Dual Point Distributor—

1973 610 MODELS

The 1973 610 is equipped with this system. The dual point distributor has two sets of breaker points which operate independently of each other and are positioned with a relative phase angle of 7° apart. This makes one set the advanced points and the other set the retarded points.

The two sets of points, which mechanically operate continuously, are connected in parallel to the primary side of the ignition circuit. One set of points controls the firing of the spark plugs and hence, the ignition timing, depending on whether or not the retarded set of points is energized.

When both sets of points are electrically energized, the first set to open (the advanced set,

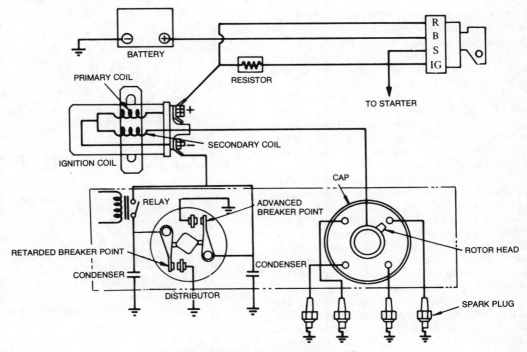

Dual point ignition system schematic

7° sooner) has no control over breaking the ignition coil primary circuit because the retarded set is still closed and maintaining a complete circuit to ground. When the retarded set of points opens, the advanced set is still open, and the primary circuit is broken causing the electromagnetic field in the coil to collapse and the ignition spark is produced.

When the retarded set of points is removed from the primary ignition circuit through the operation of a distributor relay inserted into the retraded points circuit, the advanced set of points controls the primary circuit. The retarded set of points is activated as follows:

The retarded set of points is activated only while the throttle is partially open, the temperature is above 50°F and the transmission is any gear but Fourth gear.

NOTE: *When the ambient temperature is below 30°F, the retarded set of points is removed from the ignition circuit no matter what switch is ON.*

In the case of an automatic transmission, the retarded set of points is activated at all times except under heavy acceleration and high-speed cruising (wide open throttle) with the ambient temperature above 50°F.

There are three switches which control the operation of the distributor relay. All of the switches must be ON in order to energize the distributor relay, thus energizing the retarded set of points.

The switches and their operation are as follows:

A transmission switch located in the transmission closes an electrical circuit when the transmission is all gears except Fourth gear.

A throttle switch located on the throttle linkage at the carburetor is ON when the throttle valve is removed within a 45° angle.

The temperature sensing switch is located near the hood release level inside the passenger compartment. The temperature sensing switch comes on between 41°F and 55°F when the temperature is rising and goes OFF above 34°F when the temperature falls.

The distributor vacuum advance mechanism produced a spark advance based on the amount of vacuum in the intake manifold. With a high vacuum, less air/fuel mixture enters the engine cylinders and the mixture is therefore less highly compressed. Consequently, this mixture burns more slowly and the advance mechanism gives it more time to burn. This longer burning time results in higher combustion temperatures at peak pressure and hence, more time for nitrogen to react with oxygen and form nitrogen oxides (NO_x). At the same time, this advanced timing results in less complete combustion due to the greater area of cylinder wall (quench area)

exposed at the instant of ignition. This "cooled" fuel will not burn as readily and hence, results in higher unburned hydrocarbons (HC). The production of NO_x and HC resulting from the vacuum advance is highest during the moderate acceleration in lower gears.

Retardation of the ignition timing is necessary to reduce NO_x and HC emissions. Various ways of retarding the ignition spark have been used in automobiles, all of which remove vacuum to the distributor vacuum advance mechanism at different times under certain conditions. Another way of accomplishing the same goal is the dual point distributor system.

INSPECTION AND ADJUSTMENTS

Phase Difference

1. Disconnect the wiring harness of the distributor from the engine harness.

2. Connect the black wire of the engine harness to the black wire of the distributor harness with a jumper wire. This connects the advanced set of points.

3. With the engine idling, adjust the ignition timing by rotating the distributor.

4. Disconnect the jumper wire from the black wire of the distributor harness and connect it to the yellow wire of the distributor harness. The retarded set of points is now activated.

5. With the engine idling, check the igni-

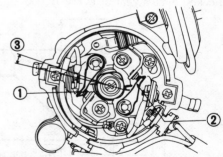

(1) Advance point set (2) Retarded point set (3) Phase difference

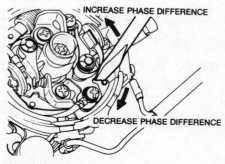

Adjusting phase difference

tion timing. The timing should be retarded from the advanced setting 7°.

6. To adjust the out-of-phase angle of the ignition timing, loosen the adjuster plate set screws on the same side as the retarded set of points.

7. Place the blade of a screwdriver in the adjusting notch of the adjuster plate and turn the adjuster plate as required to obtain the correct retarded ignition timing specification. The ignition timing is retarded when the adjuster plate is turned counterclockwise. There are graduations on the adjuster plate to make the adjustment easier; one graduation is equal to 4° of crankcase rotation.

8. Replace the distributor cap, start the engine and check the ignition timing with the retarded set of points activated (yellow wire of the distributor wiring harness connected to the black wire of the engine wiring harness).

9. Repeat the steps above as necessary to gain the proper retarded ignition timing.

Transmission Switch

Disconnect the electrical leads at the switch and connect a self-powered test light to the electrical leads. The switch should conduct electricity only when the gearshift is moved to Fourth gear.

If the switch fails to perform in the above manner, replace it with a new one.

Throttle Switch

The throttle switch located on the throttle linkage at the carburetor is checked with a self-powered test light. Disconnect the electrical leads of the switch and connect the test light. The switch should not conduct current when the throttle valve is closed or opened, up to 45°. When the throttle is fully opened, the switch should conduct current.

Temperature Sensing Switch

The temperature sensing switch mounted in the passenger compartment near the hood release lever should not conduct current when the temperature is above 55°F when connected to a self-powered test light as previously outlined for the throttle switch.

Dual Spark Plug Ignition System—Z20E, Z20S, CA20E, CA18ET

The 1980 California model and all 1981–83 Z-series and CA-series engines have two spark plugs per cylinder. This arrangement allows the engine to burn large amounts of recirculated exhaust gases without effecting performance. In fact, the system works so well it improves gas mileage under most circumstances.

Both spark plugs fire simultaneously, which substantially shortens the time required to burn the air/fuel mixture when exhaust gases (EGR) are not being recirculated. When gases are being recirculated, the dual spark plug system brings the ignition level up to that of a single plug system which is not recirculating exhaust gases.

ADJUSTMENT

The only adjustments necessary are the tune-up and maintenance procedures outlined in Chapters One and Two.

Spark Timing Control System
GASOLINE ENGINE ONLY

The spark timing control system has been used in different forms on Datsuns since 1972. The first system, Transmission Controlled Spark System (TCS) was used on most Datsuns through 1979. This system consists of a thermal vacuum valve, a vacuum switching valve, a high gear detecting switch, and a number of vacuum hoses. Basically, the system is designed to retard full spark advance except when the car is in high gear and the engine is at normal operating temperature. At all other times, the

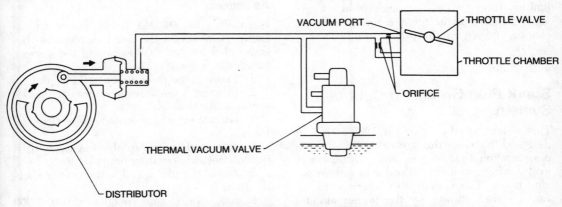

1980 and later Spark Timing Control System, CA20E engine system shown

spark advance is retarded to one degree or another.

The 1980 and later Spark Timing Control System replaces the TCS system. The major difference is that it works solely from engine water temperature changes rather than a transmission mounted switch. The system includes a thermal vacuum valve, a vacuum delay valve, and attendant hoses. It performs the same function as the earlier TCS system; to retard full spark advance at times when high levels of pollutants would otherwise be given off.

INSPECTION AND ADJUSTMENTS

Normally the TCS and Spark Timing Control systems should be trouble-free. However, if you suspect a problem in the system, first check to make sure all wiring (if so equipped) and hoses are connected and free from dirt. Also check to make sure the distributor vacuum advance is working properly. If everything appears all right, connect a timing light to the engine and make sure the initial timing is correct. On vehicles with the TCS system, run the engine until it reaches normal operating temperature, and then have an assistant sit in the car and shift the transmission through all the gears slowly. If the system is functioning properly, the timing will be 10 to 15 degrees advanced in high gear (compared to the other gear positions). If the system is still not operating correctly, you will have to check for continuity at all the connections with a test light.

To test the Spark Timing Control System, connect a timing light and check the ignition timing while the temperature gauge is in the "cold" position. Write down the reading. Allow the engine to run with the timing light attached until the temperature needle reaches the center of the gauge. As the engine is warming up, check with the timing light to make sure the ignition timing retards. When the temperature needle is in the middle of the gauge, the ignition timing should advance from its previous position. If the ignition timing does not change, replace the thermal vacuum valve.

Spark Plug Switching Control System

This system, used only on the 1982 200SX, is designed to change the ignition system from 2-plug ignition to 1-plug ignition during heavy load driving conditions in order to reduce engine noise. The system also functions to advance ignition timing by the proper amount during 1-plug ignition.

Early Fuel Evaporation System
GASOLINE ENGINES ONLY

The Early Fuel Evaporation System is used on some L-series engines. The system's purpose is to heat the air/fuel mixture when the engine is below normal operating temperature. The L-series engines use a system much akin to the old style exhaust manifold heat riser. The only adjustment necessary is to occasionally lubricate the counterweight. Other than that, the system should be trouble-free.

The 1980 and later carbureted engines use coolant water heat instead of exhaust gas heat to prewarm the fuel mixture. This system should be trouble-free.

Boost Control Deceleration Device (BCDD)
GASOLINE ENGINES ONLY

The Boost Control Deceleration Device (BCDD) used on the L-series engines to reduce hydrocarbon emissions during coasting conditions.

High manifold vacuum during coasting prevents the complete combustion of the air/fuel mixture because of the reduced amount of air. This condition will result in a large amount of HC emission. Enriching the air/fuel mixture for a short time (during the high vacuum condition) will reduce the emission of the HC.

However, enriching the air/fuel mixture with only the mixture adjusting screw will cause poor engine idle or invite an increase in the carbon monoxide (CO) content of the exhaust gases. The BCDD consists of an independent system that kicks in when the engine is coasting and enriches the air/fuel mixture, which reduces the hydrocarbon content of the exhaust gases. This is accomplished without adversely affecting engine idle and the carbon monoxide content of the exhaust gases.

Adjustment

Normally, the BCDD never needs adjustment. However, if the need should arise because of suspected malfunction of the system, proceed as follows:

1. Connect the tachometer to the engine.
2. Connect a quick-response vacuum gauge to the intake manifold.
3. Disconnect the solenoid valve electrical leads.
4. Start and warm up the engine until it reaches normal operating temperature.
5. Adjust the idle speed to the proper specification.
6. Raise the engine speed to 3,000–3,500 rpm under no-load (transmission in Neutral or

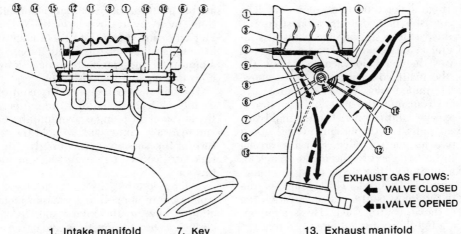

1. Intake manifold
2. Stove gasket
3. Manifold stove
4. Heat shield plate
5. Snap ring
6. Counterweight
7. Key
8. Stopper pin
9. Screw
10. Thermostat spring
11. Heat control valve
12. Control valve shaft
13. Exhaust manifold
14. Cap
15. Bushing
16. Coil spring

Typical EFE system

Park), then allow the throttle to close quickly. Take notice as to whether or not the engine rpm returns to idle speed and if it does, how long the fall in rpm is interrupted before it reaches idle speed.

At the moment the throttle is snapped closed at high engine rpm and the vacuum in the intake manifold reaches between −23 to −27.7 in. Hg and then gradually falls to about −16.5 in. Hg at idle speed. The process of the fall of the intake manifold vacuum and the engine rpm will take one of the following three forms:

a. When the operating pressure of the BCDD is too high, the system remains inoperative, and the vacuum in the intake manifold decreases without interruption just like that of an engine without a BCDD.

b. When the operating pressure is lower than that of the case given above, but still higher than the proper set pressure, the fall of vacuum in the intake manifold is interupted and kept constant at a certain level (operating pressure) for about one second and then gradually falls down to the normal vacuum at idle speed;

c. When the set of operating pressure of the BCDD is lower than the intake manifold vacuum when the throttle is suddenly released, the engine speed will not lower to idle speed.

To adjust the set operating pressure of the BCDD, remove the adjusting screw cover from the BCDD mechanism mounted on the side of the carburetor. On 810 models, the BCDD system is installed under the throttle chamber.

The adjusting screw is a left-hand threaded screw. Late models may have an adjusting nut instead of a screw. Turning the screw ⅛ of a turn in either direction will change the operation pressure about 0.79 in. Hg. Turning the screw counterclockwise will increase the amount of vacuum needed to operate the mechanism. Turning the screw clockwise will decrease the amount of vacuum needed to operate the mechanism.

The operating pressure for the BCDD on most models should be between −19.9 to −22.05 in. Hg. The decrease in intake manifold vacuum should be interrupted at these levels for about one second when the BCDD is operating correctly.

Don't forget to install the adjusting screw cover after the system is adjusted.

Intake Manifold Vacuum Control System

This system, used in 1980–81 510s, is designed to reduce the engine's oil consumption when the intake manifold vacuum increases to an ex-

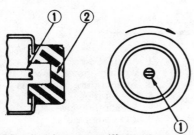

(1) BCDD adjusting screw (2) cover

tremely high level during deceleration. The system consistes of two units: a boost control unit as the vacuum sensor, and a by-pass air control unit as an actuator. The boost control unit senses the manifold vacuum. When the level of the manifold vacuum increases above the predetermined value, the boost control valve opens and transmits the manifold vacuum to the by-pass air control unit. The manifold vacuum then pulls the diaphragm in and opens the by-pass air control valve, thereby causing the air to be bypassed to the intake manifold. After completion of the air by-pass, the manifold vacuum is lowered. This results in the closing of the boost control valve and then the closing of the air control valve. This system operates in a tightly controlled circuit so that the manifold vacuum can be kept very close to the predetermined value during deceleration.

Aside from a routine check of the hoses and their connections, no service or adjustments should ever be necessary on this system. If at some time you feel that an adjustment is required, it is suggested that you take the car to a Datsun dealer or an authorized service representative.

Automatic Temperature Controlled Air Cleaner

This system is used on all Datsun models covered in this guide except the 810 and the 200SX.

The rate of fuel atomization varies with the temperature of the air that the fuel is being mixed with. The air/fuel ratio cannot be held constant for efficient fuel combustion with a wide range of air temperatures. Cold air being drawn into the engine causes a denser and richer air/fuel mixture, inefficient fuel atomization, and thus, more hydrocarbons in the exhaust gas. Hot air being drawn into the engine causes a leaner air/fuel mixture and more efficient atomization and combustion for less hydrocarbons in the exhaust gases.

The automatic temperature controlled air cleaner is designed so that the temperature of the ambient air being drawn into the engine is automatically controlled, to hold the temperature of the air and, consequently, the fuel/air ratio at a constant rate for efficient fuel combustion.

A temperature sensing vacuum switch controls vacuum applied to a vacuum motor operating a valve in the intake snorkle of the air cleaner. When the engine is cold or the air being drawn into the engine is cold, the vacuum motor opens the valve, allowing air heated by the exhaust manifold to be drawn into the engine. As the engine warms up, the temperature sensing unit shuts off the vacuum applied to vacuum motor which allows the valve to close, shutting off the heated air and allowing cooler, outside (under hood) air to be drawn into the engine.

TESTING

When the air around the temperature sensor of the unit mounted inside the air cleaner housing reaches 100°F, the sensor should block the flow of vacuum to the air control valve vacuum motor. When the temperature around the temperature sensor is below 100°F, the sensor should allow vacuum to pass onto the air valve vacuum motor thus blocking off the air cleaner snorkle to under hood (unheated) air.

When the temperature around the sensor is

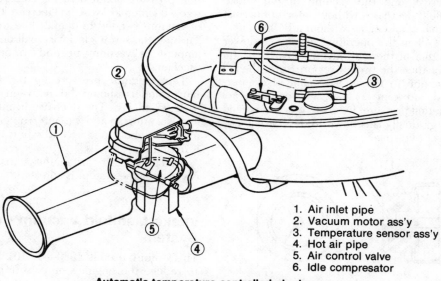

1. Air inlet pipe
2. Vacuum motor ass'y
3. Temperature sensor ass'y
4. Hot air pipe
5. Air control valve
6. Idle compresator

Automatic temperature controlled air cleaner

above 188°F, the air control valve should be completely open to under hood air.

If the air cleaner fails to operate correctly, check for loose or broken vacuum hoses. If the hoses are not the cause, replace the vacuum motor in the air cleaner.

Exhaust Gas Recirculation (EGR)

GASOLINE ENGINES

This system is used on all 1974 and later models. Exhaust gas recirculation is used to reduce combustion temperatures in the engine, thereby reducing the oxides of nitrogen emissions.

An EGR valve is mounted on the center of the intake manifold. The recycled exhaust gas is drawn into the bottom of the intake manifold riser portion through the exhaust manifold heat stove and EGR valve. A vacuum diaphragm is connected to a timed signal port at the carburetor flange.

As the throttle valve is opened, vacuum is applied to the EGR valve vacuum diaphragm. When the vacuum reaches about 2 in. Hg, the diaphragm moves against string pressure and is in a fully up position at 8 in. Hg of vacuum. As the diaphragm moves up, it opens the exhaust gas metering valve which allows exhaust gas to be pulled into the engine intake manifold. The system does not operate when the

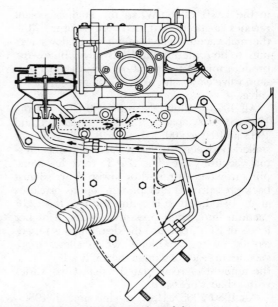

EGR system—carbureted models

engine is idling because the exhaust gas recirculation would cause a rough idle.

On 1975 and later models, a thermal vacuum valve inserted in the engine thermostat housing controls the application of the vacuum

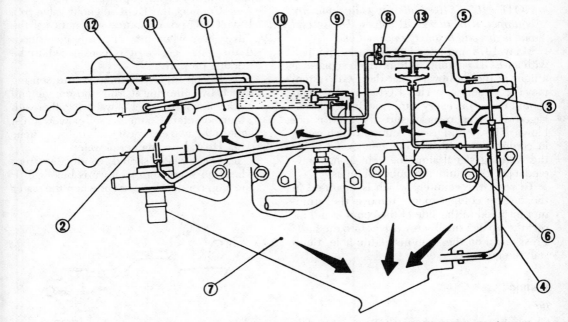

1. Intake manifold	6. B.P.T. valve control tube	9. Thermal vacuum vlave
2. Throttle chamber	7. Exhaust manifold	10. Heater housing
3. E.G.R. control valve	8. Vacuum delay valve	11. Water return tube
4. E.G.R. tube	(California automatic	12. Thermostat housing
5. B.P.T. valve	transmission models only)	13. Vacuum orifice

810 EGR system schematic

to the EGR valve. When the engine coolant reaches a predetermined temperature, the thermal vacuum valve opens and allows vacuum to be routed to the EGR valve. Below the predetermined temperature, the thermal vacuum valve closes and blocks vacuum to the EGR valve.

All 1978–79 models, the 1980 810 and the 1980–81 510(Canadian), 200 SX(Canadian) and 1983 and later 200SX have a B.P.T. valve installed between the EGR valve and the thermal vacuum valve. The B.P.T. valve has a diaphragm which is raised or lowered by exhaust back pressure. The diaphragm opens or closes an air bleed, which is connected into the EGR vacuum line. High pressure results in higher levels of EGR, because the diaphragm is raised, closing off the air bleed, which allows more vacuum to reach and open the EGR valve. Thus, the amount of recirculated exhaust gas varies with exhaust pressure.

All 1980 200SX(USA) models and all 1980–81 510(USA) models use a V.V.T. valve (venturi vacuum transducer valve) instead of the B.P.T. valve. The V.V.T. valve monitors exhaust pressure and carburetor vacuum in order to activate the diaphragm which controls the throttle vacuum applied to the EGR control valve. This system expands the operating range of the EGR flow rate as compared to the B.P.T. unit.

NOTE: *1981 510s built for California are equipped with two EGR valves. The second one is directly below the normal one.*

Many 1975 and later Datsuns are equipped with an EGR warning system which signals via a light in the dashboard that the EGR system may need service. The EGR warning light should come on every time the starter is engaged as a test to make sure the bulb is not blown. The system uses a counter which works in conjunction with the odometer, and lights the warning signal after the vehicle has traveled a pre-determined number of miles.

To reset the counter, which is mounted in the engine compartment, remove the grommet installed in the side of the counter and insert the tip of a small screwdriver into the hole. Press down on the knob inside the hole. Reinstall the grommet.

Testing

1974

Check the operation of the EGR system as follows:

1. Visually inspect the entire EGR control system. Clean the mechanism free of oil and dirt. Replace any rubber hoses found to be cracked or broken.

2. Make sure that the EGR solenoid valve is properly wired.

3. Increase the engine speed from idling to 2,000–3,500 rpm. The plate of the EGR control valve diaphragm and the valve shaft should move upward as the engine speed is increased.

4. Disconnect the EGR solenoid valve electrical leads and connect them directly to the vehicle's 12-volt electrical supply (battery). Race the engine again with the EGR solenoid valve connected to a 12-volt power source. The EGR control valve should remain stationary.

5. With the engine running at idle, push up on the EGR control valve diaphragm with your finger. When this is done, the engine idle should become rough and uneven.

Inspect the two components of the EGR system as necessary in the following manner:

a. Remove the EGR control valve from the intake manifold;

b. Apply 4.7–5.1 in. Hg of vacuum to the EGR control valve by sucking on a tube attached to the outlet on top of the valve. The valve should move to the full up position. The valve should remain open for more than 30 seconds after the application of vacuum is discontinued and the vacuum hose is blocked;

c. Inspect the EGR valve for any signs of warpage or damage;

d. Clean the EGR valve seat with a brush and compressed air to prevent clogging;

e. Connect the EGR solenoid valve to a 12-volt DC power source and notice if the valve clicks when intermittently electrified. If the valve clicks, it is considered to be working properly;

f. Check the EGR temperature sensing switch by removing it from the engine and placing it in a container of water together with a thermometer. Connect a self-powered test light to the two electrical leads of the switch;

g. Heat the container of water;

h. The switch should conduct current when the water temperature is below 77°F and stop conducting current when the water

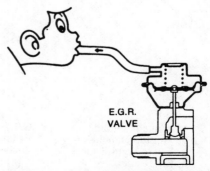

E.G.R. VALVE

You can apply vacuum to the EGR valve by sucking on the air tube which is connected to it

reaches a temperature somewhere between 88°–106°F. Replace the switch if it functions otherwise.

1975 AND LATER

1. Remove the EGR valve and apply enough vacuum to the diaphragm to open the valve.

2. The valve should remain open for over 30 seconds after the vacuum is removed.

3. Check the valve for damage, such as warpage, cracks, and excessive wear around the valve and seat.

Clean the seat of the EGR valve with a stiff brush

CA20E ENGINE

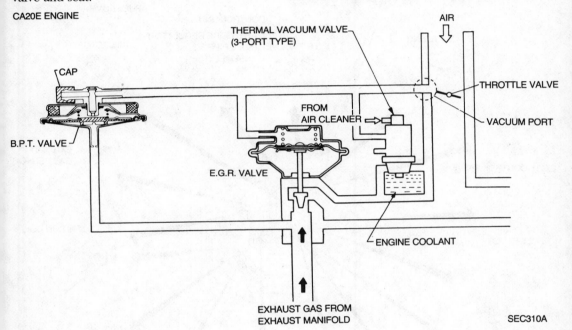

CA18ET ENGINE

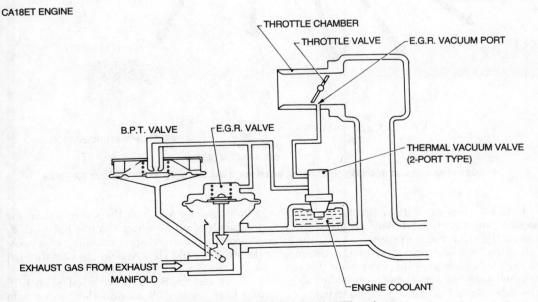

EGR systems, 1984 CA20E and CA18ET engines

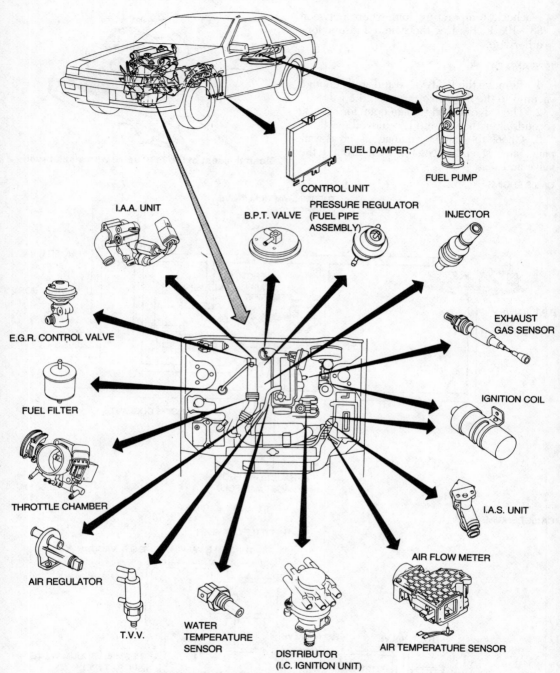

FUEL DAMPER

FUEL PUMP

CONTROL UNIT

I.A.A. UNIT

B.P.T. VALVE

PRESSURE REGULATOR (FUEL PIPE ASSEMBLY)

INJECTOR

E.G.R. CONTROL VALVE

EXHAUST GAS SENSOR

FUEL FILTER

IGNITION COIL

THROTTLE CHAMBER

I.A.S. UNIT

AIR REGULATOR

AIR FLOW METER

T.V.V.

WATER TEMPERATURE SENSOR

DISTRIBUTOR (I.C. IGNITION UNIT)

AIR TEMPERATURE SENSOR

Various emissions and injection component locations, 1984 and later 200SX and 200 SX Turbo

4. Clean the seat with a brush and compressed air and remove any deposits from around the valve and port (seat).

5. To check the operation of the thermal vacuum valve, remove the valve from the engine and apply vacuum to the ports of the valve. The valve should not allow vacuum to pass.

6. Place the valve in a container of water with a thermometer and heat the water. When the temperature of the water reaches 134°–145°F, remove the valve and apply vacuum to the ports; the valve should allow vacuum to pass through it.

7. To test the B.P.T. valve installed on 1978 and later models, disconnect the two vacuum hoses from the valve. Plug one of the ports.

While applying pressure to the bottom of the valve, apply vacuum to the unplugged port and check for leakage. If any exists, replace the valve.

8. To test the check valve installed in some 1978 and later models, remove the valve and blow into the side which connects the EGR valve. Air should flow. When air is supplied to the other side, air flow resistance should be greater. If not, replace the valve.

9. To check the V.V.T. valve which replaces the B.P.T. valve on some 1980 and later models, disconnect the top and bottom center hoses and apply a vacuum to the top hose. Check for leaks. If a leak is present, replace the valve.

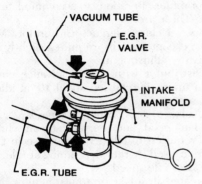

Removing the EGR valve

Removal and Installation

EGR CONTROL VALVE

1. Remove the nuts which attach the EGR tube and/or the BP tube to the EGR valve (if so equipped).

2. Unscrew the mounting bolts and remove the heat shield plate from the EGR control valve (if so equipped).

3. Tag and disconnect the EGR vacuum hose(s).

4. Unscrew the mounting bolts and remove the EGR control valve.

5. Installation is in the reverse order of removal.

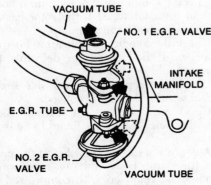

Some models have two EGR valves

NOTE: *Always be sure that the new valve is identical to the old one.*

DIESEL ENGINES

This system is designed to control the formation of NO_x emissions by recirculating the exhaust gas into the intake manifold passage through the control valve.

The EGR flow rate is controlled in three stages in accordance with the engine speed and load. The first stage, "High EGR", is obtained through the combination of a closed throttle valve and an open EGR valve. The second stage, "Low EGR", is obtained through the opening of the throttle valve. The third stage, "Zero EGR", is obtained closing the EGR valve.

The engine load signal is picked up by the potentiometer installed on the injection pump control lever. The engine speed signal is transmitted by an electromagnetic revolution sensor attached to the front cover. The throttle diaphragm and the EGR valve are both actuated by vacuum generated at the vacuum pump. Solenoids are used to convert the electrical signal from the control unit into the vacuum signal.

The EGR system is deactivated under extremely high or low coolant temperatures in order to assure good driveability.

Testing

1. Visually check the entire EGR system as detailed in the previous "Gasoline Engine" section.

2. With the engine off, check the EGR control valve and throttle body for an indication of binding or sticking by moving the diaphragm/rod upward with your finger.

3. Start the engine and place your finger on the underside of the EGR valve. You should feel the diaphragm.

CAUTION: *Be careful that your finger doesn't get caught between the diaphragm and the body of the valve.*

4. When the temperature of the engine is at

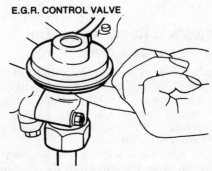

Place your finger on the EGR diaphragm

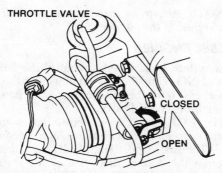

THROTTLE VALVE

CLOSED

OPEN

The position of this lever will tell you whether the throttle valve is open or closed

or below 86°F. (30°C.), make sure that the EGR valve does not operate and the throttle valve is open when the engine is revved.

5. If the EGR valve operates or the throttle valve is closed, check the water temperature sensor. If the sensor appears normal, replace the EGR control unit.

6. When the temperature of the engine is high (above 86°F), make sure that the EGR valve operates and the throttle valve is closed when the engine is idling.

7. Increase the engine speed gradually and make sure that the throttle valve opens and the EGR valve closes in this order.

8. If the EGR valve and/or the throttle valve do not operate properly in this step, check them as follows:

a. Run the engine at idle and disconnect the harness connector at the solenoid valve. Apply battery voltage to the connector and check that the EGR valve and the throttle valve operate normally.

b. If they do not, check the EGR valve and the throttle diaphragm independently. If they operate normally, check the rev sensor, the potentiometer and all electrical circuits. If they appear normal, replace the EGR control unit.

Removal and Installation

Follow the procedures given in the "Gasoline Engine" section.

Air Injection Reactor System
GASOLINE ENGINES ONLY

This system is used on 1974–79 models. In gasoline engines, it is difficult to completely burn the air/fuel mixture through normal combustion in the combustion chambers. Under certain operating conditions, unburned fuel is exhausted into the atmosphere.

The air injection reactor system is designed so that ambient air, pressurized by the air pump, is injected through the injection nozzles into the exhaust ports near each exhaust valve. The exhaust gases are at high temperatures and ignite when brought into contact with the oxygen. Unburned fuel is then burned in the exhaust ports and manifold.

In 1976 California models utilized a secondary system consisting of an air control valve which limits injection of secondary air and an emergency relief valve which controls the supply of secondary air. This system protects the catalytic converter from overheating. In 1977 the function of these two valves was taken by a single combined air control (C.A.C.) valve.

All engines with the air pump system have a series of minor alterations to accommodate the system. These are:

1. Special close-tolerance carburetor. Most engines, except the L16, require a slightly rich idle mixture adjustment.

2. Distributor with special advance curve. Ignition timing is retarded about 10° at idle in most cases.

3. Cooling system changes such as larger fan, higher fan speed, and thermostatic fan clutch. This is required to offset the increase in temperature caused by retarded timing at idle.

4. Faster idle speed.

5. Heated air intake on some engines.

The only periodic maintenance required on the air pump system is replacement of the drive belt.

Testing
AIR PUMP

If the air pump makes an abnormal noise and cannot be corrected without removing the pump from the vehicle, check the following in sequence:

1. Turn the pulley ¾ of a turn in the clockwise direction and ¼ of a turn in the counterclockwise direction. If the pulley is binding and if rotation is not smooth, a defective bearing is indicated.

2. Check the inner wall of the pump body, vanes and rotor for wear. If the rotor has abnormal wear, replace the air pump.

3. Check the needle roller bearing for wear and damage. If the bearings are defective, the air pump should be replaced.

4. Check and replace the rear side seal if abnormal wear or damage is noticed.

5. Check and replace the carbon shoes holding the vanes if they are found to be worn or damaged.

6. A deposit of carbon particles on the inner wall of the pump body and vanes is normal, but should be removed with compressed air before reassembling the air pump.

Air pump (arrow)

CHECK VALVE

Remove the check valve from the air pump discharge line. Test it for leakage by blowing air into the valve from the air pump side and from the air manifold side. Air should only pass through the valve from the air pump side if the valve is functioning normally. A small amount of air leakage from the manifold side can be overlooked. Replace the check valve if it is found to be defective.

ANTI-BACKFIRE VALVE

Disconnect the rubber hose connecting the mixture control valve with the intake manifold and plug the hose. If the mixture control valve is operating correctly, air will continue to blow out the mixture control valve for a few seconds after the accelerator pedal is fully depressed (engine running) and released quickly. If air continues to blow out for more than five seconds, replace the mixture control valve.

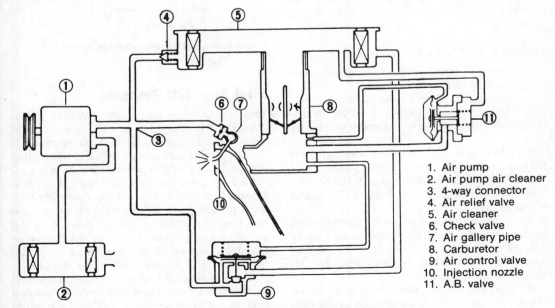

1. Air pump
2. Air pump air cleaner
3. 4-way connector
4. Air relief valve
5. Air cleaner
6. Check valve
7. Air gallery pipe
8. Carburetor
9. Air control valve
10. Injection nozzle
11. A.B. valve

Air injection system schematic—typical

AIR PUMP RELIEF VALVE

Disconnect the air pump discharge hose leading to the exhaust manifold. With the engine running, restrict the air-flow coming from the pump. The air pump relief valve should vent the pressurized air to the atmosphere if it is working properly.

NOTE: *When performing this test do not completely block the discharge line of the air pump as damage may result if the relief valve fails to function properly.*

AIR INJECTION NOZZLES

Check around the air manifold for air leakage with the engine running at 2,000 rpm. If air is leaking from the eye joint bolt, retighten or replace the gasket. Check the air nozzles for restrictions by blowing air into the nozzles.

HOSES

Check and replace hoses if they are found to be weakened or cracked. Check all hose connections and clips. Be sure that the hoses are not in contact with other parts of the engine.

EMERGENCY AIR RELIEF VALVE

1. Warm up the engine.
2. Check all hoses for leaks, kinks, improper connections, etc.
3. Run the engine up to 2000 rpm under no load. No air should be discharged from the valve.
4. Disconnect the vacuum hose from the valve. This is the hose which runs to the intake manifold. Run the engine up to 2000 rpm. Air should be discharged from the valve. If not, replace it.

COMBINED AIR CONTROL (CAC) VALVE

1. Check all hoses for leaks, kinks, and improper connections.
2. Thoroughly warm up the engine.
3. With the engine idling, check for air discharge from the relief opening in the air cleaner case.
4. Disconnect and plug the vacuum hose from the valve. Air should be discharged from the valve with the engine idling. If the disconnected vacuum hose is not plugged, the engine will stumble.
5. Connect a hand-operated vacuum pump to the vacuum fitting on the valve and apply 7.8–9.8 in. Hg. of vacuum. Run the engine speed up to 3000 rpm. No air should be discharged from the valve.
6. Disconnect and plug the air hose at the check valve, with the conditions as in the preceding step. This should cause the valve to dis-

charge air. If not, or if any of the conditions in this procedure are not met, replace the valve.

Air Induction System
GASOLINE ENGINES ONLY

Models using this system include the 1980–81 510, the 1980 200SX and the 49-state version of the 1980 810. The air induction system is used to send fresh, secondary air to the exhaust manifold by utilizing vacuum created by the exhaust pulsation in the manifold.

The exhaust pressure usually pulsates in response to the opening and closing of the exhaust valve and it periodically decreases below atmospheric pressure. If a secondary air intake pipe is opened to the atmosphere under a vacuum condition, secondary air can then be drawn into the exhaust manifold in proportion of the vacuum. Because of this, the air induction system is able to reduce the CO and HC content in the exhaust gases. The system consists of two air induction valves, a filter, hoses and E.A.I. tubes.

The only periodic maintenance required is replacement of the air induction filter as detailed in Chapter 1.

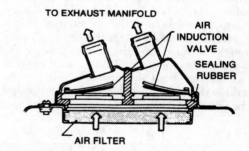

Cross section of the air induction valve

Fuel Shut-Off System

This system, used only in the 1980–81 510, is designed to reduce HC emissions and also to improve fuel economy during deceleration.

The system is operated by an anti-dieseling solenoid valve in the carburetor which is controlled by a vacuum switch. When the intake manifold vacuum increases to an extremely high level (which it does during deceleration), the fuel flow of the slow system is shut off by the anti-dieseling solenoid valve. When the intake manifold vacuum drops to a low level again, the fuel flow of the slow system is resupplied.

The fuel shut-off system is further controlled by the clutch switch and gear position switches such as the neutral switch (M/T) and the inhibitor switch (A/T) to ensure that fuel cannot be

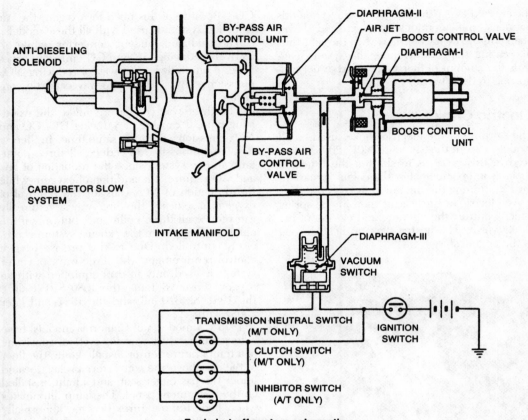

Fuel shut-off system schematic

shut off even if the manifold vacuum is high enough to trigger the normal fuel shut-off operation.

Injection Timing Advance System
DIESEL ENGINE ONLY

This system is designed to control the formation of HC emissions. It controls the amount of recirculating fuel in the fuel injection pump in order to control the injection timing.

The injection timing advance system is composed of an injection timing control solenoid valve, a potentiometer, and EGR control unit and a revolution sensor. This system is also called a Partial Load Advancer (PLA). The system operates along much the same lines as the EGR system and shares many of the same components.

High Altitude Emission Control System
DIESEL ENGINES ONLY

The high altitude emission control system is designed to control the formation of HC and

CO emissions and to improve the driveability of the car in high altitude areas. In order to ensure decreased exhaust emissions, the injection timing and EGR tube have to be changed/replaced.

There is an altitude compensator located on top of the injection pump. The altitude shaft is in contact with a pin which is connected to the control lever which is in contact with the governor lever. The higher the altitude, the lower the atmospheric pressure. Due to this fact, the pressure inside the aneroid is higher than that of the atmosphere at high altitudes, which causes

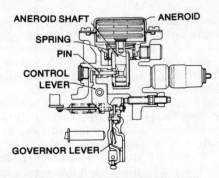

Cross-section of the altitude compensator

the aneroid to expand like a balloon. When this happens, the aneroid shaft is pushed down, changing the contact surface with the pin, thus decreasing the fuel. Hence, the system controls the amount of fuel supplied in direct proportion to the altitude.

Electric Choke

The purpose of the electric choke, used on all models, except the 810, and Z20E (200SX) covered in this guide is to shorten the time the choke is in operation after the engine is started, thus shortening the time of high HC output.

An electric heater warms the bimetal spring which controls the opening and closing of the choke valve. The heater starts to heat as soon as the engine starts.

Electric choke (arrow)

Catalytic Converter
GASOLINE ENGINES ONLY

The catalytic converter is a muffler-like container built into the exhaust system to aid in the reduction of exhaust emissions. The catalyst element consists of individual pellets or a honeycomb monolithic substrate coated with a noble metal such as platinum, palladium, rhodium or a combination. When the exhaust gases come into contact with the catalyst, a chemical reaction occurs which will reduce the pollutants into harmless substances like water and carbon dioxide.

There are essentially two types of catalytic converters: an oxidizing type is used on all 1975–79 models built for California, all 1980 200SX models, the 49-state version of the 1980 810, and all 1980–81 510s. It requires the addition of oxygen to spur the catalyst into reducing the engine's HC and CO emissions into H_2O and

CO_2. Because of this need for oxygen, the Air Injection system is used with all these models.

The oxidizing catalytic converter, while effectively reducing HC and CO emissions, does little, if anything in the way of reducing NOx emissions. Thus, the three-way catalytic converter.

The three-way converter, unlike the oxiodizing type, is capable of reducing HC, CO and NOx emissions; all at the same time. In theory, it seems impossible to reduce all three pollutants in one system since the reduction of HC and CO requires the addition of oxygen, while the reduction of NOx calls for the removal of oxygen. In actuality, the three-way system really can reduce all three pollutants, but only if the amount of oxygen in the exhaust system is precisely controlled. Due to this precise oxygen control requirement, the three-way converter system is used only in cars equipped with an oxygen sensor system—the 1980 810 (Calif.), the 1981–82 810 (all) and the 1981–and later 200SX (all).

1975–78 models (all California models) have a floor temperature warning system, consisting of a temperature sensor installed onto the floor of the car above the converter; a relay, located under the passenger seat; and a light, installed on the instrument panel. The lamp illuminates when floor temperatures become abnormally high, due to converter or engine malfunction. The light also comes on when the ignition switch is turned to Start, to check its operation. 1979 and later models do not have the warning system.

All models with the three-way converter have an oxygen sensor warning light on the dashboard, which illuminates at the first 30,000 mile interval, signaling the need for oxygen sensor replacement. The oxygen sensor is part of the Mixture Ratio Feedback System, described later in this section. The Feedback System uses the three-way converter as one of its major components.

No regular maintenance is required for the catalyic converter system, except for periodic replacement of the Air Induction System filter (if so equipped). The Air Induction System is described earlier in this chapter; filter replacement procedures are in Chapter 1. The Air Induction System is used to supply the catalytic converter with fresh air; oxygen present in the air is used in the oxidation process.

Precautions

1. Use only unleaded fuel.
2. Avoid prolonged idling; the engine should run on longer than 20 min. at curb idle and no longer than 10 min. at fast idle.

3. Do not disconnect any of the spark plug leads while the engine is running.

4. Make engine compression checks as quickly as possible.

Catalyst Testing

At the present time there is no known way to reliably test catalytic converter operation in the field. The only reliable test is a 12 hour and 40 min. "soak" test (CVS) which must be done in a laboratory.

An infrared HC/CO tester is not sensitive enough to measure the higher tailpipe emissions from a failing converter. Thus, a bad converter may allow enough emissions to escape so that the car is no longer in compliance with Federal or state standards, but will still not cause the needle on a tester to move off zero.

The chemical reactions which occur inside a catalytic converter generate a great deal of heat. Most converter problems can be traced to fuel or ignition system problems which cause unusually high emissions. As a result of the increased intensity of the chemical reactions, the converter literally burns itself up.

A completely failed converter might cause a tester to show a slight reading. As a result, it is occasionally possible to detect one of these.

As long as you avoid severe overheating and the use of leaded fuels it is reasonably safe to assume that the converter is working properly. If you are in doubt, take the car to a diagnostic center that has a tester.

Mixture Ratio Feedback System
GASOLINE ENGINES ONLY

The need for better fuel economy coupled to increasingly strict emission control regulations dictates a more exact control of the engine air/fuel mixture. Datsun has developed a Mixture Ratio Feedback System in response to these needs. The system is installed on all 1980 810s sold in California and all 1981 and later 810, Maxima, and 200SX models.

The principle of the system is to control the air/fuel mixture exactly, so that more complete combustion can occur in the engine, and more thorough oxidation and reduction of the exhaust gases can occur in the catalytic converter. The object is to maintain a stoichiometric air/fuel mixture, which is chemically correct for theoretically complete combustion. The stoichiometric ratio is 14.7:1 (air to fuel). At that point, the converter's efficiency is greatest in oxidizing and reducing HC, CO, and NOx into CO_2, H_2O, O_2, and N_2.

Components used in the system include an oxygen sensor, installed in the exhaust manifold upstream of the converter; a three-way oxidation-reduction catalytic converter; an electronic control unit, and the fuel injection system itself.

The oxygen sensor reads the oxygen content of the exhaust gases. It generates an electrical signal which is sent to the control unit. The control unit then decides how to adjust the mixture to keep it at the correct air/fuel ratio. For example, if the mixture is too lean, the control unit increases the fuel metering to the injectors. The monitoring process is a continual one, so that fine mixture adjustments are going on at all times.

The system has two modes of operation: open loop and closed loop. Open loop operation takes place when the engine is still cold. In this mode, the control unit ignores signals from the oxygen sensor and provides a fixed signal to the fuel injection unit. Closed loop operation takes place when the engine and catalytic converter have warmed to normal operating temperature. In closed loop operation, the control unit uses the oxygen sensor signals to adjust the mixture; the burned mixture's oxygen content is read by the oxygen sensor, which continues to signal the control unit, and so on. Thus, the closed loop mode is an interdependent system of information feedback.

Mixture is, of course, not readily adjustable in this system. All system adjustments require the use of a CO meter; thus, they should be entrusted to a qualified dealer with access to the equipment and special training in the system's repair. The only regularly scheduled maintenance is replacement of the oxygen sensor at 30,000 mile intervals. This procedure is covered in the following section.

It should be noted that proper operation of the system is entirely dependent on the oxygen sensor. Thus, if the sensor is not replaced at the correct interval, or if the sensor fails during normal operation, the engine fuel mixture will be incorrect, resulting in poor fuel economy, starting problems, or stumbling and stalling of the engine when warm.

Oxygen Sensor Inspection and Replacement

An exhaust gas sensor warning light will illuminate on the instrument panel when the car has reached 30,000 miles. This is a signal that the oxygen sensor must be replaced. Note that the warning light is not part of a repeating system; that is, after the first 30,000 mile service, the warning light will not illuminate again. However, it is important to replace the oxygen sensor every 30,000 miles, to ensure proper monitoring and control of the engine air/fuel mixture.

The oxygen sensor can be inspected using the following procedure:

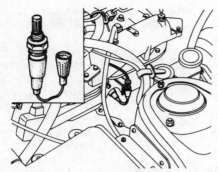

Oxygen sensor location—810 and Maxima

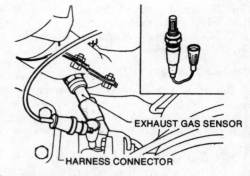

Oxygen sensor location—200SX

1. Start the engine and allow it to reach normal operating temperature.

2. Run the engine at approximately 2,000 rpm under no load. Block the front wheels and set the parking brake.

3. An inspection lamp has been provided on the bottom of the control unit, which is located in the passenger compartment on the driver's side kick panel, next to the clutch or brake pedal. If the oxygen sensor is operating correctly, the inspection lamp will go on and off more than 5 times in 10 seconds. The inspection lamp can be more easily seen with the aid of a mirror.

4. If the lamp does not go on and off as specified, the system is not operating correctly. Check the battery, ignition system, engine oil and coolant levels, all fuses, the fuel injection wiring harness connectors, all vacuum hoses, the oil filler cap and dipstick for proper seating, and the valve clearance and engine compression. If all of these parts are in good order, and the inspection lamp still does not go on and off at least 5 times in 10 seconds, the oxygen sensor is probably faulty. However, the possibility exists that the malfunction could be in the fuel injection control unit. The system should be tested by a qualified dealer with specific training in the Mixture Ratio Feedback System.

To replace the oxygen sensor:

UNDER THE RIGHT SIDE OF INSTRUMENT PANEL

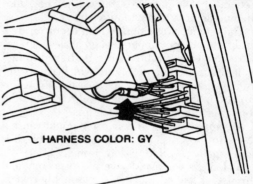

HARNESS COLOR: GY

Oxygen sensor warning lamp harness connector

1. Disconnect the sensor electrical lead. Unscrew the sensor from the exhaust manifold.

2. Coat the threads of the replacement sensor with a nickel base anti-seize compound. Do not use other types of compounds, since they may electrically insulate the sensor. Install the sensor into the manifold. Installation torque for the sensor is 29–36 ft. lbs. (40–50 kg-m). Connect the electrical lead. Be careful handling the electrical lead; it is easily damaged.

3. Connect the negative battery cable.

After the first 30,000 mile replacement, the warning lamp harness connector should be unplugged to extinguish the lamp. The connector is located under the right side of the instrument panel; the harness wire color is green with a yellow stripe.

FUEL SYSTEM—GASOLINE ENGINES

Fuel Pump—All Except 810 and 1980—and later 200SX

The fuel pump is a mechanically-operated, diaphragm-type driven by the fuel pump eccentric on the camshaft.

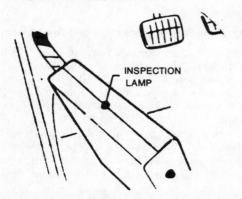

INSPECTION LAMP

Check the inspection lamp on the bottom of the control panel

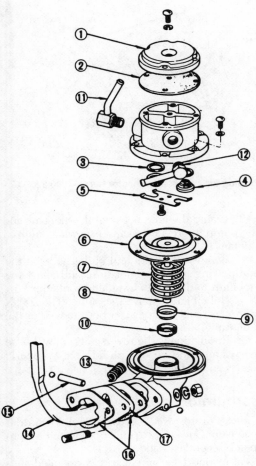

1. Fuel pump cap
2. Cap gasket
3. Valve packing assembly
4. Fuel pump valve assembly
5. Valve retainer
6. Diaphragm assembly
7. Diaphragm spring
8. Pull rod
9. Lower body seal washer
10. Lower body seal
11. Inlet connector
12. Outlet connector
13. Rocker arm spring
14. Rocker arm
15. Rocker arm side pin
16. Fuel pump packing
17. Spacer-fuel pump to cylinder block

Exploded view of the fuel pump—L-series engines

Design of the fuel pump permits disassembly, cleaning, and repair or replacement of defective parts. The fuel pump is mounted on the right side of the cylinder block, near the front.

TESTING

1. Disconnect the line between the carburetor and the pump at the carburetor.

2. Connect a fuel pump perssure gauge on the line.

3. Start the engine. The pressure should be between 3.0 and 3.9 psi. There is usually enough gas in the float bowl to perform this test.

4. If the pressure is ok, perform a capacity test. Remove the gauge from the line. Use a graduated container to catch the gas from the fuel line. Fill the carburetor float bowl with gas. Run the engine for one minute at about 1,000 rpm. The pump should deliver 1,000cc in a minute or less.

REMOVAL AND INSTALLATION

1. Disconnect the two fuel lines from the fuel pump. Be sure to keep the line leading from the fuel tank up high to prevent the excess loss of fuel.

2. Remove the two fuel pump mounting nuts and remove the fuel pump assembly from the side of the engine.

3. Install the fuel pump in the reverse order of removal, using a new gasket and sealer on the mating surface.

Fuel Pump—810, Maxima and 1980–and later 200SX

The fuel injected 810 and 200SX (1980–and later) use an electric fuel pump mounted near the fuel tank on the 810 and 1984 and later 200 SX and near the center of the car on the 200SX to 1983. The pump is of wet type construction. A vane pump and roller are directly coupled to a motor filled with fuel. A relief valve in the pump is designed to open when the pressure in the fuel line rises over 64 psi. Normal operating pressure is 36–43 psi. The pump is automatically activated when the ignition switch is burned to the "start" position. If the engine stalls for some reason, the fuel pump is cut off even though the ignition switch remains in the "on" position.

TESTING

Fuel pressure must be reduced to zero before tests are made.

On 1977–79 810's, disconnect the ground cable from the battery. Disconnect the cold start valve wiring harness at the connector. Connect two jumper wires to the terminals of the cold start valve. Touch the other ends of the jumpers to the positive and negative terminals of the battery for a few seconds to release the pressure.

For 1980–and later 810s, Maximas and 200SXs start the engine, disconnect the harness connector of fuel pump relay-2 (except on 1984 and later 200SXs—on these models, disconnect the connector in the tool box in the

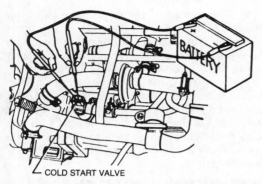

Releasing pressure at the cold start valve—810 and Maxima

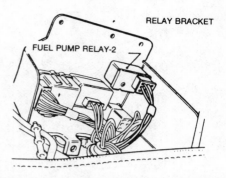

Unplug the harness connector here—1980 200SX

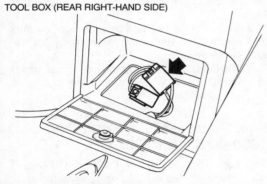

Unplug the connectors before releasing fuel pressure on the 1984 and later 200SX

rear right-hand side of the car) while the engine is running. After the engine stalls, crank it over two or three times to make sure all of the fuel pressure is released.

NOTE: *If the engine will not start, remove the fuel pump relay-2 harness connector and crank the engine for about 5 seconds.*

To test pressure:

1. Connect a fuel pressure gauge between the fuel feed pipe and the fuel filter outlet.

2. Start the engine and read the pressure. It should be 30 psi at idle, and 37 psi at the moment the accelerator pedal is fully depressed.

3. If pressure is not as specified, replace the pressure regulator and repeat the test. If the pressure is still incorrect, check for clogged or deformed fuel lines, then replace the fuel pump.

REMOVAL AND INSTALLATION

1. Reduce the fuel pressure to zero. See procedures under the "Testing" section, above.

2. Disconnect the electrical harness connector at the pump. The 810 pump is located near the fuel tank. The 200SX pump is located near the center of the car, except on 1984 and later 200SXs, on which the pump is located on the fuel tank.

3. Clamp the hose between the fuel tank and the pump to prevent gas from spewing out from the tank.

4. Remove the inlet and outlet hoses at the pump. Unclamp the inlet hose and allow the fuel lines to drain into a suitable container.

5. Unbolt and remove the pump. The 200SX pump and fuel damper can be removed at the same time.

6. Installation is the reverse of removal. Use new clamps and be sure all hoses are properly seated on the fuel pump body.

Carburetor

The carburetor used is a two-barrel down-draft type with a low-speed (primary) side and a high-speed (secondary) side.

All models have an electrically-operated anti-dieseling solenoid. As the ignition switch is turned off, the valve is energized and shuts off the supply of fuel to the idle circuit of the carburetor.

REMOVAL AND INSTALLATION

1. Remove the air cleaner.

2. Disconnect the fuel and vacuum lines from the carburetor.

3. Remove the throttle lever.

4. Remove the four nuts and washers retaining the carburetor to the manifold.

5. Lift the carburetor from the manifold.

6. Remove and discard the gasket used between the carburetor and the manifold.

7. Install the carburetor in the reverse order of removal, using a new carburetor base gasket.

THROTTLE LINKAGE ADJUSTMENT

On all models, make sure the throttle is wide open when the accelerator pedal is floored. Some models have an adjustable accelerator pedal stop to prevent strain on the linkage.

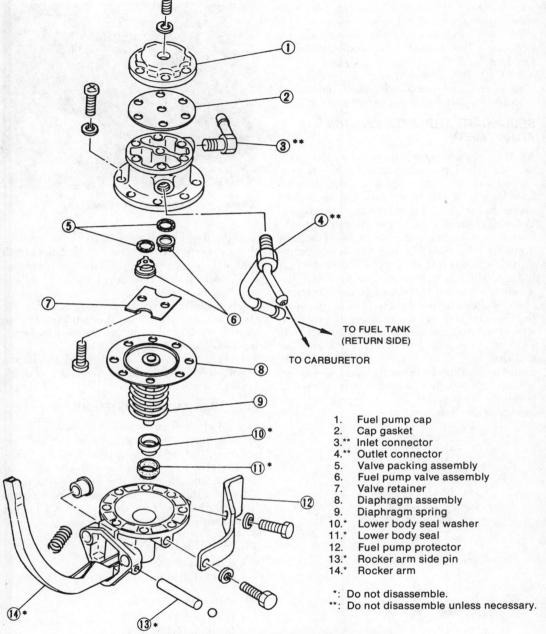

1. Fuel pump cap
2. Cap gasket
3.** Inlet connector
4.** Outlet connector
5. Valve packing assembly
6. Fuel pump valve assembly
7. Valve retainer
8. Diaphragm assembly
9. Diaphragm spring
10.* Lower body seal washer
11.* Lower body seal
12. Fuel pump protector
13.* Rocker arm side pin
14.* Rocker arm

*: Do not disassemble.
**: Do not disassemble unless necessary.

TO FUEL TANK
(RETURN SIDE)

TO CARBURETOR

Exploded view of the fuel pump—Z20S engines

DASHPOT ADJUSTMENT

A dashpot is used on carburetor of all cars with automatic transmissions and many late model manual transmission models. The dashpot slowly closes the throttle on automatic transmissions to prevent stalling and serves as an emission control device on all late model vehicles.

The dashpot should be adjusted to contact the throttle lever on deceleration at approximately 1,900–2,100 rpm for automatic trans-

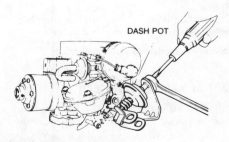

DASH POT

L-series dashpot adjustment

missions or 1,600–1,800 rpm for automatic transmissions with the L-series engines. The Z20S engine's dashpot contact point should be between 1,400–1,600 rpm for automatic transmissions.

NOTE: *Before attempting to adjust the dashpot, make sure the idle speed, timing and mixture adjustments are correct.*

SECONDARY THROTTLE LINKAGE ADJUSTMENT

All Datsun carburetors discussed in this book are two stage type carburetors. On this type of carburetor, the engine runs on the primary barrel most of the time, with the secondary barrel being used for acceleration purposes. When the throttle valve on the primary side opens to an angle of approximately 50 degrees (from its fully closed position), the secondary throttle valve is pulled open by the connecting linkage. The fifty degree angle of throttle valve opening works out to a clearance measurement of somewhere between 0.26–0.32 in. between the throttle valve and the carburetor body. The easiest way to measure this is to use a drill bit. Drill bits from size H to size P (standard letter size drill bits) should fit. Check the appendix in the back of the book for the exact size of the various drill bits. If an adjustment is necessary, bend the connecting link between the two linkage assemblies.

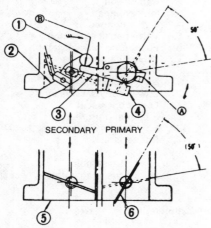

1. Roller
2. Connecting lever
3. Return plate
4. Adjust plate
5. Throttle chamber
6. Throttle valve

Secondary throttle linkage adjustment

FLOAT LEVEL ADJUSTMENT

The fuel level is normal if it is within the lines on the window glass of the float chamber (or the sight glass) when the vehicle is resting on level ground and the engine is off.

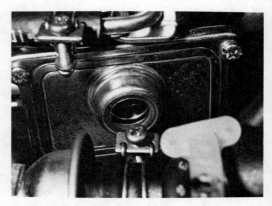

Close-up of float level sight window

If the fuel level is outside the lines, remove the float housing cover. Have an absorbent cloth under the cover to catch the fuel from the fuel bowl. Adjust the float level by bending the needle seat on the float.

The needle valve should have an effective stroke of about 0.0591 in. When necessary, the needle valve stroke can be adjusted by bending the float stopper.

NOTE: *Be careful not to bend the needle valve rod when installing the float and baffle plate, if removed.*

FAST IDLE AND ADJUSTMENT

1. With the carburetor removed from the vehicle, place the upper side of the fast idle screw on the second step (first step for 1977–81 L and Z engines) of the fast idle cam and measure the clearance between the throttle valve and the wall of the throttle valve chamber at the center of the throttle valve. Check it against the following specifications:

1973–74 610, 1974 710:

- 0.035–0.039 in. M/T
- 0.044–0.048 in. A/T

1975–76 610, 710:

- 0.040–0.048 in. M/T
- 0.049–0.052 in. A/T

1977 710, 1978–79 510, 200SX:

- 0.0370–0.0465 in. M/T
- 0.0457–0.0551 in. A/T

1980–81 510:

- 0.0299–0.0354 in. M/T
- 0.0378–0.0433 in. M/T

"M/T" means manual transmission. "A/T" means automatic transmission.

NOTE: *The first step of the fast idle adjustment procedure is not absolutely necessary.*

2. Install the carburetor on the engine.

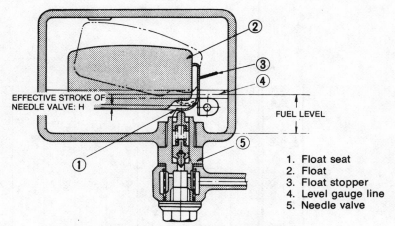

EFFECTIVE STROKE OF
NEEDLE VALVE: H

FUEL LEVEL

1. Float seat
2. Float
3. Float stopper
4. Level gauge line
5. Needle valve

Z20S, and L-series float level adjustment

3. Start the engine and measure the fast idle rpm with the engine at operating temperature. The cam should be at the 2nd step.

1974–76 710, 610:

- M/T 1,900–2,100 rpm
- A/T 2,300–2,500 rpm

1977 710, 1978–79 510, 200SX:

- M/T 1,900–2,800 rpm
- A/T 2,200–3,200 rpm

4. To adjust the fast idle speed, turn the fast idle adjusting screw counterclockwise to increase the fast idle speed and clockwise to decrease the fast idle speed.

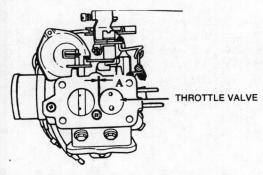

THROTTLE VALVE

FAST IDLE CAM STEPS

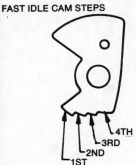

4TH
3RD
2ND
1ST

Fast idle adjustment

AUTOMATIC CHOKE ADJUSTMENT

1. With the engine cold, make sure the choke is fully closed (press the gas pedal all the way to the floor and release).

2. Check the choke linkage for binding. The choke plate should be easily opened and closed with your finger. If the choke sticks or binds, it can usually be freed with a liberal application of a carburetor cleaner made for the purpose. A couple of quick squirts of the right stuff normally does the trick.

If not, the carburetor will have to be disassembled for repairs.

3. The choke is correctly adjusted when the index mark on the choke housing (notch) aligns with the center mark on the carburetor body. If the setting is incorrect, loosen the three screws clamping the choke body in place and rotate the choke cover left or right until the marks align. Tighten the screws carefully to avoid cracking the housing.

CHOKE UNLOADER ADJUSTMENT

1. Close the choke valve completely.

2. Hold the choke valve closed by stretching a rubber band between the choke piston lever and a stationary part of the carburetor.

3. Open the throttle lever fully.

4. Adjust the gap between the choke plate and the carburetor body to:

L-series engines, 1980–81 Z20S engine:

- 1973–74, 0.173 in.
- 1975–77, 0.096 in., except:
- 1977 710: 0.0807–0.1122 in.
- 1978–80: 0.0807–0.1122 in.

OVERHAUL

Efficient carburetion depends greatly on careful cleaning and inspection during overhaul, since dirt, gum, water, or varnish in or on the

Carburetor Specifications

Year	Engine	Vehicle Model	Carb Model	Main Jet # Primary	Main Jet # Secondary	Main Air Bleed # Primary	Main Air Bleed # Secondary	Slow Jet # Primary	Slow Jet # Secondary	Float Level (in.)	Power Jet #
1973	L18	610	DCH340-2 ① DCH340-1 ②	97.5	170	65	60	48③	90③	0.906	53
1974	L18	710	DCH340-10 ① DCH340-11 ②	100	170	60	60	45③	90③	0.906	41
	L20B	610	DCH340-15 ① DCH340-14 ②	102	170	60	60	46③	160③	0.906	50
1975	L20B (California)	710	DCH340-41 ① DCH340-42 ②	99	160	70	60	48	80	0.906	43
	L20B (Federal)	710	DCH340-43 ① DCH340-44 ②	97	160	70	60	48	100	0.906	48
1976	L20B (California)	710, 610	DCH340-41A ① DCH340-42B ②	101	160	70	60	48	80	0.906	40
	L20B (Federal)	710, 610	DCH340-43A ① DCH340-44A ②	99	160	70	60	48	100	0.906	43
1977	L20B (California)	710	DCH340-41B ① DCH340-42C ②	101	160	70	60	48	80	0.91	40
	L20B (Federal)	710	DCH340-51A ① DCH340-52A ②	105	165	60	60	48	100	0.91	43
	L20B (California)	200SX	DCH340-49A ① DCH340-50A ②	101	160	70	60	48	80	0.91	43
	L20B (Federal)	200SX	DCH340-53B ① DCH340-54B ②	105	165	60	60	48	100	0.91	43

Year	Engine	Model	Carburetor								
1978	L20B (California)	200SX	DCH340-91A ① / DCH340-92A ②	102	158	70	60	48	70	0.91	40
	L20B (Federal)	200SX	DCH340-93A ① / DCH340-94A ②	104	160	60	60	48	70	0.91	43
	L20B (California)	510	DCH340-99 ① / DCH340-92A ②	103 / 102	158	70	60	48	70	0.91	35 / 40
	L20B (Federal)	510	DCH340-93A ① / DCH340-94A ②	104	160	60	60	48	70	0.91	43
1979	L20B (California)	200SX	DCH340-91C ① / DCH340-92C ②	102	158	70	60	48	70	0.91	40
	L20B (Federal)	200SX	DCH340-69 ① / DCH340-94B ②	104	160	60	60	48	70	0.91	35 / 43
	L20B (California)	510	DCH340-99C ① / DCH340-92C ②	103 / 102	158	70	60	48	70	0.91	35 / 40
	L20B (Fedral)	510	DCH340-69 ① / DCH340-94B ②	104	160	60	60	48	70	0.91	35 / 43
1980	Z20S (California)	510	All	107	170	110	60	47	100	0.91	35
	Z20S (Federal)	510	All	99	166	90	60	47	100	0.91	40
1981	Z20S (California)	510	All	112	155	90	60	47	100	0.91	35 ④
	Z20S (Federal)	510	All	112	155	90	60	47	100	0.91	35

① Manual Transmission
② Automatic Transmission
③ Slow jet air bleed: Primary #145, Secondary #100
④ Models with A/T: #45

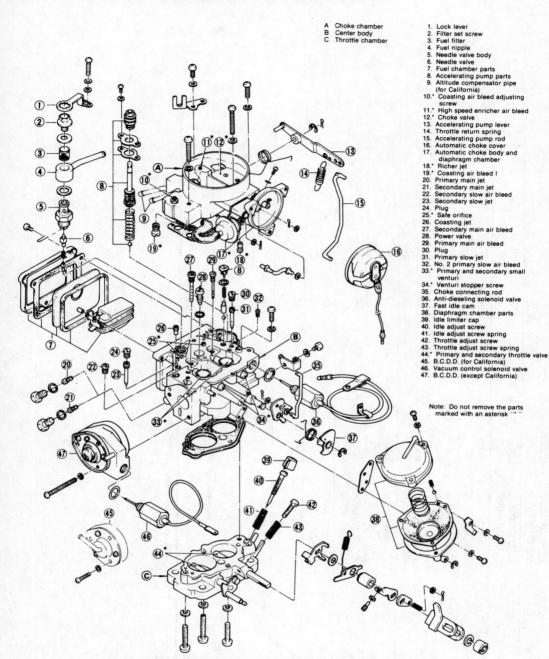

A Choke chamber
B Center body
C Throttle chamber

1. Lock lever
2. Filter set screw
3. Fuel filter
4. Fuel nipple
5. Needle valve body
6. Needle valve
7. Fuel chamber parts
8. Accelerating pump parts
9. Altitude compensator pipe (for California)
10.* Coasting air bleed adjusting screw
11.* High speed enricher air bleed
12.* Choke valve
13. Accelerating pump lever
14. Throttle return spring
15. Accelerating pump rod
16. Automatic choke cover
17. Automatic choke body and diaphragm chamber
18.* Richer jet
19.* Coasting air bleed I
20. Primary main jet
21. Secondary main jet
22. Secondary slow air bleed
23. Secondary slow jet
24. Plug
25.* Safe orifice
26. Coasting jet
27. Secondary main air bleed
28. Power valve
29. Primary main air bleed
30. Plug
31. Primary slow jet
32. No. 2 primary slow air bleed
33.* Primary and secondary small venturi
34.* Venturi stopper screw
35. Choke connecting rod
36. Anti-dieseling solenoid valve
37. Fast idle cam
38. Diaphragm chamber parts
39. Idle limiter cap
40. Idle adjust screw
41. Idle adjust screw spring
42. Throttle adjust screw
43. Throttle adjust screw spring
44.* Primary and secondary throttle valve
45. B.C.D.D. (for California)
46. Vacuum control solenoid valve
47. B.C.D.D. (except California)

Note: Do not remove the parts marked with an asterisk "*"

Exploded view of 1975 710 carburetor—other L-series similar

carburetor parts are often responsible for poor performance.

Overhaul your carburetor in a clean, dust-free area. Carefully disassemble the carburetor, referring often to the exploded views. Keep all similar and look-alike parts segregated during disassembly and cleaning to avoid accidental interchange during assembly. Make a note of all jet sizes.

When the carburetor is disassembled, wash all parts (except diaphragms, electric choke units, pump plunger, and any other plastic, leather, fiber, or rubber parts) in clean carburetor solvent. Do not leave parts in the solvent any longer than is necessary to sufficiently loosen the deposits. Excessive cleaning may remove the special finish from the float bowl and choke valve bodies, leaving these parts unfit for service. Rinse all parts in clean solvent and blow them dry with compressed air to allow them to

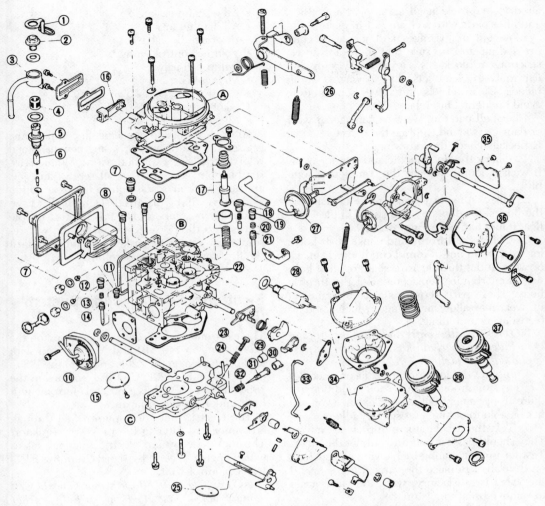

1. Lock lever
2. Filter set screw
3. Fuel nipple
4. Fuel filter
5. Needle valve body
6. Needle valve
7. Power valve
8. Secondary main air bleed
9. Primary main air bleed
10. B.C.D.D.
11. Secondary slow air bleed
12. Secondary main jet
13. Plug
14. Secondary slow jet
15. Primary throttle valve
16. Idle compensator
17. Accelerating pump parts
18. Plug for accelerating
    mechanism
19. Plug
20. Spring
21. Primary slow jet

22. Primary and secondary small
    venturi
23. Throttle adjusting screw
24. Throttle adjusting screw
    spring
25. Secondary throttle valve
26. Accelerating pump lever
27. Vacuum break diaphragm
28. Anti-dieseling solenoid valve
29. Blind plug (California)
30. Idle limiter cap (Except
    California)
31. Idle adjusting screw
32. Idle adjusting screw spring
33. Choke connecting rod
34. Diaphragm chamber parts
35. Choke valve
36. Automatic choke cover
37. F.I. pot (A/T)
38. F.I.C.D. actuator (M/T air conditioner
    equipped models only)

Exploded view of 1980 510 (Z20S) engine carburetor

air dry. Wipe clean all cork, plastic, leather, and fiber parts with a clean, lint-free cloth.

Blow out all passages and jets with compressed air and be sure that there are no restrictions or blockages. Never use wire or similar tools to clean jets, fuel passages, or air bleeds. Clean all jets and valves separately to avoid accidental interchange.

Check all parts for wear or damage. If wear or damage is found, replace the defective parts. Especially check the following:

1. Check the float needle and seat for wear. If wear is found, replace the complete assembly.

2. Check the float hinge pin for wear and the float(s) for dents or distortion. Replace the float if fuel has leaked into it.

3. Check the throttle and choke shaft bores for wear or an out-of-round condition. Damage or wear to the throttle arm, shaft, or shaft bore will often require replacement of the throttle body. These parts require a close tolerance of fit; wear may allow air leakage, which could affect starting and idling.

NOTE: *Throttle shafts and bushings are not included in overhaul kits. They can be purchased separately.*

4. Inspect the idle mixture adjusting needles for burrs or grooves. Any such condition requires replacement of the needle, since you will not be able to obtain a satisfactory idle.

5. Text the accelerator pump check valves. They should pass air one way but not the other. Test for proper seating by blowing and sucking on the valve. Replace the valve if necessary. If the valve is satisfactory, wash the valve again to remove breath moisture.

6. Check the bowl cover for warped surfaces with a straightedge.

7. Closely inspect the valves and seats for wear and damage, replacing as necessary.

8. After the carburetor is assembled, check the choke valve for freedom of operation.

Carburetor overhaul kits are recommended for each overhaul. These kits contain all gaskets and new parts to replace those that deteriorate most rapidly. Failure to replace all parts supplied with the kit (especially gaskets) can result in poor performance later.

Some carburetor manufacturers supply overhaul kits of three basic types: minor repair; major repair; and gasket kits. Basically, they contain the following:

Minor Repair Kits:
- All gaskets
- Float needle valve
- Volume control screw
- All diaphragms
- Spring for the pump diaphragm

Major Repair Kits:
- All jets and gaskets
- All diaphragms
- Float needle valve
- Volume control screw
- Pump ball valve
- Main jet carrier
- Float

Gasket Kits:
- All gaskets

After cleaning and checking all components, reassemble the carburetor, using new parts and referring to the exploded view. When reassembling, make sure that all screws and jets are tight in their seats, but do not overtighten as the tips will be distorted. Tighten all screws gradually in rotation. Do not tighten needle valves into their seats; uneven jetting will result. Always use new gaskets. Be sure to adjust the float level when reassembling.

Electronic Fuel Injection System (EFI)

The electronic fuel injection system used on the L24 engine in the 810 and Maxima and with slight alteration on the Z20E engine in the 1980–82 200SX and CA20E CA18ET engines in the 1984 and later 200SX is a Bosch L-Jetronic unit built under license in Japan.

The electric fuel pump pumps fuel through a damper and filter to the pressure regulator. The fuel injectors are electric solenoid valves which open and close by signals from the Electronic Control Unit.

NOTE: *The 1979–80 Electronic Control Unit must not be installed on 1978 or earlier models. Damage to the ECU will result. A special adapter harness must be used with the factory EFI analyzer when testing the 1979–80 ECU.*

CHECKING FUNCTIONAL PARTS

For the following tests you will need a small testing light and an ohmmeter. Be sure the car's battery is fully charged before making the tests.

ELECTRONIC CONTROL UNIT TEST

1. Connect the testing lamp to the harness-side connector of the injector.

2. Crank the engine. If the light flashes due to the pulse voltage applied to the injector, the control unit is operating.

Because two different transistors arke used in the system, you will have to test both the No. 1 and 4 cylinders.

NOTE: *The engine must be turning over at a speed of more than 80 rpm to complete the test.*

To further test 1977–79 810's, remove the

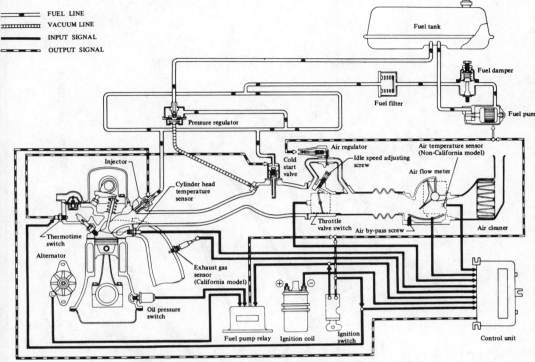

FUEL LINE
VACUUM LINE
INPUT SIGNAL
OUTPUT SIGNAL

1980 810 fuel injection system. Later 810s and Maxima similar

connector on the coolant sensor. The installed testing lamp should flash more brightly.

TESTING THE POTENTIOMETER

Except 1984 and later CA18ET Engines

The Potentiometer monitors the amount of air passing into the intake manifold and sends an appropriate signal to the control unit which in turn adjusts the fuel/air mixture for best effi-

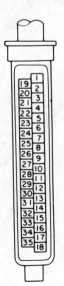

EFI connector numbering

Check air flow meter resistance between terminals ③④ and ③②, ③③, ③⑤.

③④ — ③② : Except 0 and $\infty\,\Omega$
③④ — ③③ : Approx. 100 - 400Ω
③④ — ③⑤ : Approx. 200 - 500Ω

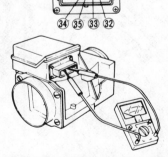

Checking airflow meter resistance, 1979–84 models except CA18ET

ciency. It is also referred to as the air flow meter.

CAUTION: *Before checking the air flow meter, or the potentiometer, remove the ground cable from the battery.*

1. Remove the air flow meter.
2. Measure the resistance between terminals 8 and 6, through 1978, or 33 and 34 for

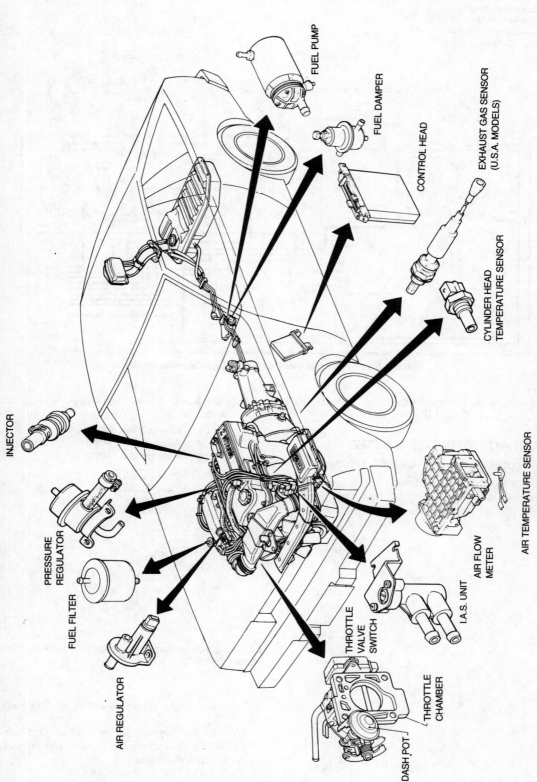

FUEL PUMP

FUEL DAMPER

CONTROL HEAD

EXHAUST GAS SENSOR
(U.S.A. MODELS)

CYLINDER HEAD
TEMPERATURE SENSOR

INJECTOR

PRESSURE
REGULATOR

FUEL FILTER

AIR REGULATOR

DASH POT

THROTTLE
CHAMBER

THROTTLE
VALVE
SWITCH

I.A.S. UNIT

AIR FLOW
METER

AIR TEMPERATURE SENSOR

1983 200SX fuel system component locations

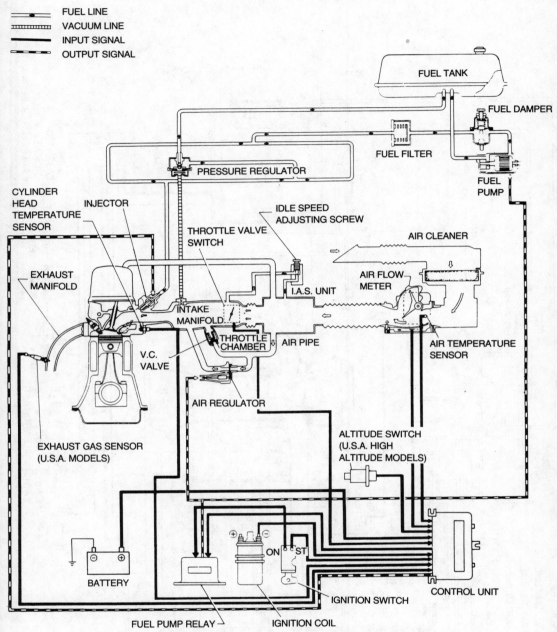

FUEL LINE
VACUUM LINE
INPUT SIGNAL
OUTPUT SIGNAL

FUEL TANK

FUEL DAMPER

FUEL FILTER

FUEL PUMP

PRESSURE REGULATOR

CYLINDER HEAD TEMPERATURE SENSOR

INJECTOR

IDLE SPEED ADJUSTING SCREW

THROTTLE VALVE SWITCH

AIR CLEANER

AIR FLOW METER

I.A.S. UNIT

EXHAUST MANIFOLD

INTAKE MANIFOLD

AIR TEMPERATURE SENSOR

V.C. VALVE

THROTTLE CHAMBER

AIR PIPE

AIR REGULATOR

EXHAUST GAS SENSOR (U.S.A. MODELS)

ALTITUDE SWITCH (U.S.A. HIGH ALTITUDE MODELS)

BATTERY

ON   ST

CONTROL UNIT

IGNITION SWITCH

FUEL PUMP RELAY

IGNITION COIL

Z22 series fuel, air flow and ignition schematic, 1983 200SX shown

1979–84 models. It should be 180 ohms through 1978 and 100–400 ohms thereafter.

3. Measure the resistance between terminals 8 and 9 through 1978, or 34 and 35 for 1979–82. Resistance should be 100 ohms through 1978, 200–500 ohms for 1979–84.

4. For models through 1978: connect a 12-volt battery to terminal 9 (positive) and terminal 6 (negative).

Connect the positive lead of a voltmeter to terminal 8 and the negative lead to terminal 7.

Reaching into the air flow meter, slowly open the flap so that the volt flow slowly decreases. If the indicator varies suddenly, the problem may be in the potentiometer.

5. For 1979–84 models: slide the flap open and measure the resistance between terminals 32 and 34. Resistance other than zero or infinite is correct.

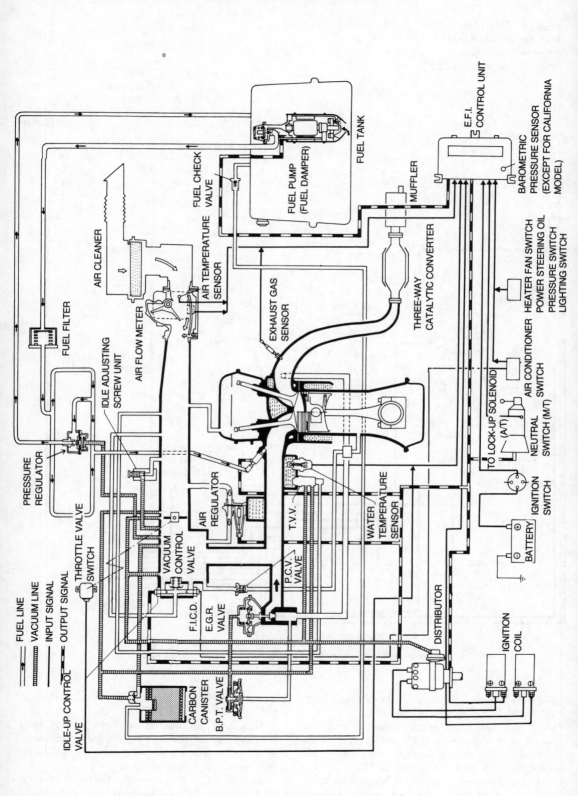

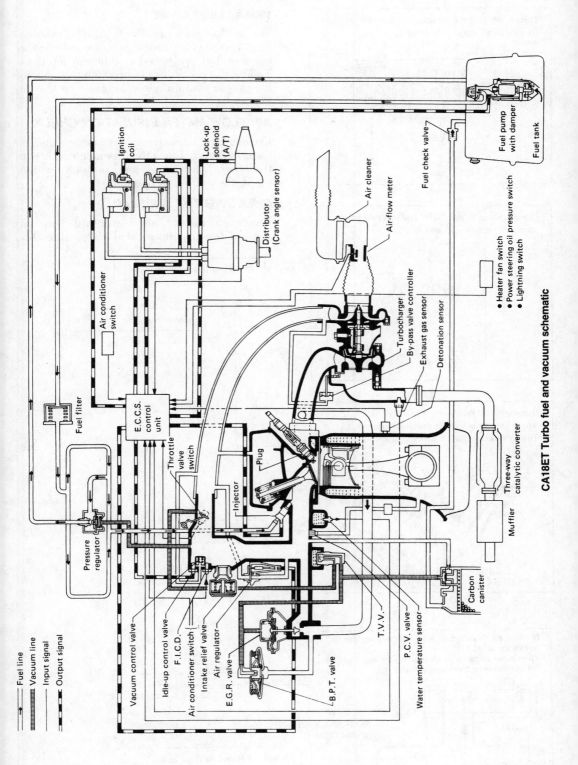

Fuel line
Vacuum line
Input signal
Output signal

Ignition coil

Lock-up solenoid (A/T)

Distributor (Crank angle sensor)

Air cleaner

Air-flow meter

Fuel check valve

Fuel pump with damper

Fuel tank

Air conditioner switch

• Heater fan switch
• Power steering oil pressure switch
• Lightning switch

Turbocharger

By-pass valve controller

Exhaust gas sensor

Detonation sensor

Fuel filter

E.C.C.S. control unit

Three-way catalytic converter

Throttle valve switch

Plug

Pressure regulator

Injector

Muffler

Vacuum control valve

Idle-up control valve

F.I.C.D.

Air conditioner switch

Intake relief valve

Air regulator

E.G.R. valve

B.P.T. valve

Water temperature sensor

P.C.V. valve

T.V.V.

Carbon canister

CA18ET Turbo fuel and vacuum schematic

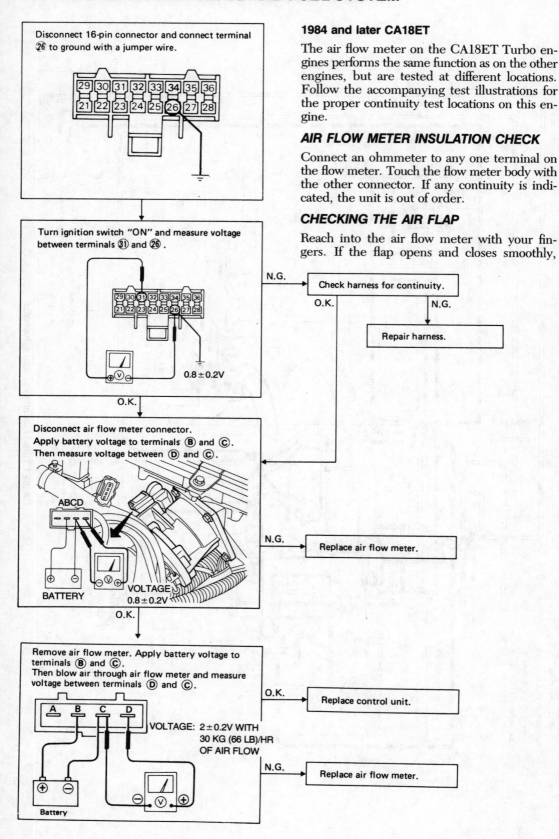

Disconnect 16-pin connector and connect terminal 26 to ground with a jumper wire.

Turn ignition switch "ON" and measure voltage between terminals 31 and 26 .

N.G. → Check harness for continuity.

O.K.

N.G. → Repair harness.

0.8±0.2V

O.K.

Disconnect air flow meter connector.
Apply battery voltage to terminals B and C.
Then measure voltage between D and C.

ABCD

BATTERY   VOLTAGE
0.8±0.2V

N.G. → Replace air flow meter.

O.K.

Remove air flow meter. Apply battery voltage to terminals B and C.
Then blow air through air flow meter and measure voltage between terminals D and C.

A B C D

VOLTAGE: 2±0.2V WITH
30 KG (66 LB)/HR
OF AIR FLOW

O.K. → Replace control unit.

N.G. → Replace air flow meter.

Battery

1984 and later CA18ET

The air flow meter on the CA18ET Turbo engines performs the same function as on the other engines, but are tested at different locations. Follow the accompanying test illustrations for the proper continuity test locations on this engine.

AIR FLOW METER INSULATION CHECK

Connect an ohmmeter to any one terminal on the flow meter. Touch the flow meter body with the other connector. If any continuity is indicated, the unit is out of order.

CHECKING THE AIR FLAP

Reach into the air flow meter with your fingers. If the flap opens and closes smoothly,

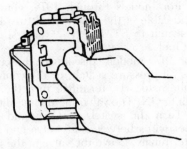

Checking the air flap

without binding, the mechanical portion of the unit is working.

AIR TEMPERATURE SENSOR—EXCEPT 1980 CALIFORNIA 810

Checking Continuity

1. Disconnect the battery ground cable.
2. Remove the air flow meter.
3. Check the temperature of your surroundings and make note of it.
4. Connect an ohmmeter to terminals 27 and 6 for models through 1978, or 25 and 34 for 1979–82 on the air flow meter connector and check the resistance indicated. Make a note of it.

The resistance values should be as indicated in the chart. Should the test results vary a great deal from the ranges provided, replace the air temperature sensor and the air flow meter as a unit.

AIR TEMPERATURE SENSOR
Air temperature sensor location

Air Flow Meter Resistance Specifications

Air Temperature °C (°F)	Resistance (kΩ)
−30 (−22)	20.3 to 33.0
−10 (−14)	7.6 to 10.8
10 (50)	3.25 to 4.15
20 (68)	2.25 to 2.75
50 (122)	0.74 to 0.94
80 (176)	0.29 to 0.36

Insulation Resistance

Connect an ohmmeter to terminal 27 of the air flow meter for models though 1978, or terminal 25 for 1979–82 models, and touch the body of the unit with the other connector. Should continuity be indicated, replace the unit.

WATER TEMPERATURE SENSOR

This test may be done either on or off the vehicle. The test should be done with the coolant both hot and cold.

NOTE: *1980–84 810s and Maximas and 1981–84 200SX's are equipped with cylinder head temperature sensors rather than water temperature sensors. However, the test is the same for both units.*

1. Disconnect the battery ground cable.
2. Disconnect the water temperature sensor harness.
3. Place a thermometer in the coolant when the engine is cold. Make note of the indication.
4. Read the resistance indicated on the meter and compare it with the chart for temperature/resistance values.

To measure the coolant temperature and resistance values when hot:

1. Connect the water temperature sensor harness.
2. Connect the battery ground cable.
3. Warm the engine and disconnect the harness and battery cable.
4. Read the sensor resistance as described in the cold process.

Sensor Check-Off the Engine

1. Remove the sensor and dip the unit into water maintained at 68°F. Read the resistance.
2. Heat the water to 176°F and check the resistance.

In either type of check, should the resistance be far outside the ranges provided, replace the sensor unit.

Water Temperature Sensor Resistance Specifications

Cooling Water Temperature °C (°F)	Resistance (kΩ)
−30 (−22)	20.3 to 33.0
−10 (−14)	7.6 to 10.8
10 (50)	3.25 to 4.15
20 (68)	2.25 to 2.75
50 (122)	0.74 to 0.94
80 (176)	0.29 to 0.36

Sensor Insulation Check

This check is done on the engine.
1. Disconnect the battery ground cable.
2. Disconnect the sensor harness connector.
3. Connect an ohmmeter to one of the terminals on the sensor and touch the engine block with the other. Any indication of continuity indicates need to replace the unit.

THERMOTIME SWITCH—810 AND MAXIMA

1. Disconnect the ground cable from the battery.
2. Disconnect the electric connector of the thermotime switch and measure the resistance between output terminal and the switch body.
The resistance should be zero with water temperatures less than 57°F.
The resistance should be zero or infinite with temperatures of 57° to 72°F.
The resistance should be infinite with a temperature of 72°F.
3. Measure the resistance between input terminal and the switch body.
70–86 ohms through 1977 . . . . OK
51–62 ohms, 1978 . . . . OK
40–70 ohms 1979–80 . . . . OK
Any different reading than shown indicates replacement.

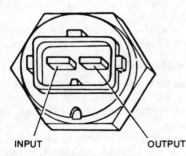

INPUT   OUTPUT

Checking the thermotime switch

COLD START VALVE—810 AND MAXIMA

Steps 1 and 2 are for models through 1978 only.
1. Disconnect the lead wire from the "S" terminal of the starter motor.
2. Turn the ignition switch to START and make sure the fuel pump is working. You should be able to hear it.
3. Disconnect the ground cable from the battery.
4. Remove the screws holding the cold start valve to the intake manifold and remove the valve.
5. Disconnect the start valve electrical connector.
6. Put the start valve into a large glass container and plug the neck of the jar.

7. For models through 1978, connect the ground cable of the battery and turn the ignition switch to START. The valve should not inject fuel.
For 1979 models, disconnect the connector at the oil pressure switch, or the connector at the alternator "L" terminal; turn the ignition switch to ON. The valve should not inject fuel.
8. Turn the switch to OFF and connect jumper wires between the valve and the battery terminals. Leave the valve in the jar.
At this point, the valve should inject fuel. If not, proceed to the next step for models through 1977 only. For 1978 and later models, replace the valve.
9. With the ignition switch in the START position, and the jumper wire installed as described, check for fuel flow. If the fuel is injected to the jar, the unit is operating. If not, replace.

FUEL INJECTION AND FUEL PUMP RELAYS

The fuel injection system is equipped with one relay and the fuel pump has two. Testing and service should be left to your Datsun dealer.
NOTE: *A faulty relay could disrupt fuel pump operation and injection performance. Be sure to have the relays checked before simply replacing them, as they are rather expensive.*

FUEL INJECTOR TEST

For continuity, remove the ground cable from the battery and disconnect the electric connectors from the injectors.
Check for continuity readings between the two terminals. If there is not an indication, the injector is faulty and must be replaced.
Check the injectors for sound as follows:
If the engine is running, run it at idle and place screwdriver tip against each injector and put your ear to the handle to check for operating sounds. You should hear a click sound at regular intervals. Note, however, that as the engine speed increases, the click intervals shorten. If no click is heard, check the Electronic Control Unit as described at the beginning of this section. If one injector sounds different from the rest, it is probably faulty: replace it.
If the engine is not running, disconnect the connector of the cold start valve (810 and Maxima only) and crank the engine. Check for the same sounds described in the above paragraph.
NOTE: *If none of the injectors is working, make sure the wiring harnesses are connected and check the fuel injection fusible link near the battery for damage. See chapter 5.*

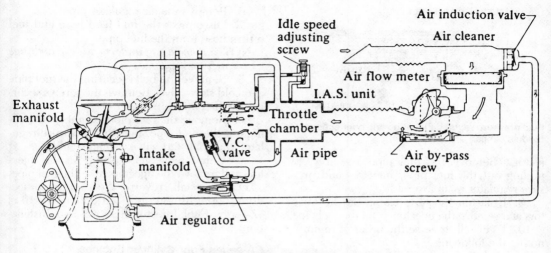

1980 200SX fuel injection system

FUEL INJECTOR REMOVAL AND INSTALLATION

Z-Series Four Cylinder Engines

1. Release fuel pressure by following the procedure in Chapter 1 under "Fuel Filter."

2. Disconnect the accelerator cable.

3. Disconnect the injector harness connector.

4. Tag and disconnect the vacuum hose at the fuel pipe connection end. Disconnect the air regulator and its harness connector, and tag and disconnect any other hoses that may hinder removal of the injection assembly.

5. Disconnect the fuel feed hose and fuel return hose from the fuel pipe.

NOTE: *Place a rag under the fuel pipe to prevent splashing of the fuel.*

6. Remove the vacuum hose connecting the pressure regulator to the intake manifold.

7. Remove the bolts securing the fuel pipe and pressure regulator.

8. Remove the screws securing the fuel in-

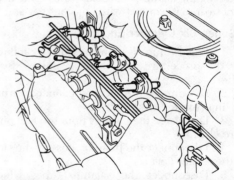

Removing the fuel pipe and injector assembly, Z-series engines

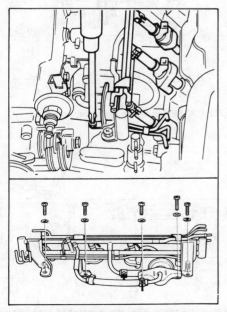

Top: Removing the Z-series fuel pressure regulator-to-fuel pipe screws. Bottom: Fuel pipe assembly securing screws

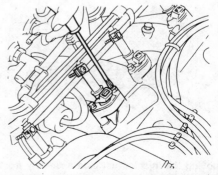

Removing the injector securing screws, all models similar

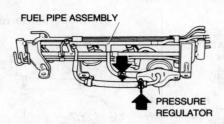

FUEL PIPE ASSEMBLY

PRESSURE REGULATOR

Fuel pressure regulator location and connections, all models similar

jectors. Remove the fuel pipe assembly, by pulling out the fuel pipe, injectors and pressure regulator as an assembly.

9. Unfasten the hose clamp on the injectors and remove the injectors from the fuel pipe.

10. To install, reverse the order of removal, noting the following:

a. When installing the injectors, check that there are no scratches or abrasion at the lower rubber insulator, and securely install it, making sure it is air-tight.

b. When installing the fuel hose, make sure the hose end is inserted onto the metal pipe until the end contacts the unit, as far as it will go. Push the end of the injector rubber hose onto the fuel pipe until it is one inch from the end of the pipe.

c. Never reuse hose clamps on the injection system. *Always renew the clamps.* When tightening clamps, make sure the screw does not come in contact with adjacent parts.

L-Series Six Cylinder Engines

1. Release fuel system pressure by following the procedure in Chapter 1 under "Fuel Filter."

2. Disconnect the electric connector from the injector and cold start valve.

3. Disengage the harness from the fuel pipe wire clamp.

4. Disconnect the blow-by hose at the side of the rocker cover.

5. Disconnect the vacuum tube, which connects the pressure regulator to the intake manifold, from the pressure regulator.

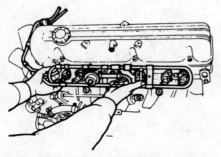

Removing the injector/fuel pipe assembly from the L24 six cylinder

6. Remove the air regulator pipe.

7. Disconnect the fuel feed hose and fuel return hose from the fuel pipe.

NOTE: *Place a rag underneath the fuel pipe to catch fuel spillage.*

8. Remove the bolts securing the fuel pipe and cold start valve. Remove the screws securing the fuel injectors.

9. Remove the fuel pipe assembly by pulling out the fuel pipe, injectors, pressure regulator and cold start valve as an assembly.

10. Unfasten the hose clamp on the injectors and remove the injectors from the fuel pipe.

11. To install, reverse the removal procedure, noting the items listed under No. 10 of "Z-series Fuel Injector Removal and Installation" above.

CA-series Four Cylinder Engines

1. On the CA20E engine, drain the engine coolant. Disconnect the fuel injection wiring harness, the ignition wires, and the collector with the throttle chamber. Tag and disconnect all related hoses.

2. On the CA18ET engine, disconnect the air intake pipe, the fuel injection wiring harness, the ignition wires and accelerator cable. Disconnect the throttle chamber.

3. On all engines, disconnect the fuel hoses and pressure regulator vacuum hoses.

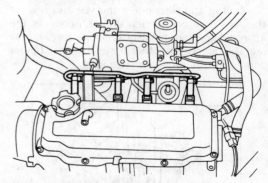

CA20E/CA18ET injector assembly location

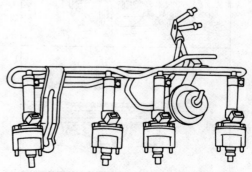

CA20E, CA18ET injector assembly including fuel pressure regulator

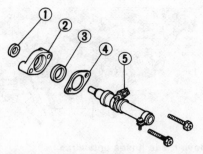

Typical fuel injector and related mounting hardware. When replacing injector, always replace the lower rubber insulator (1) and the upper rubber insulator (3)

4. Remove the injectors together with the fuel tube assembly. Remove the individual injectors from the fuel tube.

5. Installation is the reverse of removal, noting the items listed under No. 10 of "Z-series Fuel Injector Removal and Installation."

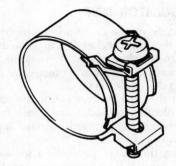

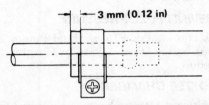

3 mm (0.12 in)

Always renew the hose clamps. Note proper installation

TO FUEL TANK   FROM FUEL TANK

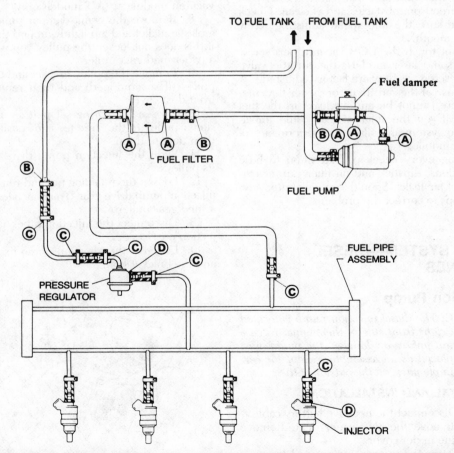

Fuel damper

FUEL FILTER

FUEL PUMP

PRESSURE
REGULATOR

FUEL PIPE
ASSEMBLY

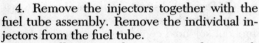

INJECTOR

Typical fuel injection hose connections. Note proper hose installation. L24E engines similar except have six injectors

AIR REGULATOR TEST

1. Start the engine and pinch the rubber hose between the throttle chamber and the air regulator. On a cold engine, the engine speed should decrease. On a warm engine the engine speed should not be affected.

To test the air regulator continuity, disconnect the electric connector and check for continuity between the terminals. If none is found, the regulator is faulty.

To open the valve, pry with a screwdriver and then close. If the operation is smooth, the valve is operating correctly. Any binding indicates replacement.

RELIEVING FUEL PRESSURE

See section under Electric Fuel Pump, Testing, or under "Fuel Filter" in Chapter 1 for procedure.

THROTTLE CHAMBER

The 810 and Maxima has a single barrel throttle chamber while the 200SX is equipped with a two barrel chamber. Check the throttle for smooth operation and make sure the by-pass port is free from obstacles and is clean. Check to make sure the idle speed adjusting screw moves smoothly.

Do not touch the EGR vacuum port screw or, on some later models, the throttle valve stopper screw, as they are factory adjusted.

Because of the sensitivity of the air flow meter, there cannot be any air leaks in the fuel system. Even the smallest leak could unbalance the system and affect the performance of the automobile.

During every check pay attention to hose connections, dipstick and oil filler cap for evidence of air leaks. Should you encounter any, take steps to correct the problem.

FUEL SYSTEM—DIESEL ENGINES

Injection Pump

NOTE: *The diesel injection pump is located at the right front side of the engine. In case of pump failure or damage, the pump must be replaced as an assembly, except for certain simple parts on the outside of the pump.*

REMOVAL AND INSTALLATION

1. Disconnect the negative battery cable.
2. Remove the air cleaner duct. Remove the engine under cover.
3. Drain the engine coolant and then remove the radiator and its shroud.

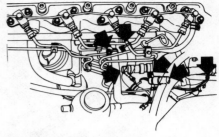

Remove these hoses and wires

4. Loosen the fan pulley nuts and then remove the drive belts (air conditioning, alternator and power steering pump).
5. Disconnect the power steering oil pump and position it out of the way.
6. Tag and disconnect the acclerator wire, the overflow hose (on the spill tube side), the fuel cut solenoid connector and the fuel return hose.
7. Tag and disconnect the potentiometer, the injection timing control solenoid valve wire, the cold start device water hoses (at the 4-way connector side) and the vacuum hoses for the vacuum modulator (A/T models only).
8. Remove the crank damper pulley. Use a plastic mallet and tap lightly around the sides, if this does not loosen the pulley you will need a two-armed gear puller.
9. Remove the pulley bracket and the idler pulley (if so equipped) and then remove the front dust cover.
10. Loosen the spring set pin, set the tensioner pulley to the "free tension" position and then tighten them.
11. Slide the injection pump drive belt off its pulleys.
12. Loosen the retaining nut and remove the injection pump drive gear. You may need a two-armed gear puller.
13. Disconnect the injection tubes at the injection nozzle side.
14. Unscrew the injection pump fixing nuts and the bracket bolt.

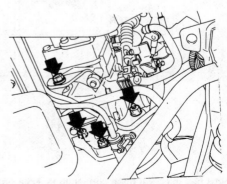

Injection pump mounting nuts and bolt

CHILTON'S
FUEL ECONOMY
& TUNE-UP TIPS

Tune-up • Spark Plug Diagnosis • Emission Controls

Fuel System • Cooling System • Tires and Wheels

General Maintenance

CHILTON'S FUEL ECONOMY & TUNE-UP TIPS

Fuel economy is important to everyone, no matter what kind of vehicle you drive. The maintenance-minded motorist can save both money and fuel using these tips and the periodic maintenance and tune-up procedures in this Repair and Tune-Up Guide.

There are more than 130,000,000 cars and trucks registered for private use in the United States. Each travels an average of 10-12,000 miles per year, and, and in total they consume close to 70 billion gallons of fuel each year. This represents nearly ⅔ of the oil imported by the United States each year. The Federal government's goal is to reduce consumption 10% by 1985. A variety of methods are either already in use or under serious consideration, and they all affect you driving and the cars you will drive. In addition to "down-sizing", the auto industry is using or investigating the use of electronic fuel delivery, electronic engine controls and alternative engines for use in smaller and lighter vehicles, among other alternatives to meet the federally mandated Corporate Average Fuel Economy (CAFE) of 27.5 mpg by 1985. The government, for its part, is considering rationing, mandatory driving curtailments and tax increases on motor vehicle fuel in an effort to reduce consumption. The government's goal of a 10% reduction could be realized — and further government regulation avoided — if every private vehicle could use just 1 less gallon of fuel per week.

How Much Can You Save?

Tests have proven that almost anyone can make at least a 10% reduction in fuel consumption through regular maintenance and tune-ups. When a major manufacturer of spark plugs sur-

TUNE-UP

1. Check the cylinder compression to be sure the engine will really benefit from a tune-up and that it is capable of producing good fuel economy. A tune-up will be wasted on an engine in poor mechanical condition.

2. Replace spark plugs regularly. New spark plugs alone can increase fuel economy 3%.

3. Be sure the spark plugs are the correct type (heat range) for your vehicle. See the Tune-Up Specifications.

Heat range refers to the spark plug's ability to conduct heat away from the firing end. It must conduct the heat away in an even pattern to avoid becoming a source of pre-ignition, yet it must also operate hot enough to burn off conductive deposits that could cause misfiring.

The heat range is usually indicated by a number on the spark plug, part of the manufacturer's designation for each individual spark plug. The numbers in bold-face indicate the heat range in each manufacturer's identification system.

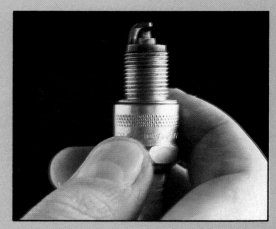

Periodically, check the spark plugs to be sure they are firing efficiently. They are excellent indicators of the internal condition of your engine.

Manufacturer	Typical Designation
AC	R **45** TS
Bosch (old)	WA **145** T30
Bosch (new)	HR **8** Y
Champion	RBL **15** Y
Fram/Autolite	**4** 15
Mopar	P-**62** PR
Motorcraft	BRF-**42**
NGK	BP **5** ES-15
Nippondenso	W **16** EP
Prestolite	14GR **5** 2A

On AC, Bosch (new), Champion, Fram/Autolite, Mopar, Motorcraft and Prestolite, a higher number indicates a hotter plug. On Bosch (old), NGK and Nippondenso, a higher number indicates a colder plug.

4. Make sure the spark plugs are properly gapped. See the Tune-Up Specifications in this book.

5. Be sure the spark plugs are firing efficiently. The illustrations on the next 2 pages show you how to "read" the firing end of the spark plug.

6. Check the ignition timing and set it to specifications. Tests show that almost all cars have incorrect ignition timing by more than 2°.

veyed over 6,000 cars nationwide, they found that a tune-up, on cars that needed one, increased fuel economy over 11%. Replacing worn plugs alone, accounted for a 3% increase. The same test also revealed that 8 out of every 10 vehicles will have some maintenance deficiency that will directly affect fuel economy, emissions or performance. Most of this mileage-robbing neglect could be prevented with regular maintenance.

Modern engines require that all of the functioning systems operate properly for maximum efficiency. A malfunction anywhere wastes fuel. You can keep your vehicle running as efficiently and economically as possible, by being aware of your vehicle's operating and performance characteristics. If your vehicle suddenly develops performance or fuel economy problems it could be due to one or more of the following:

PROBLEM	POSSIBLE CAUSE
Engine Idles Rough	Ignition timing, idle mixture, vacuum leak or something amiss in the emission control system.
Hesitates on Acceleration	Dirty carburetor or fuel filter, improper accelerator pump setting, ignition timing or fouled spark plugs.
Starts Hard or Fails to Start	Worn spark plugs, improperly set automatic choke, ice (or water) in fuel system.
Stalls Frequently	Automatic choke improperly adjusted and possible dirty air filter or fuel filter.
Performs Sluggishly	Worn spark plugs, dirty fuel or air filter, ignition timing or automatic choke out of adjustment.

Check spark plug wires on conventional point type ignition for cracks by bending them in a loop around your finger.

Be sure that spark plug wires leading to adjacent cylinders do not run too close together. (Photo courtesy Champion Spark Plug Co.)

7. If your vehicle does not have electronic ignition, check the points, rotor and cap as specified.

8. Check the spark plug wires (used with conventional point-type ignitions) for cracks and burned or broken insulation by bending them in a loop around your finger. Cracked wires decrease fuel efficiency by failing to deliver full voltage to the spark plugs. One misfiring spark plug can cost you as much as 2 mpg.

9. Check the routing of the plug wires. Misfiring can be the result of spark plug leads to adjacent cylinders running parallel to each other and too close together. One wire tends to pick up voltage from the other causing it to fire "out of time".

10. Check all electrical and ignition circuits for voltage drop and resistance.

11. Check the distributor mechanical and/or vacuum advance mechanisms for proper functioning. The vacuum advance can be checked by twisting the distributor plate in the opposite direction of rotation. It should spring back when released.

12. Check and adjust the valve clearance on engines with mechanical lifters. The clearance should be slightly loose rather than too tight.

SPARK PLUG DIAGNOSIS

Normal

APPEARANCE: This plug is typical of one operating normally. The insulator nose varies from a light tan to grayish color with slight electrode wear. The presence of slight deposits is normal on used plugs and will have no adverse effect on engine performance. The spark plug heat range is correct for the engine and the engine is running normally.

CAUSE: Properly running engine.

RECOMMENDATION: Before reinstalling this plug, the electrodes should be cleaned and filed square. Set the gap to specifications. If the plug has been in service for more than 10-12,000 miles, the entire set should probably be replaced with a fresh set of the same heat range.

Oil Deposits

APPEARANCE: The firing end of the plug is covered with a wet, oily coating.

CAUSE: The problem is poor oil control. On high mileage engines, oil is leaking past the rings or valve guides into the combustion chamber. A common cause is also a plugged PCV valve, and a ruptured fuel pump diaphragm can also cause this condition. Oil fouled plugs such as these are often found in new or recently overhauled engines, before normal oil control is achieved, and can be cleaned and reinstalled.

RECOMMENDATION: A hotter spark plug may temporarily relieve the problem, but the engine is probably in need of work.

Incorrect Heat Range

APPEARANCE: The effects of high temperature on a spark plug are indicated by clean white, often blistered insulator. This can also be accompanied by excessive wear of the electrode, and the absence of deposits.

CAUSE: Check for the correct spark plug heat range. A plug which is too hot for the engine can result in overheating. A car operated mostly at high speeds can require a colder plug. Also check ignition timing, cooling system level, fuel mixture and leaking intake manifold.

RECOMMENDATION: If all ignition and engine adjustments are known to be correct, and no other malfunction exists, install spark plugs one heat range colder.

Photos Courtesy Fram Corporation

Carbon Deposits

APPEARANCE: Carbon fouling is easily identified by the presence of dry, soft, black, sooty deposits.

CAUSE: Changing the heat range can often lead to carbon fouling, as can prolonged slow, stop-and-start driving. If the heat range is correct, carbon fouling can be attributed to a rich fuel mixture, sticking choke, clogged air cleaner, worn breaker points, retarded timing or low compression. If only one or two plugs are carbon fouled, check for corroded or cracked wires on the affected plugs. Also look for cracks in the distributor cap between the towers of affected cylinders.

RECOMMENDATION: After the problem is corrected, these plugs can be cleaned and reinstalled if not worn severely.

MMT Fouled

APPEARANCE: Spark plugs fouled by MMT (Methycyclopentadienyl Maganese Tricarbonyl) have reddish, rusty appearance on the insulator and side electrode.

CAUSE: MMT is an anti-knock additive in gasoline used to replace lead. During the combustion process, the MMT leaves a reddish deposit on the insulator and side electrode.

RECOMMENDATION: No engine malfunction is indicated and the deposits will not affect plug performance any more than lead deposits (see Ash Deposits). MMT fouled plugs can be cleaned, regapped and reinstalled.

High Speed Glazing

APPEARANCE: Glazing appears as shiny coating on the plug, either yellow or tan in color.

CAUSE: During hard, fast acceleration, plug temperatures rise suddenly. Deposits from normal combustion have no chance to fluff-off; instead, they melt on the insulator forming an electrically conductive coating which causes misfiring.

RECOMMENDATION: Glazed plugs are not easily cleaned. They should be replaced with a fresh set of plugs of the correct heat range. If the condition recurs, using plugs with a heat range one step colder may cure the problem.

Ash (Lead) Deposits

APPEARANCE: Ash deposits are characterized by light brown or white colored deposits crusted on the side or center electrodes. In some cases it may give the plug a rusty appearance.

CAUSE: Ash deposits are normally derived from oil or fuel additives burned during normal combustion. Normally they are harmless, though excessive amounts can cause misfiring. If deposits are excessive in short mileage, the valve guides may be worn.

RECOMMENDATION: Ash-fouled plugs can be cleaned, gapped and reinstalled.

Detonation

APPEARANCE: Detonation is usually characterized by a broken plug insulator.

CAUSE: A portion of the fuel charge will begin to burn spontaneously, from the increased heat following ignition. The explosion that results applies extreme pressure to engine components, frequently damaging spark plugs and pistons.

Detonation can result by over-advanced ignition timing, inferior gasoline (low octane) lean air/fuel mixture, poor carburetion, engine lugging or an increase in compression ratio due to combustion chamber deposits or engine modification.

RECOMMENDATION: Replace the plugs after correcting the problem.

Photos Courtesy Champion Spark Plug Co.

EMISSION CONTROLS

13. Be aware of the general condition of the emission control system. It contributes to reduced pollution and should be serviced regularly to maintain efficient engine operation.

14. Check all vacuum lines for dried, cracked or brittle conditions. Something as simple as a leaking vacuum hose can cause poor performance and loss of economy.

15. Avoid tampering with the emission control system. Attempting to improve fuel econ-

FUEL SYSTEM

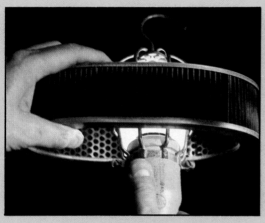

Check the air filter with a light behind it. If you can see light through the filter it can be reused.

Extremely clogged filters should be discarded and replaced with a new one.

18. Replace the air filter regularly. A dirty air filter richens the air/fuel mixture and can increase fuel consumption as much as 10%. Tests show that ⅓ of all vehicles have air filters in need of replacement.

19. Replace the fuel filter at least as often as recommended.

20. Set the idle speed and carburetor mixture to specifications.

21. Check the automatic choke. A sticking or malfunctioning choke wastes gas.

22. During the summer months, adjust the automatic choke for a leaner mixture which will produce faster engine warm-ups.

COOLING SYSTEM

29. Be sure all accessory drive belts are in good condition. Check for cracks or wear.

30. Adjust all accessory drive belts to proper tension.

31. Check all hoses for swollen areas, worn spots, or loose clamps.

32. Check coolant level in the radiator or expansion tank.

33. Be sure the thermostat is operating properly. A stuck thermostat delays engine warm-up and a cold engine uses nearly twice as much fuel as a warm engine.

34. Drain and replace the engine coolant at least as often as recommended. Rust and scale

TIRES & WHEELS

38. Check the tire pressure often with a pencil type gauge. Tests by a major tire manufacturer show that 90% of all vehicles have at least 1 tire improperly inflated. Better mileage can be achieved by over-inflating tires, but never exceed the maximum inflation pressure on the side of the tire.

39. If possible, install radial tires. Radial tires deliver as much as ½ mpg more than bias belted tires.

40. Avoid installing super-wide tires. They only create extra rolling resistance and decrease fuel mileage. Stick to the manufacturer's recommendations.

41. Have the wheels properly balanced.

omy by tampering with emission controls is more likely to worsen fuel economy than improve it. Emission control changes on modern engines are not readily reversible.

16. Clean (or replace) the EGR valve and lines as recommended.

17. Be sure that all vacuum lines and hoses are reconnected properly after working under the hood. An unconnected or misrouted vacuum line can wreak havoc with engine performance.

23. Check for fuel leaks at the carburetor, fuel pump, fuel lines and fuel tank. Be sure all lines and connections are tight.

24. Periodically check the tightness of the carburetor and intake manifold attaching nuts and bolts. These are a common place for vacuum leaks to occur.

25. Clean the carburetor periodically and lubricate the linkage.

26. The condition of the tailpipe can be an excellent indicator of proper engine combustion. After a long drive at highway speeds, the inside of the tailpipe should be a light grey in color. Black or soot on the insides indicates an overly rich mixture.

27. Check the fuel pump pressure. The fuel pump may be supplying more fuel than the engine needs.

28. Use the proper grade of gasoline for your engine. Don't try to compensate for knocking or "pinging" by advancing the ignition timing. This practice will only increase plug temperature and the chances of detonation or pre-ignition with relatively little performance gain.

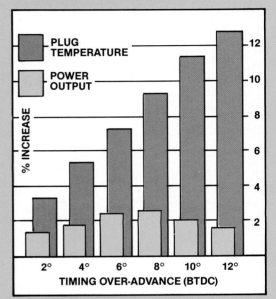

Increasing ignition timing past the specified setting results in a drastic increase in spark plug temperature with increased chance of detonation or preignition. Performance increase is considerably less. (Photo courtesy Champion Spark Plug Co.)

that form in the engine should be flushed out to allow the engine to operate at peak efficiency.

35. Clean the radiator of debris that can decrease cooling efficiency.

36. Install a flex-type or electric cooling fan, if you don't have a clutch type fan. Flex fans use curved plastic blades to push more air at low speeds when more cooling is needed; at high speeds the blades flatten out for less resistance. Electric fans only run when the engine temperature reaches a predetermined level.

37. Check the radiator cap for a worn or cracked gasket. If the cap does not seal properly, the cooling system will not function properly.

42. Be sure the front end is correctly aligned. A misaligned front end actually has wheels going in differed directions. The increased drag can reduce fuel economy by .3 mpg.

43. Correctly adjust the wheel bearings. Wheel bearings that are adjusted too tight increase rolling resistance.

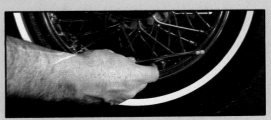

Check tire pressures regularly with a reliable pocket type gauge. Be sure to check the pressure on a cold tire.

GENERAL MAINTENANCE

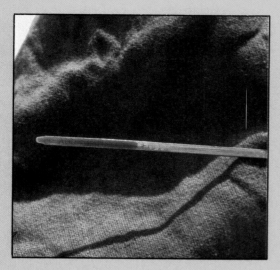

Check the fluid levels (particularly engine oil) on a regular basis. Be sure to check the oil for grit, water or other contamination.

A vacuum gauge is another excellent indicator of internal engine condition and can also be installed in the dash as a mileage indicator.

44. Periodically check the fluid levels in the engine, power steering pump, master cylinder, automatic transmission and drive axle.

45. Change the oil at the recommended interval and change the filter at every oil change. Dirty oil is thick and causes extra friction between moving parts, cutting efficiency and increasing wear. A worn engine requires more frequent tune-ups and gets progressively worse fuel economy. In general, use the lightest viscosity oil for the driving conditions you will encounter.

46. Use the recommended viscosity fluids in the transmission and axle.

47. Be sure the battery is fully charged for fast starts. A slow starting engine wastes fuel.

48. Be sure battery terminals are clean and tight.

49. Check the battery electrolyte level and add distilled water if necessary.

50. Check the exhaust system for crushed pipes, blockages and leaks.

51. Adjust the brakes. Dragging brakes or brakes that are not releasing create increased drag on the engine.

52. Install a vacuum gauge or miles-per-gallon gauge. These gauges visually indicate engine vacuum in the intake manifold. High vacuum = good mileage and low vacuum = poorer mileage. The gauge can also be an excellent indicator of internal engine conditions.

53. Be sure the clutch is properly adjusted. A slipping clutch wastes fuel.

54. Check and periodically lubricate the heat control valve in the exhaust manifold. A sticking or inoperative valve prevents engine warm-up and wastes gas.

55. Keep accurate records to check fuel economy over a period of time. A sudden drop in fuel economy may signal a need for tune-up or other maintenance.

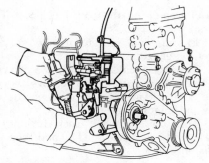

Removing the injection pump

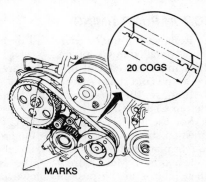

20 COGS

MARKS

Timing mark alignment on the injection pump drive belt

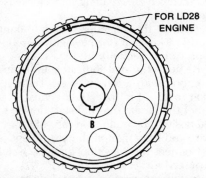

Make sure the No. 1 cam lobe is in this position

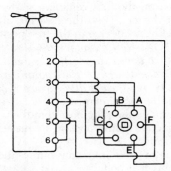

1
2
3
4
5
6

B A
C
D
F
E

Injection tube routing

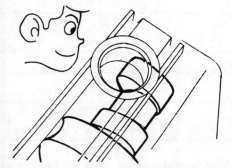

FOR LD28 ENGINE

B

Injection pump drive gear alignment marks

15. Remove the injection pump assembly with the injection tubes attached.

NOTE: *If you plan to measure plunger lift, remove the injection tubes before removing the pump.*

Installation is in the reverse order of removal. Observe the following:

1. Set the No. 1 cylinder at TDC of the compression stroke. Make sure that the grooves in the rear plate and the flywheel align and that the No. 1 cam lobe on the camshaft is in the position shown.

2. Install the injection pump and temporarily tighten the mounting bolts.

3. Use the alignment marks as shown in the illustration and install the injection pump drive gear. Tighten the nut to 43–51 ft. lbs. (59–69 Nm).

NOTE: *The injection pump drive shaft is tapered.*

If the drive gear is difficult to install, use a plastic mallet and drive it into place.

4. Make sure that the tensioner pulley is still in the free position and slide the injection drive belt over the pulleys.

5. The drive belt should have two timing marks on it. Align one with the mark on the crank pulley and the other with the mark on the drive gear. If the timing marks on the drive belt are not clear enough to read, set the marks on the drive gear and the crank pulley so that there are 20 cogs of the drive belt between them when it is installed.

6. Loosen the spring set pin and the tensioner so that the belt is automatically set to the "tension" position.

7. Adjust the injection timing as detailed later in this chapter.

8. Tighten the injection pump nuts to 12–15 ft. lbs. (16–21 Nm) and the bracket bolt to 22–26 ft. lbs. (30–35 Nm).

9. Reconnect the injection tubes. Connect them to the cylinders in this order: 4, 2, 6, 1, 5, 3.

10. Bleed the air from the fuel system as detailed later in this chapter.

INJECTION PUMP TIMING

1. Remove the under cover and drain the coolant as detailed in Chapter 1.

2. Remove the coolant hoses that are connected to the cold start device.

3. Remove the power steering pump as detailed in Chapter 8.

4. Set the No. 1 cylinder at TDC of its compression stroke. Make sure that the grooves in the rear plate and the drive plate are aligned with each other. Make sure that the No. 1 camshaft lobe is in the position shown in the illustration.

5. Using two wrenches, remove the fuel injection tubes as detailed later in this chapter.

6. Loosen the fork retaining screw on the cold start device. Turn the fork 90° and then set the cold start device in the free position.

CAUTION: *Never remove the screw on the cold start device wire. If it should be removed accidentally, the pump assembly should be readjusted at a service shop specified by the manufacturer.*

7. Remove the plug bolt from the rear side of the injection pump and, in its place, attach a dial indicator.

8. Loosen the injection pump mounting nuts and bracket bolt.

9. Turn the crankshaft counterclockwise 15

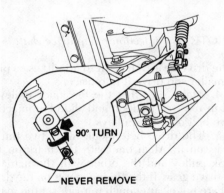

Loosen the fork retaining screw on the cold start device

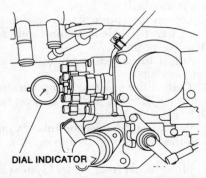

Remove the plug bolt and attach a dial indicator

to 20 degrees from the No. 1 cylinder TDC position.

10. Find the dial indicator needle rest point and set the gauge to zero.

11. Turn the crankshaft clockwise two complete revolutions in order to remove the play in the camshaft mechanism. Loosen the tensioner and then retighten it.

12. Turn the crankshaft clockwise until the No. 1 cylinder is again at TDC and then read the dial indicator.

	Plunger Lift mm (in) For Low Altitudes
M/T	0.85 ± 0.03 (0.0335 ± 0.0012)
A/T	0.81 − 0.03 (0.0319 ± 0.0012)

	For High Altitudes (Non-California Model Only)
M/T	0.90 ± 0.03 (0.0354 ± 0.0012)
A/T	0.85 ± 0.03 (0.0335 ± 0.0012)

13. If the dial indicator is not within the above range, turn the injection pump counterclockwise to increase the reading and clockwise to decrease it.

14. Tighten the injection pump mounting nuts and bracket bolt (torque figures are given in the preceding section).

15. Remove the dial indicator and reinstall the plug bolt with a new washer. Tighten the plug bolt to 10–14 ft. lbs. (14–20 Nm).

16. Set the fork at the cold start device in its original position by pulling on the cold start device wire and then tighten the fork screw.

17. Connect the injection tubes as detailed in the preceding section.

18. Install the power steering pump, connect the cold start device water hoses, refill the pump with coolant and replace the under cover.

BLEED THE FUEL SYSTEM

NOTE: *Air should be bled from the fuel system whenever the injection pump is removed or the fuel system is repaired.*

1. Loosen the priming pump vent screw and pump a few times. Make sure that the fuel overflows at the vent screw.

2. Tighten the vent screw.

3. Disconnect the fuel return hose and install a suitable hose over the overflow connector. Place a small pan under the overflow hose.

4. Prime the priming pump to make sure that the fuel overflows at the open end of the hose.

5. Remove the pan and the overflow hose and then install the return hose.

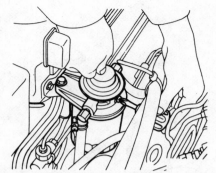

Loosen the priming pump vent screw on the fuel filter

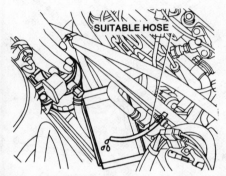

Install a suitable hose over the overflow connector

Fuel Injectors

REMOVAL AND INSTALLATION

1. Remove the injection tubes at the injector and then remove the spill tube assembly.

2. Unscrew the two mounting bolts and pull out the injectors and their washers.

3. Installation is in the reverse order of removal. Tighten the injector mounting nuts to 12–15 ft. lbs. (16–21 Nm). Tighten the injection tube-to-injector nut to 16–18 ft. lbs. (22–25 Nm). Always use a new injector small washer.

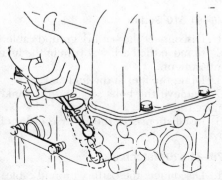

Use tweezers to remove and install injector small washer

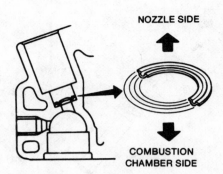

Proper positioning of the small washer

Fuel Tank

REMOVAL AND INSTALLATION

610 and 710 Station Wagon

1. Disconnect the battery ground cable.

2. Remove the inspection plate from the rear floor. Disconnect the gauge wiring.

3. Remove the spare tire.

4. Place a pan under the drain plug and remove the plug.

5. Disconnect the filler hose, ventilation lines, and the fuel line from the tank.

6. Remove the retaining bolts and remove the tank.

7. Installation is the reverse of removal.

1977–79 200SX

1. Disconnect the battery ground cable.

2. Remove the rubber plug located on the floor panel above the left side rear axle.

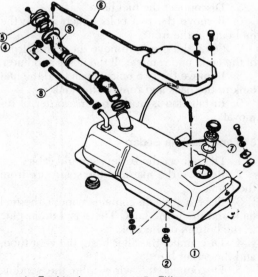

1. Fuel tank	5. Filler cap
2. Drain plug	6. Breather tube
3. Filler hose	7. Fuel gauge unit
4. Filler neck	8. Ventilation hose

710 fuel tank

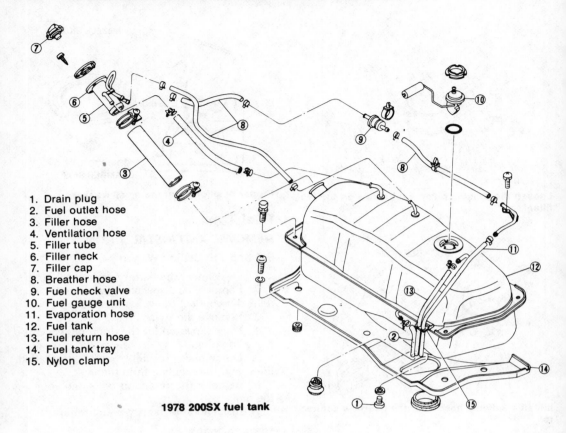

1. Drain plug
2. Fuel outlet hose
3. Filler hose
4. Ventilation hose
5. Filler tube
6. Filler neck
7. Filler cap
8. Breather hose
9. Fuel check valve
10. Fuel gauge unit
11. Evaporation hose
12. Fuel tank
13. Fuel return hose
14. Fuel tank tray
15. Nylon clamp

1978 200SX fuel tank

3. Remove the drain plug and drain the tank.

4. Detach the rear seat cushion, seat back, and rear seat backboard.

5. Disconnect the fuel hose.

6. Remove the two bolts which secure the fuel tank in the front.

7. Open the trunk, remove the trim in front of the tank, and remove all the hoses and lines.

8. Remove the two bolts which hold the fuel tank in the back and remove the tank.

9. Installation is in the reverse order of removal.

810 and Maxima Sedan

1. Disconnect the battery ground cable.

2. Remove the mat and the spare tire from the trunk.

3. Place a suitable container under the fuel tank and drain the tank. There is a drain plug in the bottom of the tank.

4. Disconnect the filler hose, the vent tube, and the outlet hose.

5. Disconnect the wires from the sending unit.

6. Remove the four belts securing the fuel tank and remove the tank.

7. Installation is in the reverse order of removal.

810 and Maxima Station Wagon

1. Disconnect the battery ground cable.

2. Loosen the tire hanger and take out the spare tire.

3. Loosen the drain plug and drain the tank.

4. Disconnect the filler hose, ventilation hose, evaporation hose, and outlet hose.

5. Remove the tire stopper. Disconnect the wiring from the gauge.

6. Remove the four bolts securing the fuel tank and remove the tank.

7. Installation is in the reverse order of removal.

1978–81 510 Sedan

1. Disconnect the battery ground cable.

2. Remove the back seat trim in the luggage compartment.

3. Drain the fuel in the fuel tank.

5. Remove the bolts securing the tank and remove the tank.

6. Installation is in the reverse order of removal.

1978–81 510 Hatchback

1. Disconnect the battery ground cable.

2. Drain the fuel from the tank, then disconnect the fuel hose.

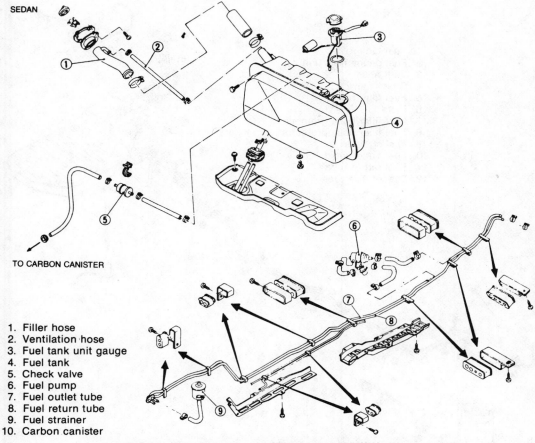

SEDAN

TO CARBON CANISTER

1. Filler hose
2. Ventilation hose
3. Fuel tank unit gauge
4. Fuel tank
5. Check valve
6. Fuel pump
7. Fuel outlet tube
8. Fuel return tube
9. Fuel strainer
10. Carbon canister

1978 810 sedan fuel tank and lines—most models similar

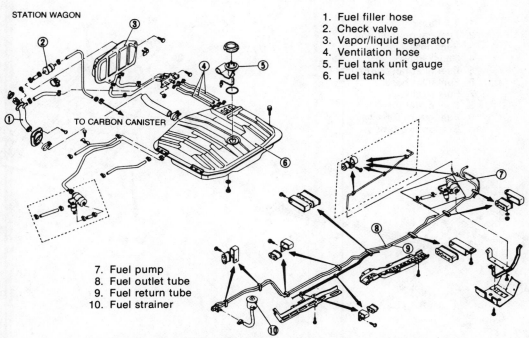

STATION WAGON

TO CARBON CANISTER

1. Fuel filler hose
2. Check valve
3. Vapor/liquid separator
4. Ventilation hose
5. Fuel tank unit gauge
6. Fuel tank

7. Fuel pump
8. Fuel outlet tube
9. Fuel return tube
10. Fuel strainer

1978 810 station wagon fuel tank and lines—most models similar

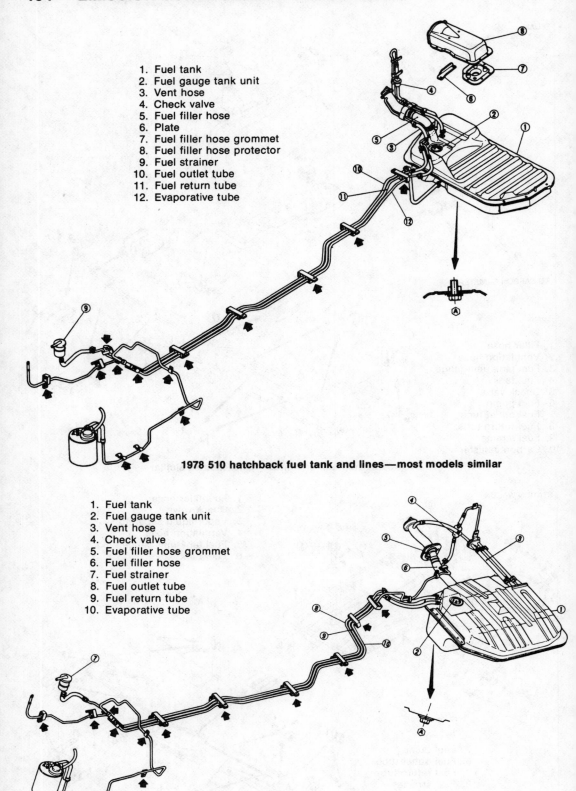

1. Fuel tank
2. Fuel gauge tank unit
3. Vent hose
4. Check valve
5. Fuel filler hose
6. Plate
7. Fuel filler hose grommet
8. Fuel filler hose protector
9. Fuel strainer
10. Fuel outlet tube
11. Fuel return tube
12. Evaporative tube

1978 510 hatchback fuel tank and lines—most models similar

1. Fuel tank
2. Fuel gauge tank unit
3. Vent hose
4. Check valve
5. Fuel filler hose grommet
6. Fuel filler hose
7. Fuel strainer
8. Fuel outlet tube
9. Fuel return tube
10. Evaporative tube

1978 510 station wagon fuel tank and lines—most models similar

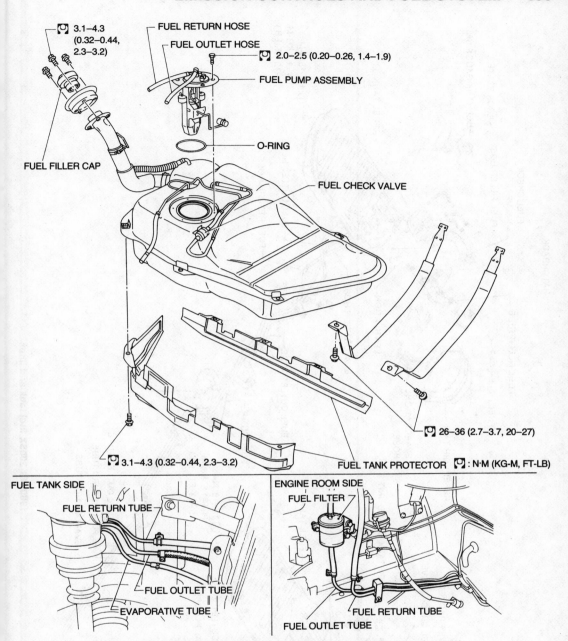

FUEL RETURN HOSE

FUEL OUTLET HOSE

3.1–4.3
(0.32–0.44,
2.3–3.2)

2.0–2.5 (0.20–0.26, 1.4–1.9)

FUEL PUMP ASSEMBLY

O-RING

FUEL CHECK VALVE

FUEL FILLER CAP

26–36 (2.7–3.7, 20–27)

3.1–4.3 (0.32–0.44, 2.3–3.2)

FUEL TANK PROTECTOR : N·M (KG-M, FT-LB)

FUEL TANK SIDE

FUEL RETURN TUBE

FUEL OUTLET TUBE

EVAPORATIVE TUBE

ENGINE ROOM SIDE

FUEL FILTER

FUEL RETURN TUBE

FUEL OUTLET TUBE

1984 and later 200SX fuel tank assembly showing fuel line connections

3. Remove the luggage carpet, luggage board, and fuel filler hose protector.

4. Disconnect all the hoses and wires to the tank.

5. Unbolt the fuel tank and remove it.

6. Installation is in the reverse order of removal.

1978–81 510 Station Wagon

1. Disconnect the battery ground cable.

2. Drain the fuel from the tank. Disconnect all the hoses and lines.

3. Remove the spare tire and fuel tank support.

4. Unbolt and remove the tank.

5. Installation is in the reverse order of removal.

1980—and Later 200SX

1. Remove the battery ground cable.

2. Drain the fuel from the fuel tank.

3. Remove the protector from the luggage compartment, and then remove the following parts:

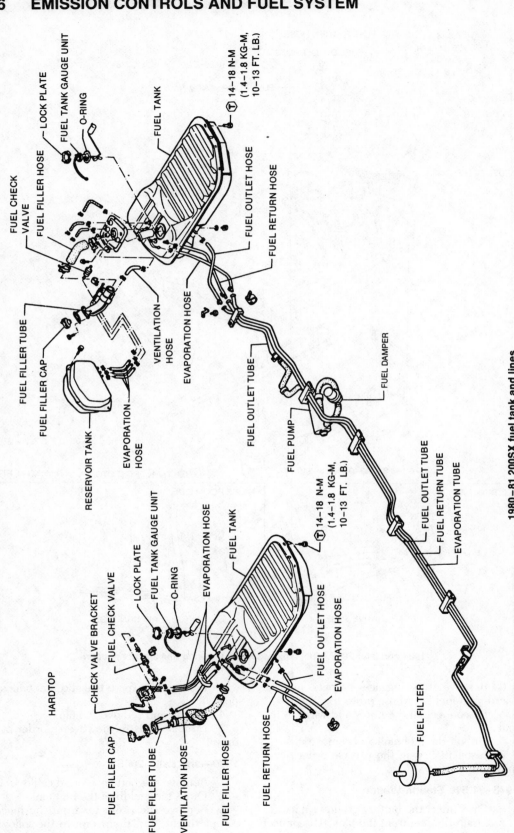

HATCHBACK

FUEL TANK GAUGE UNIT
LOCK PLATE
FUEL FILLER HOSE
O-RING
FUEL TANK

Ⓣ 14–18 N-M
(1.4–1.8 KG-M,
10–13 FT. LB.)

FUEL CHECK VALVE
FUEL FILLER HOSE

FUEL OUTLET HOSE
FUEL RETURN HOSE

FUEL FILLER TUBE
FUEL FILLER CAP

VENTILATION HOSE
EVAPORATION HOSE

RESERVOIR TANK
EVAPORATION HOSE

FUEL OUTLET TUBE

FUEL PUMP

FUEL DAMPER

FUEL OUTLET TUBE
FUEL RETURN TUBE
EVAPORATION TUBE

1980–81 200SX fuel tank and lines

HARDTOP

CHECK VALVE BRACKET
FUEL CHECK VALVE
LOCK PLATE
FUEL TANK GAUGE UNIT
O-RING
EVAPORATION HOSE
FUEL TANK

Ⓣ 14–18 N-M
(1.4–1.8 KG-M,
10–13 FT. LB.)

FUEL FILLER CAP
FUEL FILLER TUBE
VENTILATION HOSE
FUEL FILLER HOSE
FUEL RETURN HOSE

FUEL OUTLET HOSE
EVAPORATION HOSE

FUEL FILTER

a. Harness connector for the fuel tank gauge unit

b. Ventilation hose

c. Evaporation hoses

d. Fuel filler hose (Hatchback)

4. Remove the following parts from beneath the floor:

a. Fuel outlet hose

b. Fuel return hose

c. Evaporation hose

d. Fuel filler hose (Hardtop)

5. Remove the bolts which secure the fuel tank and remove the tank.

6. Installation is the reverse of removal.

To remove the Reservoir tank from the Hatchback:

1. Remove the battery cable.

2. Remove the protector from the luggage compartment. Also remove the right hand speaker and side lower finisher.

3. Remove the evaporation hoses and then remove the reservoir tank.

4. Installation is the reverse of removal.

Chassis Electrical

5

HEATER

Heater Assembly
REMOVAL AND INSTALLATION
610, 710

1. Disconnect the battery ground cable.
2. Drain the coolant.
3. Detach the coolant inlet and outlet hoses.
4. On the 610, remove the center ventilator grille from the bottom of the instrument panel.
5. Remove the heater duct hose from both sides of the heater unit. Remove the defroster hose or hoses on the 610. On the 710, remove the intake duct and defroster duct from both sides of the heater unit. Remove the console box on the 710 if so equipped.
6. Disconnect the electrical wires of the heater unit (and air conditioner, if so equipped) at their connections.
7. Disconnect and remove the heater control cables.
8. On 710 and 1974–76 610, remove the two bolts on each side of the unit and one on the top. For 1973 610's, remove one attaching bolt from each side and one from the top center of the unit.
9. Remove the unit.
10. Installation is the reverse of removal. Run the engine for a few minutes with the heater on to make sure the system is filled with coolant.

1977–79 200SX

1. Disconnect the battery cable.
2. Drain the engine coolant and remove the heater hoses from the engine side.
3. Inside the passenger compartment, disconnect the lead wires from the heater unit to the instrument harness.
4. At this point, the instrument panel must be removed in order to remove the heater assembly. To remove the panel proceed as follows:
5. Remove the steering wheel cover.
6. Disconnect the speedometer cable and the radio antenna cable.
7. After noting their position, disconnect the following connectors: instrument harness to body, harness to engine room, transistor ignition unit, and the wiring to the console.
8. Remove the bolts securing the column clamp and lower the steering column.
9. Remove the package tray.
10. Remove the bolts which attach the instrument panel to the mounting bracket on the left and right-hand sides.
11. Remove the trim on the right side windshield pillar, and remove the bolt attaching the instrument panel to the pillar.
12. Remove the trim on the top of the instrument panel.
13. Remove the bolts attaching the instrument panel.
14. Move the instrument panel to the right to remove it.
15. Remove the defroster hoses on both sides of the heater unit.
16. If the car is air-conditioned, disconnect the wires to the air-conditioner.
17. Remove the three heater retaining bolts and remove the heater assembly.
18. Installation is in the reverse order of removal.

1980–82 200SX

1. Set the TEMP lever to the HOT position and drain the coolant.
2. Disconnect the heater hoses from the driver's side of the heater unit.
3. At this point the manufacturer suggests you remove the front seats. To do this, remove the plastic covers over the ends of the seat runners, both front and back, to expose the seat

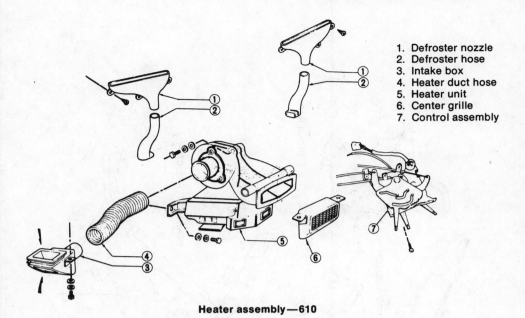

1. Defroster nozzle
2. Defroster hose
3. Intake box
4. Heater duct hose
5. Heater unit
6. Center grille
7. Control assembly

Heater assembly—610

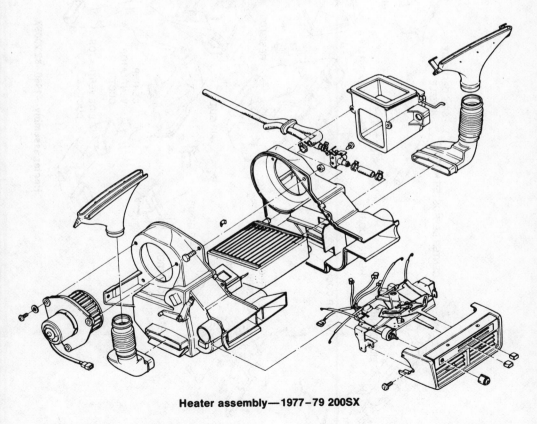

Heater assembly—1977–79 200SX

mounting bolts. Remove the bolts and remove the seats.

4. Remove the console box and the floor carpets.

5. Remove the instrument panel lower covers from both the driver's and passenger's sides of the car. Remove the lower cluster lids.

6. Remove the left hand side ventilator duct.

7. Remove the radio, sound balancer and stereo cassette deck. (See below for procedures).

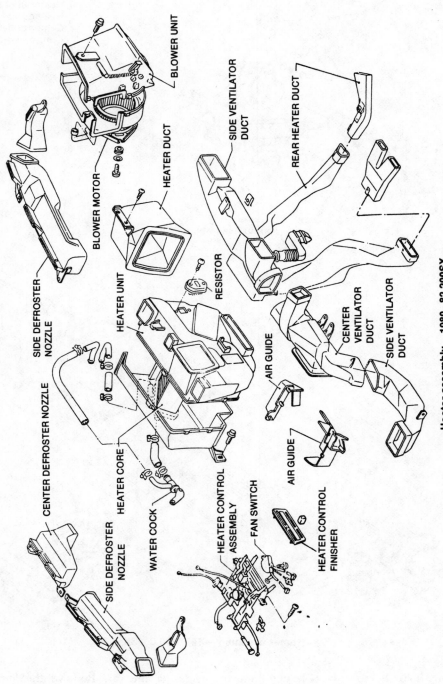

BLOWER UNIT

BLOWER MOTOR

HEATER DUCT

SIDE VENTILATOR DUCT

REAR HEATER DUCT

RESISTOR

HEATER UNIT

CENTER VENTILATOR DUCT

SIDE VENTILATOR DUCT

AIR GUIDE

AIR GUIDE

SIDE DEFROSTER NOZZLE

CENTER DEFROSTER NOZZLE

HEATER CORE

WATER COCK

HEATER CONTROL ASSEMBLY

FAN SWITCH

HEATER CONTROL FINISHER

SIDE DEFROSTER NOZZLE

Heater assembly—1980–82 200SX

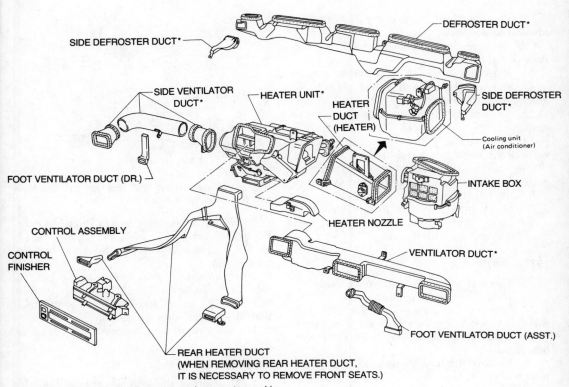

SIDE DEFROSTER DUCT*

DEFROSTER DUCT*

SIDE VENTILATOR DUCT*

HEATER UNIT*

HEATER DUCT (HEATER)

SIDE DEFROSTER DUCT*

Cooling unit (Air conditioner)

FOOT VENTILATOR DUCT (DR.)

INTAKE BOX

HEATER NOZZLE

CONTROL ASSEMBLY

VENTILATOR DUCT*

CONTROL FINISHER

FOOT VENTILATOR DUCT (ASST.)

REAR HEATER DUCT
(WHEN REMOVING REAR HEATER DUCT,
IT IS NECESSARY TO REMOVE FRONT SEATS.)

*For removal, it is necessary to remove instrument assembly.

1984 and later 200SX heater assembly

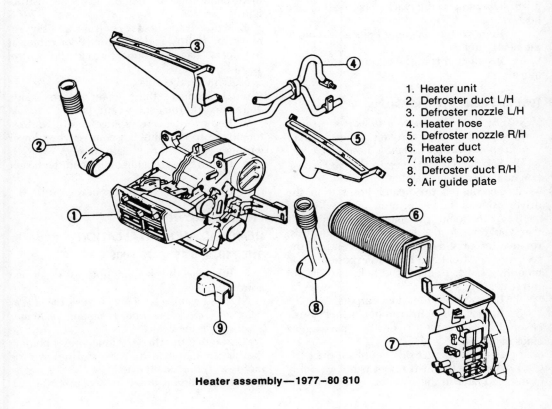

1. Heater unit
2. Defroster duct L/H
3. Defroster nozzle L/H
4. Heater hose
5. Defroster nozzle R/H
6. Heater duct
7. Intake box
8. Defroster duct R/H
9. Air guide plate

Heater assembly—1977–80 810

8. Remove the instrument panel-to-transmission tunnel stay.

9. Remove the rear heater duct from the floor of the vehicle.

10. Remove the center ventilator duct.

11. Remove the left and right-hand side air guides from the lower heater outlets.

12. Disconnect the wire harness connections.

13. Remove the two screws at the bottom sides of the heater unit and the one screw and the top of the unit and remove the unit together with the heater control assembly.

Installation is the reverse of removal.

NOTE: *You may be able to skip several of the above steps if only certain components of the heater unit need service.*

1977–80 810

1. Disconnect the battery ground cable.
2. Drain the engine coolant.
3. Remove the console box and the console box bracket. Remove the front floor mat.
4. Loosen the screws and remove the rear heater duct.
5. Remove the hose clamps and remove the inlet and outlet hoses.
6. Remove the heater duct and remove the defroster hoses from the assembly.
7. Remove the air intake door control cable.
8. Disconnect the wiring harness to the heater.
9. Remove the retaining bolts and remove the heater unit.
10. Installation is in the reverse order of removal.

1981 and Later 810 and Maxima

NOTE: *You may be able to skip several of the following steps if only certain components of the heater assembly need service.*

1. Set the TEMP lever to the HOT position and drain the coolant.
2. Disconnect the heater hoses from the driver's side of the heater unit.
3. At this point the manufacturer suggests that you remove the front seats. To do this, remove the plastic covers over the ends of the seat runners, front and back, to expose the seat mounting bolts. Remove the bolts and lift out the seats.
4. Remove the front floor carpets.
5. Remove the instrument panel lower covers from both the driver's and passenger's sides of the car.
6. Remove the left side ventilator duct.
7. Remove the instrument panel assembly as detailed later in this chapter.

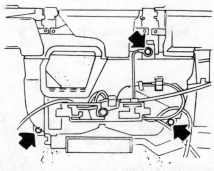

The heater vent on the 1981 and later 810 and Maxima has three mounting bolts

8. Remove the rear heater duct from the floor of the car.

9. Tag and disconnect the wire harness connectors.

10. Remove the two screws at the bottom sides of the heater unit and the one screw from the top of the unit. Lift out the heater together with the heater control assembly.

11. Installation is in the reverse order of removal.

1978–80 510

1. Disconnect the ground cable at the battery. Drain the coolant.
2. Remove the console box on the 510.
3. Remove the driver's side of the instrument panel. See the section below for instructions.
4. Remove the heater control assembly: remove the defroster ducts, vent door cables at the doors, harness connector and the control assembly.
5. Remove the radio.
6. Disconnect the heater ducts, side defrosters and the center vent duct.
7. Remove the screws attaching the defroster nozzle to the unit. Disconnect the blower wiring harness and the heater hoses.
8. Remove the retaining bolts and the heater unit.
9. Installation is the revers of removal.

Heater Blower

REMOVAL AND INSTALLATION

610, 710, and 1977–79 200SX

1. Remove the heater unit as described above.

NOTE: *You may be able to remove the blower on some models without removing the heater unit from the vehicle.*

2. Remove the three or four screws holding the blower motor in the case and remove the motor with the fan attached.
3. Installation is the reverse of removal.

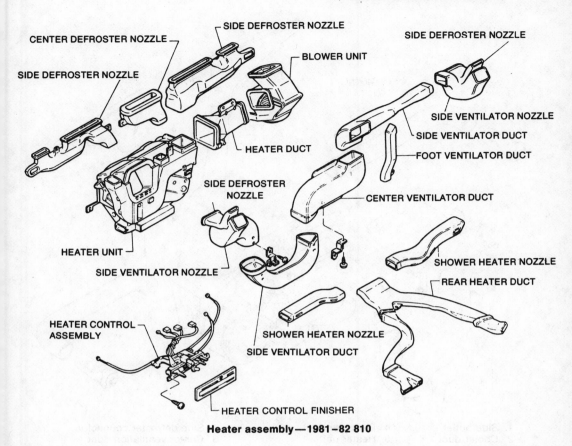

CENTER DEFROSTER NOZZLE

SIDE DEFROSTER NOZZLE

SIDE DEFROSTER NOZZLE

BLOWER UNIT

SIDE DEFROSTER NOZZLE

SIDE VENTILATOR NOZZLE

SIDE VENTILATOR DUCT

FOOT VENTILATOR DUCT

HEATER DUCT

SIDE DEFROSTER NOZZLE

CENTER VENTILATOR DUCT

HEATER UNIT

SIDE VENTILATOR NOZZLE

SHOWER HEATER NOZZLE

REAR HEATER DUCT

HEATER CONTROL ASSEMBLY

SHOWER HEATER NOZZLE

SIDE VENTILATOR DUCT

HEATER CONTROL FINISHER

Heater assembly—1981–82 810

1980–82 200SX

1. Remove the instrument panel lower cover and cluster lid on the right-hand side.

2. Disconnect the negative battery cable.

3. Disconnect the control cable and harness connector from the blower unit.

4. Remove the three bolts and remove the blower unit.

5. Remove the three screws holding the blower motor in the case, unplug the hose running from the rear of the motor into the case

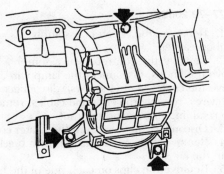

Remove the three bolts and remove the blower—1980–82 200SX

and pull the motor together with the fan out of the case.

6. Installation is the reverse of removal.

810

1. Disconnect the negative battery cable.

2. Remove the heater duct running from the blower case to the heater unit.

3. Disconnect the control cable from the blower case.

4. Disconnect the harness connector.

5. Remove the screws holding the blower case in place and remove the blower case.

6. Remove the three bolts holding the blower motor in place and remove the blower motor.

7. Installation is the reverse of removal.

1978–81 510

1. Disconnect the battery ground cable.

2. Disconnect the blower motor harness connector.

3. Remove the blower motor by removing the three outer retaining screws and pulling the motor with the fan out of the case.

NOTE: *Make sure you remove the three outer screws and not the three screws holding the motor to the backing plate.*

4. Installation is the reverse of removal.

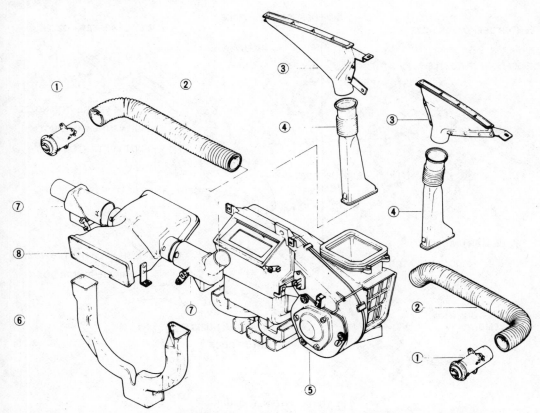

1. Side outlet
2. Cooler duct
3. Defroster nozzle
4. Defroster duct
5. Heater unit
6. Side defroster center duct
7. Side defroster connector
8. Center ventilation duct

Heater assembly—510

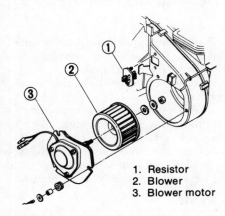

1. Resistor
2. Blower
3. Blower motor

Removing the blower—510

Heater Core
REMOVAL AND INSTALLATION
610 and 710

The heater unit need not be removed to remove the heater core. It must be removed to remove the blower motor.

1. Drain the coolant.
2. Detach the coolant hoses.
3. Disconnect the control cables on the sides of the heater unit.
4. Remove the clips and the cover from the front of the heater unit.
5. Pull out the core.
6. Reverse the procedure for installation. Run the engine with the heater on for a few minutes to make sure that the system fills with coolant.

1977–79 200SX

1. Remove the heater assembly as described earlier.
2. Remove the control lever assembly. Remove the knobs, disconnect the lamp wire, remove the center vent (4 screws), disconnect the fan wires, remove the clips and cables, remove the retaining screws and the unit.
3. Disconnect the hose from the heater cock.
4. Remove the connection rod (with bracket) from the air door.
5. Remove the clips on each side of the box, split the box, and remove the core.
6. Installation is the reverse of removal.

1980–82 200SX

1. Remove the heater unit as described earlier.

2. Remove the hoses from the heater core and remove the core.

3. Installation is the reverse of removal.

810 and Maxima

1. Remove the heater assembly as outlined earlier.

2. Loosen the clips and screws and remove the center ventilation cover and heater control assembly.

3. Remove the screws securing the door shafts.

4. Remove the clips securing the left and right heater cases, and then separate the cases.

5. Remove the heater core.

6. Installation is in the reverse order of removal.

1978–81 510

1. Remove the heater unit as outlined earlier.

2. Loosen the hose clamps and disconnect the inlet and outlet hoses.

3. Remove the clips securing the case halves and separate the cases.

4. Remove the heater core.

5. Installation is in the reverse order of removal.

RADIO

REMOVAL AND INSTALLATION

610 and 710

1. Remove the instrument cluster.

2. Detach all electrical connections.

3. Remove the radio knobs and retaining nuts.

4. Remove the rear support bracket.

5. Remove the radio.

6. Reverse the procedure for installation.

1977–79 200SX

1. The instrument panel must be removed in order to remove the radio. The instrument panel is referred to as the cluster lid in the illustrations.

2. Pull out the radio switch knobs.

3. In order to remove the instrument panel, first remove the steering wheel and cover.

4. Remove the control knobs on the instrument panel by pushing in on them and turning them counterclockwise. Once the knobs are removed, remove the nuts.

5. Remove the instrument panel screws. See the illustration for their location.

6. Disconnect the switch wires (after noting their location) and remove the panel.

7. Loosen the screws and remove the radio from its bracket. Disconnect the wires and pull the radio free.

8. Installation is in the reverse order of removal.

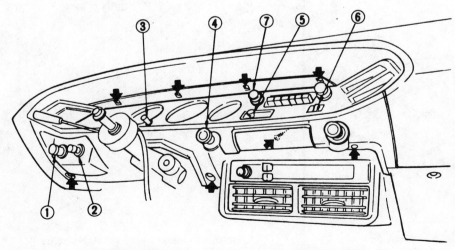

1. Light switch
2. Illumination control knob
3. Trip meter knob
4. Windshield wiper and washer switch knob
5. Hazard switch
6. Rear defogger switch
7. Radio knob

Instrument panel removal points—1977–79 200SX

1980–82 200SX

1. Disconnect the battery. Before removing the radio (audio assembly), you must remove the center instrument cluster which holds the heater controls, etc. Remove the two side screws in the cluster. Remove the heater control and the control panel. Remove the two bolts behind the heater control panel and the two bolts at the case of the cluster. Pull the cluster out of the way after disconnecting the lighter wiring and any other control cables.

2. Remove the radio knobs and fronting panel.

3. Remove the five screws holding the radio assembly in place.

4. Remove the radio after unplugging all connections.

5. Installation is the reverse of removal.

810 and Maxima

1. Disconnect the battery ground cable.

2. Remove the knobs and nuts on the radio and the choke control wire. Remove the ash tray.

3. Remove the steering column cover, and disconnect the main harness connectors.

4. Remove the retaining screws and remove the instrument panel cover.

5. Disconnect the wires from the radio and remove the radio from the bracket.

6. Installation is in the reverse order of removal.

1978–81 510

1. Disconnect the battery ground cable.

2. Remove the steering column covers and disconnect the hazard warning switch connector.

3. Loosen the wiper switch attaching screws and remove the wiper switch.

4. Pull out the ash tray and the heater control knobs.

5. Remove the heater control finisher. See the illustration. Insert a screwdriver into the FAN lever slit to remove the finisher. Remove finisher A. (see the illustration.)

6. Remove the radio knobs, nuts and washers.

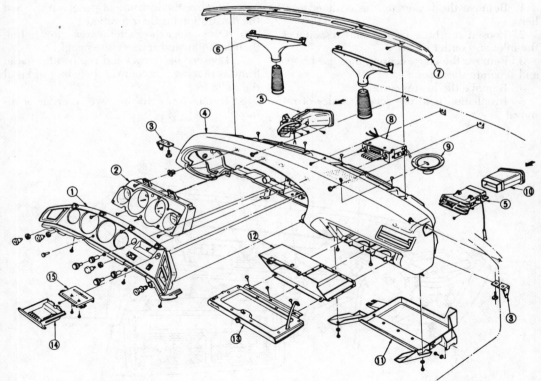

1. Cluster lid	6. Defroster nozzle	11. Package tray
2. Meter assembly	7. Instrument garnish	12. Glove box
3. Instrument mounting lower bracket	8. Radio	13. Glove box lid
4. Instrument pad	9. Speaker	14. Ash tray
5. Ventilation grille	10. Ventilation duct	15. Outer case

1977–79 200SX instrument panel

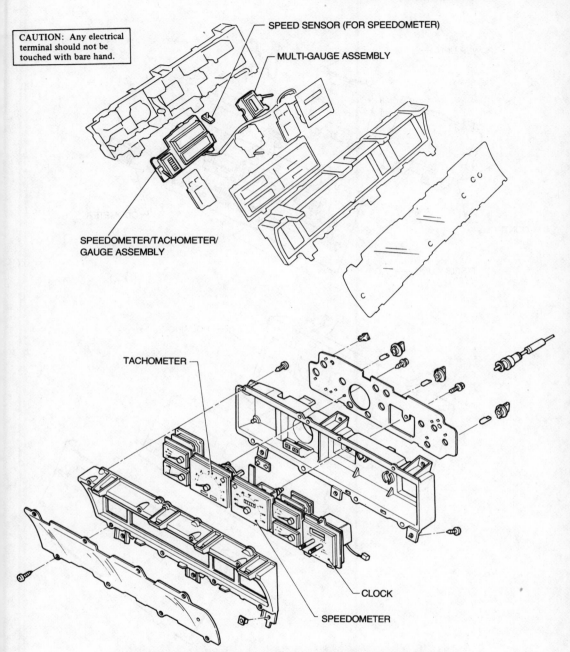

CAUTION: Any electrical terminal should not be touched with bare hand.

SPEED SENSOR (FOR SPEEDOMETER)

MULTI-GAUGE ASSEMBLY

SPEEDOMETER/TACHOMETER/ GAUGE ASSEMBLY

TACHOMETER

CLOCK

SPEEDOMETER

1984 Maxima instrument cluster, electronic cluster (optional) at top

7. Remove the manual choke knob and the defroster control knob.

8. Disconnect the following connectors:
   a. center illumination light
   b. cigarette lighter
   c. clock
   d. turn signal switch

9. Remove the screws from the instrument panel (referred to as cluster lid A in the illustration). The black arrows mark the screws locations.

10. Remove the instrument panel cover. Remove the connections from the radio and remove the radio from its bracket.

11. Installation is in the reverse order of removal.

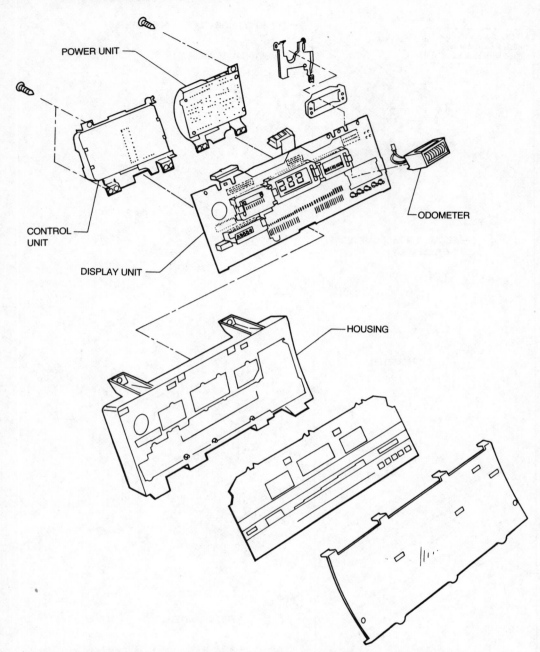

POWER UNIT

CONTROL UNIT

DISPLAY UNIT

ODOMETER

HOUSING

1984 200SX electronic digital instrument cluster. No user-serviceable equipment is found here

WINDSHIELD WIPER MOTOR AND LINKAGE

REMOVAL AND INSTALLATION

610, 710, 810, Maxima 1977–79 200SX

1. Disconnect the battery ground cable.
2. The wiper motor and linkage are accessible from under the hood. Raise the wiper blade from the windshield and remove the retaining nut. Remove the wiper blades and arms.
3. Remove the nuts holding the wiper pivots to the body.
4. Remove the screws holding the wiper motor to the firewall.
5. Disconnect the wiper motor wiring connector.
6. Remove the cowl air intake grille.

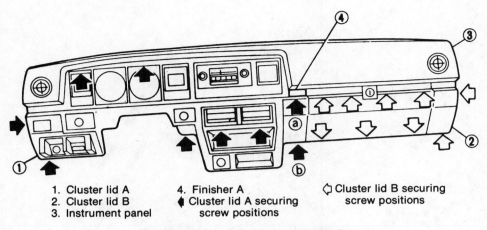

1. Cluster lid A
2. Cluster lid B
3. Instrument panel
4. Finisher A
◀ Cluster lid A securing screw positions
◇ Cluster lid B securing screw positions

1978 510 instrument panel removal points

7. Disconnect the wiper motor from the linkage.
8. Remove the linkage assembly through the cowl top.
9. Installation is the reverse of removal.
NOTE: *If the wipers do not park correctly, adjust the position of the automatic stop cover of the wiper motor, if so equipped.*

1978–81 510

1. Disconnect the battery ground cable.
2. Remove the wiper motor.
3. Remove the wiper link inspection cover under the hood.
4. Remove the wiper arms from the pivot shafts by lifting the arms then removing the attaching nuts.
5. Loosen and remove the large nuts securing the pivot shafts to the body.
6. Remove the linkage through the inspection hole.

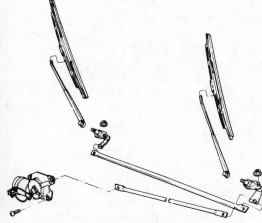

Windshield wiper motor and linkage—710, 810 and Maxima similar

7. Installation is the reverse of removal.
NOTE: *Make sure you install the wiper arms in the correct positions by running the system without the arms on, stopping it, then attaching the arms.*

1980–84 200SX

1. Disconnect the battery ground cable.
2. Open the hood and disconnect the motor wiring connection.
3. Unbolt the motor from the body.
4. Disconnect the wiper linkage from the motor and remove the motor.
5. Installation is the reverse of removal.

INSTRUMENT CLUSTER

REMOVAL AND INSTALLATION

610 and 710

1. Disconnect the battery ground cable.
2. Remove the four screws and the steering column cover.
3. Remove the screws which attach the cluster face. Two are just above the steering column, and there is one inside each of the outer instrument recesses.
4. Pull the cluster lid forward.
5. Disconnect the multiple connector.
6. Disconnect the speedometer cable.
7. Disconnect any other wiring.
8. Remove the cluster face.
9. Remove the odometer knob if the vehicle has one.
10. Remove the six screws and the cluster.
11. Instruments may now be readily replaced.
12. Reverse the procedure for installation.
NOTE: *It may be necessary to drop the steering column to aid removal.*

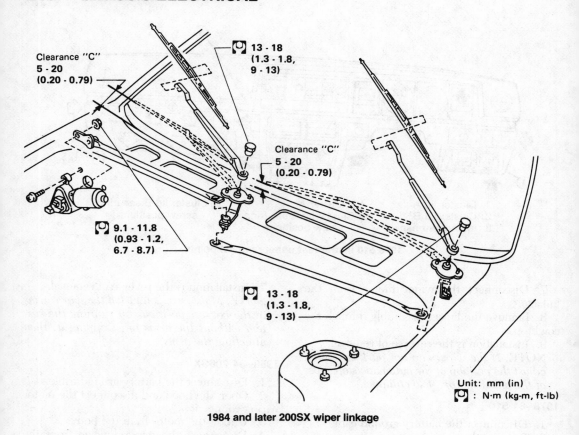

Clearance "C"
5 - 20
(0.20 - 0.79)

13 - 18
(1.3 - 1.8,
9 - 13)

Clearance "C"
5 - 20
(0.20 - 0.79)

9.1 - 11.8
(0.93 - 1.2,
6.7 - 8.7)

13 - 18
(1.3 - 1.8,
9 - 13)

Unit: mm (in)
: N·m (kg-m, ft-lb)

1984 and later 200SX wiper linkage

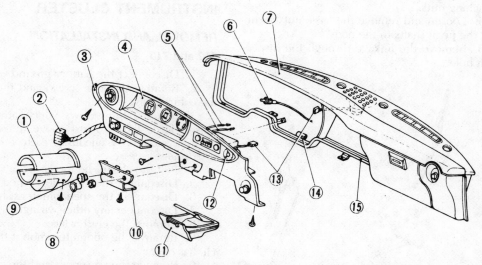

1. Steering column covers	6. Speedometer cable	11. Ash tray
2. Instrument harness	7. Upper instrument pad	12. Clock
3. Cluster cover	8. Wiper/washer switch knob	13. Speaker harness
4. Gauges	9. Light control switch	14. Illumination bulb
5. Light monitor	10. Cluster cover	15. Instrument panel

710 instrument cluster removal

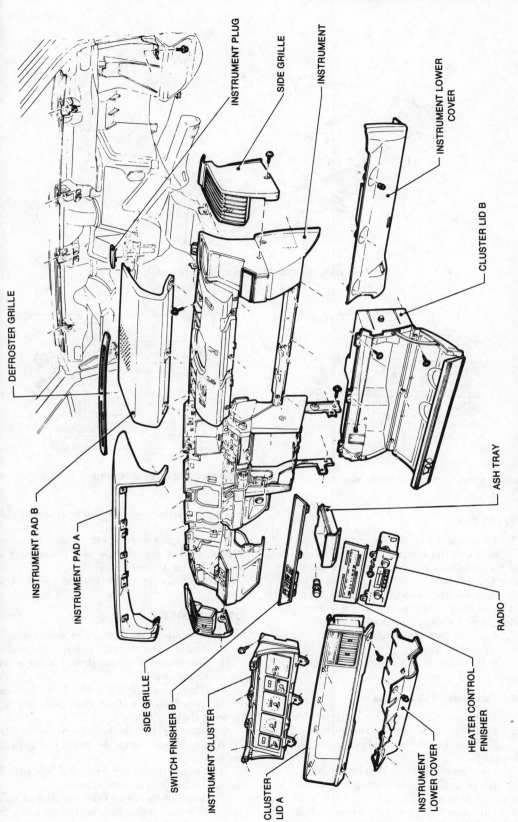

INSTRUMENT PLUG

SIDE GRILLE

INSTRUMENT

INSTRUMENT LOWER COVER

CLUSTER LID B

DEFROSTER GRILLE

INSTRUMENT PAD B

INSTRUMENT PAD A

SIDE GRILLE

SWITCH FINISHER B

INSTRUMENT CLUSTER

CLUSTER LID A

INSTRUMENT LOWER COVER

HEATER CONTROL FINISHER

ASH TRAY

RADIO

1981 and later 810 and Maxima instrument panel

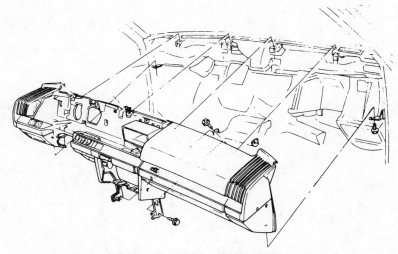

Removing the 1984 Maxima instrument panel

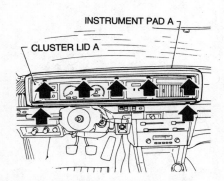

Maxima instrument panel/cluster screws

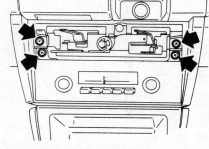

Radio securing screws, Maxima

1977–80 810

1. Disconnect the battery ground cable.
2. Remove the knobs and nuts on the radio and the knob on the choke control wire. Remove the ash tray.
3. Remove the steering column covers.
4. Disconnect the harness connectors after noting their location and marking them.
5. Remove the retaining screws and remove the instrument panel.
6. Installation is in the reverse order of removal.

1981– and later 810 and Maxima

1. Disconnect the negative battery cable.
2. Remove the instrument lower cover.
3. Remove the steering wheel as detailed in Chapter 8.
4. Disconnect the speedometer cable.
5. Remove the six mounting screws and lift out the cluster lid.
6. Unscrew the mounting bolts and lift off the left side instrument pad (this is the hooded

part of the dashboard that the instrument cluster sits in).
7. Loosen the instrument cluster mounting screws, pull it out slightly and disconnect all wiring. Remove the cluster.
8. Installation is in the reverse order of removal.

1977–79 200SX

1. Disconnect the battery ground cable.
2. Remove the steering column covers.
3. Disconnect the speedometer cable and the radio antenna.
4. Disconnect all the wires from the back of the panel after noting their location and marking them.
5. Remove the bolts which secure the steering column clamp. Remove the package tray.
6. Unbolt the panel from the brackets on the left and right-hand sides.
7. Remove the right-side windshield pillar trim and remove the bolt which attaches the panel to the pillar.

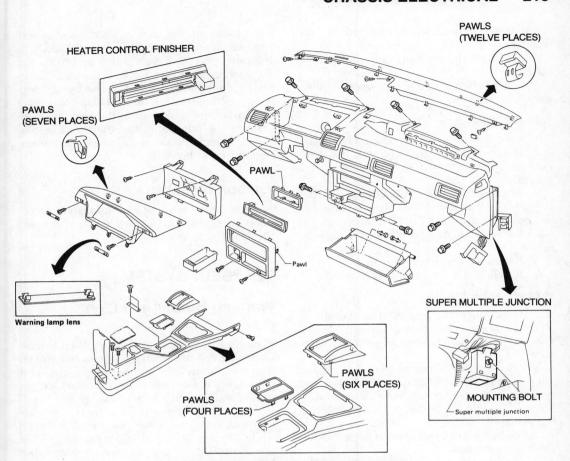

HEATER CONTROL FINISHER

PAWLS (TWELVE PLACES)

PAWLS (SEVEN PLACES)

PAWL

Pawl

Warning lamp lens

PAWLS (SIX PLACES)

PAWLS (FOUR PLACES)

SUPER MULTIPLE JUNCTION

MOUNTING BOLT

Super multiple junction

1984 and later 200SX instrument panel assembly

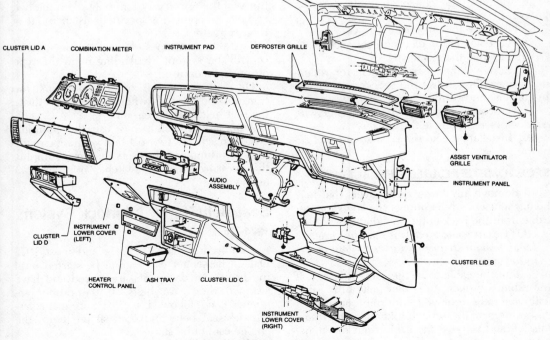

CLUSTER LID A

COMBINATION METER

INSTRUMENT PAD

DEFROSTER GRILLE

ASSIST VENTILATOR GRILLE

INSTRUMENT PANEL

CLUSTER LID D

INSTRUMENT LOWER COVER (LEFT)

CLUSTER LID C

AUDIO ASSEMBLY

HEATER CONTROL PANEL

ASH TRAY

CLUSTER LID B

INSTRUMENT LOWER COVER (RIGHT)

1980–82 200SX instrument panel

8. Remove the instrument garnish (see the illustration).

9. Remove the retaining bolts and remove the panel.

10. Installation is in the reverse order of removal.

1980–82 200SX

1. Disconnect the battery ground terminal.

2. It may be necessary to remove the steering wheel and covers to remove the instrument cluster.

3. Remove the five bolts holding the cluster in place and pull the cluster out, then remove all connections from its back. Make sure you mark the wiring to avoid confusion during reassembly.

5. Remove the instrument cluster.

6. Installation is the reverse of removal.

1978 and Later 510

1. Disconnect the battery ground cable.

2. Remove the steering column covers. Disconnect the hazard warning switch connector.

3. Remove the wiper switch. Pull out the ash tray, remove the heater, control knobs, and remove the heater control plate by inserting a screwdriver into the fan lever slit and levering the plate out.

4. Remove the finish plate to the left of the glove compartment.

5. Pull off the radio knobs and remove the nuts and washers.

6. Remove the choke and side defroster knobs.

7. Remove the cluster lid screws.

8. Disconnect the electrical connectors.

9. Remove the cluster lid.

10. Remove the instrument cluster retaining screws. Disconnect the speedometer cable by pushing and turning counterclockwise.

11. Disconnect the instrument cluster wire connectors and remove the cluster.

12. Installation is in the reverse order of removal.

SPEEDOMETER CABLE REPLACEMENT

1. Remove any lower dash covers that may be in the way and disconnect the speedometer cable from the back of the speedometer.

NOTE: *On some models it may be easier to remove the instrument cluster to gain access to the cable.*

2. Pull the cable from the cable housing. If the cable is broken, the other half of the cable will have to be removed from the transmission end. Unscrew the retaining knob at the transmission and remove the cable from the transmission extension housing.

3. Lubricate the cable with graphite power (sold as speedometer cable lubricant) and feed the cable into the housing. It is best to start at the speedometer end and feed the cable down towards the transmission. It is also usually necessary to unscrew the transmission connection and install the cable end to the gear, then reconnect the housing to the transmission. Slip the cable end into the speedometer and reconnect the cable housing.

Ignition Switch

Ignition switch removal and installation procedures are covered in Chapter 8; Suspension and Steering.

SEATBELT SYSTEM

Warning Buzzer and Light

610

Beginning in 1972, all cars are required to have a warning system which operates a buzzer and warning system light if either of the front seat belts are not fastened when the seats are occupied and the car is in a forward gear.

A light with the words "Seat Belts," or "Fasten Seat Belts" is located on the dash board while a buzzer is located under the dash. They are controlled by pressure-sensitive switches hidden in the front bench or bucket seats. A switch in each of the front seat belt retractors turns off the warning system only when the belt or belts are pulled a specified distance out of their retractors.

Two different types of switches are used to control the system, depending upon the type of transmission used:

On manual transmission-equipped cars, the transmission neutral switch is used to activate the seat belt warning circuit.

Automatic transmissions use the inhibitor switch to activate the seat belt warning circuit.

When removing the seats, be sure to unplug the pressure-sensitive switches at their connections.

Seat Belt/Starter Interlock System

1974–75

As required by law, all 1974 and most 1975 Datsun passenger cars cannot be started until the front seat occupants are seated and have fastened their seat belts. If the proper sequence is not followed, e.g., the occupants fasten the seat belts and *then* sit on them, the engine cannot be started.

The shoulder harness and lap belt are permanently fastened together, so that they both must be worn. The shoulder harness uses an inertia-lock reel to allow freedom of movement under normal driving conditions.

NOTE: *This type of reel locks up when the car decelerates rapidly, as during a crash.*

The switches for the interlock system have been removed from the lap belt retractors and placed in the belt buckles. The seat sensors remain the same as those used in 1973.

For ease of service, the car may be started from outside, by reaching in and turning the key, but without depressing the seat sensors.

In case of system failure, an override switch is located under the hood. This is a "one start" switch and it must be reset each time it is used.

LIGHTING

Headlights

REMOVAL AND INSTALLATION

All Except 1984 and later 200SX

NOTE: *Many Datsuns have radiator grilles which are unit-constructed to also serve as headlight frames. In this case, it will be necessary to remove the grille to gain access to the headlights.*

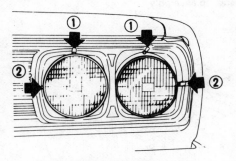

1. Vertical adjustment
2. Horizontal adjustment

Headlight adjusting screws—most models similar

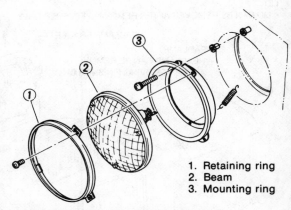

1. Retaining ring
2. Beam
3. Mounting ring

Exploded view of standard headlight

1. Remove the grille, if necessary.
2. Remove the headlight retaining ring screws. These are the three or four short screws in the assembly. There are also two longer screws at the top and side of the headlight which are used to aim the headlight. Do not tamper with these or the headlight will have to be re-aimed.
3. Remove the ring on round headlights by turning it clockwise.
4. Pull the headlight bulb from its socket and disconnect the electrical plug.
5. Connect the plug to the new bulb.
6. Position the headlight in the shell. Make sure that the word "TOP" is, indeed, at the top and that the knobs in the headlight lens engage the slots in the mounting shell.
7. Place the retaining ring over the bulb and install the screws.
8. Install the grille, if removed.

1984 and later 200SX

NOTE: *If headlamps do not open on these models, first check the fusible link for the headlight motor. Also check the retract switch. If headlamps do not retract, check the retract control relay. The headlamp can*

Fusible Links

Year	Model	Number	Location
1973–74	610	2	At positive battery terminal
1976 1974–77	610 710	4	On relay bracket, front right side of engine compartment
1977–82	810	6	On relay bracket, in engine compartment ①
1977–79	200SX	2	At positive battery terminal
1980–84	200SX	4	At positive battery terminal
1978–81	510	2	At positive battery terminal

① The fusible links for the fuel injection and the glow plugs (diesel) are located at the positive battery terminal

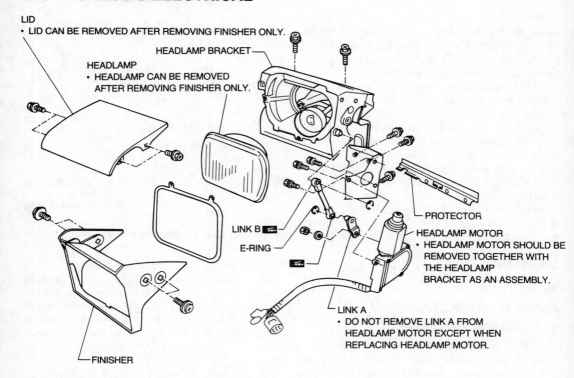

LID
• LID CAN BE REMOVED AFTER REMOVING FINISHER ONLY.

HEADLAMP BRACKET

HEADLAMP
• HEADLAMP CAN BE REMOVED
  AFTER REMOVING FINISHER ONLY.

LINK B

E-RING

PROTECTOR

HEADLAMP MOTOR
• HEADLAMP MOTOR SHOULD BE
  REMOVED TOGETHER WITH
  THE HEADLAMP
  BRACKET AS AN ASSEMBLY.

LINK A
• DO NOT REMOVE LINK A FROM
  HEADLAMP MOTOR EXCEPT WHEN
  REPLACING HEADLAMP MOTOR.

FINISHER

: GREASING POINT

1984 and later 200SX headlamp assembly

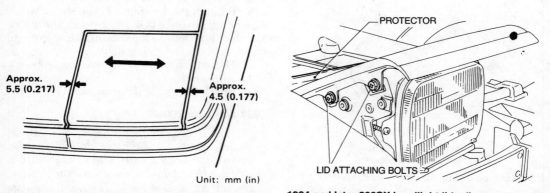

Approx.
5.5 (0.217)

Approx.
4.5 (0.177)

Unit: mm (in)

Adjust the lid to these dimensions at the joints, and so it is flush with the hood and fenders

PROTECTOR

LID ATTACHING BOLTS

1984 and later 200SX headlight lid adjustment

be opened and closed manually by using the knob on the headlamp motor.

1. Open the headlamp.
2. Unbolt and remove the finisher, shown in the accompanying illustration.
3. Remove the headlamp lid.
4. Remove the bulb retaining ring. Unplug and remove the headlamp bulb.
5. Reverse the removal procedure to install. Adjust the headlamp lid so it is flush with the hood and fender, and so the lid joint is as shown in the accompanying illustration. This is done by adjusting the lid mounting screws while you open and close the headlamp by operating the manual knob on the headlamp motor. Make sure the lid is not interfering with the protector. Adjust the headlights.

CIRCUIT PROTECTION

Fusible Links

A fusible link is a protective device used in an electrical circuit. When current increases beyond a certain amperage, the fusible metal wire of the link melts, thus breaking the electrical

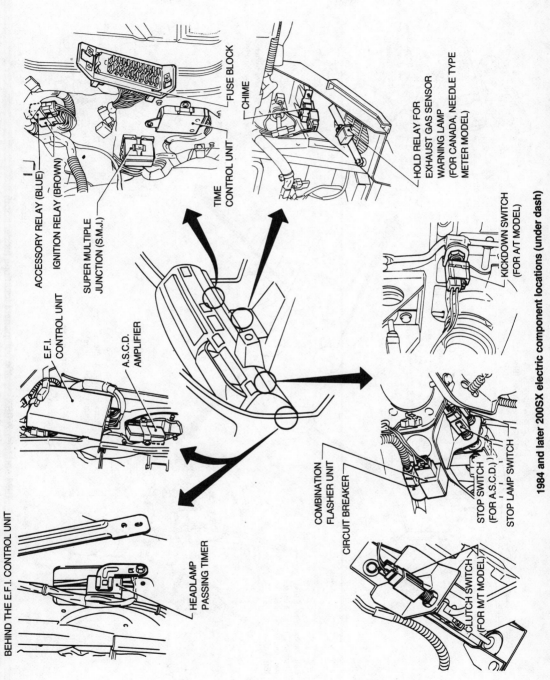

ACCESSORY RELAY (BLUE)
IGNITION RELAY (BROWN)
SUPER MULTIPLE JUNCTION (S.M.J.)
FUSE BLOCK
CHIME
TIME CONTROL UNIT
HOLD RELAY FOR EXHAUST GAS SENSOR WARNING LAMP (FOR CANADA, NEEDLE TYPE METER MODEL)
KICKDOWN SWITCH (FOR A/T MODEL)
E.F.I. CONTROL UNIT
A.S.C.D. AMPLIFIER
COMBINATION FLASHER UNIT
CIRCUIT BREAKER
STOP SWITCH (FOR A.S.C.D.)
STOP LAMP SWITCH
CLUTCH SWITCH (FOR M/T MODEL)
BEHIND THE E.F.I. CONTROL UNIT
HEADLAMP PASSING TIMER

1984 and later 200SX electric component locations (under dash)

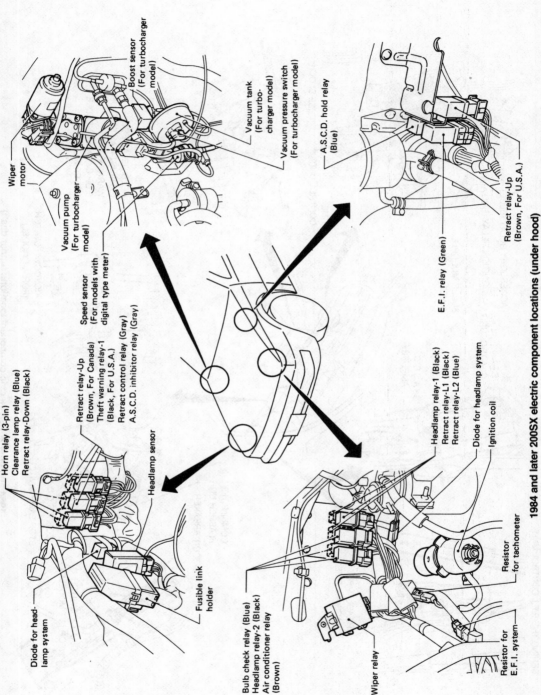

Wiper motor

Vacuum pump (For turbocharger model)

Boost sensor (For turbocharger model)

Vacuum tank (For turbo-charger model)

Vacuum pressure switch (For turbocharger model)

A.S.C.D. hold relay (Blue)

Retract relay-Up (Brown, For U.S.A.)

E.F.I. relay (Green)

Speed sensor (For models with digital type meter)

Retract control relay (Gray)
A.S.C.D. inhibitor relay (Gray)

Retract relay-Up (Brown, For Canada)
Theft warning relay-1 (Black, For U.S.A.)

Horn relay (3-pin)
Clearance lamp relay (Blue)
Retract relay-Down (Black)

Headlamp sensor

Diode for head-lamp system

Fusible link holder

Headlamp relay-1 (Black)
Retract relay-L1 (Black)
Retract relay-L2 (Blue)

Diode for headlamp system

Ignition coil

Resistor for tachometer

Bulb check relay (Blue)
Headlamp relay-2 (Black)
Air conditioner relay (Brown)

Wiper relay

Resistor for E.F.I. system

Resistor for E.F.I. system

1984 and later 200SX electric component locations (under hood)

circuit and preventing further damage to the other components and wiring. Whenever a fusible link is melted because of a short circuit, correct the cause before installing a new link.

Use the following chart to locate the fusible link(s) on your Datsun.

All Datsun fusible links are the plug in kind. To replace them, simply unplug the bad link and insert the new one.

WIRING DIAGRAMS

Wiring diagrams have been left out of this book. As cars have become more complex, and available with longer and longer option lists, wiring diagrams have grown in size and complexity also. It has become virtually impossible to provide a readable reproduction in a reasonable number of pages.

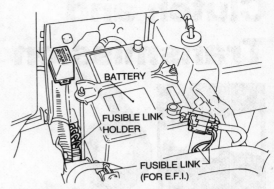

Most fusible links are found beside the battery

Fuse Box and Flasher Location

Year	Model	Fuse Box Location	Flasher Location
1973–77	610, 710	Under instrument panel	Top of pedal assembly ①
1977–80	810	Right side kick panel	Under driver's side of dashboard ①
1981–82	810	Underneath glove box	Under driver's side of dashboard, near steering column
1977–79	200SX	Underneath glove box	Turn signal: Behind radio Hazard: Behind glove box
1980–84	200SX	Underneath glove box	Under driver's side dashboard ①
1978–81	510	Under instrument panel, Next to hood release	Under driver's side dashboard ①

① Both the turn signal and the hazard flashers are side by side
NOTE: The original turn signal flasher unit is pink, and larger than the original hazard flasher unit, which is gold.

Clutch and Transmission

6

MANUAL TRANSMISSION

LINKAGE AND SHIFTER ADJUSTMENT

All models are equipped with an integral linkage system; no adjustments are either possible or necessary.

REMOVAL AND INSTALLATION

1. Disconnect the negative battery cable.
2. Disconnect the accelerator linkage on the 1980–82 200SX and the 1981 and later 810 and Maxima.
3. Raise the car and support it with jack stands.
4. Disconnect the exhaust pipe from the manifold and bracket.

5. Tag and disconnect any switches that are connected to the transmission case (back-up, neutral, top gear or overdrive).
6. Disconnect the speedometer cable where it attaches to the transmission.
7. Remove the drive shaft as detailed in Chapter 7. Don't forget to plug the opening in the rear extension so that oil won't flow out.
8. Remove the clutch slave cylinder as detailed later in this chapter.
9. Remove the rubber boot and console box (if so equipped). Place the shift lever in neutral, remove the E-ring (later models only) and then remove the shifter.
10. Support the engine by placing a jack un-

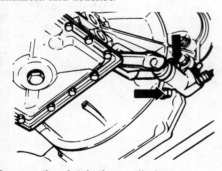

Remove the clutch slave cylinder

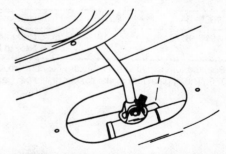

Later models used an E-ring to secure the shifter

Early models used nuts to secure the shifter

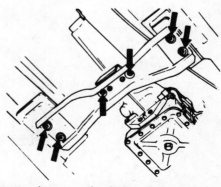

Crossmember mounting bolts—610 and 710

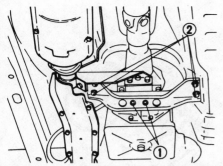

Rear engine mount nuts (1), crossmember mounting nuts (2)—510

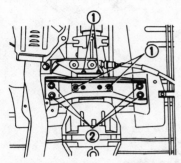

Rear engine mount nuts (1), crossmember mounting nuts (2)—200SX

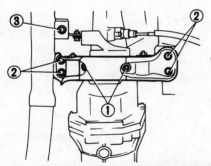

Rear engine mount nuts (1), crossmember mounting nuts (2), exhaust bracket mounting nut (3)—810

der the oil pan with a wooden block used between the jack and the pan.

CAUTION: *Do not place a jack directly under the drain plug with a block of wood between the jack and the transmission.*

11. Support the transmission with a transmission jack.

12. Loosen the rear engine mount securing nuts temporarily and then remove the crossmember mounting nuts.

13. Lower the rear of the engine slightly to allow additional clearance.

14. Remove the starter motor.

15. Remove the transmission-to-engine mounting bolts, lower the transmission and remove it toward the rear.

16. Installation is in the reverse order of removal.

CLUTCH

The purpose of the clutch is to disconnect and connect engine power from the transmission. A car at rest requires a lot of engine torque to get all that weight moving. An internal-combustion engine does not develop a high starting torque (unlike steam engines), so it must be allowed to operate without any load until it builds up enough torque to move the car. Torque increases with engine rpm. The clutch allows the engine to build up torque by physically disconnecting the engine from the transmission, relieving the engine of any load or resistance. The transfer of engine power to the transmission (the load) must be smooth and gradual; if it wasn't driveline components would wear out or break quickly. This gradual power transfer is made possible by gradually releasing the clutch pedal. The clutch disc and pressure plate are the connecting link between the engine and transmission. When the clutch pedal is released, the disc and plate contact each other (clutch engagement), physically joining the engine and transmission. When the pedal is pushed in, the disc and plate separate (the clutch is disengaged), disconnecting the engine from the transmission.

The clutch assembly consists of the flywheel, the clutch disc, the clutch pressure plate, the throwout bearing and fork, the clutch master cylinder, slave cylinder and connecting line, and the pedal. The flywheel and clutch pressure plate (driving members) are connected to the engine crankshaft and rotate with it. The clutch disc is located between the flywheel and pressure plate, and splined to the transmission shaft. A driving member is one that is attached to the engine and transfers engine power to a driven member (clutch disc) on the transmission shaft. A driving member (pressure plate) rotates (drives) a driven member (clutch disc) on contact and, in so doing, turns the transmission shaft. There is a circular diaphragm spring within the pressure plate cover (transmission side). In a relaxed state (when the clutch pedal is fully released), this spring is convex; that is, it is dished outward toward the transmission. Pushing in the clutch pedal actuates the slave cylinder. Connected to the other end of the slave cylinder rod is the throwout bearing fork. The throwout bearing is attached to the fork. When the clutch pedal is depressed, the slave cylinder pushes the fork and bearing forward to

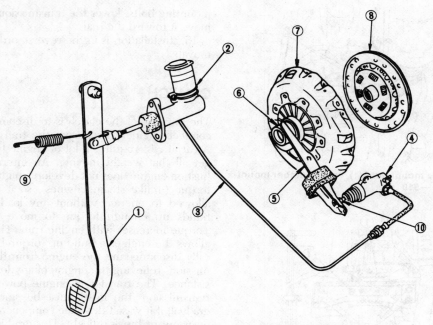

1. Clutch pedal
2. Clutch master cylinder
3. Clutch piping
4. Operating cylinder
5. Withdrawal lever
6. Release bearing
7. Clutch cover
8. Clutch disc
9. Return spring
10. Push rod

510, 610 and 710 clutch control system

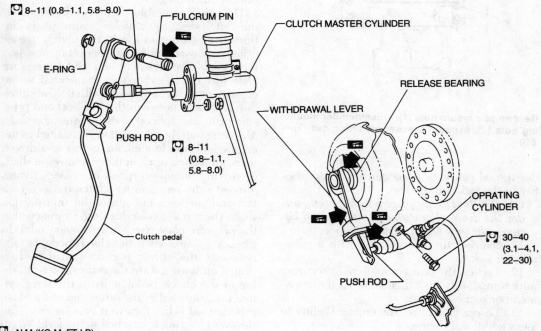

8–11 (0.8–1.1, 5.8–8.0)

FULCRUM PIN

CLUTCH MASTER CYLINDER

E-RING

RELEASE BEARING

WITHDRAWAL LEVER

PUSH ROD

8–11
(0.8–1.1,
5.8–8.0)

Clutch pedal

OPRATING
CYLINDER

30–40
(3.1–4.1,
22–30)

PUSH ROD

: N·M (KG-M, FT-LB)

1984 and later 200SX clutch operating mechanism

contact the diaphragm spring of the pressure plate. The outer edges of the spring are secured to the pressure plate and are pivoted on rings so that when the center of the spring is compressed by the throwout bearing, the outer edges bow outward, and, by so doing, pull the pressure plate in the same direction—away from the clutch disc. This action separates the disc from the plate, disengaging the clutch and allowing the transmission to be shifted into another gear. Releasing the pedal allows the throwout bearing to pull away from the diaphragm spring resulting in a reversal of spring position. As bearing pressure is gradually released from the spring center, the outer edges of the spring bow inward, pushing the pressure plate into closer contact with the clutch disc. As the disc and plate move closer together, friction between the two increases and slippage is reduced until, when full spring pressure is applied (by fully releasing the pedal), the speed of the disc and plate are the same. This stops all slipping, creating a direct connection between the plate and disc which results in the transfer of power from the engine to the transmission. The clutch disc is now rotting with the pressure plate at engine speed and, because it is splined to the transmission shaft, the shaft now turns at the same engine speed.

All Datsun models included in this guide are equipped with hydraulic clutch control. This system consists of the clutch pedal and return spring, master cylinder, connecting hydraulic line, and slave (operating) cylinder.

CLUTCH OPERATION

The clutch is operating properly if:

1. It will stall the engine when released with the vehicle held stationary.

2. The shift lever can be moved freely between first and reverse gears when the vehicle is stationary and the clutch is disengaged.

A clutch pedal free-play adjustment is incorporated in the linkage. If there is about 1–2 in. of motion before the pedal begins to release the clutch, it is adjusted properly. Inadequate free-play wears all parts of the clutch releasing mechanisms and may cause slippage. Excessive free-play may cause inadequate release and hard shifting of gears.

If the clutch fails to release, fill the clutch master cylinder with fluid to the proper level and pump the clutch pedal to fill the system with fluid. Bleed the system in the same way as a brake system is bled. If leaks are located, tighten loose connections or overhaul the master or slave cylinder as necessary.

Clutch Specifications

Model	Pedal Height Above Floor (in.)	Pedal Free-Play (in.)
510	6.5	0.04–0.20
610	6.9	0.04–0.12
710	7.09	0.04–0.20
1977–80 810	6.9	0.04–0.20
1981–83 810, Maxima	7.25	0.04–0.20
1977–79 200SX	7.60	0.04–0.12
1980–83 200SX	6.70	0.04–0.20
1984 200SX	7.60	0.04–0.06
1984 Maxima	6.9	0.04–0.20

ADJUSTMENT

Refer to the Clutch Specifications Chart for clutch pedal height above floor and pedal free play.

All models have a hydraulically operated clutch. Pedal height is usually adjusted with a stopper limiting the upward travel of the pedal. Pedal free-play is adjusted at the master cylinder pushrod. If the pushrod is nonadjustable, free-play is adjusted by placing shims between the master cylinder and the firewall.

REMOVAL AND INSTALLATION

1. Remove the transmission from the engine as detailed earlier in this chapter.

2. Insert a clutch aligning bar or similar tool all the way into the clutch disc hub. This must be done so as to support the weight of the clutch disc during removal. Mark the clutch assembly-to-flywheel relationship with paint or a center punch so that the clutch assembly can be assembled in the same position from which it is removed.

3. Loosen the bolts in sequence, a turn at a time. Remove the bolts.

4. Remove the pressure plate and clutch disc.

5. Remove the release mechanism from the transmission housing. Apply lithium-based molybdenum-disulfide grease to the bearing sleeve inside groove, the contact point of the withdrawal lever and bearing sleeve, the contact surface of the lever ball pin and lever. Replace the release mechanism.

6. Inspect the pressure plate for wear, scoring, etc., and reface or replace as necessary. Inspect the release bearing and replace as necessary. Apply a small amount of grease to the transmission splines. Install the disc on the splines and slide back and forth a few times.

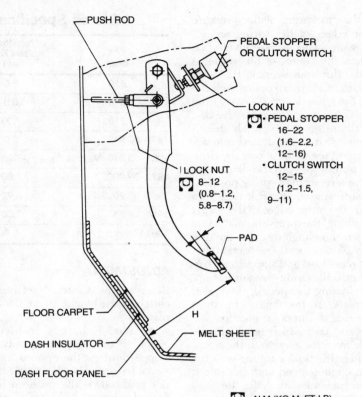

PUSH ROD

PEDAL STOPPER
OR CLUTCH SWITCH

LOCK NUT
• PEDAL STOPPER
16–22
(1.6–2.2,
12–16)
• CLUTCH SWITCH
12–15
(1.2–1.5,
9–11)

LOCK NUT
8–12
(0.8–1.2,
5.8–8.7)

A

PAD

FLOOR CARPET

H

DASH INSULATOR

MELT SHEET

DASH FLOOR PANEL

: N·M (KG-M, FT-LB)

Clutch adjusting points

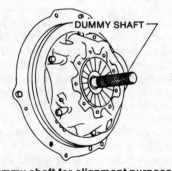

DUMMY SHAFT

Use a dummy shaft for alignment purposes

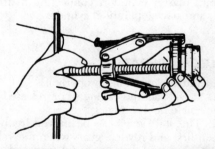

Use a universal puller and adapter to pull the release bearing out of the bearing sleeve

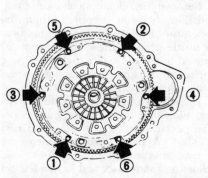

Loosen the bolts in sequence, one turn at a time

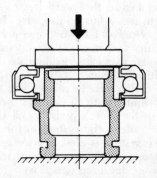

Install the release bearing on the sleeve using a press

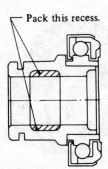

Pack this recess.

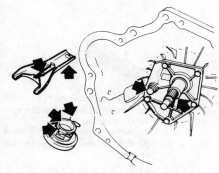

Apply grease to the release bearing here

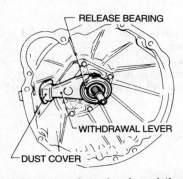

Grease these points before installing the clutch

RELEASE BEARING

WITHDRAWAL LEVER

DUST COVER

Withdrawal lever-to-release bearing relationship

Remove the disc and remove excess grease on hub. Be sure no grease contacts the disc or pressure plate.

7. Install the disc, aligning it with a splined dummy shaft.

8. Install the pressure plate and torque the bolts to 11–16 ft. lbs. (16–22 ft. lbs. on 1984 and later 200SX).

9. Remove the dummy shaft.

10. Replace the transmission.

Clutch Master Cylinder
REMOVAL AND INSTALLATION

1. Disconnect the clutch pedal arm from the pushrod.

2. Disconnect the clutch hydraulic line from the master cylinder.

NOTE: *Take precautions to keep brake fluid from coming in contact with any painted surfaces.*

3. Remove the nuts attaching the master cylinder and remove the master cylinder and pushrod toward the engine compartment side.

4. Install the master cylinder in the reverse order of removal and bleed the clutch hydraulic system.

OVERHAUL

1. Remove the master cylinder from the vehicle.

2. Drain the clutch fluid from the master cylinder reservoir.

3. Remove the boot and circlip and remove the pushrod.

4. Remove the stopper, piston, cup and return spring.

5. Clean all of the parts in clean brake fluid.

6. Check the master cylinder and piston for wear, corrosion and scores and replace the parts as necessary. Light scoring and glaze can be removed with crocus cloth soaked in brake fluid.

7. Generally, the cup seal should be replaced each time the master cylinder is disassembled. Check the cup and replace it if it is worn, fatigued, or damaged.

8. Check the clutch fluid reservoir, filler cap, dust cover and the pipe for distortion and damage and replace the parts as necessary.

9. Lubricate all new parts with clean brake fluid.

10. Reassemble the master cylinder parts in the reverse order of disassembly, taking note of the following:

    a. Reinstall the cup seal carefully to prevent damaging the lipped portions;

    b. Adjust the height of the clutch pedal after installing the master cylinder in position on the vehicle;

    c. Fill the master cylinder and clutch fluid reservoir and then bleed the clutch hydraulic system.

Clutch Slave Cylinder
REMOVAL AND INSTALLATION

1. Remove the slave cylinder attaching bolts and the pushrod from the shift fork.

2. Disconnect the flexible fluid hose from the slave cylinder and remove the unit from the vehicle.

3. Install the slave cylinder in the reverse order of removal and bleed the clutch hydraulic system.

1. Disc
2, 3. Clutch cover assembly with pressure plate
4. Bolt
5. Lockwasher
6. Withdrawal lever
7. Retainer spring
8. Bearing sleeve

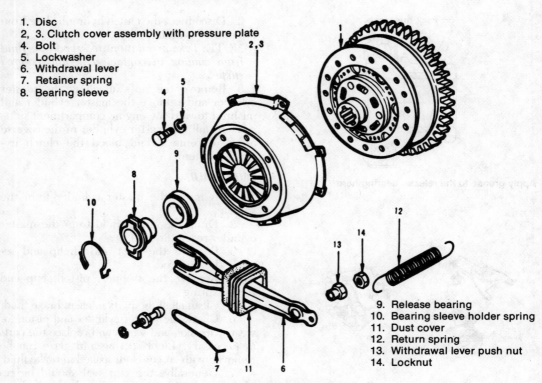

9. Release bearing
10. Bearing sleeve holder spring
11. Dust cover
12. Return spring
13. Withdrawal lever push nut
14. Locknut

Typical clutch assembly

OVERHAUL

1. Remove the slave cylinder from the vehicle.
2. Remove the pushrod and boot.
3. Force out the piston by blowing compressed air into the slave cylinder at the hose connection.

NOTE: *Be careful not to apply excess air pressure to avoid possible injury.*

4. Clean all of the parts in clean brake fluid.

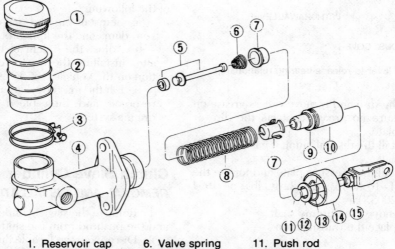

1. Reservoir cap	6. Valve spring	11. Push rod
2. Reservoir	7. Spring seat	12. Stopper
3. Reservoir band	8. Return spring	13. Stopper ring
4. Cylinder body	9. Piston cup	14. Dust cover
5. Valve assembly	10. Piston	15. Nut

Exploded view of typical master cylinder

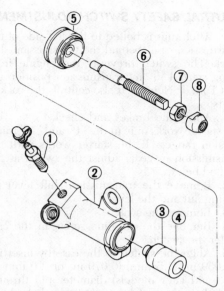

1. Bleeder screw   5. Dust cover
2. Cylinder body   6. Push rod
3. Piston cup   7. Lock nut
4. Piston   8. Push nut

Exploded view of a typical slave cylinder

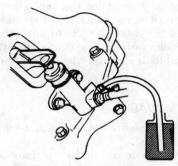

Run a hose from the bleeder screw into a clear container filled with brake fluid

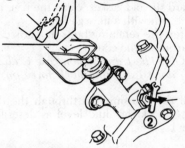

Pump the clutch pedal several times and then open the bleeder screw

5. Check and replace the slave cylinder bore and piston if wear or severe scoring exists. Light scoring and glaze can be removed with crocus cloth soaked in brake fluid.

6. Normally the piston cup should be replaced when the slave cylinder is disassembled. Check the piston cup and replace it if it is found to be worn, fatigued or scored.

7. Replace the rubber boot if it is cracked or broken.

8. Lubricate all of the new parts in clean brake fluid and reassemble in the reverse order of diassembly, taking note of the following:

a. Use care when reassembling the piston cup to prevent damaging the lipped portion of the piston cup;

b. Fill the master cylinder with brake fluid and bleed the clutch hydraulic system;

c. Adjust the clearance between the pushrod and the shift fork to 5/64 in.

Bleeding the Clutch Hydraulic System

1. Check and fill the clutch fluid reservoir to the specified level as necessary. During the bleeding process, continue to check and replenish the reservoir to prevent the fluid level from getting lower than 1/2 the specified level.

2. Remove the dust cap from the bleeder screw on the clutch slave cylinder and connect a tube to the bleeder screw and insert the other

end of the tube into a clean glass or metal container.

NOTE: *Take precautionary measures to prevent the brake fluid from getting on any painted surfaces.*

3. Pump the clutch pedal several times, hold it down and loosen the bleeder screw slowly.

4. Tighten the bleeder screw and release the clutch pedal gradually. Repeat this operation until air bubbles disappear from the brake fluid being expelled out through the bleeder screw.

5. Repeat until all evidence of air bubbles completely disappears from the brake fluid being pumped out through the tube.

6. When the air is completely removed, securely tighten the bleeder screw and replace the dust cap.

7. Check and refill the master cylinder reservoir as necessary.

8. Depress the clutch pedal several times to check the operation of the clutch and check for leaks.

AUTOMATIC TRANSMISSION

All Datsuns covered in this book can be optionally equipped with an automatic three-speed transmission. Except for the procedures outlined here, it is recommended that automatic transmission service be left to an authorized Datsun dealer or transmission specialist who has the special tools and expertise to work on these units.

PAN REMOVAL

1. Jack up the front of the car and support it safely on stands.
2. Slide a drain pan under the transmission. Loosen the rear oil pan bolts first, to allow most of the fluid to drain off without making a mess on your garage floor.
3. Remove the remaining bolts and drop the pan.
4. Discard the old gasket, clean the pan, and reinstall the pan with a new gasket.
5. Tighten the retaining bolts in a crisscross pattern starting at the center.
CAUTION: *The transmission case is aluminum, so don't exert too much force on the bolts.*
6. Refill the transmission through the dipstick tube. Check the fluid level as described in Chapter 1.

BRAKE BAND ADJUSTMENT

1. Remove the oil pan as previously described.
2. Loosen the locknut on the piston stem. Tighten the piston stem to *exactly* 9–11 ft. lbs. (1.2–1.5 kg-m).
3. Loosen the piston stem *exactly* two turns. Hold the stem and tighten the locknut to 11–29 ft. lbs. (1.5–4.0 kg-m) on 1973–79 models, 14 ft. lbs. (2 kg-m) on 1980–and later models. If the stem turns when the locknut is tightened, loosen the locknut and repeat the adjustment.
4. Replace the oil pan and refill the transmission as described above.

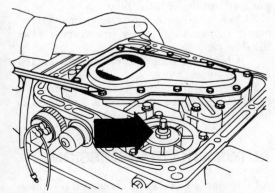

Brake band piston stem and locknut (arrow)

NEUTRAL SAFETY SWITCH ADJUSTMENT

The switch unit is bolted to the left-side of the transmission case, behind the transmission shift level. The switch prevents the engine from being started in any transmission position except Park or Neutral. It also controls the backup lights.

1. Apply the brakes and check to see that the starter works only in the "P" and "N" transmission ranges. If the starter works with the transmission in gear, adjust the switch as described below.
2. Remove the transmission shift level retaining nut and the lever.
3. Remove the switch.
4. Remove the machine screw in the case under the switch.
5. Align the switch to the case by inserting a 0.059 in. (1.5 mm) (0.079 in. or 2.0 mm on 1983 and later models) diameter pin through the hole in the switch into the screw hole. Mark the switch location.
6. Remove the pin, replace the machine screw, install the switch as marked, and replace the transmission shift lever and retaining nut.
7. Make sure while holding the brakes on, that the engine will start only in Park or Neutral. Check that the backup lights go only in Reverse.

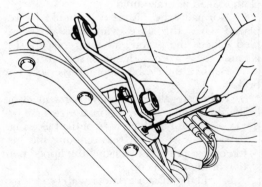

After removing the screw, insert the alignment pin into the hole for neutral safety switch alignment

SHIFT LINKAGE ADJUSTMENT

1973–78

1. Loosen the trunnion locknuts at the lower end of the control level. Remove the selector level knob and console.
2. Put the transmission selector in "N" and put the transmission shift level in the Neutral position by pushing it all the way back, then moving it forward two stops.
3. Check the vertical clearance between the top of the shift level pin and transmission con-

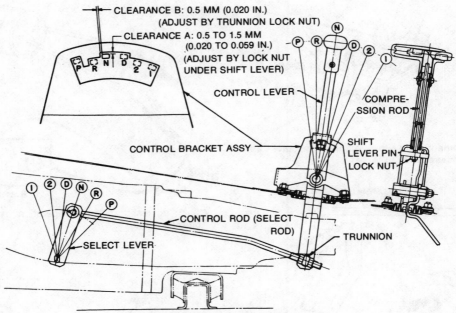

Shift linkage adjustment—1973–78

trol bracket ("A" in the illustration). It should be 0.026–0.059 in. (0.5–1.5 mm). Adjust the nut at the lower end of the selector lever compression rod, as necessary.

4. Check the horizontal clearance ("B") between the shift lever pin and transmission control bracket. It should be 0.020 in. (0.5 mm). Adjust the trunion locknuts as necessary to get this clearance.

5. Replace the console with the shift pointer correctly aligned. Install the shift knob.

1979—and Later

Adjustment is made at the locknuts at the base of the shifter, which control the length of the shift control rod.

1. Place the shift lever in "D".

2. Loosen the locknuts and move the shift lever until it is firmly in the "D" range, the pointer is aligned, and the transmission is in "D" range.

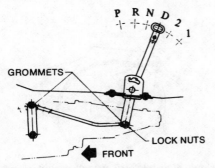

Shift linkage adjustment—1979 and later models

3. Tighten the locknuts.

4. Check the adjustment. Start the car and apply the parking brake. Shift through all the ranges, starting in "P". As the lever is moved from "P" to "1", you should be able to feel the detents in each range. If proper adjustment is not possible, the grommets are probably worn and should be replaced.

CHECKING KICK-DOWN SWITCH AND SOLENOID

1. Turn the key to the normal ON position, and depress the accelerator all the way. The solenoid in the transmission should make an audible click.

2. If the solenoid does not work, inspect the wiring, and test it electrically to determine whether the problem is in the wiring, the kick-down switch, or the solenoid.

3. If the solenoid requires replacement, drain a little over 2 pts (1 liter) of fluid from the transmission before removing it.

REMOVAL AND INSTALLATION

1. Disconnect the battery cable.

2. Remove the accelerator linkage.

3. Detach the shift linkage.

4. Disconnect the neutral safety switch and downshift solenoid wiring.

5. Drain the transmission.

6. Remove the front exhaust pipe.

7. Remove the vacuum tube and speedometer cable.

8. Disconnect the fluid cooler tubes.

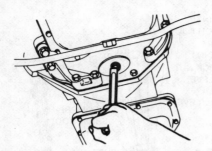

Disconnecting the torque converter bolts through the access hole

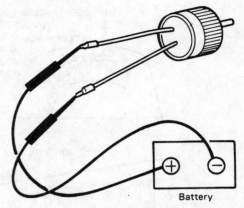

Check downshift solenoid operation by applying battery voltage

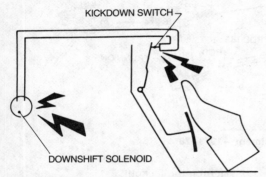

Kickdown switch and downshift solenoid

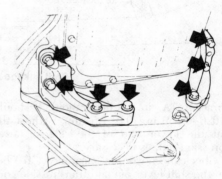

Remove the transmission gussets

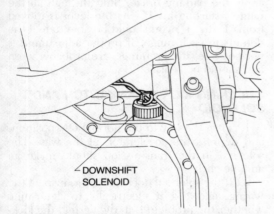

The downshift solenoid is located on the side of the transmission just above the pan

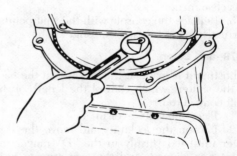

Removing the bolts securing the torque converter to the drive plate

9. Remove the driveshaft and starter.

10. Support the transmission with a jack under the oil pan. Support the engine also.

11. Remove the rear crossmember.

12. Mark the relationship between the torque converter and the drive plate (flywheel). Remove the four bolts holding the converter to the drive plate through the hole at the front, under the engine. Unbolt the transmission from the engine.

13. Reverse the procedure for installation. Refill the torque converter with 2⅛ qts. of automatic transmission fluid. Make sure that the

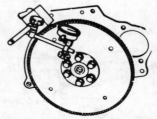

Checking drive plate (flywheel) runout with a dial gauge

Refill the torque converter before installation

drive plate is warped no more than 0.020 in. Torque the drive plate-to-torque converter and converter housing-to-engine bolts to 29–36 ft. lbs. Drive plate-to-crankshaft bolt torque is 101–116 ft. lbs.

14. Refill the transmission and check the fluid level.

Drive Train

+7

DRIVELINE

Driveshaft and Universal Joints

The driveshaft transfers power from the engine and transmission to the differential and rear axles and then to the rear wheels to drive the car. All of the models covered in this book utilize a conventional driveshaft. Except on the 610 wagon, the 810, Maxima, and the 200SX (manual transmission only—1977–79, all transmissions—1980–82) models, the driveshaft assembly has two universal joints—one at each end—and a slip yoke at the front of the assembly which fits into the back of the transmission. The 610, 810, Maxima, and 200SX incorporate an additional universal joint at the center of the driveshaft with a support bearing.

REMOVAL AND INSTALLATION

510, 610 (Except Station Wagon), 710, 1977–79 200SX (with Automatic Trans.)

These driveshafts are the one-piece type with a U-joint and flange at the rear, and a U-joint and a splined sleeve yoke which fits into the rear of the transmission, at the front. The U-joints must be disassembled for lubrication at 24,000 mile intervals. The splines are lubricated by transmission oil.

1. Release the handbrake.
2. Loosen the 510 muffler and rotate it out of the way.
3. On the 510, remove the handbrake rear cable adjusting nut and disconnect the left handbrake cable from the adjuster.
4. Unbolt the rear flange.
5. Pull the driveshaft down and back.
6. Plug the transmission extension housing.
7. Reverse the procedure to install, oiling the splines. Flange bolt torque is 15–24 ft. lbs.

610 Station Wagon, 810, Maxima 200SX (Manual Trans. Only–1977–79)

These models use a driveshaft with three U-joints and a center support bearing. The driveshaft is balanced as an assembly.

1. Mark the relationship of the driveshaft flange to the differential flange.
2. Unbolt the center bearing bracket.
3. Unbolt the driveshaft back under the rear axle. Plug the rear of the transmission to prevent oil or fluid loss.
5. On installation, align the marks made in Step 1. Torque the flange bolts to 15–24 ft. lbs.

U-JOINT OVERHAUL

Disassembly

1. Mark the relationship of all components for reassembly.
2. Remove the snap-rings. On early units, the snap-rings are seated in the yokes. On later units, the snap-rings seat in the needle bearing races.
3. Tap the yoke with brass or rubber mallet to release one bearing cap. Be careful not to lose the needle rollers.
4. Remove the other bearing caps. Remove the U-joint spiders from the yokes.

Inspection

1. Spline backlash should not exceed 0.0197 in. (0.5 mm).
2. Driveshaft run-out should not exceed 0.015 in. (0.4 mm).
3. On later model with snap-rings seated in the needle bearing races, different thicknesses of snap-rings are available for U-joint adjustment. Play should not exceed 0.0008 in. (0.02 mm).
4. U-joint spiders must be replaced if their

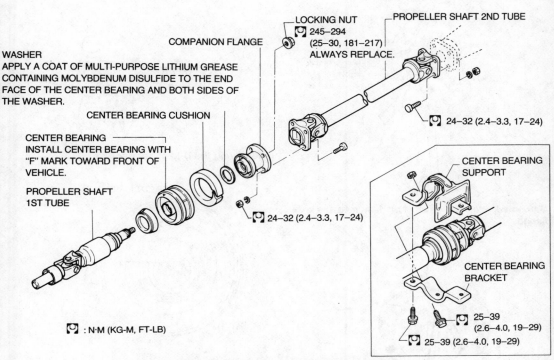

WASHER
APPLY A COAT OF MULTI-PURPOSE LITHIUM GREASE
CONTAINING MOLYBDENUM DISULFIDE TO THE END
FACE OF THE CENTER BEARING AND BOTH SIDES OF
THE WASHER.

LOCKING NUT
245–294
(25–30, 181–217)
ALWAYS REPLACE.

PROPELLER SHAFT 2ND TUBE

COMPANION FLANGE

CENTER BEARING CUSHION

CENTER BEARING
INSTALL CENTER BEARING WITH
"F" MARK TOWARD FRONT OF
VEHICLE.

PROPELLER SHAFT
1ST TUBE

24–32 (2.4–3.3, 17–24)

24–32 (2.4–3.3, 17–24)

CENTER BEARING
SUPPORT

CENTER BEARING
BRACKET

25–39
(2.6–4.0, 19–29)

25–39 (2.6–4.0, 19–29)

: N·M (KG-M, FT-LB)

Exploded view of the two-piece driveshaft (3 U-joints)

bearing journals are worn more than 0.0059 in. (0.15 mm) from their original diameter.

Assembly

1. Place the needle rollers in the races and hold them in place with grease.
2. Put the spider into place in its yokes.
3. Replace all seals.
4. Tap the races into position and secure them with snap-rings.

CENTER BEARING REPLACEMENT

The center bearing is a sealed unit which must be replaced as an assembly if defective.

1. Remove the driveshaft.
2. Paint a matchmark across where the flanges behind the center yoke are joined. This is for assembly purposes. If you don't paint or somehow mark the relationship between the two shafts, they may be out of balance when you put them back together.
3. Remove the bolts and separate the shafts. Make a matchmark on the front driveshaft half which lines up with the mark you made on the flange half.
4. You must devise a way to hold the driveshaft while unbolting the companion flange from the front driveshaft. Do not place the front

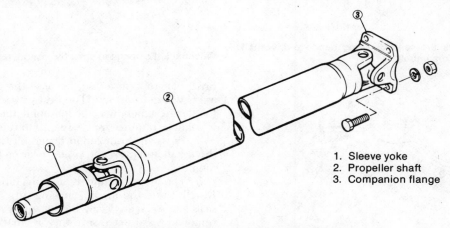

1. Sleeve yoke
2. Propeller shaft
3. Companion flange

Exploded view of the one-piece driveshaft (2 U-joints)

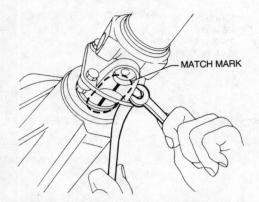

Matchmark the rear drive shaft flange to the axle flange

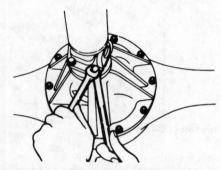

Disconnecting the rear driveshaft flange

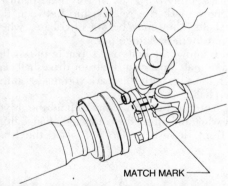

Matchmark the center bearing flange-to-driveshaft flange before unbolting

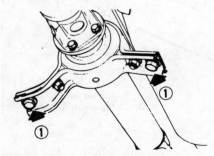

Remove the center bearing bracket

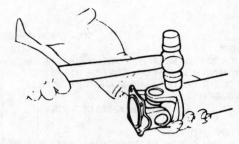

Removing the U-joint bearings

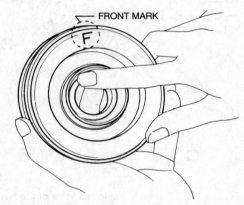

Before installing the center bearing, position the "F" mark so it is facing the front of the car

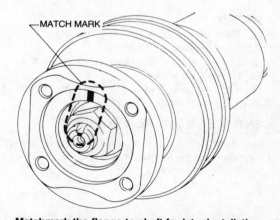

Matchmark the flange-to-shaft for later installation

driveshaft tube in a vise, because the chances are it will get crushed. The best way is to grip the flange somehow while loosening the nut. It is going to require some strength to remove.

5. Press the companion flange off the front driveshaft and press the center bearing from its mount.

6. The new bearing is already lubricated. Install it into the mount, making sure that the seals and so on are facing the same way as when removed. Also make sure the "F" mark is facing the front of the car.

Always use a new nut, and stake it after tightening

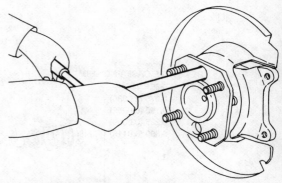

Removing the brake backing plate nuts

7. Slide the companion flange on to the front driveshaft, aligning the marks made during removal. Install the washer and lock nut. If the washer and locknut are separate pieces, tighten them to 145–175 ft. lbs. If they are a unit, tighten it to 180–217 ft. lbs. Check that the bearing rotates freely around the driveshaft. Stake the nut (always use a *new* nut).

8. Connect the companion flange to the other half of the driveshaft, aligning the marks made during removal. Tighten the bolts securely.

9. Install the driveshaft.

Rear Axle

There are several different types of rear axles used on the cars covered in this guide. A solid rear axle is used on all 200SX except Turbo models, 710, and all station wagon models. The 1978–81 510 uses a solid rear axle with either coil springs or leaf springs, depending on whether it is a sedan or a wagon. Independent rear suspension is used on the 610 sedans, turbocharged 200SXs, and the 810 and Maxima sedan. In this design, separate axle driveshafts are used to transmit power from the differential to the wheels.

Axle Shaft—Solid Rear Axle Models

REMOVAL AND INSTALLATION

NOTE: *Bearings must be pressed on and off the shaft with an arbor press. Unless you have access to one, it is inadvisable to attempt any repair work on the axle shaft and bearing assemblies.*

1. Remove the hub cap or wheel cover. Loosen the lug nuts.

2. Raise the rear of the car and support it safely on stands.

3. Remove the rear wheel. Remove the four brake backing plate retaining nuts. Detach the parking brake linkage from the brake backing plate.

4. Attach a slide hammer to the axle shaft and remove it. Use a slide hammer and a two-pronged puller to remove the oil seal from the housing.

NOTE: *If a slide hammer is not available, the axle can sometimes be pried out using pry bars on opposing sides of the hub.*

If end-play is found to be excessive, the bearing should be replaced. Shimming the bearing is not recommended as this ignores end-play of the bearing itself and could result in improper seating of the bearing.

5. Using a chisel, carefully nick the bearing retainer in three or four places. The retainer does not have to be cut, only collapsed enough to allow the bearing retainer to be slid off the shaft.

6. Pull or press the old bearing off and install the new one by pressing it into position.

7. Install the outer bearing retainer with its raised surface facing the wheel hub, and then install the bearing and the inner bearing retainer in that order on the axle shaft.

8. With the smaller chamfered side of the inner bearing retainer facing the bearing, press on the retainer. The edge of the retainer should fully touch the bearing.

9. Clean the oil seal seat in the rear axle housing. Apply a thin coat of chassis grease.

10. Using a seal installation tool, drive the

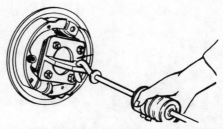

Use a slide hammer to remove the axle shaft— solid rear axle models

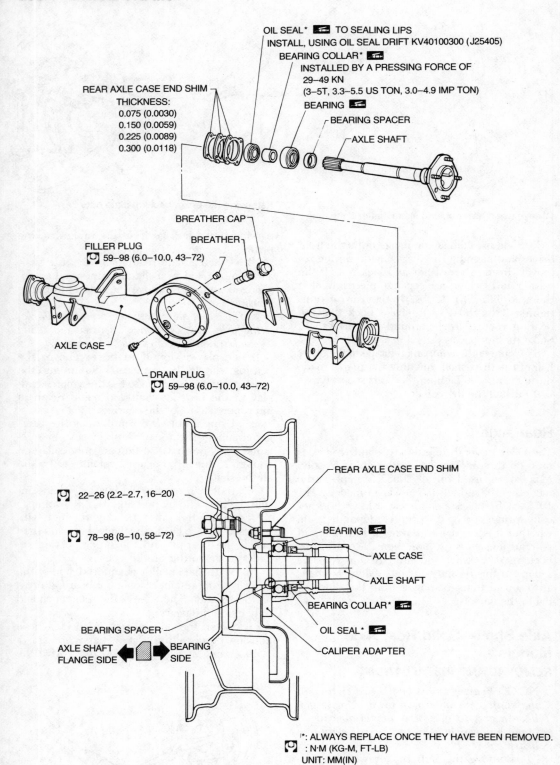

OIL SEAL* ⬛ TO SEALING LIPS
INSTALL, USING OIL SEAL DRIFT KV40100300 (J25405)
BEARING COLLAR* ⬛
INSTALLED BY A PRESSING FORCE OF
29–49 KN
(3–5T, 3.3–5.5 US TON, 3.0–4.9 IMP TON)
BEARING ⬛
BEARING SPACER
AXLE SHAFT

REAR AXLE CASE END SHIM
THICKNESS:
0.075 (0.0030)
0.150 (0.0059)
0.225 (0.0089)
0.300 (0.0118)

BREATHER CAP
BREATHER
FILLER PLUG
🔧 59–98 (6.0–10.0, 43–72)

AXLE CASE

DRAIN PLUG
🔧 59–98 (6.0–10.0, 43–72)

REAR AXLE CASE END SHIM

🔧 22–26 (2.2–2.7, 16–20)

🔧 78–98 (8–10, 58–72)

BEARING ⬛
AXLE CASE
AXLE SHAFT
BEARING COLLAR* ⬛
OIL SEAL* ⬛
CALIPER ADAPTER

BEARING SPACER
AXLE SHAFT
FLANGE SIDE ◄ ► BEARING
SIDE

*: ALWAYS REPLACE ONCE THEY HAVE BEEN REMOVED.
🔧 : N·M (KG-M, FT-LB)
UNIT: MM(IN)

Axle shaft, rear axle and bearing assemblies

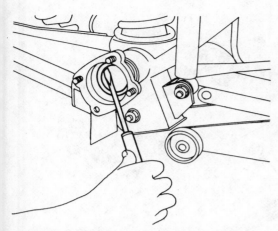

Carefully remove the oil seal. Replace the seal before axle shaft installation

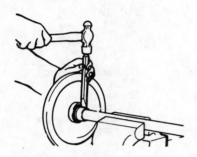

Use a chisel to cut the bearing retainer

oil seal into the rear axle housing. Wipe a thin coat of bearing grease on the lips of the seal.

11. Determine the number of retainer gaskets which will give the correct bearing-to-outer retainer clearance of 0.01 in.

12. Insert the axle shaft assembly into the axle housing, being careful not to damage the seal. Ensure that the shaft splines engage those of the differential pinion. Align the vent holes of the gasket and the outer bearing retainer. Install the retaining bolts.

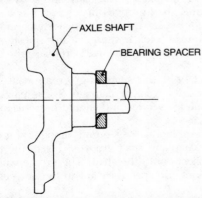

Install the bearing spacer with the chamfer side facing the axle shaft flange

13. Install the nuts on the bolts and tighten them evenly, and in a criss-cross pattern, to 20 ft. lbs.

Half-Shaft—Independent Rear Suspension Models

ALL EXCEPT 1982 AND LATER 810, MAXIMA, AND 1984 AND LATER 200SX TURBO

Removal and Installation

1. Raise and support the car.
2. Remove the U-joint yoke flange bolts at the outside. Remove the U-joint center bolt at the differential.
3. Remove the axle shaft.
4. Installation is the reverse. Torque the outside flange bolts to 36–43 ft. lbs. (5.0–6.0 kg-m). Tighten the four differential side flange bolts to 36–43 ft. lbs. (5.0–6.0 kg-m). On axle shafts retained to the differential with a single center bolt, tighten the bolt to 17–23 ft. lbs. (2.4–3.2 kg-m), 1973–77, or 23–31 ft. lbs. (3.2–4.3 kg-m), 1978–81.

Inspection

Before disassembling the axle shaft, inspect it as follows:

1. Check the parts for wear or damage. Replace the shaft as an assembly if defects are found.
2. Extend and compress the axle shaft (full stroke). Check the action for smoothness.

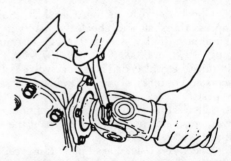

Removing the yoke flange center bolt at the differential

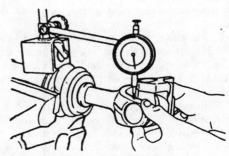

Measuring the play in the half shaft

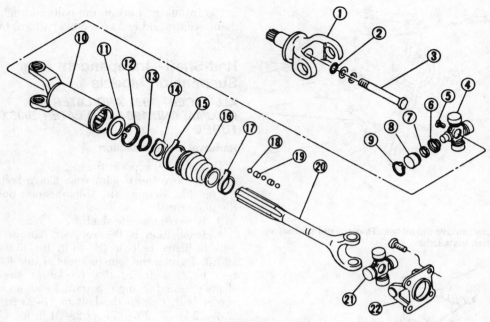

1. Side yoke
2. O-ring
3. Side yoke bolt
4. Spider journal
5. Filler plug
6. Dust cover
7. Oil seal
8. Bearing race assembly
9. Bearing race snap ring
10. Sleeve yoke
11. Sleeve yoke stopper
12. Snap ring
13. Drive shaft snap ring
14. Drive shaft stopper
15. Boot band (long)
16. Rubber boot
17. Boot band (short)
18. Ball
19. Ball spacer
20. Driveshaft
21. Spider assembly
22. Flange yoke

Exploded view of the halfshaft—all except the 1982 and later 810 and Maxima, and the 1984 and later 200SX Turbo

3. Check the play in the axle shaft. Fully compress the shaft and check the play with a dial indicator. If play exceeds 0.004 in. (0.1 mm) through 1978, or 0.008 (0.2 mm), 1979–80, the shaft must be replaced. The sleeve yoke, balls, spacers and outer shaft are *not* available as service parts.

4. Check the U-joints for smoothness. If movement is notchy or loose, overhaul the U-joints.

5. Check the U-joint axial play. If it exceeds 0.0008 in. (0.02 mm), overhaul the U-joints.

Overhaul

You will need a pair of snap ring pliers for this job.

1. Matchmark the parts across the U-joint journals, and across the sliding yoke (outer shaft to sleeve yoke). The axle shaft was balanced as a unit and must be rebuilt as originally assembled.

2. Remove the snap ring from the U-joints and disassemble them as outlined in the "U-joint Overhaul" procedure in this chapter.

3. Cut the boot band and remove the boot from the sleeve yoke.

4. Remove the snap ring from the sleeve yoke at the boot end.

5. Remove the outer shaft carefully; do not lose any of the balls or spacers.

6. It is not necessary to remove the snap ring and sleeve yoke plug at the differential end of the sleeve yoke, because the parts are not available for service. If any damage is present, the entire axle shaft must be replaced.

7. Clean the spacers, balls, and sleeve yoke and outer shaft grooves in solvent. Check the parts for wear, brinelling, distortion, cracks, straightness, etc. If there is any question as to the integrity of the part, replace the axle shaft.

8. Check the snap ring, grease seal, and dust seal for wear or damage. These parts are available for service and should be replaced as necessary.

9. Apply a fairly generous amount of grease to the yoke and shaft grooves. Install the balls and spacers onto the shaft. The grease will retain them. Be sure they are in the correct sequence.

10. Before assembling the shaft and sleeve yoke, apply a large glob of grease to the inner

end of the sleeve yoke. You can put a blob of grease on the end of the shaft, too.

11. Align the parts according to the matchmarks made in Step 1. Slide the shaft into the sleeve yoke, making sure none of the balls or spacers is displaced.

12. Compress the shaft and check the play again. Refer to the inspections procedure. Replace the shaft if necessary.

13. Install the boot onto the sleeve yoke and retain with a new boot band.

14. Clean, repack, and assemble the U-joints. Select snap rings which will yield 0.0008 in. (0.02 mm) of axial play. Be certain to use the same thickness snap ring on opposite sides of the journals to retain driveline balance, and to keep the stresses evenly distributed.

15. Install the axle shaft.

1982 AND LATER 810 AND MAXIMA, AND 1984 AND LATER 200SX TURBO

Removal and Installation

1. Raise and support the rear of the car.

2. Disconnect the half shaft on the wheel side by removing the four flange bolts.

3. Grasp the half shaft at the center and extract it from the differential carrier by prying it with a suitable pry bar.

4. Installation is in the reverse order of removal. Install the differential end first and then the wheel end. Tighten the four flange bolts to 20–27 ft. lbs. (2.3–3.8 kg).

CAUTION: *Take care not to damage the oil seal or either end of the half shaft during installation.*

Overhaul

1. Clamp the half shaft in a vise using "soft" jaws.

2. Using pliers, pry the plug from the wheel side of the half shaft.

3. Remove the plug seal, spring, spring cap and the boot bands.

NOTE: *Never resuse boot bands once they have been removed.*

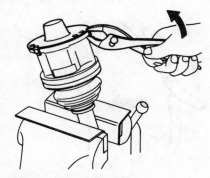

Use pliers to remove the plug

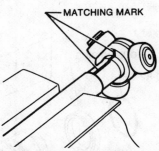

MATCHING MARK

Matchmark the spider assembly to the half shaft

4. Scribe a matchmark on the spider assembly and the half shaft.

5. Remove the spider assembly with a press. Do not attempt to touch the contact surface of the half shaft end at the spring cap or housing subassembly. Always support the half shaft with your hand while you are removing the spider assembly.

6. Draw out the slide joint boot and the boot bands.

7. Loosen the vise and turn the half shaft around so that the differential end is up.

8. Using a hacksaw, cut off the hold joint boot assembly and then remove the housing sub-assembly.

NOTE: *When cutting the hold joint boot assembly, make sure that the half shaft is pushed into the housing sub-assembly in order to prevent the spider assembly from being scratched. Never reuse the boot assembly after it has been removed.*

9. Remove and discard the boot band and then remove the spider assembly as detailed in Steps 4–5.

10. Cut off the remaining part of the hold joint boot assembly and remove it from the housing sub-assembly. Be careful not to scratch the housing ring or assembly.

11. Remove and discard the housing cover and the O-ring.

12. Remove the housing ring.

13. Remove all remaining parts of the hold joint boot assembly and the boot band from the half shaft.

To install:

1. Attach a housing ring, an O ring, a housing sub-assembly and a housing cover to a new hold joint boot assembly. Place the assembled unit flange in a vise. Don't forget to grease the O-ring.

2. Place a board on a housing cover to prevent it from being scratched. Use a mallet and bend the edge over along the entire circumference.

3. Withdraw the housing sub-assembly, install a new boot band and then hold the joint boot assembly on the half shaft.

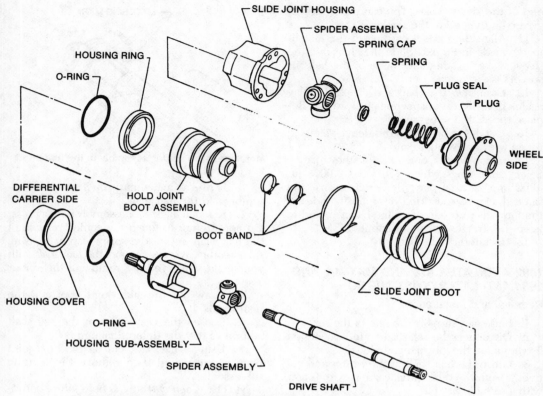

Exploded view of the halfshaft—1982 and later 810 and Maxima

4. Install the spider assembly securely, making sure that the matchmarks are aligned. Make sure that when press-fitting the assembly, the serration chamfer faces the shaft.

5. Stake the serration sides evenly at three places, avoiding areas that have been previously staked. Always stake two or three teeth in an area where the staked gap is more than 0.004 in.

6. Pack with grease.

7. Install the greased O-ring to the housing assembly and then place the hold joint boot assembly so that its flange is in the vise. Be sure that no other part of the assembly is in the vise.

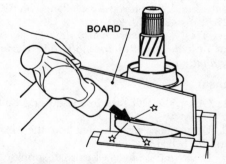

Bending the housing cover

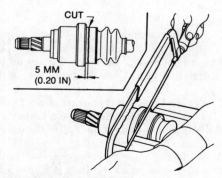

Cutting the hold joint boot

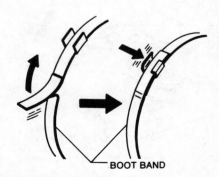

Installing the boot bands

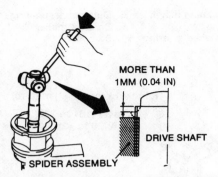

You must stake the serrated sides of the spider assembly upon installation

8. Insert the housing sub-assembly into place and then bend the edge as detailed in Step 2 for the housing cover.

9. Apply sealant. Set the boot and install the boot bands.

10. Turn the half shaft in the vise so that the wheel side is up.

11. Install the new boot bands, slide joint boot and slide joint housing on the half shaft. Be careful not to scratch the boot with the end of the shaft.

12. Install the spider assembly as previously detailed.

13. Install the large diameter boot band and then pack with grease.

14. Install the spring cap, spring and plug seal. Install the plug and secure with dummy bolts. Lock the plug by bending it and then remove the dummy bolts.

15. Install the small diameter boot band and replace the half shaft.

Stub Axle and Rear Wheel Bearings—Independent Rear Suspension Models

REMOVAL AND INSTALLATION

1. Block the front wheels. Loosen the wheel nuts, raise and support the car, and remove the wheel.

2. Remove the half shaft.

3. On cars with rear disc brakes, unbolt the caliper and move it aside. See Chapter 9. Do not allow the caliper to hang by the hose; support the caliper with a length of wire or rest it on a suspension member.

4. Remove the brake disc on models with rear disc brakes. Remove the brake drum on cars with drum brakes. See Chapter 9.

5. Remove the stub axle nut. You will have to hold the stub axle at the outside while removing the nut from the axle shaft side. The nut will require a good deal of force to remove, so be sure to hold the stub axle firmly.

6. Remove the stub axle with a slide hammer and an adapter. The outer wheel bearing will come off with the stub axle.

7. Remove the companion flange from the lower arm.

8. Remove and discard the grease seal and inner bearing from the lower arm using a drift made for the purpose or a length of pipe of the proper diameter.

The outer bearing can be removed from the stub axle with a puller. If the grease seal or the bearings are removed, new parts must be used on assembly.

9. Clean all the parts to be reused in solvent.

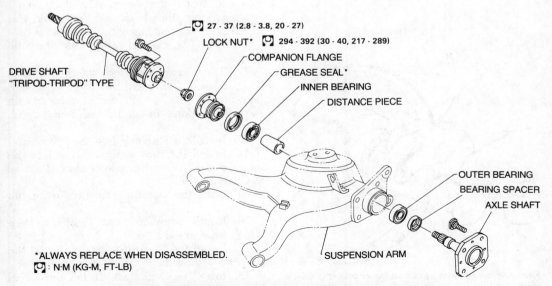

810, Maxima and 200SX Turbo halfshaft, bearings and stub shaft assembly

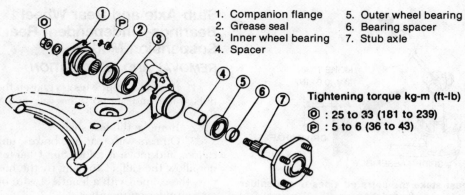

1. Companion flange
2. Grease seal
3. Inner wheel bearing
4. Spacer
5. Outer wheel bearing
6. Bearing spacer
7. Stub axle

Tightening torque kg-m (ft-lb)

Ⓞ : 25 to 33 (181 to 239)
Ⓟ : 5 to 6 (36 to 43)

Stub axle and rear wheel bearings—all models similar

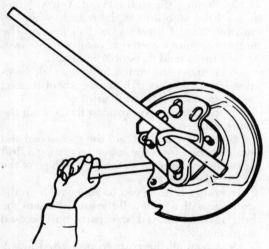

Hold the stub axle while removing the nut from the half shaft side

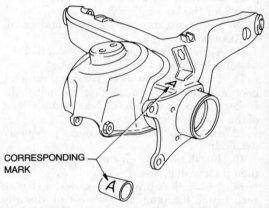

CORRESPONDING MARK

Make sure you install a spacer which is marked the same as the mark on the bearing housing

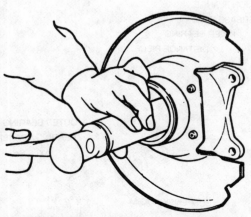

Remove the grease seal and inner bearing with a drift or driver

10. Sealed-type bearings are used. When the new bearings are installed, the sealed side must face out. Install the sealed side of the outer bearing facing the wheel, and the sealed side of the inner bearing facing the differential.

11. Press the outer bearing onto the stub axle.

12. The bearing housing is stamped with an "A," "B," or "C," through 1978. 1979–82 models have an "N," "M," or "P." Select a spacer with the same marking. Install the spacer on the stub axle.

13. Install the stub axle into the lower arm.

14. Install the new inner bearing into the lower arm with the stub axle in place. Install a new grease seal.

15. Install the companion flange onto the stub axle.

16. Install the sub axle nut. Tighten to 181–239 ft. lbs. (25–33 kg-m).

17. Install the brake disc or drum, and the caliper if removed.

18. Install the half shaft. Install the wheel and lower the car.

Suspension and Steering

8

FRONT SUSPENSION

All models covred in this book use Mac-Pherson strut front suspension. In this type of suspension, each strut combines the function of coil spring and shock absorber. The spindle is mounted to the lower part of the strut through a single ball joint. No upper suspension arm is required in this design. The lower suspension arm is bolted to the front subframe assembly. The spindle and lower control arm are located fore and aft by tension rods which attach to the chassis.

Springs and Shock Absorbers
TESTING SHOCK ABSORBER ACTION

Shock absorbers require replacement if the vehicle fails to recover quickly after a large bump is encountered, if there is a tendency for the vehicle to sway or nose dive excessively, or, sometimes, if the suspension is overly susceptible to vibration.

A good way to test the shocks is to intermittently apply downward pressure to one corner of the vehicle until it is moving up and down for almost the full suspension travel, then release it and watch the recovery. If the vehicle bounces slightly about one more time and then comes to rest, the shock absorbers are serviceable. If the vehicle goes on bouncing, the shocks require replacement.

Strut
REMOVAL AND INSTALLATION

The struts are precision parts and retain the springs under tremendous pressure even when removed from the car. For these reasons, several expensive special tools and substantial specialized knowledge are required to safely and effectively work on these parts. We recommend that if spring or shock absorber repair

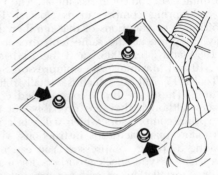

Remove the top strut nuts

work is required, you remove the strut or struts involved and take them to a repair facility which is fully equipped and familiar with the car.

1. Jack up the car and support it safely. Remove the wheel.

2. Remove the brake caliper as outlined in Chapter 9. Remove the disc and hub as described in this chapter.

3. Disconnect the tension rod and stabilizer bar from the transverse link.

4. Unbolt the steering arm. Pry the control arm down to detach it from the strut.

5. Place a jack under the bottom of the strut.

6. Open the hood and remove the nuts holding the top of the strut.

7. Lower the jack slowly and cautiously until the strut assembly can be removed.

8. Reverse the procedure to install. The self-locking nuts holding the top of the strut must be replaced. Bleed the brakes.

STRUT CARTRIDGE REPLACEMENT

CAUTION: *The coil springs are under considerable tension, and can exert enough force to cause serious injury. Disassemble the struts only if the proper tools are available, and use extreme caution.*

Coil springs on all models must be removed

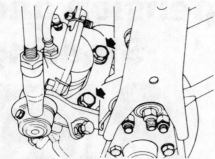

Brake caliper-to-strut mounting bolts

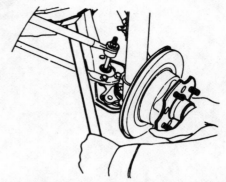

Pry the control arm down to separate the strut from the knuckle

with the aid of a coil spring compressor. If you don't have one, don't try to improvise by using something else: you could risk injury. The Datsun coil spring compressor is Special Tool ST3565S001 or variations of that number. Basically, they are all the same tool, except for the 1980–and later 200SX and the 1981–and later 810 and Maxima spring compressor, Special Tool HT71730000, which is a totally different unit. These are the recommended compressors, although they are probably not the only spring compressors which will work. Always follow manufacturer's instructions when operating a spring compressor. You can now buy cartridge type shock absorbers for many Datsuns: installation procedures are not the same as those given here. In this case, follow the instructions that come with the shock absorbers.

To remove the coil spring, you must first remove the strut assembly from the vehicle. See above for procedures.

1. Secure the strut assembly in a vise.
2. Attach the spring compressor to the spring, leaving the top few coils free.
3. Remove the dust cap from the top of the strut to expose the center nut, if a dust cap is provided.
4. Compress the spring just far enough to permit the strut insulator to be turned by hand. Remove the self-locking center nut.
5. Take out the strut insulator, strut bearing, oil seal, upper spring seat and bound bumper rubber from the top of the strut. Note their sequence of removal and be sure to assemble them in the same order.
6. Remove the spring with the spring compressor still attached.

Assembly is the reverse of disassembly. Observe the following: Make sure you assemble the unit with the shock absorber piston rod fully

1. Strut mounting insulator
2. Coil spring
3. Strut assembly
4. Suspension cross member
5. Stabilizer
6. Tension rod
7. Transverse link
8. Steering knuckle arm

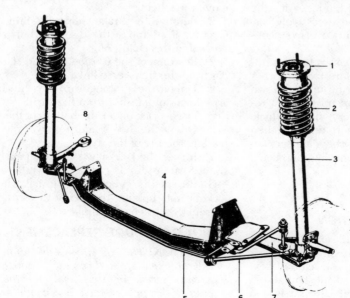

Front suspension—610 and 710

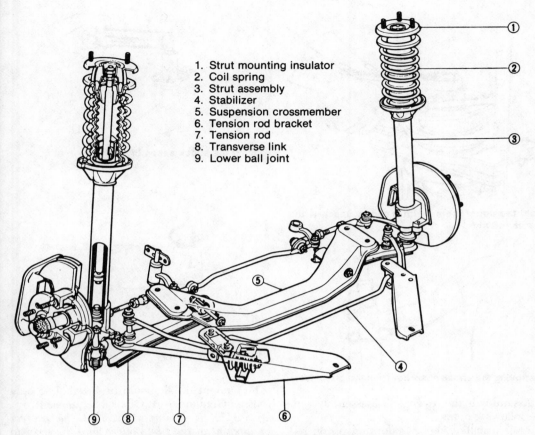

1. Strut mounting insulator
2. Coil spring
3. Strut assembly
4. Stabilizer
5. Suspension crossmember
6. Tension rod bracket
7. Tension rod
8. Transverse link
9. Lower ball joint

Front suspension—200SX; 510, 810 and Maxima similar

extended. When assembling, take care that the rubber spring seats, both top and bottom, and the spring are positioned in their grooves before releasing the spring.

7. To remove the shock absorber: Remove the dust cap, if so equipped, and push the piston rod down until it bottoms. With the piston in this position, loosen and remove the gland packing shock absorber retainer. This calls for Datsun Special Tool ST35500001, but you should be able to loosen it either with a pipe wrench or by tapping it around with a drift.

NOTE: *If the gland tube is dirty, clean it before removing it to prevent dirt from contaminating the fluid inside the strut tube.*

8. Remove the O-ring from the top of the piston rod guide and lift out the piston rod together with the cylinder. Drain all of the fluid from the strut and shock components into a suitable container. Clean all parts.

NOTE: *The piston rod, piston rod guide and cylinder are a matched set: single parts of this shock assembly should not be exchanged with parts of other assemblies.*

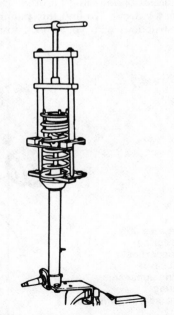

Spring compressor installed on the coil spring for removal

Hold the upper mount with a rod to unscrew the piston rod nut

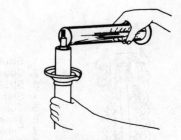

Filling the shock assembly with oil

Removing the shock absorber from the gland tube

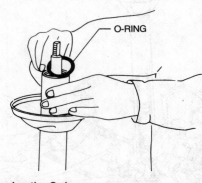

O-RING

Removing the O-ring

Assembly is the reverse of disassembly with the following notes.

After installing the cylinder and piston rod assembly (the shock absorber kit) in the outer casing, remove the piston rod guide, if so equipped, from the cylinder and pour the correct amount of new fluid into the cylinder and strut outer casing. To find this amount consult the instructions with your shock absorber kit.

The amount of oil should be listed. Use only Nissan Genuine Strut Oil or its equivalent.

NOTE: *It is important that the correct amount of fluid be poured into the strut to assure correct shock absorber damping force.*

Install the O-ring, fluid and any other cylinder components. Fit the gland packing and tighten it after greasing the gland packing-to-piston rod mating surfaces.

NOTE: *When tightening the gland packing,*

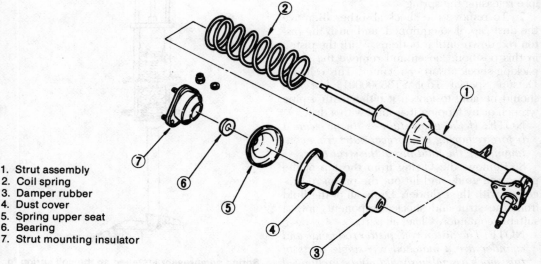

1. Strut assembly
2. Coil spring
3. Damper rubber
4. Dust cover
5. Spring upper seat
6. Bearing
7. Strut mounting insulator

Exploded view of the typical strut assembly

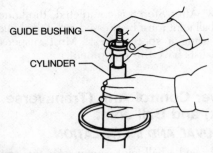

Installing the guide bushing

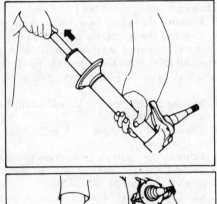

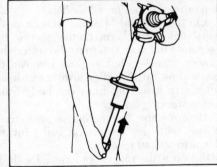

Bleeding air from the assembled strut

extend the piston rod about 3 to 5 inches from the end of the outer casing to expel most of the air from the strut.

After the kit is installed, bleed the air from the system in the following manner: hold the strut with its bottom end facing down. Pull the piston rod out as far as it will go. Turn the strut upside down and push the piston in as far as it will go. Repeat this procedure several times until an equal pressure is felt on both the pull out and the push in strokes of the piston rods. The remaining assembly is the reverse of disassembly.

Ball Joint

INSPECTION

The lower ball joint should be replaced when play becomes excessive. Datsun does not pub-

lish specifications on just what constitutes excessive play, relying instead on a method of determining the force (in inch pounds) required to keep the ball joint turning. This method is not very helpful to the backyard mechanic since it involves removing the ball joint, which is what we are trying to avoid in the first place. An effective way to determine ball joint play is to jack up the car until the wheel is just a couple of inches off the ground and the ball joint is unloaded (meaning you can't jack directly underneath the ball joint). Place a long bar under the tire and move the wheel and tire assembly up and down. Keep one hand on top of the tire while you are going this. If there is over ¼ inch of play at the top of the tire, the ball joint is probably bad. This is assuming that the wheel bearings are in good shape and properly adjusted. As a double check on this, have someone watch the ball joint while you move the tire up and down with the bar. If you can see

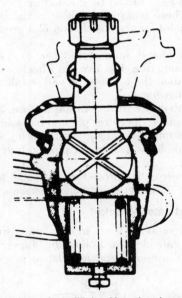

Cross section of a ball joint. Note the plug at the bottom for a grease nipple. Make sure the rubber boot is in good condition; if not, replace it

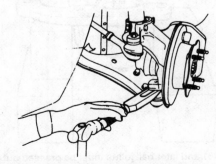

Separate the ball joint from the knuckle

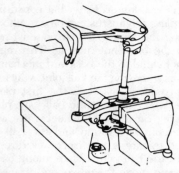

Removing the ball joint, all models except 1981 and later 810, Maxima and 200SX

considerable play, besides feeling play at the top of the wheel, the ball joint needs replacing.

REMOVAL AND INSTALLATION

Except 1981 and Later

The ball joint should be greased every 30,000 miles. There is a plugged hole in the bottom for the joint for the installation of a grease fitting.

1. Raise and support the car so that the wheels hang free. Remove the wheel.
2. Unbolt the tension rod and stabilizer bar from transverse link.
3. Unbolt the strut from the steering arm.
4. Remove the cotter pin and ball joint stud nut. Separate the ball joint and steering arm.
5. Unbolt the ball joint from the transverse link.
6. Reverse the procedure to install a new ball joint. Grease the joint after installation.

1981 and Later Models

The ball joints on these models are a press-fit into the knuckle arm. Follow the "Lower Control Arm" removal and installation procedure

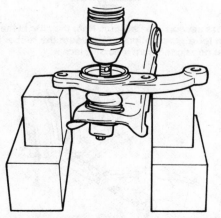

The 1981 and later ball joints must be pressed out of the knuckle

below. After Step 8 is completed, the knuckle arm ball joint must be pressed out of the knuckle arm using a special press. Most suspension specialists have this equipment.

Lower Control Arm (Transverse Link) and Ball Joint

REMOVAL AND INSTALLATION

You'll need a ball joint remover for this operation.

1. Jack up the vehicle and support it with jack stands; remove the wheel.
2. Remove the splash board, if so equipped.
3. Remove the cotter pin and castle nut from the side rod (steering arm) ball joint and separate the ball joint from the side rod. You'll need either a fork type or puller type ball joint remover.
4. Separate the steering knuckle arm from the MacPherson strut.
5. Remove the tension rod and stabilizer bar from the lower arm.
6. Remove the nuts or bolts connecting the lower control arm (transverse link) to the suspension crossmember on all models.
7. On the 810 and Maxima, to remove the transverse link (control arm) on the steering gear side, separate the gear arm from the sector shaft and lower steering linkage; to remove the transverse link on the idler arm side, detach the idler arm assembly from the body frame and lower steering linkage.
8. Remove the lower control arm (transverse link) with the suspension ball joint and knuckle arm still attached.

Installation is the reverse of removal with the following notes.

9. When installing the control arm, temporarily tighten the nuts and/or bolts securing the control arm to the suspension crossmember. Tighten them fully only after the car is sitting on its wheels.
10. Lubricate the ball joints after assembly.

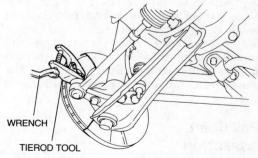

WRENCH

TIEROD TOOL

Separating the knuckle from the tie-rod using a tie-rod removal tool

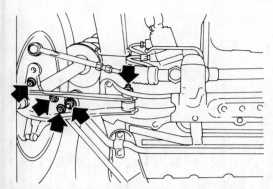

Removing the knuckle arm from the strut (left arrows) and the control arm (transverse link) from the car

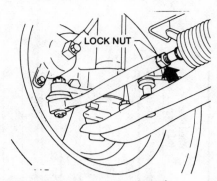

Toe adjustment is made at the tie-rod

Front End Alignment

CASTER AND CAMBER

Caster is the forward or rearward tilt of the upper end of the kingpin, or the upper ball joint, which results in a slight tilt of the steering axis forward or backward. Rearward tilt is referred to as a positive caster, while forward tilt is referred to as negative caster.

Camber is the inward or outward tilt from the vertical, measured in degrees of the front wheels at the top. An outward tilt gives the wheel positive camber. Proper camber is critical to assure even tire wear.

Since caster and camber are adjusted traditionally by adding or subtracting shims behind the upper control arms, and the Datsuns covered in this guide have replaced the upper control arm with the MacPherson strut, the only way to adjust caster and camber is to replace bent or worn parts of the front suspension.

TOE

Toe is the amount, measured in a fraction of an inch, that the wheels are closer together at one end than the other. Toe-in means that the front wheels are closer together at the front than the rear; toe-out means the rears are closer than the front. Datsuns are adjusted to have a slight amount of toe-in. Toe-in is adjusted by turning the tie-rod, which has a right-hand thread on one end and a left-hand thread on the other.

You can check your vehicle's toe-in yourself without special equipment if you make careful measurements. The wheels must be straight ahead.

1. Toe-in can be determined by measuring the distance between the center of the tire treads, at the front of the tire and at the rear. If the tread pattern of your car's tires makes this impossible, you can measure between the edges of the wheel rims, but make sure to move the car forward and measure in a couple of places to void errors caused by bent rims or wheel runout.

2. If the measurement is not within specifications, loosen the locknuts at both ends of the tie-rod (the driver's side locknut is left-hand threaded).

3. Turn the top of the tie-rod toward the front of the car to reduce toe-in, or toward the rear to increase it. When the correct dimension is reached, tighten the locknuts and check the adjustment.

NOTE: *The length of the tie-rods must always be equal to each other.*

STEERING ANGLE ADJUSTMENT

The maximum steering angle is adjusted by stopper bolts on the steering arms. Loosen the locknut on the stopper bolt, turn the stopped bolt in or out as required to obtain the proper maximum steering angle and retighten the locknut.

SUSPENSION HEIGHT

Suspension height is adjusted by replacing the springs. Various springs are available for adjustment.

REAR SUSPENSION

There are several different types of rear suspensions used on the Datsuns covered in this guide. All 710 and 1977–79 200SX models are equipped with solid rear axles suspended by leaf springs. The 610 sedan and the 810 sedan have independent rear suspensions which incorporate semi-trailing arms and coil springs.

The 1978–81 510 sedans and hatchbacks, the 1982 and later Maxima wagon, and the 1980–84 200SX (except Turbo) are equipped with four-link type solid rear axles with coil springs. All station wagons up to 1981 use a solid rear axle supported by leaf springs.

CAUTION: *Before doing any rear suspen-*

Wheel Alignment Specifications

Year	Model	Caster Range (deg)	Caster Preferred Setting (deg)	Camber Range (deg)	Camber Preferred Setting (deg)	Toe-In (in.)	Steering Axis Inclination (deg)	Wheel Pivot Ratio (deg) Inner Wheel	Wheel Pivot Ratio (deg) Outer Wheel
1973	610	1¼–2¾	2	1½–2¾	2	½	6²¹⁄₃₂	32½+	30½
	610 Station Wagon	1¼–2¾	2	1½–3	2¼	½	6²¹⁄₃₂	32½+	30½
1974	610	1¼–2¾	2	1¼–2¾	2	½	6²¹⁄₃₂	32½+	30½
	610 Station Wagon	1¼–2¾	2	1½–3	2¼	½	6²¹⁄₃₂	32½+	30½
	710	1³⁄₁₆–2¹¹⁄₁₆	1¹⁵⁄₁₆	1⁷⁄₁₆–2¹⁵⁄₁₆	1⅛	⅝	6¹³⁄₃₂	37½+	31²⁷⁄₃₂
1975	610 (Front)	1¼–2¾	2	1¼–2¾	2	½	6²¹⁄₃₂	32½+	30½
	610 (Rear)	—	—	¾–2¼	1½	⁵⁄₁₆	—	—	—
	610 Station Wagon	1¼–2¾	2	1½–3	2¼	½	6²¹⁄₃₂	32½+	30½
	710	1³⁄₁₆–2¹¹⁄₁₆	1¹⁵⁄₁₆	2¹⁵⁄₁₆	2¹⁵⁄₁₆	⅜	6¹³⁄₃₂	32½+	30½
1976–77	610, 710 (Bias Tires)	—	—	—	—	¼	7	32½+	30½
	610, 710 (Radials)	1¹⁄₁₆–2⁹⁄₁₆	1¹³⁄₁₆	1¼–2¾	2	⁷⁄₃₂	7	32½+	30½
1977	200SX	1¹⁄₃₂–2¼	1²¹⁄₃₂	½–1½	1	⅛	7¹³⁄₁₆	35	30
1977–80	810 (Front)	1³⁄₁₆–2¹¹⁄₁₆	2¼	0–1½	¾	⅛	7²⁹⁄₃₂	20	18²⁰⁄₃₂
	810 (Rear)	—	—	—	—	³⁄₁₆	—	—	—
1978–79	200SX	1¹⁄₁₆–2⁹⁄₁₆	1¹³⁄₁₆	⁵⁄₁₆–1¹³⁄₁₆	¹⁷⁄₁₆	⅛	7¹³⁄₁₆	35	30
1978–81	510 Station Wagon	¹⁵⁄₁₆–2⁷⁄₁₆	1⁹⁄₁₆	¹⁄₁₆–1⁹⁄₁₆	¾	¹⁄₁₆	8⁵⁄₃₂	20	19½
1979–81	510	1¹⁄₁₆–2⁹⁄₁₆	1¹³⁄₁₆	−¼–1¼	½	¹⁄₁₆	8²⁷⁄₃₂	20	19½
1981–83	810 (Front)	2¹⁵⁄₁₆–4⁷⁄₁₆	3¹¹⁄₁₆	−⁵⁄₁₆–1³⁄₁₆	⁷⁄₁₆	¹⁄₃₂	12⅛	20	18¹¹⁄₁₆
	810 (Rear)	—	—	¹⁵⁄₁₆–2⁷⁄₁₆	1¹¹⁄₁₆	⁷⁄₃₂	—	—	—
1980–83	200SX	1¾–3¼	2½	−¹¹⁄₁₆–¹³⁄₁₆	¹⁄₁₆	³⁄₆₄	8⁵⁄₃₂	20	18⁴⁵⁄₆₄
1984	Maxima (Front)	2¹⁵⁄₁₆–4⁷⁄₁₆	3¹¹⁄₁₆	−⁵⁄₁₆–1³⁄₁₆	⁷⁄₁₆	¹⁄₃₂	12⅛	20	18¹¹⁄₁₆
	Maxima (Rear)	—	—	1¼–2¾	2	⁵⁄₃₂	—	—	—
1984	200SX	2¾–4¼	3½	−⅜–1¹⁄₁₆	1⅞	³⁄₆₄	11¹¹⁄₁₆	20	18¹¹⁄₁₆

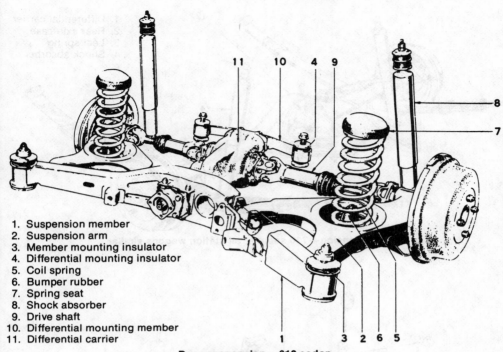

1. Suspension member
2. Suspension arm
3. Member mounting insulator
4. Differential mounting insulator
5. Coil spring
6. Bumper rubber
7. Spring seat
8. Shock absorber
9. Drive shaft
10. Differential mounting member
11. Differential carrier

Rear suspension—610 sedan

sion work, block the front wheels of the vehicle to insure that it won't move or shift while you are under it. Remember, you are dealing with spring steel that has enough force to physically damage you if you don't follow the removal and installation procedures exactly.

Springs

REMOVAL AND INSTALLATION

Leaf Spring Type

610 STATION WAGON AND ALL 710 AND 1977–79 200SX MODELS

1. Raise the rear axle until the wheels hang free. Support the car on stands. Support the rear axle with a floor jack.
2. Remove the spare tire.
3. Unbolt the bottom end of the shock absorber.
4. Unbolt the axle from the spring leaves.
5. Unbolt the front spring bracket from the body, Lower the spring end and bracket to the floor.
6. Unbolt and remove the rear shackle.
7. Unbolt the bracket from the spring.
8. Before reinstallation, coat the front bracket pin and bushing, and the shackle pin and bushing with a soap solution.
9. Reverse the procedure to install. The front pin nut and the shock absorber mounting should be tightened after the vehicle is lowered to the

floor. Make sure that the elongated flange of the rubber bumper is to the rear.

510 AND 810 STATION WAGONS

1. Raise the rear of the car and support it with jackstands.
2. Remove the wheels and tires.
3. Disconnect the lower end of the shcok absorber and remove the U-bolt nuts.
4. Place a jack under the rear axle.
5. Disconnect the spring shackle bolts at the front and rear of the spring.
6. Lower the jack slowly and remove the spring.
7. Installation is in the reverse order of removal.

Coil Spring Type

610 SEDAN

1. Raise the rear of the vehicle and support it on stands.
2. Remove the wheels.
3. Disconnect the handbrake linkage and return spring.
4. Unbolt the axle drive shaft flange at the wheel end.
5. Unbolt the rubber bumper inside the bottom of the coil spring.
6. Jack up the suspension arm and unbolt the shock absorber lower mounting
7. Lower the jack slowly and cautiously. Re-

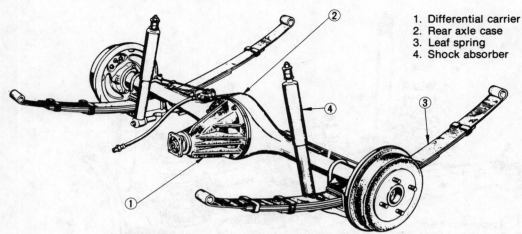

1. Differential carrier
2. Rear axle case
3. Leaf spring
4. Shock absorber

Rear suspension—710 sedans; all station wagons similar

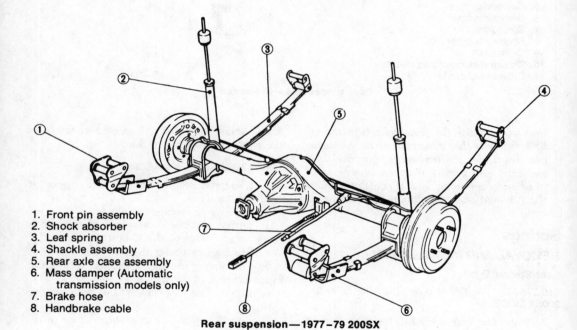

1. Front pin assembly
2. Shock absorber
3. Leaf spring
4. Shackle assembly
5. Rear axle case assembly
6. Mass damper (Automatic transmission models only)
7. Brake hose
8. Handbrake cable

Rear suspension—1977–79 200SX

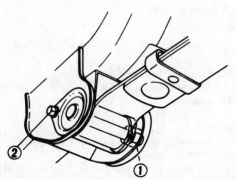

Remove the spring pin by removing the nuts (1) and (2)—all leaf spring rear suspension cars

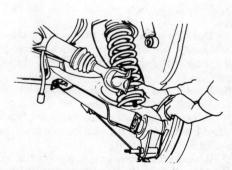

Coil spring removal, all independent rear suspension cars except 810 and Maxima

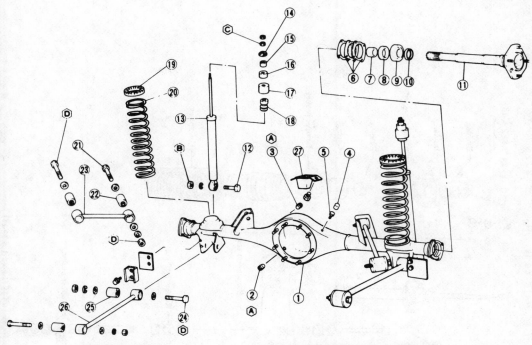

1. Rear axle case
2. Drain plug
3. Filler plug
4. Breather cap
5. Breather
6. Rear axle case end shim
7. Bearing collar
8. Oil seal
9. Rear axle bearing
10. Bearing spacer
11. Rear axle shaft
12. Shock absorber lower end bolt
13. Shock absorber assembly
14. Special washer
15. Shock absorber mounting bushing A
16. Shock absorber mounting bushing B
17. Bound bumper cover
18. Bound bumper rubber
19. Shock absorber mounting insulator
20. Coil spring
21. Upper link bushing bolt
22. Upper link bushing

Rear suspension—510 sedan; 1980 and later 200SX (non-Turbo) similar

move the coil spring, spring seat, and rubber bumper.

8. Reverse the procedure to install, making sure that the flat face of the spring is at the top.

810 AND MAXIMA SEDAN MODELS

These models utilizes MacPherson struts in the rear suspension. The struts are removed as a unit; disassembly of the strut requires a spring compressor. For strut disassembly, follow the procedure given for front suspension Mac-Pherson struts.

1. Raise the car and safely support the rear end with jackstands and a floor jack.

2. Open the trunk and remove the three nuts which secure the top of the strut to the body.

3. Disconnect the strut at the bottom by removing the bolt at the suspension arm.

4. Service the strut as detailed under "Front Suspension".

5. Installation is the reverse of removal. Install the strut so that the larger hole on the lower end faces out.

510 SEDAN AND HATCHBACK, 1980–84 200SX

1. Raise the car and support it with jackstands.

2. Support the center of the differential with a jack or other suitable tool.

3. Remove the rear wheels.

4. Remove the bolts securing the lower ends of the shock absorbers.

5. Lower the jack under the differential slowly and carefully and remove the coil springs after they are fully extended.

6. Installation is in the reverse order of removal.

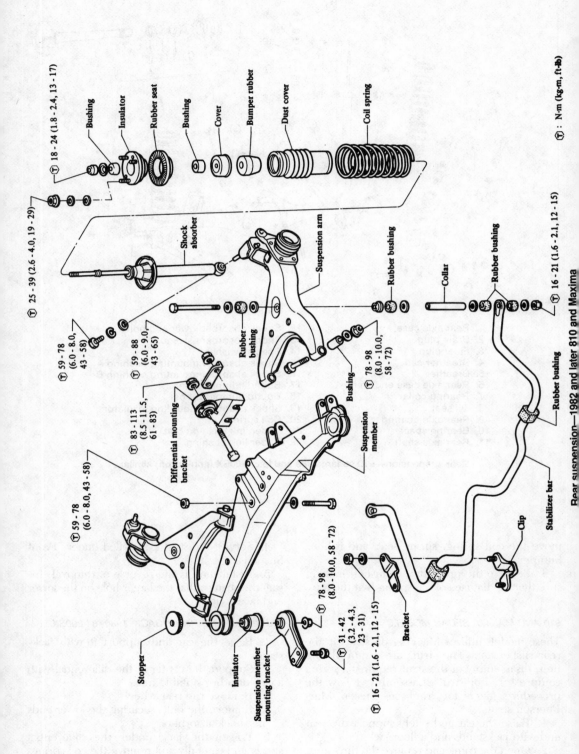

Bushing

Insulator

Rubber seat

Bushing

Cover

Bumper rubber

Dust cover

Coil spring

Ⓣ 18 - 24 (1.8 - 2.4, 13 - 17)

Ⓣ : N·m (kg·m, ft-lb)

Ⓣ 25 - 39 (2.6 - 4.0, 19 - 29)

Shock absorber

Suspension arm

Rubber bushing

Rubber bushing

Collar

Ⓣ 16 - 21 (1.6 - 2.1, 12 - 15)

Ⓣ 59 - 78 (6.0 - 8.0, 43 - 58)

Ⓣ 59 - 88 (6.0 - 9.0, 43 - 65)

Rubber bushing

Ⓣ 78 - 98 (8.0 - 10.0, 58 - 72)

Bushing

Rubber bushing

Ⓣ 83 - 113 (8.5 - 11.5, 61 - 83)

Differential mounting bracket

Suspension member

Ⓣ 59 - 78 (6.0 - 8.0, 43 - 58)

Rubber bushing

Stabilizer bar

Clip

Stopper

Insulator

Suspension member mounting bracket

Ⓣ 78 - 98 (8.0 - 10.0, 58 - 72)

Ⓣ 31 - 42 (3.2 - 4.3, 23 - 31)

Ⓣ 16 - 21 (1.6 - 2.1, 12 - 15)

Bracket

Rear suspension—1982 and later 810 and Maxima

WHEEL ALIGNMENT
- CAMBER CANNOT BE ADJUSTED.
- VEHICLE REQUIRES ONLY TOE-IN ADJUSTMENT.
  - 2 TO 0 MM (− 0.08 TO 0 IN), (− 12′ TO 0)

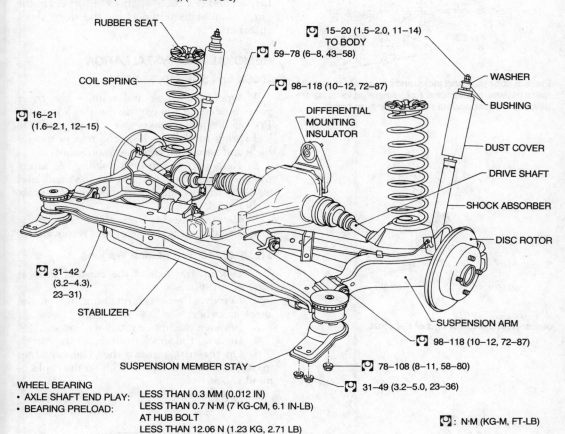

RUBBER SEAT

COIL SPRING

15–20 (1.5–2.0, 11–14) TO BODY

59–78 (6–8, 43–58)

98–118 (10–12, 72–87)

16–21 (1.6–2.1, 12–15)

DIFFERENTIAL MOUNTING INSULATOR

WASHER

BUSHING

DUST COVER

DRIVE SHAFT

SHOCK ABSORBER

DISC ROTOR

31–42 (3.2–4.3, 23–31)

STABILIZER

SUSPENSION ARM

98–118 (10–12, 72–87)

SUSPENSION MEMBER STAY

78–108 (8–11, 58–80)

31–49 (3.2–5.0, 23–36)

WHEEL BEARING
- AXLE SHAFT END PLAY: LESS THAN 0.3 MM (0.012 IN)
- BEARING PRELOAD: LESS THAN 0.7 N·M (7 KG-CM, 6.1 IN-LB)
  AT HUB BOLT
  LESS THAN 12.06 N (1.23 KG, 2.71 LB)

: N·M (KG-M, FT-LB)

1984 and later 200SX rear suspension

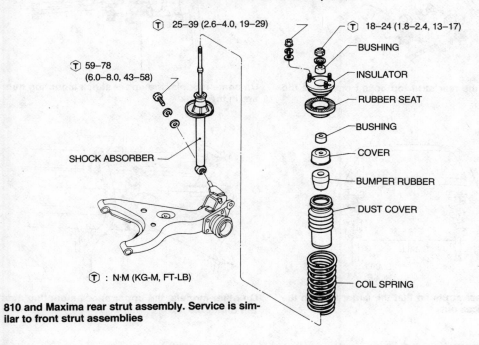

25–39 (2.6–4.0, 19–29)

18–24 (1.8–2.4, 13–17)

BUSHING

INSULATOR

RUBBER SEAT

BUSHING

COVER

BUMPER RUBBER

DUST COVER

COIL SPRING

59–78 (6.0–8.0, 43–58)

SHOCK ABSORBER

: N·M (KG-M, FT-LB)

810 and Maxima rear strut assembly. Service is similar to front strut assemblies

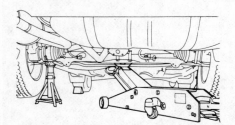

Place a floor jack and jackstands securely under the rear suspension member. Note where jackstands are placed for independent rear suspension cars

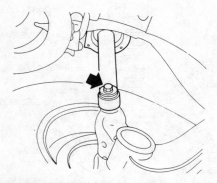

Disconnect the lower end of the strut

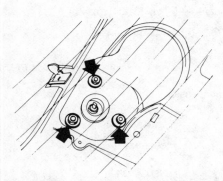

Disconnect the rear strut top bolts from inside the trunk

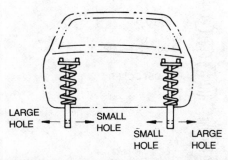

Install the rear struts so that the larger hole on the lower end faces out

Shock Absorber

INSPECTION AND TESTING

Inspect and test the rear shock absorbers in the same manner as outlined for the front shock absorbers.

REMOVAL AND INSTALLATION

200SX and 510, 610, 710 Sedans

1. Open the trunk and remove the cover panel if necessary to expose the shock mounts. Pry off the mount covers, if so equipped. On leaf spring models, jack up the rear of the vehicle and support the rear axle on stands.

2. Remove the two nuts holding the top of the shock absorber (one nut on 1984 and later 200SX). Unbolt the bottom of the shock absorber.

3. Remove the shock absorber.

4. Installation is the reverse of removal.

510, 610, 710, 810 Station Wagons

1. Jack up the rear of the car and support the axle on stands.

2. Remove the lower retaining nut on the shock absorber.

3. Remove the upper retaining bolt(s).

4. Remove the shock from under the car.

5. On the 610, remove the retaining strap from the old shock and install it on the replacement shock.

6. Installation is the reverse of removal.

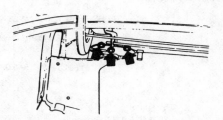

On some models, the upper shock mounting nuts are in the trunk

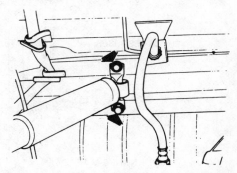

On other models, the upper shock mounting nuts are under the car

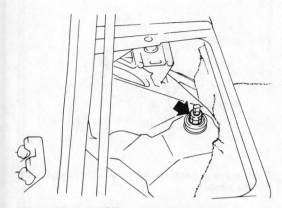

1984 and later 200SX top rear shock nut

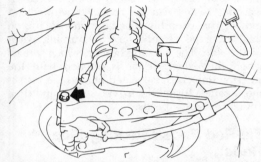

Rear shock bottom mounting bolt, 1984 and later 200SX

810 Sedans

The shock absorber is actually a MacPherson strut on these models. See "Spring Removal" in this chapter. Disassembly of the strut unit on the rear of this vehicle is similar to the disassembly procedures for the front struts. You will need a spring compressor. See the section above.

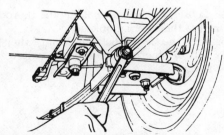

Removing the lower shock mounting nut

STEERING

Steering Wheel

REMOVAL AND INSTALLATION

1. Position the wheels in the straight-ahead direction. The steering wheel should be right-side up and level.

2. Disconnect the battery ground cable.

3. Look at the back of your steering wheel. If there are countersunk screws in the back of the spokes, remove the screws and pull off the horn pad. Some models have a horn wire running from the pad to the steering wheel. Disconnect it.

There are three other types of horn buttons or rings on Datsuns. The first simply pulls off. The second, which is usually a large, semi-triangular pad, must be pushed up, then pulled off. The third must be pushed in and turned clockwise.

4. Remove the rest of the horn switching mechanism, noting the relative location of the parts. Remove the mechanism only if it hinders subsequent wheel removal procedures.

5. Match-mark the top of the steering column shaft and the steering wheel flange.

610 horn pad removal

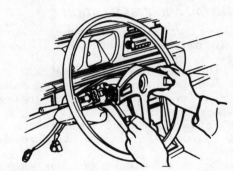

Horn pads on later models pull right off

ST27180001

Use a puller to remove the steering wheel

6. Remove the attaching nut and remove the steering wheel with a puller.

CAUTION: *Do not strike the shaft with a hammer, which may cause the column to collapse.*

7. Install the steering wheel in the reverse order of removal, aligning the punch marks. Do not drive or hammer the wheel into place, or you may cause the collapsible steering column to collapse; in which case you'll have to buy a whole new steering column unit.

8. Tighten the steering wheel nut to 22–25 ft. lbs. on the 1977–79 200SX. Tighten all other steering wheel nuts to 28–36 ft. lbs. except the 1984 200 SX wheel nut, which is tightened to 22–29 ft. lbs.

9. Reinstall the horn button, pad, or ring.

Turn Signal Switch
REMOVAL AND INSTALLATION

On some later model Datsuns, the turn signal switch is part of a combination switch. The whole unit is removed together.

1. Disconnect the battery ground cable.

2. Remove the steering wheel as previously outlined. Observe the "caution" on the collapsible steering column.

3. Remove the steering column covers.

4. Disconnect the electrical plugs from the switch.

5. Remove the retaining screws and remove the switch.

6. Installation is the reverse of removal. Many models have turn signal switches that have a tab which must fit into a hole in the steering shaft in order for the system to return the switch to the neutral position after the turn has been made. Be sure to align the tab and the hole when installing.

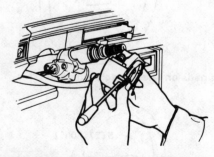

Removing the turn signal switch—610 shown

Steering Lock
REMOVAL AND INSTALLATION

The steering lock/ignition switch/warning buzzer assembly is attached to the steering column by special screws whose heads shear off on instal-

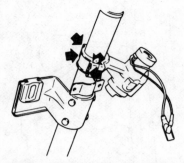

Steering lock securing screws—1977–79 200SX, others similar

lation. The screws must be drilled out to remove the assembly. The ignition switch or warning switch can be replaced without removing the assembly. The ignition switch is on the back of the assembly, and the warning switch on the side. The warning buzzer, which sounds when the driver's door is opened with the steering unlocked, is located behind the instrument panel. Install shear-type screws and then cut off the screw heads.

Tie-Rod Ends (Steering Side Rods)
REMOVAL AND INSTALLATION

You will need a ball joint remover for this operation.

1. Jack up the front of the vehicle and support it on jack stands.

2. Locate the faulty tie-rod end. It will have a lot of play in it and the dust cover will probably be ripped.

3. Remove the cotter key and nut from the tie-rod stud. Note the position of the tie-rod end in relation to the rest of the steering linkage.

4. Loosen the locknut holding the tie-rod to the rest of the steering linkage.

5. Free the tie-rod ball joint from either the relay rod or steering knuckle by using a ball joint remover.

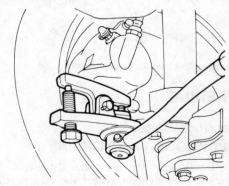

Tie-rod puller

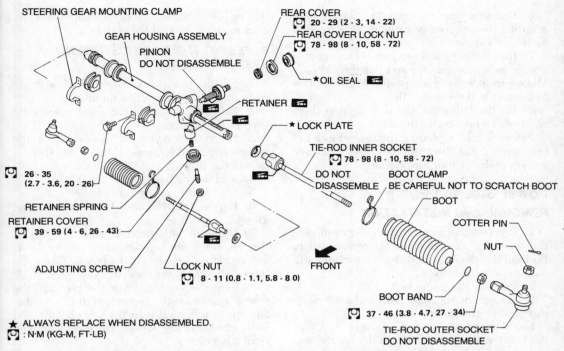

STEERING GEAR MOUNTING CLAMP

GEAR HOUSING ASSEMBLY

PINION
DO NOT DISASSEMBLE

REAR COVER
20 - 29 (2 - 3, 14 - 22)

REAR COVER LOCK NUT
78 - 98 (8 - 10, 58 - 72)

★OIL SEAL

RETAINER

★ LOCK PLATE

TIE-ROD INNER SOCKET
78 - 98 (8 - 10, 58 - 72)

DO NOT
DISASSEMBLE

BOOT CLAMP
BE CAREFUL NOT TO SCRATCH BOOT

BOOT

COTTER PIN

NUT

26 - 35
(2.7 - 3.6, 20 - 26)

RETAINER SPRING

RETAINER COVER
39 - 59 (4 - 6, 26 - 43)

ADJUSTING SCREW

LOCK NUT
8 - 11 (0.8 - 1.1, 5.8 - 8 0)

FRONT

BOOT BAND

37 - 46 (3.8 - 4.7, 27 - 34)

TIE-ROD OUTER SOCKET
DO NOT DISASSEMBLE

★ ALWAYS REPLACE WHEN DISASSEMBLED.
: N·M (KG-M, FT-LB)

200SX rack and pinion system showing tie rod ends. Other models' rack and pinion systems similar

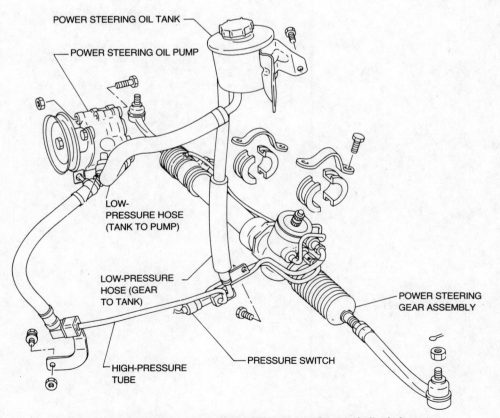

POWER STEERING OIL TANK

POWER STEERING OIL PUMP

LOW-
PRESSURE HOSE
(TANK TO PUMP)

LOW-PRESSURE
HOSE (GEAR
TO TANK)

HIGH-PRESSURE
TUBE

PRESSURE SWITCH

POWER STEERING
GEAR ASSEMBLY

Typical power steering system, 1984 200SX shown. Others similar in layout

6. Unscrew and remove the tie-rod end, counting the number of turns it takes to completely free it.

7. Install the new tie-rod end, turning it in exactly as far as you screwed out the old one. Make sure it is correctly positioned in relation to the rest of the steering linkage.

8. Fit the ball joint and nut, tighten them and install a new cotter pin.

Before finally tightening the tie-rod lock nut or clamp, adjust the toe-in of the vehicle. See section under "Front Suspension."

Power Steering Pump
REMOVAL AND INSTALLATION

1. Remove the hoses at the pump and plug the openings shut to prevent contamination. Position the disconnected lines in a raised attitude to prevent leakage.

2. Remove the pump belt.

3. Loosen the retaining bolts and any braces, and remove the pump.

Installation is the reverse of removal. Adjust the belt tension by referring to the "Belts" section in Chapter one, "General Information and Maintenance." Bleed the system.

BLEEDING THE POWER STEERING SYSTEM

1. Fill the pump reservoir and allow to remain undisturbed for a few minutes.

2. Raise the car until the front wheels are clear of the ground.

3. With the engine off, quickly turn the wheels right and left several times, lightly contacting the stops.

4. Add fluid if necessary.

5. Start the engine and let it idle.

6. Repeat Steps 3 and 4 with the engine idling.

7. With the steering wheel all the way to the left, open the bleeder screw on the steering gear to allow the air to bleed. Close the screw when fluid is expelled.

8. Stop the engine, lover the car until the wheels just touch the ground. Start the engine, allow it to idle, and turn the wheels back and forth several times. Check the fluid level and refill if necessary.

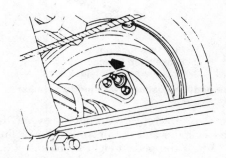

BRAKE SYSTEM

Adjustment

Front disc brakes are used on all Datsuns covered in this manual. All models are equipped with independent front and rear hydraulic systems with a warning light to indicate loss of pressure in either system. All models except the 1980–83 200SX, the 1984 and later 200SX Turbo, and the Maxima/810 (some models) have rear drum brakes. (Rear disc brakes are available as an option on certain other models). The 1980–82 200SX is equipped with rear disc brakes with the parking brake system activating the main brake pads via a mechanical lever assembly. All models have a vacuum booster system to lessen the required pedal pressure. The parking brake on all models operates the rear brakes through a cable system.

> NOTE: *Only certain types of drum brakes require adjustment; some drum brakes are automatically adjusted when the parking brake is applied. No disc brakes need adjustment—they are self adjusting.*

To adjust the brakes, raise the wheels, disconnect the parking brake linkage from the rear wheels, apply the brakes hard a few times to center the drums, and proceed as follows:

BOLT-TYPE ADJUSTER

Turn the adjuster bolt on the backing plate until the wheel can no longer be turned, then back off until the wheel is free of drag. Repeat the procedure on the other adjuster bolt on the same wheel. Some models may have only one adjuster bolt per wheel.

Some models incorporate a "click" arrangement with the bolt adjuster. The adjustment proceeds in clicks or notches. The wheel will often be locked temporarily as the adjuster passes over the center for each click. Thus, the adjuster is alternately hard and easy to turn.

710 rear brake adjuster

When the wheel is fully locked, back off 1–3 clicks.

TOOTHED ADJUSTING NUT

Remove the rubber cover from the backing plate. Align the hole in the brake backing plate with the adjusting nut. To spread the brake shes, turn the toothed adjusting nut with a conventional screwdriver. Stop turning when a considerable drag is felt. Back off the nut a few notches so that the correct clearance is reached between the brake drum and the brake shoes. Make sure that the wheel rotates freely.

AUTOMATIC ADJUSTERS

No manual adjustment is necessary. The self adjuster operates whenever the hand or foot brake brakes (on some models) are used.

After Adjustment—All Models

After adjusting the brakes, reconnect the handbrake linkage. Make sure that there is no rear wheel drag with the handbrake released. Loosen the handbrake adjustment if necessary.

BRAKE PEDAL ADJUSTMENT

Before adjusting the pedal, make sure that the wheelbrakes are correctly adjusted. Adjust the pedal free play by means of the adjustable

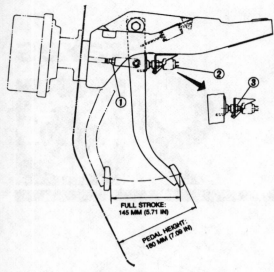

1. Push rod lock nut
2. Brake lamp switch
3. Brake lamp switch lock nut

Brake pedal adjustment—all models similar

pushrod or by replacing shims between the master cylinder and the brake booster or firewall. Adjust the pedal height by means of the adjustable pedal arm stop pad in the driver's compartment. Free play should be approximately 0.04–0.20 in. on all models. Pedal height (floorboard-to-pedal pad) should be approximately 6 in. for all 510s and the 1980–81 200SX. Pedal height should be about 6½ in. for the 1981–84 810 and Maxima and the 1982 200SX; 7 in. for all 1977–79 200SX, 610s, 710s and the 1977–80 810; 7½ in. for the 1984 and later 200SX with manual transmission, and 7½ to 8 in. for the 1984 and later 200SX with automatic transmission.

HYDRAULIC SYSTEM

Master Cylinder
REMOVAL AND INSTALLATION

Clean the outside of the cylinder thoroughly, particularly around the cap and fluid lines. Disconnect the fluid lines and cap them to exclude dirt. Remove the clevis pin connecting the pushrod to the brake pedal arm inside the vehicle. This pin need not be removed if the car is equipped with a vacuum booster. Unbolt the master cylinder from the firewall (or vacuum booster) and remove. The adjustable pushrod is used to adjust brake pedal free-play. If the pushrod is not adjustable, there will be shims between the cylinder and the mount. These shims, or the adjustable pushrod, are used to

adjust brake pedal free play. The 1980–83 200SX's pushrod is not adjustable, as the rod between the brake booster and the master cylinder is secured by adhesion. After installation, bleed the system and check the pedal free-play.

NOTE: *Ordinary brake fluid will boil and cause brake failure under the high temperatures developed in disc brake systems. DOT 3 or 4 brake fluid for disc brake systems must be used.*

OVERHAUL

CAUTION: *Master cylinders are supplied to Datsun by two manufacturers: Nabco and Tokico. Parts between these manufacturers are not interchangeable. Be sure you obtain the correct rebuilding kit for your master cylinder.*

The master cylinder can be disassembled using the illustrations as a guide. Clean all parts in clean brake fluid. Replace the cylinder or piston as necessary if clearance between the two exceeds 0.006 in. Lubricate all parts with clean brake fluid on assembly. Master cylinder rebuilding kits, containing all the wearing parts, are available to simplify overhaul.

Brake Proportioning Valve

All Datsuns covered in this guide are equipped with brake proportioning valves of several different types. The valves all do the same job, which is to separate the front and rear brake lines, allowing them to function independently, and preventing the rear brakes from locking before the front brakes. Damage, such as brake line leakage, in either the front or rear brake system will not affect the normal operation of the unaffected system. If, in the event of a panic stop, the rear brakes lock up before the front brakes, it could mean the proportioning valve is defective. In that case, replace the entire proportioning valve.

REMOVAL AND INSTALLATION

1. Disconnect and plug the brake lines at the valve.
2. Unscrew the mounting bolt(s) and remove the valve.

NOTE: *Do not disassemble the valve.*

3. Installation is in the reverse order of removal. Bleed the system.

Bleeding

The purpose of bleeding the brakes is to expel air trapped in the hydraulic system. The system must be bled whenever the pedal feels spongy, indicating that compressible air has entered the system. It must also be bled when-

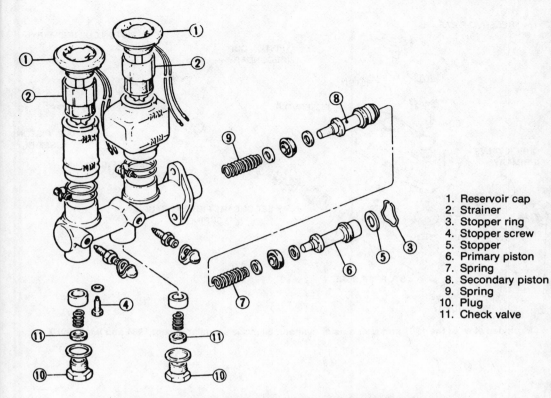

1. Reservoir cap
2. Strainer
3. Stopper ring
4. Stopper screw
5. Stopper
6. Primary piston
7. Spring
8. Secondary piston
9. Spring
10. Plug
11. Check valve

Exploded view of the 1973–80 master cylinder—all models similar

ever the system has been opened or repaired. You will need a helper for this job.

CAUTION: *Never reuse brake fluid which has been bled from the system.*

The sequence for bleeding is as follows: Right rear, left rear, right front, left front.

1. Clean all dirt from around the master cyl-inder reservoir caps. Remove the caps and fill the master cylinder to the proper level with clean, fresh brake fluid meeting DOT 3 speci-fications.

NOTE: *Brake fluid picks up moisture from the air, which reduces its effectiveness and causes brake line corrosion. Don't leave the*

Brake Identification Chart

Match the numbers on the chart with those below to identify your brake system

Model	1973	1974	1975	1976	1977	1978	1979	1980	1981	1982	1983	1984
610	②⑦	②⑦	①⑦	①⑦								
710		②⑦	②⑦	③⑦	③⑦							
810, Maxima					③⑧	③⑧	③⑧	③⑧	④⑧⑥	④⑧⑥	④⑧⑥	④⑧⑥
200SX					①⑧	①⑧	①⑧	③⑨	③⑨	③⑤	③⑤	⑩⑪⑧
510						③⑧	③⑧	③⑧	③⑧			

① Annette-type front disc brakes
② SC-type front disc brakes
③ N20, N22, N22A, N32, N34L front disc brakes
④ CL22V front disc brakes
⑤ CL11H rear disc brakes with parking brake assembly
⑥ CL11H rear disc brakes with parking brake assembly—optional
⑦ Rear drum brakes with bolt-type adjuster
⑧ Rear drum brakes with automatic adjustment
⑨ AN12H rear disc brakes with parking brake assembly
⑩ AD22V front disc brakes
⑪ CL11H rear disc brakes on 200SX Turbo

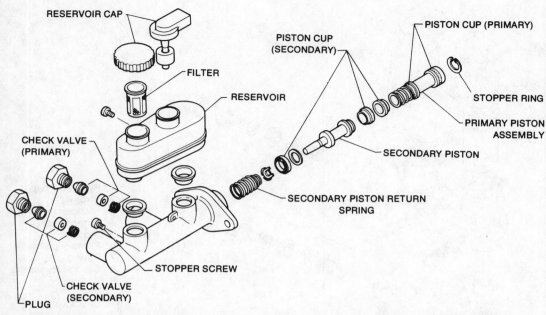

Exploded view of the 1981 and later master cylinder, all models similar except 1984 and later 200SX

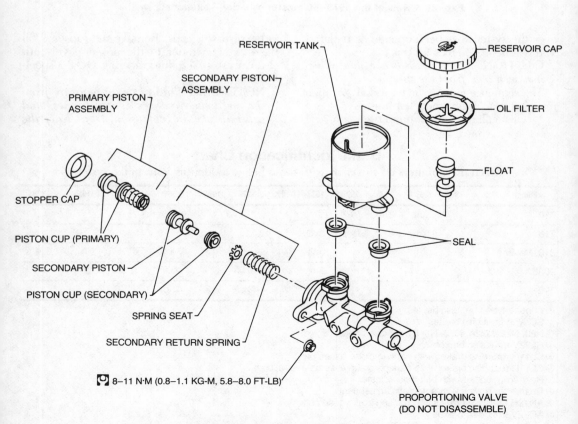

8–11 N·M (0.8–1.1 KG-M, 5.8–8.0 FT-LB)

1984 and later 200SX master cylinder

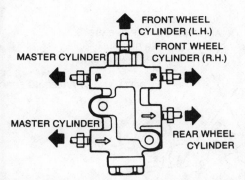

FRONT WHEEL CYLINDER (L.H.)

FRONT WHEEL CYLINDER (R.H.)

MASTER CYLINDER

MASTER CYLINDER

REAR WHEEL CYLINDER

Cross section of the proportioning valve—most models similar

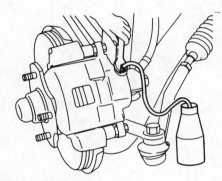

Bleeding the brakes

master cylinder or the fluid container open any longer than necessary. Be careful not to spill brake fluid on painted surfaces; wipe up any spilled fluid immediately and rinse the area with clear water.

2. Clean all the bleeder screws. You may want to give each one a shot of penetrating solvent to loosen it up; seizure is a common problem with bleeder screws, which then break off, sometimes requiring replacement of the part to which they are attached.

3. Attach a length of clear vinyl tubing to the bleeder screw on the wheel cylinder. Insert the other end of the tube into a clear, clean jar half filled with brake fluid.

4. Have your helper slowly depress the brake pedal. As this is done, open the bleeder screw ⅓–½ of a turn, and allow the fluid to run through the tube. Close the bleeder screw before the pedal reaches the end of its travel. Have your assistant slowly release the pedal. Repeat this process until no air bubbles appear in the expelled fluid.

NOTE: *Some front drum brakes have two hydraulic cylinders and two bleeder screws. Both cylinders must be bled.*

5. Repeat the procedure on the other three brakes, checking the fluid level in the master cylinder reservoirs often. Do not allow the res-

ervoirs to run dry, or the bleeding process will have to be repeated.

FRONT DISC BRAKES

Disc Brake Pads

INSPECTION

You should be able to check the pad lining thickness without removing the pads. Check the "Brake Specifications" chart at the end of this chapter to find the manufacturer's pad wear limit. However, this measurement may disagree with your state inspection laws. When replacing pads, always check the surface of the rotors for scoring or wear. The rotors should be removed for resurfacing if badly scored.

REMOVAL AND INSTALLATION

All four front brake pads must always be replaced as a set.

NOTE: *Use the Brake Identification Chart in this section to find the brake system your vehicle uses.*

Types N20, N22, N22A, N32, N34L

1. Raise and support the front of the car or truck. Remove the wheels.

2. Remove the retaining clip from the outboard pad.

3. Remove the pad pins retaining the antisqueal springs.

4. Remove the pads.

5. To install, open the bleeder screw slightly and push the outer piston into the cylinder until the dust seal groove aligns with the end of the seal retaining ring, then close the bleed screw. Be careful because the piston can be pushed too far, requiring disassembly of the caliper to repair. Install the inner pad.

6. Pull the yoke to push the inner piston into place. Install the outer pad.

7. Lightly coat the areas where the pins touch the pads, and where the pads touch the caliper (at the top) with grease. Do not allow grease to get on the pad friction surfaces.

8. Install the anti-squeal springs and pad pins. Install the clip.

9. Apply the brakes a few times to seat the pads. Check the master cylinder level; add fluid if necessary. Bleed the brakes if necessary.

Annette Type

1. Raise and support the front of the car. Remove the wheels.

2. Remove the clip, pull out the pins, and remove the pad springs.

3. Remove the pads by pulling them out with pliers.

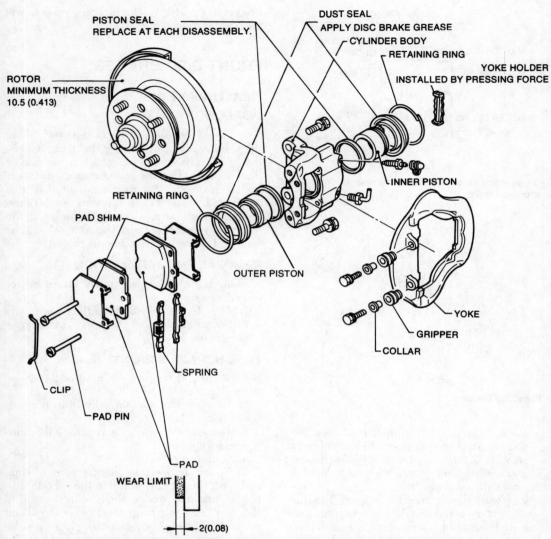

PISTON SEAL
REPLACE AT EACH DISASSEMBLY.

DUST SEAL
APPLY DISC BRAKE GREASE
CYLINDER BODY
RETAINING RING

YOKE HOLDER
INSTALLED BY PRESSING FORCE

ROTOR
MINIMUM THICKNESS
10.5 (0.413)

INNER PISTON

RETAINING RING

PAD SHIM

OUTER PISTON

YOKE

GRIPPER

COLLAR

SPRING

CLIP

PAD PIN

PAD

WEAR LIMIT

2(0.08)

Exploded view of the N22 disc brake assembly—N20, N22A, N32 and N34L similar

4. To install, first lightly coat the yoke groove and end surface of the piston with grease. Do not allow grease to contact the pads or rotor.

5. Open the bleeder screw slightly and push the outer piston into the cylinder until its end aligns with the end of the boot retaining ring.

Do not push too far, which will require caliper disassembly to correct. Install the inner pad.

6. Pull the yoke toward the outside of the car to push the inner piston into place. Install the outer pad.

7. Apply the brakes a few times to seat the

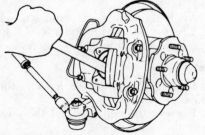

Pushing the inner piston in to install new brake pads (all calipers)

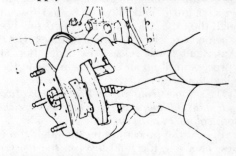

Don't push the piston in too far

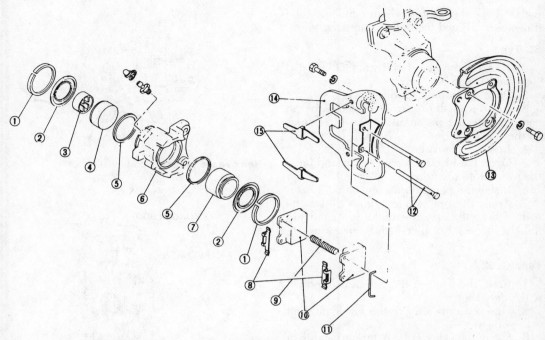

1. Retaining ring
2. Boot
3. Bias ring
4. Piston A (inner piston)
5. Piston seal
6. Cylinder body
7. Piston B (outer piston)
8. Hanger spring
9. Spring
10. Pad
11. Clip
12. Clevis pin
13. Buffle plate
14. Yoke
15. Yoke spring

Exploded view of the Annette disc brake assembly

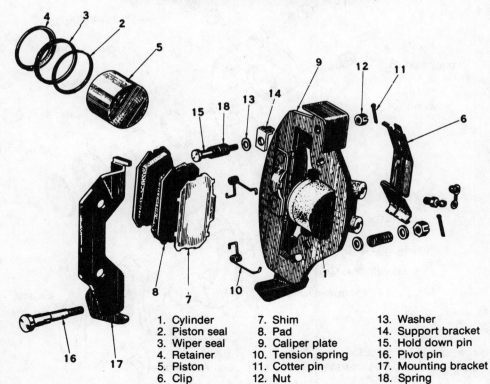

1. Cylinder
2. Piston seal
3. Wiper seal
4. Retainer
5. Piston
6. Clip
7. Shim
8. Pad
9. Caliper plate
10. Tension spring
11. Cotter pin
12. Nut
13. Washer
14. Support bracket
15. Hold down pin
16. Pivot pin
17. Mounting bracket
18. Spring

Exploded view of the SC disc brake assembly

pads. Check the master cylinder and add fluid
if necessary. Bleed the brakes if necessary.

SC Type

1. Raise and support the front of the car.
Remove the wheels.

2. Push up on the clip to remove.

3. Insert a small prybar into the back of the
pad opposite the piston and move the caliper
all the way out.

4. Remove the pads.

5. Open the bleeder screw slightly and press
the piston into the caliper.

6. Install the pads, shims, and clips.

7. Apply the brakes a few times to seat the
pads. Check the master cylinder level and add
fluid if necessary. Bleed the brakes as required.

Type CL22V

1. Raise the front of the car and support it
with safety stands.

2. Unscrew and remove the lower pin bolt
(sub pin).

3. Swing the cylinder body upward and then
remove the pad retainer, the inner and outer
shims and the pads themselves.

NOTE: *Do not depress the brake pedal when*

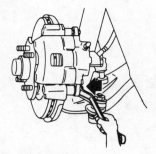

Remove the lower pin bolt

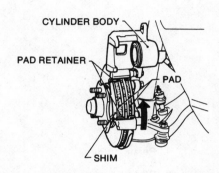

Raise the cylinder body to remove the pads

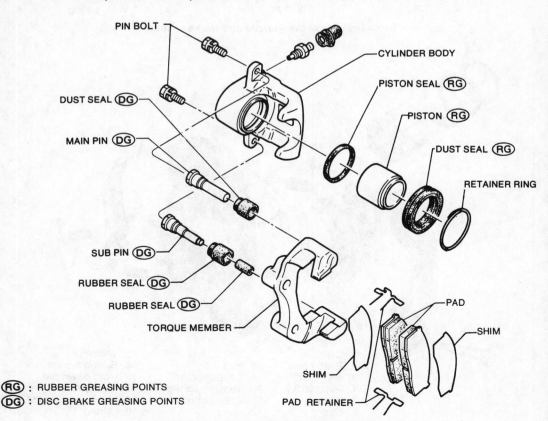

(RG) : RUBBER GREASING POINTS
(DG) : DISC BRAKE GREASING POINTS

Exploded view of the CL22V disc brake assembly

the cylinder body is in the raised position or the piston will pop out.

4. Clean the piston end of the cylinder body and the pin bolt holes. Be careful not to get oil on the rotor.

5. Pull the cylinder body to the outer side and install the inner pad.

6. Install the outer pad, the shim and the pad retainer.

7. Re-position the cylinder body and then tighten the pin bolt to 12–15 ft. lbs. (16–21 Nm).

8. Apply the brakes a few times to seat the new pads. Check the fluid level and bleed the brakes as required.

Type AD22V

1. Remove the road wheel.

2. Remove the lower caliper guide pin. See the accompanying illustration.

3. Rotate the brake caliper body upward.

4. Remove the brake pad retainer and the inner and outer pad shims.

5. Remove the brake pads.

NOTE: *Do not depress the brake pedal when the caliper body is raised; the brake piston will be forced out of the caliper.*

6. Clean the piston end of the caliper body and the pin bolt holes. Be careful not to get oil on the brake rotor.

7. Pull the caliper body to the outer side and install the inner brake pad. Make sure both new pads are kept clean!

8. Install the outer pad, shim and pad retainer.

9. Reposition the caliper body and then tighten the guide pin bolt to 23–30 ft. lbs.

10. Apply the brakes a few times to seat the pads before driving out on the road.

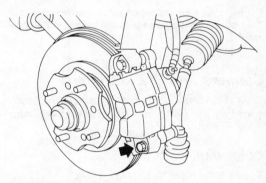

Remove the AD22V guide pin . . .

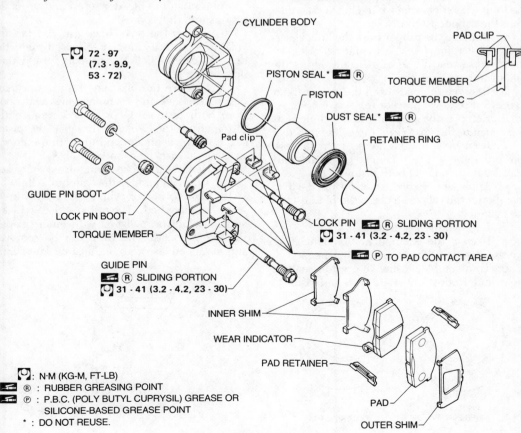

AD22V brake caliper

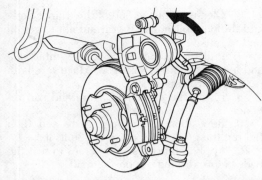

. . . and rotate the caliper up and away from the rotor. Do not apply the brakes with the caliper in this position!

Calipers and Brake Discs

NOTE: *Use the Brake Identification Chart in this section to find the brake system your vehicle uses.*

OVERHAUL

Types N20, N22, N22A, N32, N34L

1. With the vehicle supported safely and the front wheels off, remove the brake fluid tube from the caliper assembly.

2. Remove the caliper from the knuckle assembly by removing the mounting bolts, located at the rear of the caliper, and lifting the caliper from the rotor.

3. Remove the pads from the caliper (refer to the pad removal procedure).

4. Remove the gripper pin attaching nuts and separate the yoke from the cylinder body.

5. Remove the yoke holder from the piston and remove the retaining rings and dust seals from the ends of both pistons.

6. Apply air pressure *gradually* into the fluid chamber of the caliper, to force the pistons from the cylinders.

7. Remove the piston seals.

8. Inspect the components for damage or excessive wear. Replace or repair as needed.

9. To assemble, install the piston seals in the cylinder bore. Lubricate seals and pistons.

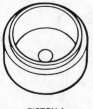

PISTON A
(INNER PISTON)

PISTON B
(OUTER PISTON)

Piston comparison (inner and outer)

10. Slide the "A" piston into the cylinder, followed by the "B" piston so that its yoke groove coincides with the yoke groove of the cylinder.

11. Install the dust seal and clamp tightly with the retaining ring.

12. Install the yoke holder on the "A" piston and install the gripper to yoke.

NOTE: *The use of soapy water will aid in the installation of the gripper pins.*

13. Support the end of "B" piston and press the yoke into the yoke holder.

14. Install the pads, anti squeal springs, pad pins and retain with the clip.

15. Tighten the gripper pin attaching nuts to 12–15 ft. lbs. and install the caliper on the spindle knuckle. Torque the caliper mounting bolts to 53–72 ft. lbs.

16. Bleed the system, check the fluid level, install the wheels and lower the vehicle.

Annette Type

1. Remove the pads.

2. Disconnect the brake tube.

3. Remove the two bottom strut assembly installation bolts to provide clearance.

4. Remove the caliper assembly mounting bolts.

5. Loosen the bleeder screw and press the pistons into their bores.

6. Clamp the yoke in a vise and tap the yoke head with a hammer to loosen the cylinder. Be careful that the primary piston does not fall out.

7. Remove the bias ring from the primary piston. Remove the retaining rings and boots from both pistons. Depress and remove the pistons from the cylinder. Remove the piston seal from the cylinder carefully with the fingers so as not to mar the cylinder wall.

8. Remove the yoke springs from the yoke.

9. Wash all parts with clean brake fluid.

10. If the piston or cylinder is badly worn or scored, replace both. The piston surface is plated and must not be polished with emery paper. Replace all seals. The rotor can be removed and machined if scored, but final thickness must

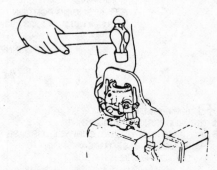

Tapping the yoke head with a hammer

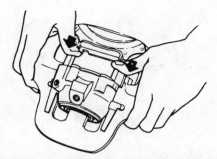

Assembling the yoke and cylinder (Annette type)

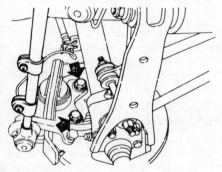

Caliper removal

be at least 0.331 in. Runout must not exceed 0.001 in.

11. Lubricate the cylinder bore with clean brake fluid and install the piston seal.

12. Insert the bias ring into primary piston so that the rounded ring portion comes to the bottom of the piston. Primary piston has a small depression inside, while secondary does not.

13. Lubricate the pistons with clean brake fluid and insert into the cylinder. Install the boot and retaining ring. The yoke groove of the bias ring of primary piston must align with the yoke groove of the cylinder.

14. Install the yoke springs to the yoke so the projecting portion faces to the disc (rotor).

15. Lubricate the sliding portion of the cylinder and yoke. Assemble the cylinder and yoke by tapping the yoke lightly.

16. Replace the caliper assembly and pads. Torque the mounting bolts to 33–41 ft. lbs. Rotor bolt torque is 20–27 ft.lbs. Strut bolt torque is 33–44 ft. lbs. Bleed the system of air.

SC Type

1. Remove the brake pads.
2. Disconnect the brake hose.
3. Remove the cotter pins from the hold down and pivot pins. Remove the retaining nuts.
4. Remove the caliper plate from its mounting bracket.
5. Remove the torsion spring and remove the cylinder assembly from the caliper plate.

6. Apply air into the fluid chamber of the caliper and force the piston from the cylinder.

7. Remove the wiper seal and piston seal retainer.

8. Inspect the components for abnormal wear or damage. Repair or replace as necessary.

9. Fit the seal into its groove in the cylinder. Lubricate the seal and piston. Install the piston into the cylinder.

10. Place the caliper plate over the cylinder assembly and install the torsion spring.

11. Install the caliper plate on the mounting bracket and install the nuts and cotter pins.

12. Bleed the system and check the reservoir level.

Type CL22V and Type AD22V

1. Disconnect and plug the brake line.
2. Unscrew the two mounting bolts and remove the caliper.
3. Remove the main pin and the sub pin and then separate the cylinder body from the torque member.
4. Remove the piston dust cover.
5. Apply compressed air gradually to the fluid chamber until the piston pops out.
6. Carefully pry out the piston seal.
7. Inspect the components for damage or excessive wear. Replace or repair as necessary.
8. Install the piston seal in the cylinder bore. Lubricate the seals and pistons.
9. Fit the dust seal onto the piston, insert the dust seal into the groove on the cylinder body and then install the piston.
10. Place the cylinder body and torque member together, grease the main and sub pins, install the pins and tighten them to 12–15 ft. lbs. (16–21 Nm) on the CL22V, and 23–30 ft. lbs. on the AD22V.
11. Install the caliper and tighten the mounting bolts to 36–51 ft. lbs. (49–69 Nm) on the CL22V, and 53–72 ft. lbs. on the AD22V. Reconnect the brake line and install the wheels.
12. Bleed the system, check the fluid level and lower the vehicle.

OVERHAUL

NOTE: *Datsun obtains parts from two manufacturers: Nabco and Tokico. Parts are not interchangeable. The name of the manufacturer is usually on the wheel cylinder.*

1. Remove the wheel cylinder from the backing plate.
2. Remove the dust boot and take out the piston. Discard the piston cup. The dust boot can be reused, if necessary, but it is better to replace it.
3. Wash all of the components in clean brake fluid.

4. Inspect the piston and piston bore. Replace any components which are severely corroded, scored, or worn. The piston and piston bore can be polished lightly with crocus cloth. Move the crocus cloth around the piston bore; *not* in and out of the piston bore.

5. Wash the wheel cylinder and piston thoroughly in clean brake fluid, allowing them to remain lubricated for assembly.

6. Coat all of the new components to be installed in the wheel cylinder with clean brake fluid prior to assembly.

7. Assemble the wheel cylinder and install it in the reverse order of removal. Assemble the remaining components and bleed the brake hydraulic system.

Front Wheel Bearings
ADJUSTMENT

The factory procedures for wheel bearing adjustment is of little use to the backyard mechanic, since it involves the use of a spring scale, an inch pound torque wrench, and a ft. lb. torque wrench. For the following procedure, you will only need a ft. lb. torque wrench.

1. Jack up the car and remove the wheel.
2. Remove the bearing dust cap and the cotter pin.
3. Torque the spindle nut to 18–22 ft. lbs. on the 610, 710, 810, and 200SX; 22–25 ft. lbs. on the 510.
4. Turn the hub a few times to seat the bearing and check the torque on the nut again.
5. Loosen the nut about 60° on all models except the 1978–81 510. Loosen the nut about 90° on the 1978–81 510.
6. Install the adjusting cap and a new cotter pin. It is permissible to loosen the nut 15° to allow the holes to align, on all models except the 1978–81 510. On this model, tighten the nut up to 15° to align the cotter pin holes.
7. Reinstall the tire and the wheel and rotate the whole assembly. There should be no roughness or binding. Grasp the top of the wheel

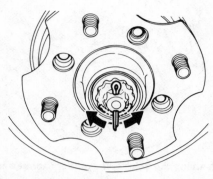

Split and spread the cotter pin

and move it in and out. There should be negligible play. If there is excessive play, the wheel bearings must be retightened. If roughness persists, check the wheel bearing condition.

8. Install the cap and lower the car.

WHEEL BEARING PACKING AND REPLACEMENT

The most important thing to remember when working with the wheel bearings is that although they are basically durable, in some ways they are remarkably fragile. Mishandling, grit, misalignment, scratches, improper preload, etc. will quickly destroy any roller bearing, no matter how well hardened during manufacture.

1. Loosen the wheel nuts, raise the car, and remove the wheel and tire. Remove the brake drum or brake caliper, following the procedure in this chapter.

2. It is not necessary to remove the drum or disc from the hub. The outer wheel bearing will come off with the hub. Simply pull the hub and disc or drum assembly toward you off the spindle. Be sure to catch the bearing before it falls to the ground.

3. From the inner side of the hub, remove the inner grease seal, and lift the inner bearing from the hub. Discard the grease seal.

4. Clean the bearings in solvent and allow them to air dry. You risk leaving bits of lint in the races if you dry them with a rag. Clean the grease cap, nuts, spindle, and the races in the hub thoroughly, and allow the parts to dry.

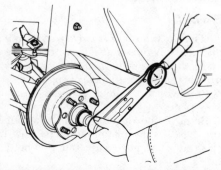

Tightening the hub nut with a torque wrench during wheel bearing adjustment

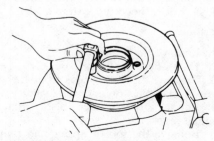

Separating the brake rotor and hub

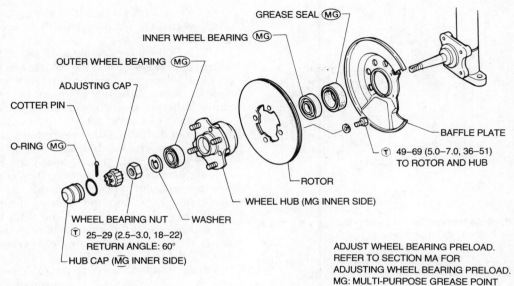

GREASE SEAL (MG)
INNER WHEEL BEARING (MG)
OUTER WHEEL BEARING (MG)
ADJUSTING CAP
COTTER PIN
O-RING (MG)

BAFFLE PLATE

(T) 49–69 (5.0–7.0, 36–51)
TO ROTOR AND HUB

ROTOR

WHEEL HUB (MG INNER SIDE)

WHEEL BEARING NUT — WASHER

(T) 25–29 (2.5–3.0, 18–22)
RETURN ANGLE: 60°

HUB CAP (MG INNER SIDE)

ADJUST WHEEL BEARING PRELOAD.
REFER TO SECTION MA FOR
ADJUSTING WHEEL BEARING PRELOAD.
MG: MULTI-PURPOSE GREASE POINT

(T) : N·M (KG-M, FT-LB)

Maxima front hub assembly showing wheel bearings. Other models similar

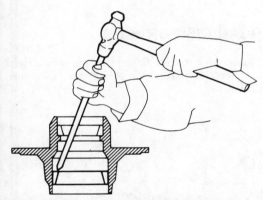

If the outer bearing race needs replacement, drive it out of the hub with a mallet and brass drift

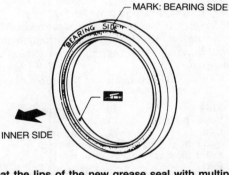

MARK: BEARING SIDE

INNER SIDE

Coat the lips of the new grease seal with multipurpose grease

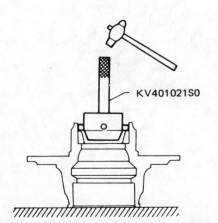

KV401021S0

Drive the new bearing seat in with a special bearing installation tool until it seats

Packing the wheel bearings. Pack 'em full!

5. Inspect the bearings carefully. If they are worn, cracked, brinelled, pitted, burned, scored, etc., they should be replaced, along with the bearing cups in which they run in the hub. Do not mix old and new parts.

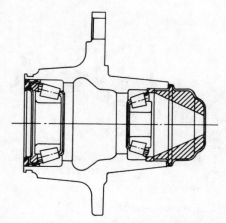

Pack the hub and hub cap with wheel bearing grease up to the shaded portions

6. If the cups are worn, remove them from the hub, by using a brass rod as a drift.

To install:

7. If the old cups were removed, install the new inner and outer cups into the hub, using either a tool made for the purpose, or a socket or piece of pipe of a large enough diameter to press on the outside rim of the cup only.

CAUTION: *Use care not to cock the bearing cups in the hub. If they are not fully seated, the bearings will be impossible to adjust properly.*

8. Pack the inside area of the hub and cups with grease. Pack the inside of the grease cap while you're at it, but do not install the cap into the hub.

9. Pack the inner bearing with grease. Place a large glob of grease into the palm of one hand and push the inner bearing through it with a sliding motion. The grease must be forced through the side of the bearing and in between each roller. Continue until the grease begins to ooze out the other side through the gaps between the rollers; the bearing must be completely packed with grease. Install the inner bearing into its cup in the hub, then press a new grease seal into place over it.

10. Install the hub and rotor or drum assembly onto the spindle. Pack the outer bearing with grease in the same manner as the inner bearing, then install the outer bearing into place in the hub.

11. Apply a thin coat of grease to the washer and the threaded portion of the spindle, then loosely install the washer and adjusting nut. Go on to the bearing preload adjustment.

REAR DISC BRAKES

Please refer to the "Brake Identification" chart to determine which type of rear disc brake your car uses.

1. Yoke
2. Yoke spring
3. Clip
4. Pad pin
5. Anti-squeal spring
6. Pad
7. Retaining ring
8. Dust seal
9. Outer piston
10. Oil seal
11. Adjusting nut
12. Bearing
13. Spacer
14. Wave washer
15. Snap ring B
16. Piston seal
17. Cylinder body
18. Retainer
19. Snap ring A
20. Spring cover
21. Spring
22. Spring seat
23. Snap ring C
24. Key plate
25. Push rod
26. O-ring
27. Strut
28. Inner piston
29. Cam
30. Toggle lever
31. Spring
32. Washer
33. Nut

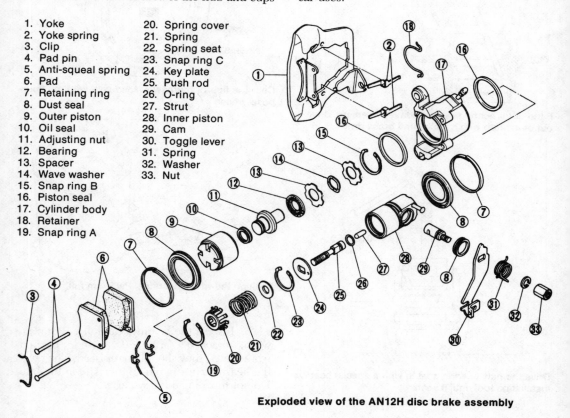

Exploded view of the AN12H disc brake assembly

Brake Pads

REMOVAL AND INSTALLATION

Type AN12H

1. Raise and support the rear of the car. Remove the wheels.
2. Remove the clip at the outside of the pad pins.
3. Remove the pad pins. Hold the anti-squeal springs in place with your finger.
4. Remove the pads.
5. To install, first clean the end of the piston with clean brake fluid.
6. Lightly coat the caliper-to-pad, the yoke-to-pad, retaining pin-to-pad, and retaining pin-to-bracket surfaces with grease. Do not allow grease to get on the rotor or pad surfaces.
7. Push the piston into place with a screwdriver by pushing in on the piston while at the same time turning it clockwise into the bore. Then, with a lever between the rotor and yoke, push the yoke over until the clearance to install the pads is equal.
8. Install the shims and pads, anti-squeal springs and pins. Install the clip. Note that the inner pad has a tab which must fit into the piston notch. Therefore, be sure that the piston notch is centered to allow proper pad installation.
9. Apply the brake a few times to center the pads. Check the master cylinder fluid level and add if necessary.

Type CL11H

1. Raise the rear of the car and support it with safety stands.
2. Remove the pin bolts and lift off the caliper body.
3. Pull out the pad springs and then remove the pads and their shims.
4. Clean the piston end of the caliper body and the area around the pin holes. Be careful not to get oil on the rotor.

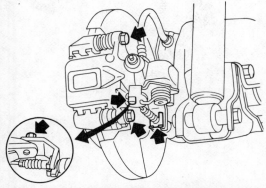

On the 200SX, remove the parking brake cable stay fixing bolt, pin bolts and lock spring before removing the pads and shims. 1984 model shown

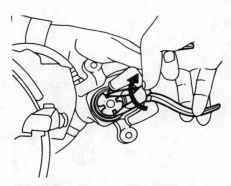

Use needle-nosed pliers to retract the piston

5. Using a pair of needle-nosed pliers, carefully turn the piston clockwise back into the caliper body. Take care not to damage the piston boot.
6. Coat the pad contact area on the mounting support with a silicone-based grease.
7. Install the pads, shims and the pad springs. NOTE: *Always use new shims.*
8. Position the caliper body in the mounting support and tighten the pin bolts to 16–23 ft. lbs. (22–31 Nm.).
9. Replace the wheel, lower the car and bleed the system.

Caliper

OVERHAUL

Type AN12H

1. Disconnect the brake hose from the caliper. Plug the hose and caliper to prevent fluid loss.
2. Disconnect the parking brake cable.
3. Remove the mounting bolts and remove the caliper from the suspension arm.
4. Remove the pads.
5. Stand the caliper assembly on end, large end down, and push on the caliper to separate it from the yoke.
6. Remove the retaining rings and dust seals from both pistons.
7. Push in on the outer piston to force out the piston assembly. Remove the piston seals.
8. Remove the yoke spring from the yoke.
9. Disengage the piston assembly by turning the outer piston counterclockwise.
10. Disassemble the outer piston by removing the snap ring.
11. Disassemble the inner piston by removing the snap ring. This will allow the spring cover, spring, and spring seat to come out. Remove the inner snap ring to remove the key plate, push rod, and strut.
12. To install, assemble the pistons in reverse order of disassembly. Apply a thin coat of grease to the groove in the push rod, its O-

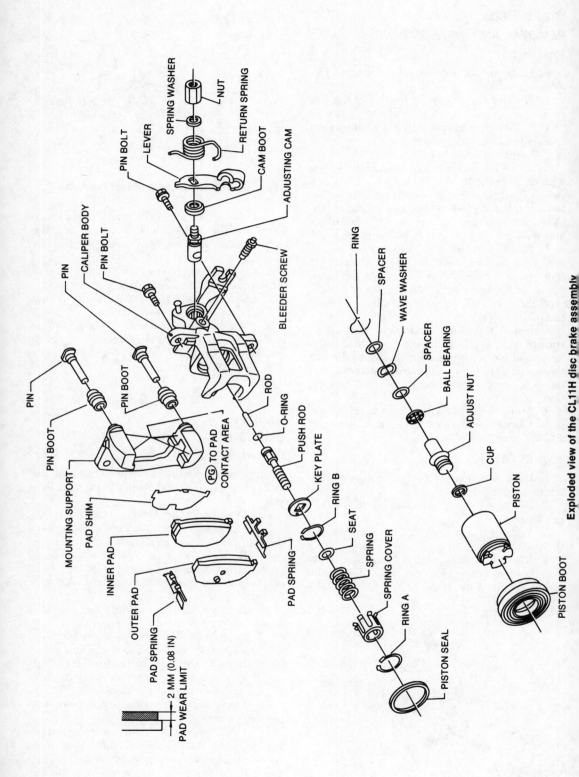

Exploded view of the CL11H disc brake assembly

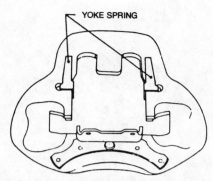

Yoke showing the yoke springs—AN12H

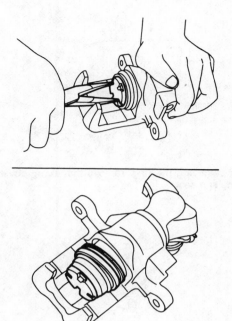

Turn the piston counterclockwise to remove it from the caliper body

ring, the strut ends, oil seal, piston seal, and the inside of the dust seal.

13. Install the piston seals. Apply a thin coat of grease to the sliding surfaces of the piston and caliper bore. Install the pistons into the caliper. Install the retainers onto the dust seals.

14. Install the yoke springs on the yoke.

15. Lightly coat the yoke and caliper body contact surfaces, and the pad pin hole, with silicone grease. Assemble the yoke to the caliper.

16. Install the pads.

17. Install the caliper to the suspension arm (28–38 ft. lbs.). Connect the parking brake cable. Connect the brake hose. Apply the brakes a few times to center the pads. Bleed the system.

Type CL11H

1. Disconnect the parking brake cable. Disconnect and plug the brake line.

2. Unscrew the mounting bolts and remove the caliper assembly.

3. Remove the pin bolts and separate the caliper body from the mounting support.

4. Using needle-nosed pliers, turn the piston counterclockwise and remove it.

5. Pry out the ring from inside the piston.

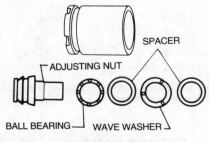

Prying off the CL11H ring from inside the piston. Some rings may be the snap-ring type

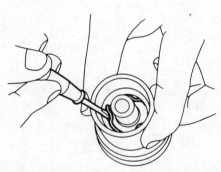

Various CL11H caliper components

You can now remove the adjusting nut, the ball bearing, the wave washer and the spacers.

6. Installation is in the reverse order of removal. Tighten the caliper mounting bolts to 28–38 ft. lbs. (38–52 Nm.).

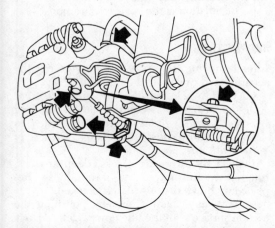

Disconnecting the 200SX parking brake, 1984 shown

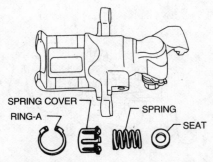

After removing the ring, remove the spring cover, spring and seat

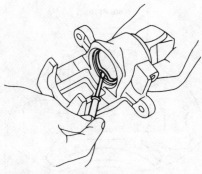

Carefully remove the oil seal, and replace it during assembly

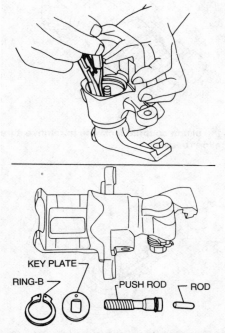

Remove the ring "B" with snap-ring pliers, then remove the key plate, push rod and rod

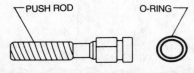

Remove the O-ring from the push rod. Replace the O-ring during installation

REAR DRUM BRAKES

Brake Drums

REMOVAL AND INSTALLATION

1. Raise the rear of the vehicle and support it on jack stands.

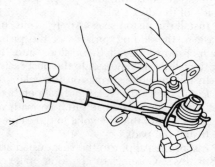

Removing the return spring

2. Remove the wheels.
3. Release the parking brake.
4. Pull off the brake drums. On some models there are two threaded service holes in each brake drum. If the drum will not come off, fit two correct size bolts in the service holes and screw them in: this will force the drum away from the axle.
5. If the drum cannot be easily removed, back off the brake adjustment.

NOTE: *Never depress the brake pedal while the brake drum is removed.*

6. Installation is the reverse of removal.

INSPECTION

After removing the brake drum, wipe out the accumulated dust with a damp cloth.

CAUTION: *Do not blow the brake dust out of the drums with compressed air or lung power. Brake linings contain asbestos, a known cancer causing substance. Dispose of the cloth after use.*

Inspect the drum for cracks, deep grooves, roughness, scoring, or out-of-roundness. Replace any brake drum which is cracked.

Smooth any slight scores by polishing the friction surface with the fine emery cloth. Heavy or extensive scoring will cause excessive brake

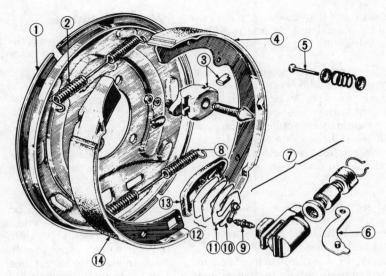

1. Brake disc
2. Return spring adjuster side
3. Brake shoe adjuster
4. Brake shoe assembly-fore
5. Anti-rattler pin
6. Lever
7. Rear wheel cylinder
8. Return spring cylinder side
9. Bleeder
10. Lock plate A
11. Lock plate B
12. Lock plate C and D
13. Dust cover
14. Brake shoe assembly-after

Exploded view of the rear drum brake—610, 710

lining wear and should be removed from the brake drum through resurfacing.

Brake Shoes

REMOVAL AND INSTALLATION

1. Raise the vehicle and remove the wheels.
2. Release the parking brake. Disconnect the cross rod from the lever of the brake cylinder. Remove the brake drum. Place a heavy rubber band around the cylinder to prevent the piston from coming out.
3. Remove the return springs and shoes.
4. Clean the backing plate and check the wheel cylinder for leaks. To remove the wheel cylinder, remove the brake line, dust cover, securing nuts or plates and adjusting shims. Clearance between the cylinder and the piston should not exceed 0.006 in.
5. The drums must be machined if scored

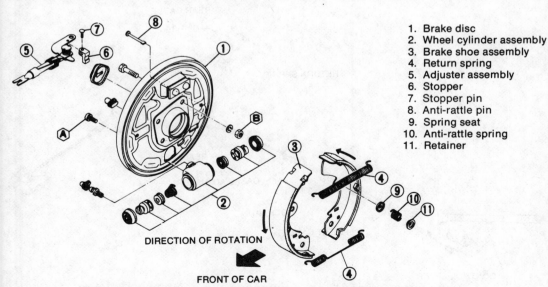

1. Brake disc
2. Wheel cylinder assembly
3. Brake shoe assembly
4. Return spring
5. Adjuster assembly
6. Stopper
7. Stopper pin
8. Anti-rattle pin
9. Spring seat
10. Anti-rattle spring
11. Retainer

DIRECTION OF ROTATION

FRONT OF CAR

Exploded view of the rear drum brake—510; 810 and 200SX similar

or out of round more than 0.002 in. The drum inside diameter should not be machined beyond 9.04 in. Minimum safe lining thickness is 0.059 in.

6. Hook the return springs into the new shoes. The springs should be between the shoes and the backing plate. The longer return spring must be adjacent to the wheel cylinder. A very thin film of grease may be applied to the pivot points at the ends of the brake shoes. Grease the shoe locating buttons on the backing plate, also. Be careful not to get grease on the linings or drums.

7. Place one shoe in the adjuster and piston slots, and pry the other shoe into position.

8. Replace the drums and wheels. Adjust the brakes. Bleed the hydraulic system of air if the brake lines were disconnected.

9. Reconnect the handbrake, making sure that it does not cause the shoes to drag when it is released.

Wheel Cylinder

Procedures for removing the rear wheel cylinders are detailed in the preceding "Brake Shoe" section.

PARKING BRAKE

ADJUSTMENT

Handbrake adjustments are generally not needed, unless the cables have stretched.

All Models

There is an adjusting nut on the cable under the car, usually at the end of the front cable and near the point at which the two cables from the rear wheels come together (the equalizer). Some models also have a turnbuckle in the rear cable to compensate for cable stretching.

To adjust, proceed as follows:

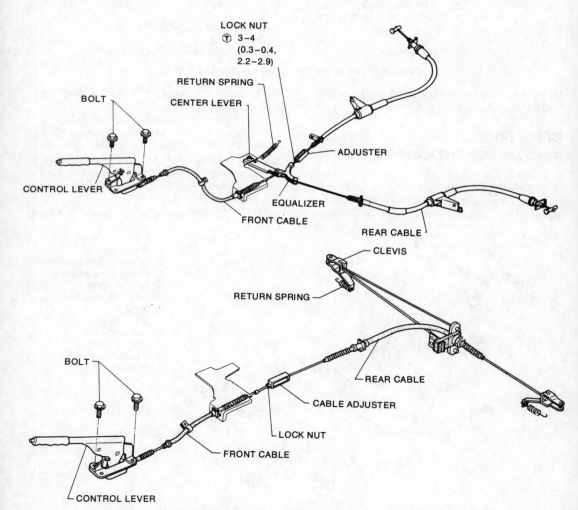

Two types of parking brake cable routing—most models similar

1. Adjust the rear brakes with the parking brake fully released.

2. Apply the hand brake lever so that it is approximately 3–3¼ in. from its fully released position.

3. Adjust the parking brake turnbuckle, locknuts, or equalizer so that the rear brakes are locked.

4. Release the parking brake. The wheels should turn freely. If not, loosen the parking brake adjuster until the wheels turn with no drag.

Brake Specifications

All measurements given are in inches unless noted

Model	Year	Lug Nut Torque (ft. lbs.)	Master Cylinder Bore	Brake Disc●		Drum		Minimum Lining Thickness●	
				Minimum Thickness	Maximum Run-Out	Diameter	Max. Wear Limit	Front	Rear
510	1978–81	58–72	0.8125	0.331	0.0047	9.000	9.060	0.080	0.059
610	1973–74	58–65	0.750	0.331	0.0048	9.000	9.055	0.039	0.059
	1975	58–65	0.750	0.331	0.0048	9.000	9.055	0.063	0.059
	1976–77	58–65	0.750	0.331	0.0048	9.000	9.055	0.079	0.059
710	1974–75	58–65	0.750	0.331	0.0047	9.000	9.055	0.039	0.059
	1976–77	58–65	0.750	0.331	0.0047	9.000	9.055	0.079	0.059
810	1977–80	58–72	0.8125	0.413	0.0059	9.000	9.060	0.080	0.059
	1981–84	58–72	0.8125	0.630/ 0.339	0.0059/① 0.0059	9.000	9.060	0.079/ 0.079	0.059
200SX	1977–79	58–65	0.750	0.331	0.0047	9.000	9.060	0.059	0.059
	1980–83	58–72	0.8750	0.413/ 0.339	0.0047/ 0.0059	—	—	0.079	0.079
	1984	58–72	0.938	0.630/ 0.354	0.0028/ 0.0028	—	9.060	—	—

—Not Applicable

●Second figure is for rear disc

NOTE: Minimum lining thickness is as recommended by the manufacturer. Due to variation in state inspection regulations, the minimum allowable thickness may be different than recommended by the manufacturer.

① 0.0028 in. on 1983 and later, on front and rear

Troubleshooting 10

This section is designed to aid in the quick, accurate diagnosis of automotive problems. While automotive repairs can be made by many people, accurate troubleshooting is a rare skill for the amateur and professional alike.

In its simplest state, troubleshooting is an exercise in logic. It is essential to realize that an automobile is really composed of a series of systems. Some of these systems are interrelated; others are not. Automobiles operate within a framework of logical rules and physical laws, and the key to troubleshooting is a good understanding of all the automotive systems.

This section breaks the car or truck down into its component systems, allowing the problem to be isolated. The charts and diagnostic road maps list the most common problems and the most probable causes of trouble. Obviously it would be impossible to list every possible problem that could happen along with every possible cause, but it will locate MOST problems and eliminate a lot of unnecessary guesswork. The systematic format will locate problems within a given system, but, because many automotive systems are interrelated, the solution to your particular problem may be found in a number of systems on the car or truck.

USING THE TROUBLESHOOTING CHARTS

This book contains all of the specific information that the average do-it-yourself mechanic needs to repair and maintain his or her car or truck. The troubleshooting charts are designed to be used in conjunction with the specific procedures and information in the text. For instance, troubleshooting a point-type ignition system is fairly standard for all models, but you may be directed to the text to find procedures for troubleshooting an individual type of electronic ignition. You will also have to refer to the specification charts throughout the book for specifications applicable to your car or truck.

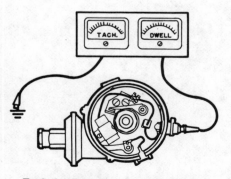

Tach-dwell hooked-up to distributor

TOOLS AND EQUIPMENT

The tools illustrated in Chapter 1 (plus two more diagnostic pieces) will be adequate to troubleshoot most problems. The two other tools needed are a voltmeter and an ohmmeter. These can be purchased separately or in combination, known as a VOM meter.

In the event that other tools are required, they will be noted in the procedures.

Troubleshooting Engine Problems

See Chapters 2, 3, 4 for more information and service procedures.

Index to Systems

System	To Test	Group
Battery	Engine need not be running	1
Starting system	Engine need not be running	2
Primary electrical system	Engine need not be running	3
Secondary electrical system	Engine need not be running	4
Fuel system	Engine need not be running	5
Engine compression	Engine need not be running	6
Engine vacuum	Engine must be running	7
Secondary electrical system	Engine must be running	8
Valve train	Engine must be running	9
Exhaust system	Engine must be running	10
Cooling system	Engine must be running	11
Engine lubrication	Engine must be running	12

Index to Problems

Problem: Symptom	Begin at Specific Diagnosis, Number ___
Engine Won't Start:	
Starter doesn't turn	1.1, 2.1
Starter turns, engine doesn't	2.1
Starter turns engine very slowly	1.1, 2.4
Starter turns engine normally	3.1, 4.1
Starter turns engine very quickly	6.1
Engine fires intermittently	4.1
Engine fires consistently	5.1, 6.1
Engine Runs Poorly:	
Hard starting	3.1, 4.1, 5.1, 8.1
Rough idle	4.1, 5.1, 8.1
Stalling	3.1, 4.1, 5.1, 8.1
Engine dies at high speeds	4.1, 5.1
Hesitation (on acceleration from standing stop)	5.1, 8.1
Poor pickup	4.1, 5.1, 8.1
Lack of power	3.1, 4.1, 5.1, 8.1
Backfire through the carburetor	4.1, 8.1, 9.1
Backfire through the exhaust	4.1, 8.1, 9.1
Blue exhaust gases	6.1, 7.1
Black exhaust gases	5.1
Running on (after the ignition is shut off)	3.1, 8.1
Susceptible to moisture	4.1
Engine misfires under load	4.1, 7.1, 8.4, 9.1
Engine misfires at speed	4.1, 8.4
Engine misfires at idle	3.1, 4.1, 5.1, 7.1, 8.4

Sample Section

Test and Procedure	Results and Indications	Proceed to
4.1—Check for spark: Hold each spark plug wire approximately ¼″ from ground with gloves or a heavy, dry rag. Crank the engine and observe the spark.	→ If no spark is evident:	→ **4.2**
	→ If spark is good in some cases:	→ **4.3**
	→ If spark is good in all cases:	→ **4.6**

Specific Diagnosis

This section is arranged so that following each test, instructions are given to proceed to another, until a problem is diagnosed.

Section 1—Battery

Test and Procedure	Results and Indications	Proceed to
1.1—Inspect the battery visually for case condition (corrosion, cracks) and water level. 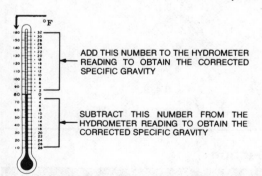 DIRT ON TOP OF BATTERY CORROSION PLUGGED VENT LOOSE CABLE OR POSTS CRACKS LOW WATER LEVEL **Inspect the battery case**	If case is cracked, replace battery: If the case is intact, remove corrosion with a solution of baking soda and water (**CAUTION:** *do not get the solution into the battery*), and fill with water:	**1.4** **1.2**
1.2—Check the battery cable connections: Insert a screwdriver between the battery post and the cable clamp. Turn the headlights on high beam, and observe them as the screwdriver is gently twisted to ensure good metal to metal contact. TESTING BATTERY CABLE CONNECTIONS USING A SCREWDRIVER	If the lights brighten, remove and clean the clamp and post; coat the post with petroleum jelly, install and tighten the clamp: If no improvement is noted:	**1.4** **1.3**
1.3—Test the state of charge of the battery using an individual cell tester or hydrometer.	If indicated, charge the battery. **NOTE:** *If no obvious reason exists for the low state of charge (i.e., battery age, prolonged storage), proceed to:*	**1.4**

°F

ADD THIS NUMBER TO THE HYDROMETER READING TO OBTAIN THE CORRECTED SPECIFIC GRAVITY

SUBTRACT THIS NUMBER FROM THE HYDROMETER READING TO OBTAIN THE CORRECTED SPECIFIC GRAVITY

Specific Gravity (@ 80° F.)

Minimum	Battery Charge
1.260	100% Charged
1.230	75% Charged
1.200	50% Charged
1.170	25% Charged
1.140	Very Little Power Left
1.110	Completely Discharged

The effects of temperature on battery specific gravity (left) and amount of battery charge in relation to specific gravity (right)

Test and Procedure	Results and Indications	Proceed to
1.4—Visually inspect battery cables for cracking, bad connection to ground, or bad connection to starter.	If necessary, tighten connections or replace the cables:	**2.1**

Section 2—Starting System
See Chapter 3 for service procedures

Test and Procedure	Results and Indications	Proceed to
Note: Tests in Group 2 are performed with coil high tension lead disconnected to prevent accidental starting.		
2.1—Test the starter motor and solenoid: Connect a jumper from the battery post of the solenoid (or relay) to the starter post of the solenoid (or relay).	If starter turns the engine normally:	2.2
	If the starter buzzes, or turns the engine very slowly:	2.4
	If no response, replace the solenoid (or relay).	3.1
	If the starter turns, but the engine doesn't, ensure that the flywheel ring gear is intact. If the gear is undamaged, replace the starter drive.	3.1
2.2—Determine whether ignition override switches are functioning properly (clutch start switch, neutral safety switch), by connecting a jumper across the switch(es), and turning the ignition switch to "start".	If starter operates, adjust or replace switch:	3.1
	If the starter doesn't operate:	2.3
2.3—Check the ignition switch "start" position: Connect a 12V test lamp or voltmeter between the starter post of the solenoid (or relay) and ground. Turn the ignition switch to the "start" position, and jiggle the key.	If the lamp doesn't light or the meter needle doesn't move when the switch is turned, check the ignition switch for loose connections, cracked insulation, or broken wires. Repair or replace as necessary:	3.1
	If the lamp flickers or needle moves when the key is jiggled, replace the ignition switch.	3.3

Checking the ignition switch "start" position

STARTER RELAY
(IF EQUIPPED)

2.4—Remove and bench test the starter, according to specifications in the engine electrical section.	If the starter does not meet specifications, repair or replace as needed:	3.1
	If the starter is operating properly:	2.5
2.5—Determine whether the engine can turn freely: Remove the spark plugs, and check for water in the cylinders. Check for water on the dipstick, or oil in the radiator. Attempt to turn the engine using an 18″ flex drive and socket on the crankshaft pulley nut or bolt.	If the engine will turn freely only with the spark plugs out, and hydrostatic lock (water in the cylinders) is ruled out, check valve timing:	9.2
	If engine will not turn freely, and it is known that the clutch and transmission are free, the engine must be disassembled for further evaluation:	Chapter 3

Section 3—Primary Electrical System

Test and Procedure	Results and Indications	Proceed to
3.1—Check the ignition switch "on" position: Connect a jumper wire between the distributor side of the coil and ground, and a 12V test lamp between the switch side of the coil and ground. Remove the high tension lead from the coil. Turn the ignition switch on and jiggle the key.	If the lamp lights:	**3.2**
	If the lamp flickers when the key is jiggled, replace the ignition switch:	**3.3**
	If the lamp doesn't light, check for loose or open connections. If none are found, remove the ignition switch and check for continuity. If the switch is faulty, replace it:	**3.3**

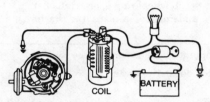

Checking the ignition switch "on" position

3.2—Check the ballast resistor or resistance wire for an open circuit, using an ohmmeter. See Chapter 3 for specific tests.	Replace the resistor or resistance wire if the resistance is zero. **NOTE:** *Some ignition systems have no ballast resistor.*	**3.3**

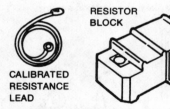

Two types of resistors

3.3—On point-type ignition systems, visually inspect the breaker points for burning, pitting or excessive wear. Gray coloring of the point contact surfaces is normal. Rotate the crankshaft until the contact heel rests on a high point of the distributor cam and adjust the point gap to specifications. On electronic ignition models, remove the distributor cap and visually inspect the armature. Ensure that the armature pin is in place, and that the armature is on tight and rotates when the engine is cranked. Make sure there are no cracks, chips or rounded edges on the armature.	If the breaker points are intact, clean the contact surfaces with fine emery cloth, and adjust the point gap to specifications. If the points are worn, replace them. On electronic systems, replace any parts which appear defective. If condition persists:	**3.4**

Test and Procedure	Results and Indications	Proceed to
3.4—On point-type ignition systems, connect a dwell-meter between the distributor primary lead and ground. Crank the engine and observe the point dwell angle. On electronic ignition systems, conduct a stator (magnetic pickup assembly) test. See Chapter 3.	On point-type systems, adjust the dwell angle if necessary. **NOTE:** *Increasing the point gap decreases the dwell angle and vice-versa.*	**3.6**
	If the dwell meter shows little or no reading;	**3.5**
	On electronic ignition systems, if the stator is bad, replace the stator. If the stator is good, proceed to the other tests in Chapter 3.	

Dwell is a function of point gap

3.5—On the point-type ignition systems, check the condenser for short: connect an ohmeter across the condenser body and the pigtail lead.	If any reading other than infinite is noted, replace the condenser	**3.6**

Checking the condenser for short

3.6—Test the coil primary resistance: On point-type ignition systems, connect an ohmmeter across the coil primary terminals, and read the resistance on the low scale. Note whether an external ballast resistor or resistance wire is used. On electronic ignition systems, test the coil primary resistance as in Chapter 3.	Point-type ignition coils utilizing ballast resistors or resistance wires should have approximately 1.0 ohms resistance. Coils with internal resistors should have approximately 4.0 ohms resistance. If values far from the above are noted, replace the coil.	**4.1**

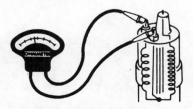

Check the coil primary resistance

Section 4—Secondary Electrical System
See Chapters 2–3 for service procedures

Test and Procedure	Results and Indications	Proceed to
4.1—Check for spark: Hold each spark plug wire approximately ¼″ from ground with gloves or a heavy, dry rag. Crank the engine, and observe the spark.	If no spark is evident:	**4.2**
	If spark is good in some cylinders:	**4.3**
	If spark is good in all cylinders:	**4.6**

Check for spark at the plugs

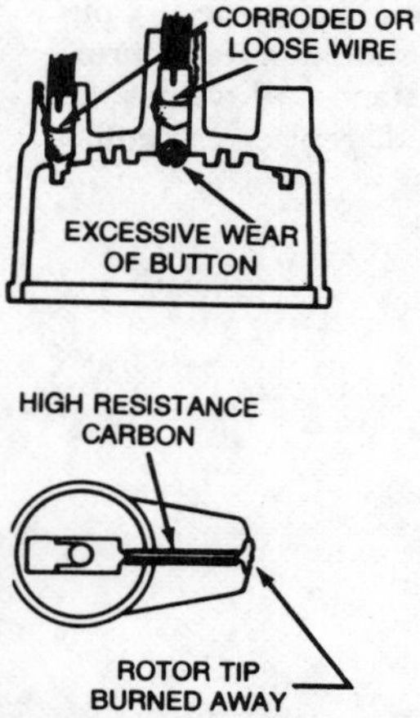

Test and Procedure	Results and Indications	Proceed to
4.2—Check for spark at the coil high tension lead: Remove the coil high tension lead from the distributor and position it approximately ¼″ from ground. Crank the engine and observe spark. **CAUTION: *This test should not be performed on engines equipped with electronic ignition.***	If the spark is good and consistent:	**4.3**
	If the spark is good but intermittent, test the primary electrical system starting at 3.3:	**3.3**
	If the spark is weak or non-existent, replace the coil high tension lead, clean and tighten all connections and retest. If no improvement is noted:	**4.4**
4.3—Visually inspect the distributor cap and rotor for burned or corroded contacts, cracks, carbon tracks, or moisture. Also check the fit of the rotor on the distributor shaft (where applicable).	If moisture is present, dry thoroughly, and retest per 4.1:	**4.1**
	If burned or excessively corroded contacts, cracks, or carbon tracks are noted, replace the defective part(s) and retest per 4.1:	**4.1**
	If the rotor and cap appear intact, or are only slightly corroded, clean the contacts thoroughly (including the cap towers and spark plug wire ends) and retest per 4.1:	
	If the spark is good in all cases:	**4.6**
	If the spark is poor in all cases:	**4.5**

CORRODED OR LOOSE WIRE

EXCESSIVE WEAR OF BUTTON

HIGH RESISTANCE CARBON

ROTOR TIP BURNED AWAY

Inspect the distributor cap and rotor

Test and Procedure	Results and Indications	Proceed to
4.4—Check the coil secondary resistance: On point-type systems connect an ohmmeter across the distributor side of the coil and the coil tower. Read the resistance on the high scale of the ohmmeter. On electronic ignition systems, see Chapter 3 for specific tests.	The resistance of a satisfactory coil should be between 4,000 and 10,000 ohms. If resistance is considerably higher (i.e., 40,000 ohms) replace the coil and retest per 4.1. **NOTE:** *This does not apply to high performance coils.*	

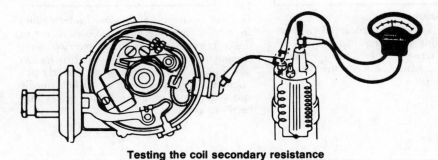

Testing the coil secondary resistance

4.5—Visually inspect the spark plug wires for cracking or brittleness. Ensure that no two wires are positioned so as to cause induction firing (adjacent and parallel). Remove each wire, one by one, and check resistance with an ohmmeter.	Replace any cracked or brittle wires. If any of the wires are defective, replace the entire set. Replace any wires with excessive resistance (over $8000\,\Omega$ per foot for suppression wire), and separate any wires that might cause induction firing.	**4.6**

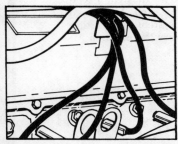

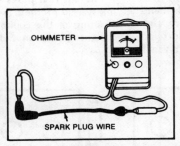

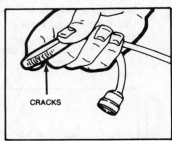

Misfiring can be the result of spark plug leads to adjacent, consecutively firing cylinders running parallel and too close together

On point-type ignition systems, check the spark plug wires as shown. On electronic ignitions, do not remove the wire from the distributor cap terminal; instead, test through the cap

Spark plug wires can be checked visually by bending them in a loop over your finger. This will reveal any cracks, burned or broken insulation. Any wire with cracked insulation should be replaced

4.6—Remove the spark plugs, noting the cylinders from which they were removed, and evaluate according to the color photos in the middle of this book.	See following.	**See following.**

Test and Procedure	Results and Indications	Proceed to
4.7—Examine the location of all the plugs.	The following diagrams illustrate some of the conditions that the location of plugs will reveal.	4.8

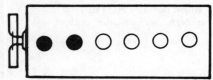

Two adjacent plugs are fouled in a 6-cylinder engine, 4-cylinder engine or either bank of a V-8. This is probably due to a blown head gasket between the two cylinders

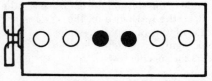

The two center plugs in a 6-cylinder engine are fouled. Raw fuel may be "boiled" out of the carburetor into the intake manifold after the engine is shut-off. Stop-start driving can also foul the center plugs, due to overly rich mixture. Proper float level, a new float needle and seat or use of an insulating spacer may help this problem

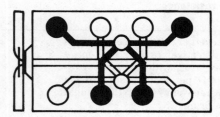

An unbalanced carburetor is indicated. Following the fuel flow on this particular design shows that the cylinders fed by the right-hand barrel are fouled from overly rich mixture, while the cylinders fed by the left-hand barrel are normal

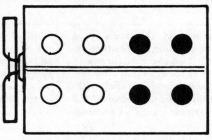

If the four rear plugs are overheated, a cooling system problem is suggested. A thorough cleaning of the cooling system may restore coolant circulation and cure the problem

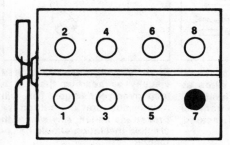

Finding one plug overheated may indicate an intake manifold leak near the affected cylinder. If the overheated plug is the second of two adjacent, consecutively firing plugs, it could be the result of ignition cross-firing. Separating the leads to these two plugs will eliminate cross-fire

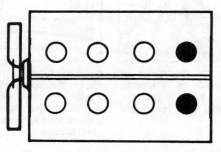

Occasionally, the two rear plugs in large, lightly used V-8's will become oil fouled. High oil consumption and smoky exhaust may also be noticed. It is probably due to plugged oil drain holes in the rear of the cylinder head, causing oil to be sucked in around the valve stems. This usually occurs in the rear cylinders first, because the engine slants that way

Test and Procedure	Results and Indications	Proceed to
4.8—Determine the static ignition timing. Using the crankshaft pulley timing marks as a guide, locate top dead center on the compression stroke of the number one cylinder.	The rotor should be pointing toward the No. 1 tower in the distributor cap, and, on electronic ignitions, the armature spoke for that cylinder should be lined up with the stator.	**4.8**
4.9—Check coil polarity: Connect a voltmeter negative lead to the coil high tension lead, and the positive lead to ground (**NOTE: *Reverse the hook-up for positive ground systems***). Crank the engine momentarily. **Checking coil polarity**	If the voltmeter reads up-scale, the polarity is correct:	**5.1**
	If the voltmeter reads down-scale, reverse the coil polarity (switch the primary leads):	**5.1**

Section 5—Fuel System
See Chapter 4 for service procedures

Test and Procedure	Results and Indications	Proceed to
5.1—Determine that the air filter is functioning efficiently: Hold paper elements up to a strong light, and attempt to see light through the filter.	Clean permanent air filters in solvent (or manufacturer's recommendation), and allow to dry. Replace paper elements through which light cannot be seen:	**5.2**
5.2—Determine whether a flooding condition exists: Flooding is identified by a strong gasoline odor, and excessive gasoline present in the throttle bore(s) of the carburetor.	If flooding is not evident:	**5.3**
	If flooding is evident, permit the gasoline to dry for a few moments and restart.	
	If flooding doesn't recur:	**5.7**
	If flooding is persistent:	**5.5**

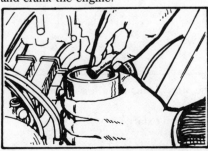

If the engine floods repeatedly, check the choke butterfly flap

Test and Procedure	Results and Indications	Proceed to
5.3—Check that fuel is reaching the carburetor: Detach the fuel line at the carburetor inlet. Hold the end of the line in a cup (not styrofoam), and crank the engine.	If fuel flows smoothly:	**5.7**
	If fuel doesn't flow (**NOTE: *Make sure that there is fuel in the tank***), or flows erratically:	**5.4**

Check the fuel pump by disconnecting the output line (fuel pump-to-carburetor) at the carburetor and operating the starter briefly

Test and Procedure	Results and Indications	Proceed to
5.4—Test the fuel pump: Disconnect all fuel lines from the fuel pump. Hold a finger over the input fitting, crank the engine (with electric pump, turn the ignition or pump on); and feel for suction.	If suction is evident, blow out the fuel line to the tank with low pressure compressed air until bubbling is heard from the fuel filler neck. Also blow out the carburetor fuel line (both ends disconnected):	**5.7**
	If no suction is evident, replace or repair the fuel pump: **NOTE:** *Repeated oil fouling of the spark plugs, or a no-start condition, could be the result of a ruptured vacuum booster pump diaphragm, through which oil or gasoline is being drawn into the intake manifold (where applicable).*	**5.7**
5.5—Occasionally, small specks of dirt will clog the small jets and orifices in the carburetor. With the engine cold, hold a flat piece of wood or similar material over the carburetor, where possible, and crank the engine.	If the engine starts, but runs roughly the engine is probably not run enough. If the engine won't start:	**5.9**
5.6—Check the needle and seat: Tap the carburetor in the area of the needle and seat.	If flooding stops, a gasoline additive (e.g., Gumout) will often cure the problem:	**5.7**
	If flooding continues, check the fuel pump for excessive pressure at the carburetor (according to specifications). If the pressure is normal, the needle and seat must be removed and checked, and/or the float level adjusted:	**5.7**
5.7—Test the accelerator pump by looking into the throttle bores while operating the throttle.	If the accelerator pump appears to be operating normally:	**5.8**
	If the accelerator pump is not operating, the pump must be reconditioned. Where possible, service the pump with the carburetor(s) installed on the engine. If necessary, remove the carburetor. Prior to removal:	**5.8**

Check for gas at the carburetor by looking down the carburetor throat while someone moves the accelerator

Test and Procedure	Results and Indications	Proceed to
5.8—Determine whether the carburetor main fuel system is functioning: Spray a commercial starting fluid into the carburetor while attempting to start the engine.	If the engine starts, runs for a few seconds, and dies:	**5.9**
	If the engine doesn't start:	**6.1**

CHILTON'S
AUTO BODY
REPAIR TIPS

Tools and Materials • Step-by-Step Illustrated Procedures
How To Repair Dents, Scratches and Rust Holes
Spray Painting and Refinishing Tips

With a little practice, basic body repair procedures can be mastered by any do-it-yourself mechanic. The step-by-step repairs shown here can be applied to almost any type of auto body repair.

TOOLS & MATERIALS

You may already have basic tools, such as hammers and electric drills. Other tools unique to body repair — body hammers, grinding attachments, sanding blocks, dent puller, half-round plastic file and plastic spreaders — are relatively inexpensive and can be obtained wherever auto parts or auto body repair parts are sold. Portable air compressors and paint spray guns can be purchased or rented.

Auto Body Repair Kits

The best and most often used products are available to the do-it-yourselfer in kit form, from major manufacturers of auto body repair products. The same manufacturers also merchandise the individual products for use by pros.

Kits are available to make a wide variety of repairs, including holes, dents and scratches and fiberglass, and offer the advantage of buying the materials you'll need for the job. There is little waste or chance of materials going bad from not being used. Many kits may also contain basic body-working tools such as body files, sanding blocks and spreaders. Check the contents of the kit before buying your tools.

BODY REPAIR TIPS

Safety

Many of the products associated with auto body repair and refinishing contain toxic chemicals. Read all labels before opening containers and store them in a safe place and manner.

• Wear eye protection (safety goggles) when using power tools or when performing any operation that involves

the removal of any type of material.

• Wear lung protection (disposable mask or respirator) when grinding, sanding or painting.

Sanding

1 Sand off paint before using a dent puller. When using a non-adhesive sanding disc, cover the back of the disc with an overlapping layer or two of masking tape and trim the edges. The disc will last considerably longer.

2 Use the circular motion of the sanding disc to grind *into* the edge of the repair. Grinding or sanding away from the jagged edge will only tear the sandpaper.

3 Use the palm of your hand flat on the panel to detect high and low spots. Do not use your fingertips. Slide your hand slowly back and forth.

WORKING WITH BODY FILLER

Mixing The Filler

Cleanliness and proper mixing and application are extremely important. Use a clean piece of plastic or glass or a disposable artist's palette to mix body filler.

1 Allow plenty of time and follow directions. No useful purpose will be served by adding more hardener to make it cure (set-up) faster. Less hardener means more curing time, but the mixture dries harder; more hardener means less curing time but a softer mixture.

2 Both the hardener and the filler should be thoroughly kneaded or stirred before mixing. Hardener should be a solid paste and dispense like thin toothpaste. Body filler should be smooth, and free of lumps or thick spots.

Getting the proper amount of hardener in the filler is the trickiest part of preparing the filler. Use the same amount of hardener in cold or warm weather. For contour filler (thick coats), a bead of hardener twice the diameter of the filler is about right. There's about a 5% margin on either side, but, if in doubt use less hardener.

3 Mix the body filler and hardener by wiping across the mixing surface, picking the mixture up and wiping it again. Colder weather requires longer mixing times. Do not mix in a circular motion; this will trap air bubbles which will become holes in the cured filler.

Applying The Filler

1 For best results, filler should not be applied over 1/4" thick.

Apply the filler in several coats. Build it up to above the level of the repair surface so that it can be sanded or grated down.

The first coat of filler must be pressed on with a firm wiping motion.

Apply the filler in one direction only. Working the filler back and forth will either pull it off the metal or trap air bubbles.

REPAIRING DENTS

Before you start, take a few minutes to study the damaged area. Try to visualize the shape of the panel before it was damaged. If the damage is on the left fender, look at the right fender and use it as a guide. If there is access to the panel from behind, you can reshape it with a body hammer. If not, you'll have to use a dent puller. Go slowly and work the metal a little at a time. Get the panel as straight as possible before applying filler.

1 This dent is typical of one that can be pulled out or hammered out from behind. Remove the headlight cover, headlight assembly and turn signal housing.

2 Drill a series of holes ½ the size of the end of the dent puller along the stress line. Make some trial pulls and assess the results. If necessary, drill more holes and try again. Do not hurry.

3 If possible, use a body hammer and block to shape the metal back to its original contours. Get the metal back as close to its original shape as possible. Don't depend on body filler to fill dents.

4 Using an 80-grit grinding disc on an electric drill, grind the paint from the surrounding area down to bare metal. Use a new grinding pad to prevent heat buildup that will warp metal.

5 The area should look like this when you're finished grinding. Knock the drill holes in and tape over small openings to keep plastic filler out.

6 Mix the body filler (see Body Repair Tips). Spread the body filler evenly over the entire area (see Body Repair Tips). Be sure to cover the area completely.

7 Let the body filler dry until the surface can just be scratched with your fingernail. Knock the high spots from the body filler with a body file ("Cheesegrater"). Check frequently with the palm of your hand for high and low spots.

8 Check to be sure that trim pieces that will be installed later will fit exactly. Sand the area with 40-grit paper.

9 If you wind up with low spots, you may have to apply another layer of filler.

10 Knock the high spots off with 40-grit paper. When you are satisfied with the contours of the repair, apply a thin coat of filler to cover pin holes and scratches.

11 Block sand the area with 40-grit paper to a smooth finish. Pay particular attention to body lines and ridges that must be well-defined.

12 Sand the area with 400 paper and then finish with a scuff pad. The finished repair is ready for priming and painting (see Painting Tips).

Materials and photos courtesy of Ritt Jones Auto Body, Prospect Park, PA.

REPAIRING RUST HOLES

There are many ways to repair rust holes. The fiberglass cloth kit shown here is one of the most cost efficient for the owner because it provides a strong repair that resists cracking and moisture and is relatively easy to use. It can be used on large and small holes (with or without backing) and can be applied over contoured areas. Remember, however, that short of replacing an entire panel, no repair is a guarantee that the rust will not return.

1 Remove any trim that will be in the way. Clean away all loose debris. Cut away all the rusted metal. But be sure to leave enough metal to retain the contour or body shape.

2 Grind away all traces of rust with a 24-grit grinding disc. Be sure to grind back 3-4 inches from the edge of the hole down to bare metal and be sure all traces of paint, primer and rust are removed.

3 Block sand the area with 80 or 100 grit sandpaper to get a clear, shiny surface and feathered paint edge. Tap the edges of the hole inward with a ball peen hammer.

4 If you are going to use release film, cut a piece about 2-3″ larger than the area you have sanded. Place the film over the repair and mark the sanded area on the film. Avoid any unnecessary wrinkling of the film.

5 Cut 2 pieces of fiberglass matte to match the shape of the repair. One piece should be about 1″ smaller than the sanded area and the second piece should be 1″ smaller than the first. Mix enough filler and hardener to saturate the fiberglass material (see Body Repair Tips).

6 Lay the release sheet on a flat surface and spread an even layer of filler, large enough to cover the repair. Lay the smaller piece of fiberglass cloth in the center of the sheet and spread another layer of filler over the fiberglass cloth. Repeat the operation for the larger piece of cloth.

7 Place the repair material over the repair area, with the release film facing outward. Use a spreader and work from the center outward to smooth the material, following the body contours. Be sure to remove all air bubbles.

8 Wait until the repair has dried tack-free and peel off the release sheet. The ideal working temperature is 60°-90° F. Cooler or warmer temperatures or high humidity may require additional curing time. Wait longer, if in doubt.

9 Sand and feather-edge the entire area. The initial sanding can be one with a sanding disc on an electric rill if care is used. Finish the sanding with a block sander. Low spots can be lled with body filler; this may require everal applications.

10 When the filler can just be scratched with a fingernail, nock the high spots down with a body le and smooth the entire area with 80-rit. Feather the filled areas into the surounding areas.

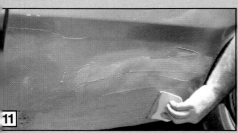

11 When the area is sanded smooth, mix some topcoat and hardener nd apply it directly with a spreader. his will give a smooth finish and prent the glass matte from showing hrough the paint.

12 Block sand the topcoat smooth with finishing sandpaper (200 grit), and 400 grit. The repair is ready for masking, priming and painting (see Painting Tips).

Materials and photos courtesy Marson Corporation, Chelsea, Massachusetts

PAINTING TIPS

Preparation

1 SANDING — Use a 400 or 600 grit wet or dry sandpaper. Wet-sand the area with a 1/4 sheet of sandpaper soaked in clean water. Keep the paper wet while sanding. Sand the area until the repaired area tapers into the original finish.

2 CLEANING — Wash the area to be painted thoroughly with water and a clean rag. Rinse it thoroughly and wipe the surface dry until you're sure it's completely free of dirt, dust, fingerprints, wax, detergent or other foreign matter.

3 MASKING — Protect any areas you don't want to overspray by covering them with masking tape and newspaper. Be careful not get fingerprints on the area to be painted.

4 PRIMING — All exposed metal should be primed before painting. Primer protects the metal and provides an excellent surface for paint adhesion. When the primer is dry, wet-sand the area again with 600 grit wet-sandpaper. Clean the area again after sanding.

Painting Techniques

P aint applied from either a spray gun or a spray can (for small areas) will provide good results. Experiment on an old piece of metal to get the right combination before you begin painting.

SPRAYING VISCOSITY (SPRAY GUN ONLY) — Paint should be thinned to spraying viscosity according to the directions on the can. Use only the recommended thinner or reducer and the same amount of reduction regardless of temperature.

AIR PRESSURE (SPRAY GUN ONLY) — This is extremely important. Be sure you are using the proper recommended pressure.

TEMPERATURE — The surface to be painted should be approximately the same temperature as the surrounding air. Applying warm paint to a cold surface, or vice versa, will completely upset the paint characteristics.

THICKNESS — Spray with smooth strokes. In general, the thicker the coat of paint, the longer the drying time. Apply several thin coats about 30 seconds apart. The paint should remain wet long enough to flow out and no longer; heavier coats will only produce sags or wrinkles. Spray a light (fog) coat, followed by heavier color coats.

DISTANCE — The ideal spraying distance is 8″-12″ from the gun or can to the surface. Shorter distances will produce ripples, while greater distances will result in orange peel, dry film and poor color match and loss of material due to overspray.

OVERLAPPING — The gun or can should be kept at right angles to the surface at all times. Work to a wet edge at an even speed, using a 50% overlap and direct the center of the spray at the lower or nearest edge of the previous stroke.

RUBBING OUT (BLENDING) FRESH PAINT — Let the paint dry thoroughly. Runs or imperfections can be sanded out, primed and repainted.

Don't be in too big a hurry to remove the masking. This only produces paint ridges. When the finish has dried for at least a week, apply a small amount of fine grade rubbing compound with a clean, wet cloth. Use lots of water and blend the new paint with the surrounding area.

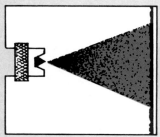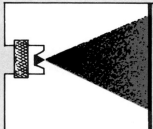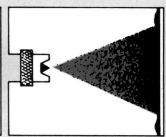

WRONG   **CORRECT**   **WRONG**

Thin coat. Stroke too fast, not enough overlap, gun too far away.

Medium coat. Proper distance, good stroke, proper overlap.

Heavy coat. Stroke too slow, too much overlap, gun too close.

Test and Procedure	Results and Indications	Proceed to
5.9—Uncommon fuel system malfunctions: See below:	If the problem is solved:	6.1
	If the problem remains, remove and recondition the carburetor.	

Condition	Indication	Test	Prevailing Weather Conditions	Remedy
Vapor lock	Engine will not restart shortly after running.	Cool the components of the fuel system until the engine starts. Vapor lock can be cured faster by draping a wet cloth over a mechanical fuel pump.	Hot to very hot	Ensure that the exhaust manifold heat control valve is operating. Check with the vehicle manufacturer for the recommended solution to vapor lock on the model in question.
Carburetor icing	Engine will not idle, stalls at low speeds.	Visually inspect the throttle plate area of the throttle bores for frost.	High humidity, 32–40° F.	Ensure that the exhaust manifold heat control valve is operating, and that the intake manifold heat riser is not blocked.
Water in the fuel	Engine sputters and stalls; may not start.	Pump a small amount of fuel into a glass jar. Allow to stand, and inspect for droplets or a layer of water.	High humidity, extreme temperature changes.	For droplets, use one or two cans of commercial gas line anti-freeze. For a layer of water, the tank must be drained, and the fuel lines blown out with compressed air.

Section 6—Engine Compression
See Chapter 3 for service procedures

6.1—Test engine compression: Remove all spark plugs. Block the throttle wide open. Insert a compression gauge into a spark plug port, crank the engine to obtain the maximum reading, and record.	If compression is within limits on all cylinders:	7.1
	If gauge reading is extremely low on all cylinders:	6.2
	If gauge reading is low on one or two cylinders: (If gauge readings are identical and low on two or more adjacent cylinders, the head gasket must be replaced.)	6.2

Checking compression

6.2—Test engine compression (wet): Squirt approximately 30 cc. of engine oil into each cylinder, and retest per 6.1.	If the readings improve, worn or cracked rings or broken pistons are indicated:	See Chapter 3
	If the readings do not improve, burned or excessively carboned valves or a jumped timing chain are indicated:	7.1
	NOTE: *A jumped timing chain is often indicated by difficult cranking.*	

Section 7—Engine Vacuum
See Chapter 3 for service procedures

Test and Procedure	Results and Indications	Proceed to
7.1—Attach a vacuum gauge to the intake manifold beyond the throttle plate. Start the engine, and observe the action of the needle over the range of engine speeds.	See below.	**See below**

INDICATION: normal engine in good condition

Proceed to: 8.1

Normal engine
Gauge reading: steady, from 17–22 in./Hg.

INDICATION: sticking valves or ignition miss

Proceed to: 9.1, 8.3

Sticking valves
Gauge reading: intermittent fluctuation at idle

INDICATION: late ignition or valve timing, low compression, stuck throttle valve, leaking carburetor or manifold gasket

Proceed to: 6.1

Incorrect valve timing
Gauge reading: low (10–15 in./Hg) but steady

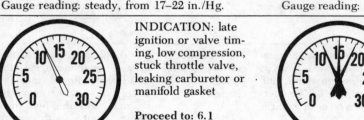

INDICATION: improper carburetor adjustment or minor intake leak.

Proceed to: 7.2

Carburetor requires adjustment
Gauge reading: drifting needle

INDICATION: ignition miss, blown cylinder head gasket, leaking valve or weak valve spring

Proceed to: 8.3, 6.1

Blown head gasket
Gauge reading: needle fluctuates as engine speed increases

INDICATION: burnt valve or faulty valve clearance. Needle will fall when defective valve operates

Proceed to: 9.1

Burnt or leaking valves
Gauge reading: steady needle, but drops regularly

INDICATION: choked muffler, excessive back pressure in system

Proceed to: 10.1

Clogged exhaust system
Gauge reading: gradual drop in reading at idle

INDICATION: worn valve guides

Proceed to: 9.1

Worn valve guides
Gauge reading: needle vibrates excessively at idle, but steadies as engine speed increases

White pointer = steady gauge hand   Black pointer = fluctuating gauge hand

Test and Procedure	Results and Indications	Proceed to
7.2—Attach a vacuum gauge per 7.1, and test for an intake manifold leak. Squirt a small amount of oil around the intake manifold gaskets, carburetor gaskets, plugs and fittings. Observe the action of the vacuum gauge.	If the reading improves, replace the indicated gasket, or seal the indicated fitting or plug: If the reading remains low:	**8.1** **7.3**
7.3—Test all vacuum hoses and accessories for leaks as described in 7.2. Also check the carburetor body (dashpots, automatic choke mechanism, throttle shafts) for leaks in the same manner.	If the reading improves, service or replace the offending part(s): If the reading remains low:	**8.1** **6.1**

Section 8—Secondary Electrical System
See Chapter 2 for service procedures

Test and Procedure	Results and Indications	Proceed to
8.1—Remove the distributor cap and check to make sure that the rotor turns when the engine is cranked. Visually inspect the distributor components.	Clean, tighten or replace any components which appear defective.	**8.2**
8.2—Connect a timing light (per manufacturer's recommendation) and check the dynamic ignition timing. Disconnect and plug the vacuum hose(s) to the distributor if specified, start the engine, and observe the timing marks at the specified engine speed.	If the timing is not correct, adjust to specifications by rotating the distributor in the engine: (Advance timing by rotating distributor opposite normal direction of rotor rotation, retard timing by rotating distributor in same direction as rotor rotation.)	**8.3**
8.3—Check the operation of the distributor advance mechanism(s): To test the mechanical advance, disconnect the vacuum lines from the distributor advance unit and observe the timing marks with a timing light as the engine speed is increased from idle. If the mark moves smoothly, without hesitation, it may be assumed that the mechanical advance is functioning properly. To test vacuum advance and/or retard systems, alternately crimp and release the vacuum line, and observe the timing mark for movement. If movement is noted, the system is operating.	If the systems are functioning: If the systems are not functioning, remove the distributor, and test on a distributor tester:	**8.4** **8.4**
8.4—Locate an ignition miss: With the engine running, remove each spark plug wire, one at a time, until one is found that doesn't cause the engine to roughen and slow down.	When the missing cylinder is identified:	**4.1**

Section 9—Valve Train
See Chapter 3 for service procedures

Test and Procedure	Results and Indications	Proceed to
9.1—Evaluate the valve train: Remove the valve cover, and ensure that the valves are adjusted to specifications. A mechanic's stethoscope may be used to aid in the diagnosis of the valve train. By pushing the probe on or near push rods or rockers, valve noise often can be isolated. A timing light also may be used to diagnose valve problems. Connect the light according to manufacturer's recommendations, and start the engine. Vary the firing moment of the light by increasing the engine speed (and therefore the ignition advance), and moving the trigger from cylinder to cylinder. Observe the movement of each valve.	Sticking valves or erratic valve train motion can be observed with the timing light. The cylinder head must be disassembled for repairs.	**See Chapter 3**
9.2—Check the valve timing: Locate top dead center of the No. 1 piston, and install a degree wheel or tape on the crankshaft pulley or damper with zero corresponding to an index mark on the engine. Rotate the crankshaft in its direction of rotation, and observe the opening of the No. 1 cylinder intake valve. The opening should correspond with the correct mark on the degree wheel according to specifications.	If the timing is not correct, the timing cover must be removed for further investigation.	**See Chapter 3**

Section 10—Exhaust System

Test and Procedure	Results and Indications	Proceed to
10.1—Determine whether the exhaust manifold heat control valve is operating: Operate the valve by hand to determine whether it is free to move. If the valve is free, run the engine to operating temperature and observe the action of the valve, to ensure that it is opening.	If the valve sticks, spray it with a suitable solvent, open and close the valve to free it, and retest. If the valve functions properly: If the valve does not free, or does not operate, replace the valve:	**10.2** **10.2**
10.2 —Ensure that there are no exhaust restrictions: Visually inspect the exhaust system for kinks, dents, or crushing. Also note that gases are flowing freely from the tailpipe at all engine speeds, indicating no restriction in the muffler or resonator.	Replace any damaged portion of the system:	**11.1**

Section 11—Cooling System
See Chapter 3 for service procedures

Test and Procedure	Results and Indications	Proceed to
11.1—Visually inspect the fan belt for glazing, cracks, and fraying, and replace if necessary. Tighten the belt so that the longest span has approximately ½″ play at its mid-point under thumb pressure (see Chapter 1).	Replace or tighten the fan belt as necessary:	**11.2**

Checking belt tension

11.2—Check the fluid level of the cooling system.	If full or slightly low, fill as necessary: If extremely low:	**11.5** **11.3**
11.3—Visually inspect the external portions of the cooling system (radiator, radiator hoses, thermostat elbow, water pump seals, heater hoses, etc.) for leaks. If none are found, pressurize the cooling system to 14–15 psi.	If cooling system holds the pressure:	**11.5**
	If cooling system loses pressure rapidly, reinspect external parts of the system for leaks under pressure. If none are found, check dipstick for coolant in crankcase. If no coolant is present, but pressure loss continues:	**11.4**
	If coolant is evident in crankcase, remove cylinder head(s), and check gasket(s). If gaskets are intact, block and cylinder head(s) should be checked for cracks or holes. If the gasket(s) is blown, replace, and purge the crankcase of coolant: NOTE: *Occasionally, due to atmospheric and driving conditions, condensation of water can occur in the crankcase. This causes the oil to appear milky white. To remedy, run the engine until hot, and change the oil and oil filter.*	**12.6**
11.4—Check for combustion leaks into the cooling system: Pressurize the cooling system as above. Start the engine, and observe the pressure gauge. If the needle fluctuates, remove each spark plug wire, one at a time, noting which cylinder(s) reduce or eliminate the fluctuation.	Cylinders which reduce or eliminate the fluctuation, when the spark plug wire is removed, are leaking into the cooling system. Replace the head gasket on the affected cylinder bank(s).	

Pressurizing the cooling system

Test and Procedure	Results and Indications	Proceed to
11.5—Check the radiator pressure cap: Attach a radiator pressure tester to the radiator cap (wet the seal prior to installation). Quickly pump up the pressure, noting the point at which the cap releases.	If the cap releases within ± 1 psi of the specified rating, it is operating properly:	**11.6**
	If the cap releases at more than ± 1 psi of the specified rating, it should be replaced:	**11.6**

Checking radiator pressure cap

Test and Procedure	Results and Indications	Proceed to
11.6—Test the thermostat: Start the engine cold, remove the radiator cap, and insert a thermometer into the radiator. Allow the engine to idle. After a short while, there will be a sudden, rapid increase in coolant temperature. The temperature at which this sharp rise stops is the thermostat opening temperature.	If the thermostat opens at or about the specified temperature:	**11.7**
	If the temperature doesn't increase: (If the temperature increases slowly and gradually, replace the thermostat.)	**11.7**
11.7—Check the water pump: Remove the thermostat elbow and the thermostat, disconnect the coil high tension lead (to prevent starting), and crank the engine momentarily.	If coolant flows, replace the thermostat and retest per 11.6:	**11.6**
	If coolant doesn't flow, reverse flush the cooling system to alleviate any blockage that might exist. If system is not blocked, and coolant will not flow, replace the water pump.	

Section 12—Lubrication
See Chapter 3 for service procedures

Test and Procedure	Results and Indications	Proceed to
12.1—Check the oil pressure gauge or warning light: If the gauge shows low pressure, or the light is on for no obvious reason, remove the oil pressure sender. Install an accurate oil pressure gauge and run the engine momentarily.	If oil pressure builds normally, run engine for a few moments to determine that it is functioning normally, and replace the sender.	—
	If the pressure remains low:	**12.2**
	If the pressure surges:	**12.3**
	If the oil pressure is zero:	**12.3**
12.2—Visually inspect the oil: If the oil is watery or very thin, milky, or foamy, replace the oil and oil filter.	If the oil is normal:	**12.3**
	If after replacing oil the pressure remains low:	**12.3**
	If after replacing oil the pressure becomes normal:	—

Test and Procedure	Results and Indications	Proceed to
12.3—Inspect the oil pressure relief valve and spring, to ensure that it is not sticking or stuck. Remove and thoroughly clean the valve, spring, and the valve body.	If the oil pressure improves: If no improvement is noted:	— **12.4**
12.4—Check to ensure that the oil pump is not cavitating (sucking air instead of oil): See that the crankcase is neither over nor underfull, and that the pickup in the sump is in the proper position and free from sludge.	Fill or drain the crankcase to the proper capacity, and clean the pickup screen in solvent if necessary. If no improvement is noted:	**12.5**
12.5—Inspect the oil pump drive and the oil pump:	If the pump drive or the oil pump appear to be defective, service as necessary and retest per 12.1: If the pump drive and pump appear to be operating normally, the engine should be disassembled to determine where blockage exists:	**12.1** **See Chapter 3**
12.6—Purge the engine of ethylene glycol coolant: Completely drain the crankcase and the oil filter. Obtain a commercial butyl cellosolve base solvent, designated for this purpose, and follow the instructions precisely. Following this, install a new oil filter and refill the crankcase with the proper weight oil. The next oil and filter change should follow shortly thereafter (1000 miles).		

TROUBLESHOOTING EMISSION CONTROL SYSTEMS

See Chapter 4 for procedures applicable to individual emission control systems used on specific combinations of engine/transmission/model.

TROUBLESHOOTING THE CARBURETOR
See Chapter 4 for service procedures

Carburetor problems cannot be effectively isolated unless all other engine systems (particularly ignition and emission) are functioning properly and the engine is properly tuned.

Condition	Possible Cause
Engine cranks, but does not start	1. Improper starting procedure 2. No fuel in tank 3. Clogged fuel line or filter 4. Defective fuel pump 5. Choke valve not closing properly 6. Engine flooded 7. Choke valve not unloading 8. Throttle linkage not making full travel 9. Stuck needle or float 10. Leaking float needle or seat 11. Improper float adjustment
Engine stalls	1. Improperly adjusted idle speed or mixture **Engine hot** 2. Improperly adjusted dashpot 3. Defective or improperly adjusted solenoid 4. Incorrect fuel level in fuel bowl 5. Fuel pump pressure too high 6. Leaking float needle seat 7. Secondary throttle valve stuck open 8. Air or fuel leaks 9. Idle air bleeds plugged or missing 10. Idle passages plugged **Engine Cold** 11. Incorrectly adjusted choke 12. Improperly adjusted fast idle speed 13. Air leaks 14. Plugged idle or idle air passages 15. Stuck choke valve or binding linkage 16. Stuck secondary throttle valves 17. Engine flooding—high fuel level 18. Leaking or misaligned float
Engine hesitates on acceleration	1. Clogged fuel filter 2. Leaking fuel pump diaphragm 3. Low fuel pump pressure 4. Secondary throttle valves stuck, bent or misadjusted 5. Sticking or binding air valve 6. Defective accelerator pump 7. Vacuum leaks 8. Clogged air filter 9. Incorrect choke adjustment (engine cold)
Engine feels sluggish or flat on acceleration	1. Improperly adjusted idle speed or mixture 2. Clogged fuel filter 3. Defective accelerator pump 4. Dirty, plugged or incorrect main metering jets 5. Bent or sticking main metering rods 6. Sticking throttle valves 7. Stuck heat riser 8. Binding or stuck air valve 9. Dirty, plugged or incorrect secondary jets 10. Bent or sticking secondary metering rods. 11. Throttle body or manifold heat passages plugged 12. Improperly adjusted choke or choke vacuum break.
Carburetor floods	1. Defective fuel pump. Pressure too high. 2. Stuck choke valve 3. Dirty, worn or damaged float or needle valve/seat 4. Incorrect float/fuel level 5. Leaking float bowl

Condition	Possible Cause
Engine idles roughly and stalls	1. Incorrect idle speed 2. Clogged fuel filter 3. Dirt in fuel system or carburetor 4. Loose carburetor screws or attaching bolts 5. Broken carburetor gaskets 6. Air leaks 7. Dirty carburetor 8. Worn idle mixture needles 9. Throttle valves stuck open 10. Incorrectly adjusted float or fuel level 11. Clogged air filter
Engine runs unevenly or surges	1. Defective fuel pump 2. Dirty or clogged fuel filter 3. Plugged, loose or incorrect main metering jets or rods 4. Air leaks 5. Bent or sticking main metering rods 6. Stuck power piston 7. Incorrect float adjustment 8. Incorrect idle speed or mixture 9. Dirty or plugged idle system passages 10. Hard, brittle or broken gaskets 11. Loose attaching or mounting screws 12. Stuck or misaligned secondary throttle valves
Poor fuel economy	1. Poor driving habits 2. Stuck choke valve 3. Binding choke linkage 4. Stuck heat riser 5. Incorrect idle mixture 6. Defective accelerator pump 7. Air leaks 8. Plugged, loose or incorrect main metering jets 9. Improperly adjusted float or fuel level 10. Bent, misaligned or fuel-clogged float 11. Leaking float needle seat 12. Fuel leak 13. Accelerator pump discharge ball not seating properly 14. Incorrect main jets
Engine lacks high speed performance or power	1. Incorrect throttle linkage adjustment 2. Stuck or binding power piston 3. Defective accelerator pump 4. Air leaks 5. Incorrect float setting or fuel level 6. Dirty, plugged, worn or incorrect main metering jets or rods 7. Binding or sticking air valve 8. Brittle or cracked gaskets 9. Bent, incorrect or improperly adjusted secondary metering rods 10. Clogged fuel filter 11. Clogged air filter 12. Defective fuel pump

TROUBLESHOOTING FUEL INJECTION PROBLEMS

Each fuel injection system has its own unique components and test procedures, for which it is impossible to generalize. Refer to Chapter 4 of this Repair & Tune-Up Guide for specific test and repair procedures, if the vehicle is equipped with fuel injection.

TROUBLESHOOTING ELECTRICAL PROBLEMS

See Chapter 5 for service procedures

For any electrical system to operate, it must make a complete circuit. This simply means that the power flow from the battery must make a complete circle. When an electrical component is operating, power flows from the battery to the component, passes through the component causing it to perform its function (lighting a light bulb), and then returns to the battery through the ground of the circuit. This ground is usually (but not always) the metal part of the car or truck on which the electrical component is mounted.

Perhaps the easiest way to visualize this is to think of connecting a light bulb with two wires attached to it to the battery. If one of the two wires attached to the light bulb were attached to the negative post of the battery and the other were attached to the positive post of the battery, you would have a complete circuit. Current from the battery would flow to the light bulb, causing it to light, and return to the negative post of the battery.

The normal automotive circuit differs from this simple example in two ways. First, instead of having a return wire from the bulb to the battery, the light bulb returns the current to the battery through the chassis of the vehicle. Since the negative battery cable is attached to the chassis and the chassis is made of electrically conductive metal, the chassis of the vehicle can serve as a ground wire to complete the circuit. Secondly, most automotive circuits contain switches to turn components on and off as required.

Every complete circuit from a power source must include a component which is using the power from the power source. If you were to disconnect the light bulb from the wires and touch the two wires together (don't do this) the power supply wire to the component would be grounded before the normal ground connection for the circuit.

Because grounding a wire from a power source makes a complete circuit—less the required component to use the power—this phenomenon is called a short circuit. Common causes are: broken insulation (exposing the metal wire to a metal part of the car or truck), or a shorted switch.

Some electrical components which require a large amount of current to operate also have a relay in their circuit. Since these circuits carry a large amount of current, the thickness of the wire in the circuit (gauge size) is also greater. If this large wire were connected from the component to the control switch on the instrument panel, and then back to the component, a voltage drop would occur in the circuit. To prevent this potential drop in voltage, an electromagnetic switch (relay) is used. The large wires in the circuit are connected from the battery to one side of the relay, and from the opposite side of the relay to the component. The relay is normally open, preventing current from passing through the circuit. An additional, smaller, wire is connected from the relay to the control switch for the circuit. When the control switch is turned on, it grounds the smaller wire from the relay and completes the circuit. This closes the relay and allows current to flow from the battery to the component. The horn, headlight, and starter circuits are three which use relays.

It is possible for larger surges of current to pass through the electrical system of your car or truck. If this surge of current were to reach an electrical component, it could burn it out. To prevent this, fuses, circuit breakers or fusible links are connected into the current supply wires of most of the major electrical systems. When an electrical current of excessive power passes through the component's fuse, the fuse blows out and breaks the circuit, saving the component from destruction.

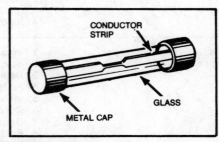

Typical automotive fuse

A circuit breaker is basically a self-repairing fuse. The circuit breaker opens the circuit the same way a fuse does. However, when either the short is removed from the circuit or the surge subsides, the circuit breaker resets itself and does not have to be replaced as a fuse does.

A fuse link is a wire that acts as a fuse. It is normally connected between the starter relay and the main wiring harness. This connection is usually under the hood. The fuse link (if installed) protects all the

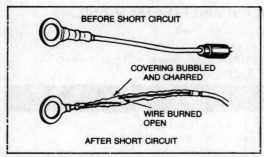

Most fusible links show a charred, melted insulation when they burn out

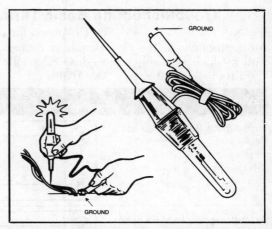

The test light will show the presence of current when touched to a hot wire and grounded at the other end

chassis electrical components, and is the probable cause of trouble when none of the electrical components function, unless the battery is disconnected or dead.

Electrical problems generally fall into one of three areas:

1. The component that is not functioning is not receiving current.

2. The component itself is not functioning.

3. The component is not properly grounded.

The electrical system can be checked with a test light and a jumper wire. A test light is a device that looks like a pointed screwdriver with a wire attached to it and has a light bulb in its handle. A jumper wire is a piece of insulated wire with an alligator clip attached to each end.

If a component is not working, you must follow a systematic plan to determine which of the three causes is the villain.

1. Turn on the switch that controls the inoperable component.

2. Disconnect the power supply wire from the component.

3. Attach the ground wire on the test light to a good metal ground.

4. Touch the probe end of the test light to the end of the power supply wire that was disconnected from the component. If the component is receiving current, the test light will go on.

NOTE: *Some components work only when the ignition switch is turned on.*

If the test light does not go on, then the problem is in the circuit between the battery and the component. This includes all the switches, fuses, and relays in the system. Follow the wire that runs back to the battery. The problem is an open circuit between the

battery and the component. If the fuse is blown and, when replaced, immediately blows again, there is a short circuit in the system which must be located and repaired. If there is a switch in the system, bypass it with a jumper wire. This is done by connecting one end of the jumper wire to the power supply wire into the switch and the other end of the jumper wire to the wire coming out of the switch. If the test light lights with the jumper wire installed, the switch or whatever was bypassed is defective.

NOTE: *Never substitute the jumper wire for the component, since it is required to use the power from the power source.*

5. If the bulb in the test light goes on, then the current is getting to the component that is not working. This eliminates the first of the three possible causes. Connect the power supply wire and connect a jumper wire from the component to a good metal ground. Do this with the switch which controls the component turned on, and also the ignition switch turned on if it is required for the component to work. If the component works with the jumper wire installed, then it has a bad ground. This is usually caused by the metal area on which the component mounts to the chassis being coated with some type of foreign matter.

6. If neither test located the source of the trouble, then the component itself is defective. Remember that for any electrical system to work, all connections must be clean and tight.

Troubleshooting Basic Turn Signal and Flasher Problems
See Chapter 5 for service procedures

Most problems in the turn signals or flasher system can be reduced to defective flashers or bulbs, which are easily replaced. Occasionally, the turn signal switch will prove defective.

F = Front   R = Rear   ● = Lights off   ○ = Lights on

Condition		Possible Cause
Turn signals light, but do not flash	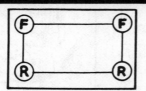	Defective flasher
No turn signals light on either side	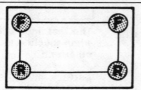	Blown fuse. Replace if defective. Defective flasher. Check by substitution. Open circuit, short circuit or poor ground.
Both turn signals on one side don't work	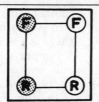	Bad bulbs. Bad ground in both (or either) housings.
One turn signal light on one side doesn't work	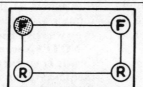	Defective bulb. Corrosion in socket. Clean contacts. Poor ground at socket.
Turn signal flashes too fast or too slowly	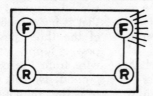	Check any bulb on the side flashing too fast. A heavy-duty bulb is probably installed in place of a regular bulb. Check the bulb flashing too slowly. A standard bulb was probably installed in place of a heavy-duty bulb. Loose connections or corrosion at the bulb socket.
Indicator lights don't work in either direction		Check if the turn signals are working. Check the dash indicator lights. Check the flasher by substitution.
One indicator light doesn't light		On systems with one dash indicator: See if the lights work on the same side. Often the filaments have been reversed in systems combining stoplights with taillights and turn signals. Check the flasher by substitution. On systems with two indicators: Check the bulbs on the same side. Check the indicator light bulb. Check the flasher by substitution.

Troubleshooting Lighting Problems
See Chapter 5 for service procedures

Condition	Possible Cause
One or more lights don't work, but others do	1. Defective bulb(s) 2. Blown fuse(s) 3. Dirty fuse clips or light sockets 4. Poor ground circuit
Lights burn out quickly	1. Incorrect voltage regulator setting or defective regulator 2. Poor battery/alternator connections
Lights go dim	1. Low/discharged battery 2. Alternator not charging 3. Corroded sockets or connections 4. Low voltage output
Lights flicker	1. Loose connection 2. Poor ground. (Run ground wire from light housing to frame) 3. Circuit breaker operating (short circuit)
Lights "flare"—Some flare is normal on acceleration—If excessive, see "Lights Burn Out Quickly"	High voltage setting
Lights glare—approaching drivers are blinded	1. Lights adjusted too high 2. Rear springs or shocks sagging 3. Rear tires soft

Troubleshooting Dash Gauge Problems
Most problems can be traced to a defective sending unit or faulty wiring. Occasionally, the gauge itself is at fault. See Chapter 5 for service procedures.

Condition	Possible Cause
COOLANT TEMPERATURE GAUGE	
Gauge reads erratically or not at all	1. Loose or dirty connections 2. Defective sending unit. 3. Defective gauge. To test a bi-metal gauge, remove the wire from the sending unit. Ground the wire for an instant. If the gauge registers, replace the sending unit. To test a magnetic gauge, disconnect the wire at the sending unit. With ignition ON gauge should register COLD. Ground the wire; gauge should register HOT.
AMMETER GAUGE—TURN HEADLIGHTS ON (DO NOT START ENGINE). NOTE REACTION	
Ammeter shows charge Ammeter shows discharge Ammeter does not move	1. Connections reversed on gauge 2. Ammeter is OK 3. Loose connections or faulty wiring 4. Defective gauge

Condition	Possible Cause

OIL PRESSURE GAUGE

Gauge does not register or is inaccurate	1. On mechanical gauge, Bourdon tube may be bent or kinked. 2. Low oil pressure. Remove sending unit. Idle the engine briefly. If no oil flows from sending unit hole, problem is in engine. 3. Defective gauge. Remove the wire from the sending unit and ground it for an instant with the ignition ON. A good gauge will go to the top of the scale. 4. Defective wiring. Check the wiring to the gauge. If it's OK and the gauge doesn't register when grounded, replace the gauge. 5. Defective sending unit.

ALL GAUGES

All gauges do not operate	1. Blown fuse
	2. Defective instrument regulator
All gauges read low or erratically	3. Defective or dirty instrument voltage regulator
All gauges pegged	4. Loss of ground between instrument voltage regulator and frame
	5. Defective instrument regulator

WARNING LIGHTS

Light(s) do not come on when ignition is ON, but engine is not started	1. Defective bulb 2. Defective wire 3. Defective sending unit. Disconnect the wire from the sending unit and ground it. Replace the sending unit if the light comes on with the ignition ON.
Light comes on with engine running	4. Problem in individual system 5. Defective sending unit

Troubleshooting Clutch Problems

It is false economy to replace individual clutch components. The pressure plate, clutch plate and throwout bearing should be replaced as a set, and the flywheel face inspected, whenever the clutch is overhauled. See Chapter 6 for service procedures.

Condition	Possible Cause
Clutch chatter	1. Grease on driven plate (disc) facing 2. Binding clutch linkage or cable 3. Loose, damaged facings on driven plate (disc) 4. Engine mounts loose 5. Incorrect height adjustment of pressure plate release levers 6. Clutch housing or housing to transmission adapter misalignment 7. Loose driven plate hub
Clutch grabbing	1. Oil, grease on driven plate (disc) facing 2. Broken pressure plate 3. Warped or binding driven plate. Driven plate binding on clutch shaft
Clutch slips	1. Lack of lubrication in clutch linkage or cable (linkage or cable binds, causes incomplete engagement) 2. Incorrect pedal, or linkage adjustment 3. Broken pressure plate springs 4. Weak pressure plate springs 5. Grease on driven plate facings (disc)

Troubleshooting Clutch Problems (cont.)

Condition	Possible Cause
Incomplete clutch release	1. Incorrect pedal or linkage adjustment or linkage or cable binding 2. Incorrect height adjustment on pressure plate release levers 3. Loose, broken facings on driven plate (disc) 4. Bent, dished, warped driven plate caused by overheating
Grinding, whirring grating noise when pedal is depressed	1. Worn or defective throwout bearing 2. Starter drive teeth contacting flywheel ring gear teeth. Look for milled or polished teeth on ring gear.
Squeal, howl, trumpeting noise when pedal is being released (occurs during first inch to inch and one-half of pedal travel)	Pilot bushing worn or lack of lubricant. If bushing appears OK, polish bushing with emery cloth, soak lube wick in oil, lube bushing with oil, apply film of chassis grease to clutch shaft pilot hub, reassemble. NOTE: Bushing wear may be due to misalignment of clutch housing or housing to transmission adapter
Vibration or clutch pedal pulsation with clutch disengaged (pedal fully depressed)	1. Worn or defective engine transmission mounts 2. Flywheel run out. (Flywheel run out at face not to exceed 0.005") 3. Damaged or defective clutch components

Troubleshooting Manual Transmission Problems
See Chapter 6 for service procedures

Condition	Possible Cause
Transmission jumps out of gear	1. Misalignment of transmission case or clutch housing. 2. Worn pilot bearing in crankshaft. 3. Bent transmission shaft. 4. Worn high speed sliding gear. 5. Worn teeth or end-play in clutch shaft. 6. Insufficient spring tension on shifter rail plunger. 7. Bent or loose shifter fork. 8. Gears not engaging completely. 9. Loose or worn bearings on clutch shaft or mainshaft. 10. Worn gear teeth. 11. Worn or damaged detent balls.
Transmission sticks in gear	1. Clutch not releasing fully. 2. Burred or battered teeth on clutch shaft, or sliding sleeve. 3. Burred or battered transmission mainshaft. 4. Frozen synchronizing clutch. 5. Stuck shifter rail plunger. 6. Gearshift lever twisting and binding shifter rail. 7. Battered teeth on high speed sliding gear or on sleeve. 8. Improper lubrication, or lack of lubrication. 9. Corroded transmission parts. 10. Defective mainshaft pilot bearing. 11. Locked gear bearings will give same effect as stuck in gear.
Transmission gears will not synchronize	1. Binding pilot bearing on mainshaft, will synchronize in high gear only. 2. Clutch not releasing fully. 3. Detent spring weak or broken. 4. Weak or broken springs under balls in sliding gear sleeve. 5. Binding bearing on clutch shaft, or binding countershaft. 6. Binding pilot bearing in crankshaft. 7. Badly worn gear teeth. 8. Improper lubrication. 9. Constant mesh gear not turning freely on transmission mainshaft. Will synchronize in that gear only.

Condition	Possible Cause
Gears spinning when shifting into gear from neutral	1. Clutch not releasing fully. 2. In some cases an extremely light lubricant in transmission will cause gears to continue to spin for a short time after clutch is released. 3. Binding pilot bearing in crankshaft.
Transmission noisy in all gears	1. Insufficient lubricant, or improper lubricant. 2. Worn countergear bearings. 3. Worn or damaged main drive gear or countergear. 4. Damaged main drive gear or mainshaft bearings. 5. Worn or damaged countergear anti-lash plate.
Transmission noisy in neutral only	1. Damaged main drive gear bearing. 2. Damaged or loose mainshaft pilot bearing. 3. Worn or damaged countergear anti-lash plate. 4. Worn countergear bearings.
Transmission noisy in one gear only	1. Damaged or worn constant mesh gears. 2. Worn or damaged countergear bearings. 3. Damaged or worn synchronizer.
Transmission noisy in reverse only	1. Worn or damaged reverse idler gear or idler bushing. 2. Worn or damaged mainshaft reverse gear. 3. Worn or damaged reverse countergear. 4. Damaged shift mechanism.

TROUBLESHOOTING AUTOMATIC TRANSMISSION PROBLEMS

Keeping alert to changes in the operating characteristics of the transmission (changing shift points, noises, etc.) can prevent small problems from becoming large ones. If the problem cannot be traced to loose bolts, fluid level, misadjusted linkage, clogged filters or similar problems, you should probably seek professional service.

Transmission Fluid Indications

The appearance and odor of the transmission fluid can give valuable clues to the overall condition of the transmission. Always note the appearance of the fluid when you check the fluid level or change the fluid. Rub a small amount of fluid between your fingers to feel for grit and smell the fluid on the dipstick.

If the fluid appears:	It indicates:
Clear and red colored	Normal operation
Discolored (extremely dark red or brownish) or smells burned	Band or clutch pack failure, usually caused by an overheated transmission. Hauling very heavy loads with insufficient power or failure to change the fluid often result in overheating. Do not confuse this appearance with newer fluids that have a darker red color and a strong odor (though not a burned odor).
Foamy or aerated (light in color and full of bubbles)	1. The level is too high (gear train is churning oil) 2. An internal air leak (air is mixing with the fluid). Have the transmission checked professionally.
Solid residue in the fluid	Defective bands, clutch pack or bearings. Bits of band material or metal abrasives are clinging to the dipstick. Have the transmission checked professionally.
Varnish coating on the dipstick	The transmission fluid is overheating

TROUBLESHOOTING DRIVE AXLE PROBLEMS

First, determine when the noise is most noticeable.

Drive Noise: Produced under vehicle acceleration.

Coast Noise: Produced while coasting with a closed throttle.

Float Noise: Occurs while maintaining constant speed (just enough to keep speed constant) on a level road.

External Noise Elimination

It is advisable to make a thorough road test to determine whether the noise originates in the rear axle or whether it originates from the tires, engine, transmission, wheel bearings or road surface. Noise originating from other places cannot be corrected by servicing the rear axle.

ROAD NOISE

Brick or rough surfaced concrete roads produce noises that seem to come from the rear axle. Road noise is usually identical in Drive or Coast and driving on a different type of road will tell whether the road is the problem.

TIRE NOISE

Tire noise can be mistaken as rear axle noise, even though the tires on the front are at fault. Snow tread and mud tread tires or tires worn unevenly will frequently cause vibrations which seem to originate elsewhere; *temporarily, and for test purposes only,* inflate the tires to 40–50 lbs. This will significantly alter the noise produced by the tires, but will not alter noise from the rear axle. Noises from the rear axle will normally cease at speeds below 30 mph on coast, while tire noise will continue at lower tone as speed is decreased. The rear axle noise will usually change from drive conditions to coast conditions, while tire noise will not. Do not forget to lower the tire pressure to normal after the test is complete.

ENGINE/TRANSMISSION NOISE

Determine at what speed the noise is most pronounced, then stop in a quiet place. With the transmission in Neutral, run the engine through speeds corresponding to road speeds where the noise was noticed. Noises produced with the vehicle standing still are coming from the engine or transmission.

FRONT WHEEL BEARINGS

Front wheel bearing noises, sometimes confused with rear axle noises, will not change when comparing drive and coast conditions. While holding the speed steady, lightly apply the footbrake. This will often cause wheel bearing noise to lessen, as some of the weight is taken off the bearing. Front wheel bearings are easily checked by jacking up the wheels and spinning the wheels. Shaking the wheels will also determine if the wheel bearings are excessively loose.

REAR AXLE NOISES

Eliminating other possible sources can narrow the cause to the rear axle, which normally produces noise from worn gears or bearings. Gear noises tend to peak in a narrow speed range, while bearing noises will usually vary in pitch with engine speeds.

Noise Diagnosis

The Noise Is:	Most Probably Produced By:
1. Identical under Drive or Coast	Road surface, tires or front wheel bearings
2. Different depending on road surface	Road surface or tires
3. Lower as speed is lowered	Tires
4. Similar when standing or moving	Engine or transmission
5. A vibration	Unbalanced tires, rear wheel bearing, unbalanced driveshaft or worn U-joint
6. A knock or click about every two tire revolutions	Rear wheel bearing
7. Most pronounced on turns	Damaged differential gears
8. A steady low-pitched whirring or scraping, starting at low speeds	Damaged or worn pinion bearing
9. A chattering vibration on turns	Wrong differential lubricant or worn clutch plates (limited slip rear axle)
10. Noticed only in Drive, Coast or Float conditions	Worn ring gear and/or pinion gear

Troubleshooting Steering & Suspension Problems

Condition	Possible Cause
Hard steering (wheel is hard to turn)	1. Improper tire pressure 2. Loose or glazed pump drive belt 3. Low or incorrect fluid 4. Loose, bent or poorly lubricated front end parts 5. Improper front end alignment (excessive caster) 6. Bind in steering column or linkage 7. Kinked hydraulic hose 8. Air in hydraulic system 9. Low pump output or leaks in system 10. Obstruction in lines 11. Pump valves sticking or out of adjustment 12. Incorrect wheel alignment
Loose steering (too much play in steering wheel)	1. Loose wheel bearings 2. Faulty shocks 3. Worn linkage or suspension components 4. Loose steering gear mounting or linkage points 5. Steering mechanism worn or improperly adjusted 6. Valve spool improperly adjusted 7. Worn ball joints, tie-rod ends, etc.
Veers or wanders (pulls to one side with hands off steering wheel)	1. Improper tire pressure 2. Improper front end alignment 3. Dragging or improperly adjusted brakes 4. Bent frame 5. Improper rear end alignment 6. Faulty shocks or springs 7. Loose or bent front end components 8. Play in Pitman arm 9. Steering gear mountings loose 10. Loose wheel bearings 11. Binding Pitman arm 12. Spool valve sticking or improperly adjusted 13. Worn ball joints
Wheel oscillation or vibration transmitted through steering wheel	1. Low or uneven tire pressure 2. Loose wheel bearings 3. Improper front end alignment 4. Bent spindle 5. Worn, bent or broken front end components 6. Tires out of round or out of balance 7. Excessive lateral runout in disc brake rotor 8. Loose or bent shock absorber or strut
Noises (see also "Troubleshooting Drive Axle Problems")	1. Loose belts 2. Low fluid, air in system 3. Foreign matter in system 4. Improper lubrication 5. Interference or chafing in linkage 6. Steering gear mountings loose 7. Incorrect adjustment or wear in gear box 8. Faulty valves or wear in pump 9. Kinked hydraulic lines 10. Worn wheel bearings
Poor return of steering	1. Over-inflated tires 2. Improperly aligned front end (excessive caster) 3. Binding in steering column 4. No lubrication in front end 5. Steering gear adjusted too tight
Uneven tire wear (see "How To Read Tire Wear")	1. Incorrect tire pressure 2. Improperly aligned front end 3. Tires out-of-balance 4. Bent or worn suspension parts

HOW TO READ TIRE WEAR

The way your tires wear is a good indicator of other parts of the suspension. Abnormal wear patterns are often caused by the need for simple tire maintenance, or for front end alignment.

Excessive wear at the center of the tread indicates that the air pressure in the tire is consistently too high. The tire is riding on the center of the tread and wearing it prematurely. Occasionally, this wear pattern can result from outrageously wide tires on narrow rims. The cure for this is to replace either the tires or the wheels.

This type of wear usually results from consistent under-inflation. When a tire is under-inflated, there is too much contact with the road by the outer treads, which wear prematurely. When this type of wear occurs, and the tire pressure is known to be consistently correct, a bent or worn steering component or the need for wheel alignment could be indicated.

Feathering is a condition when the edge of each tread rib develops a slightly rounded edge on one side and a sharp edge on the other. By running your hand over the tire, you can usually feel the sharper edges before you'll be able to see them. The most common causes of feathering are incorrect toe-in setting or deteriorated bushings in the front suspension.

When an inner or outer rib wears faster than the rest of the tire, the need for wheel alignment is indicated. There is excessive camber in the front suspension, causing the wheel to lean too much putting excessive load on one side of the tire. Misalignment could also be due to sagging springs, worn ball joints, or worn control arm bushings. Be sure the vehicle is loaded the way it's normally driven when you have the wheels aligned.

Cups or scalloped dips appearing around the edge of the tread almost always indicate worn (sometimes bent) suspension parts. Adjustment of wheel alignment alone will seldom cure the problem. Any worn component that connects the wheel to the suspension can cause this type of wear. Occasionally, wheels that are out of balance will wear like this, but wheel imbalance usually shows up as bald spots between the outside edges and center of the tread.

Second-rib wear is usually found only in radial tires, and appears where the steel belts end in relation to the tread. It can be kept to a minimum by paying careful attention to tire pressure and frequently rotating the tires. This is often considered normal wear but excessive amounts indicate that the tires are too wide for the wheels.

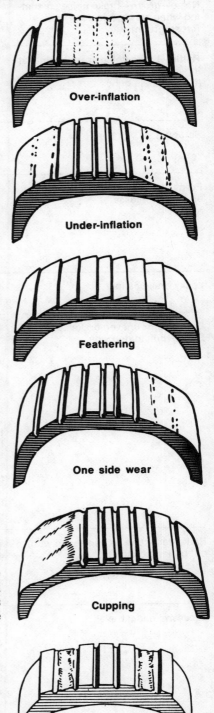

Over-inflation

Under-inflation

Feathering

One side wear

Cupping

Second-rib wear

Troubleshooting Disc Brake Problems

Condition	Possible Cause
Noise—groan—brake noise emanating when slowly releasing brakes (creep-groan)	Not detrimental to function of disc brakes—no corrective action required. (This noise may be eliminated by slightly increasing or decreasing brake pedal efforts.)
Rattle—brake noise or rattle emanating at low speeds on rough roads, (front wheels only).	1. Shoe anti-rattle spring missing or not properly positioned. 2. Excessive clearance between shoe and caliper. 3. Soft or broken caliper seals. 4. Deformed or misaligned disc. 5. Loose caliper.
Scraping	1. Mounting bolts too long. 2. Loose wheel bearings. 3. Bent, loose, or misaligned splash shield.
Front brakes heat up during driving and fail to release	1. Operator riding brake pedal. 2. Stop light switch improperly adjusted. 3. Sticking pedal linkage. 4. Frozen or seized piston. 5. Residual pressure valve in master cylinder. 6. Power brake malfunction. 7. Proportioning valve malfunction.
Leaky brake caliper	1. Damaged or worn caliper piston seal. 2. Scores or corrosion on surface of cylinder bore.
Grabbing or uneven brake action—Brakes pull to one side	1. Causes listed under "Brakes Pull". 2. Power brake malfunction. 3. Low fluid level in master cylinder. 4. Air in hydraulic system. 5. Brake fluid, oil or grease on linings. 6. Unmatched linings. 7. Distorted brake pads. 8. Frozen or seized pistons. 9. Incorrect tire pressure. 10. Front end out of alignment. 11. Broken rear spring. 12. Brake caliper pistons sticking. 13. Restricted hose or line. 14. Caliper not in proper alignment to braking disc. 15. Stuck or malfunctioning metering valve. 16. Soft or broken caliper seals. 17. Loose caliper.
Brake pedal can be depressed without braking effect	1. Air in hydraulic system or improper bleeding procedure. 2. Leak past primary cup in master cylinder. 3. Leak in system. 4. Rear brakes out of adjustment. 5. Bleeder screw open.
Excessive pedal travel	1. Air, leak, or insufficient fluid in system or caliper. 2. Warped or excessively tapered shoe and lining assembly. 3. Excessive disc runout. 4. Rear brake adjustment required. 5. Loose wheel bearing adjustment. 6. Damaged caliper piston seal. 7. Improper brake fluid (boil). 8. Power brake malfunction. 9. Weak or soft hoses.

Troubleshooting Disc Brake Problems (cont.)

Condition	Possible Cause
Brake roughness or chatter (pedal pumping)	1. Excessive thickness variation of braking disc. 2. Excessive lateral runout of braking disc. 3. Rear brake drums out-of-round. 4. Excessive front bearing clearance.
Excessive pedal effort	1. Brake fluid, oil or grease on linings. 2. Incorrect lining. 3. Frozen or seized pistons. 4. Power brake malfunction. 5. Kinked or collapsed hose or line. 6. Stuck metering valve. 7. Scored caliper or master cylinder bore. 8. Seized caliper pistons.
Brake pedal fades (pedal travel increases with foot on brake)	1. Rough master cylinder or caliper bore. 2. Loose or broken hydraulic lines/connections. 3. Air in hydraulic system. 4. Fluid level low. 5. Weak or soft hoses. 6. Inferior quality brake shoes or fluid. 7. Worn master cylinder piston cups or seals.

Troubleshooting Drum Brakes

Condition	Possible Cause
Pedal goes to floor	1. Fluid low in reservoir. 2. Air in hydraulic system. 3. Improperly adjusted brake. 4. Leaking wheel cylinders. 5. Loose or broken brake lines. 6. Leaking or worn master cylinder. 7. Excessively worn brake lining.
Spongy brake pedal	1. Air in hydraulic system. 2. Improper brake fluid (low boiling point). 3. Excessively worn or cracked brake drums. 4. Broken pedal pivot bushing.
Brakes pulling	1. Contaminated lining. 2. Front end out of alignment. 3. Incorrect brake adjustment. 4. Unmatched brake lining. 5. Brake drums out of round. 6. Brake shoes distorted. 7. Restricted brake hose or line. 8. Broken rear spring. 9. Worn brake linings. 10. Uneven lining wear. 11. Glazed brake lining. 12. Excessive brake lining dust. 13. Heat spotted brake drums. 14. Weak brake return springs. 15. Faulty automatic adjusters. 16. Low or incorrect tire pressure.

Condition	Possible Cause
Squealing brakes	1. Glazed brake lining. 2. Saturated brake lining. 3. Weak or broken brake shoe retaining spring. 4. Broken or weak brake shoe return spring. 5. Incorrect brake lining. 6. Distorted brake shoes. 7. Bent support plate. 8. Dust in brakes or scored brake drums. 9. Linings worn below limit. 10. Uneven brake lining wear. 11. Heat spotted brake drums.
Chirping brakes	1. Out of round drum or eccentric axle flange pilot.
Dragging brakes	1. Incorrect wheel or parking brake adjustment. 2. Parking brakes engaged or improperly adjusted. 3. Weak or broken brake shoe return spring. 4. Brake pedal binding. 5. Master cylinder cup sticking. 6. Obstructed master cylinder relief port. 7. Saturated brake lining. 8. Bent or out of round brake drum. 9. Contaminated or improper brake fluid. 10. Sticking wheel cylinder pistons. 11. Driver riding brake pedal. 12. Defective proportioning valve. 13. Insufficient brake shoe lubricant.
Hard pedal	1. Brake booster inoperative. 2. Incorrect brake lining. 3. Restricted brake line or hose. 4. Frozen brake pedal linkage. 5. Stuck wheel cylinder. 6. Binding pedal linkage. 7. Faulty proportioning valve.
Wheel locks	1. Contaminated brake lining. 2. Loose or torn brake lining. 3. Wheel cylinder cups sticking. 4. Incorrect wheel bearing adjustment. 5. Faulty proportioning valve.
Brakes fade (high speed)	1. Incorrect lining. 2. Overheated brake drums. 3. Incorrect brake fluid (low boiling temperature). 4. Saturated brake lining. 5. Leak in hydraulic system. 6. Faulty automatic adjusters.
Pedal pulsates	1. Bent or out of round brake drum.
Brake chatter and shoe knock	1. Out of round brake drum. 2. Loose support plate. 3. Bent support plate. 4. Distorted brake shoes. 5. Machine grooves in contact face of brake drum (Shoe Knock). 6. Contaminated brake lining. 7. Missing or loose components. 8. Incorrect lining material. 9. Out-of-round brake drums. 10. Heat spotted or scored brake drums. 11. Out-of-balance wheels.

Troubleshooting Drum Brakes (cont.)

Condition	Possible Cause
Brakes do not self adjust	1. Adjuster screw frozen in thread. 2. Adjuster screw corroded at thrust washer. 3. Adjuster lever does not engage star wheel. 4. Adjuster installed on wrong wheel.
Brake light glows	1. Leak in the hydraulic system. 2. Air in the system. 3. Improperly adjusted master cylinder pushrod. 4. Uneven lining wear. 5. Failure to center combination valve or proportioning valve.

Mechanic's Data

General Conversion Table

Multiply By	To Convert	To	
		LENGTH	
2.54	Inches	Centimeters	.3937
25.4	Inches	Millimeters	.03937
30.48	Feet	Centimeters	.0328
.304	Feet	Meters	3.28
.914	Yards	Meters	1.094
1.609	Miles	Kilometers	.621
		VOLUME	
.473	Pints	Liters	2.11
.946	Quarts	Liters	1.06
3.785	Gallons	Liters	.264
.016	Cubic inches	Liters	61.02
16.39	Cubic inches	Cubic cms.	.061
28.3	Cubic feet	Liters	.0353
		MASS (Weight)	
28.35	Ounces	Grams	.035
.4536	Pounds	Kilograms	2.20
—	To obtain	From	Multiply by

Multiply By	To Convert	To	
		AREA	
.645	Square inches	Square cms.	.155
.836	Square yds.	Square meters	1.196
		FORCE	
4.448	Pounds	Newtons	.225
.138	Ft./lbs.	Kilogram/meters	7.23
1.36	Ft./lbs.	Newton-meters	.737
.112	In./lbs.	Newton-meters	8.844
		PRESSURE	
.068	Psi	Atmospheres	14.7
6.89	Psi	Kilopascals	.145
		OTHER	
1.104	Horsepower (DIN)	Horsepower (SAE)	.9861
.746	Horsepower (SAE)	Kilowatts (KW)	1.34
1.60	Mph	Km/h	.625
.425	Mpg	Km/1	2.35
—	To obtain	From	Multiply by

Tap Drill Sizes

National Coarse or U.S.S.

Screw & Tap Size	Threads Per Inch	Use Drill Number
No. 5	40	39
No. 6	32	36
No. 8	32	29
No. 10	24	25
No. 12	24	17
1/4	20	8
5/16	18	F
3/8	16	5/16
7/16	14	U
1/2	13	27/64
9/16	12	31/64
5/8	11	17/32
3/4	10	21/32
7/8	9	49/64

National Coarse or U.S.S.

Screw & Tap Size	Threads Per Inch	Use Drill Number
1	8	7/8
1 1/8	7	63/64
1 1/4	7	1 7/64
1 1/2	6	1 11/32

National Fine or S.A.E.

Screw & Tap Size	Threads Per Inch	Use Drill Number
No. 5	44	37
No. 6	40	33
No. 8	36	29
No. 10	32	21

National Fine or S.A.E.

Screw & Tap Size	Threads Per Inch	Use Drill Number
No. 12	28	15
1/4	28	3
5/16	24	1
3/8	24	Q
7/16	20	W
1/2	20	29/64
9/16	18	33/64
5/8	18	37/64
3/4	16	11/16
7/8	14	13/16
1 1/8	12	1 3/64
1 1/4	12	1 11/64
1 1/2	12	1 27/64

Drill Sizes In Decimal Equivalents

Inch	Decimal	Wire	mm
1/64	.0156		.39
	.0157		.4
	.0160	78	
	.0165		.42
	.0173		.44
	.0177		.45
	.0180	77	
	.0181		.46
	.0189		.48
	.0197		.5
	.0200	76	
	.0210	75	
	.0217		.55
	.0225	74	
	.0236		.6
	.0240	73	
	.0250	72	
	.0256		.65
	.0260	71	
	.0276		.7
	.0280	70	
	.0292	69	
	.0295		.75
	.0310	68	
1/32	.0312		.79
	.0315		.8
	.0320	67	
	.0330	66	
	.0335		.85
	.0350	65	
	.0354		.9
	.0360	64	
	.0370	63	
	.0374		.95
	.0380	62	
	.0390	61	
	.0394		1.0
	.0400	60	
	.0410	59	
	.0413		1.05
	.0420	58	
	.0430	57	
	.0433		1.1
	.0453		1.15
	.0465	56	
3/64	.0469		1.19
	.0472		1.2
	.0492		1.25
	.0512		1.3
	.0520	55	
	.0531		1.35
	.0550	54	
	.0551		1.4
	.0571		1.45
	.0591		1.5
	.0595	53	
	.0610		1.55
1/16	.0625		1.59
	.0630		1.6
	.0635	52	
	.0650		1.65
	.0669		1.7
	.0670	51	
	.0689		1.75
	.0700	50	
	.0709		1.8
	.0728		1.85

Inch	Decimal	Wire	mm
	.0730	49	
	.0748		1.9
	.0760	48	
	.0768		1.95
5/64	.0781		1.98
	.0785	47	
	.0787		2.0
	.0807		2.05
	.0810	46	
	.0820	45	
	.0827		2.1
	.0846		2.15
	.0860	44	
	.0866		2.2
	.0886		2.25
	.0890	43	
	.0906		2.3
	.0925		2.35
	.0935	42	
3/32	.0938		2.38
	.0945		2.4
	.0960	41	
	.0965		2.45
	.0980	40	
	.0981		2.5
	.0995	39	
	.1015	38	
	.1024		2.6
	.1040	37	
	.1063		2.7
	.1065	36	
	.1083		2.75
7/64	.1094		2.77
	.1100	35	
	.1102		2.8
	.1110	34	
	.1130	33	
	.1142		2.9
	.1160	32	
	.1181		3.0
	.1200	31	
	.1220		3.1
1/8	.1250		3.17
	.1260		3.2
	.1280		3.25
	.1285	30	
	.1299		3.3
	.1339		3.4
	.1360	29	
	.1378		3.5
	.1405	28	
9/64	.1406		3.57
	.1417		3.6
	.1440	27	
	.1457		3.7
	.1470	26	
	.1476		3.75
	.1495	25	
	.1496		3.8
	.1520	24	
	.1535		3.9
	.1540	23	
5/32	.1562		3.96
	.1570	22	
	.1575		4.0
	.1590	21	
	.1610	20	

Inch	Decimal	Wire & Letter	mm
	.1614		4.1
	.1654		4.2
	.1660	19	
	.1673		4.25
	.1693		4.3
	.1695	18	
11/64	.1719		4.36
	.1730	17	
	.1732		4.4
	.1770	16	
	.1772		4.5
	.1800	15	
	.1811		4.6
	.1820	14	
	.1850	13	
	.1850		4.7
	.1870		4.75
3/16	.1875		4.76
	.1890		4.8
	.1890	12	
	.1910	11	
	.1929		4.9
	.1935	10	
	.1960	9	
	.1969		5.0
	.1990	8	
	.2008		5.1
	.2010	7	
13/64	.2031		5.16
	.2040	6	
	.2047		5.2
	.2055	5	
	.2067		5.25
	.2087		5.3
	.2090	4	
	.2126		5.4
	.2130	3	
	.2165		5.5
7/32	.2188		5.55
	.2205		5.6
	.2210	2	
	.2244		5.7
	.2264		5.75
	.2280	1	
	.2283		5.8
	.2323		5.9
	.2340	A	
15/64	.2344		5.95
	.2362		6.0
	.2380	B	
	.2402		6.1
	.2420	C	
	.2441		6.2
	.2460	D	
	.2461		6.25
	.2480		6.3
1/4	.2500	E	6.35
	.2520		6.
	.2559		6.5
	.2570	F	
	.2598		6.6
	.2610	G	
	.2638		6.7
17/64	.2656		6.74
	.2657		6.75
	.2660	H	
	.2677		6.8

Inch	Decimal	Letter	mm
	.2717		6.9
	.2720	I	
	.2756		7.0
	.2770	J	
	.2795		7.1
	.2810	K	
9/32	.2812		7.14
	.2835		7.2
	.2854		7.25
	.2874		7.3
	.2900	L	
	.2913		7.4
	.2950	M	
	.2953		7.5
19/64	.2969		7.54
	.2992		7.6
	.3020	N	
	.3031		7.7
	.3051		7.75
	.3071		7.8
	.3110		7.9
5/16	.3125		7.93
	.3150		8.0
	.3160	O	
	.3189		8.1
	.3228		8.2
	.3230	P	
	.3248		8.25
	.3268		8.3
21/64	.3281		8.33
	.3307		8.4
	.3320	Q	
	.3346		8.5
	.3386		8.6
	.3390	R	
	.3425		8.7
11/32	.3438		8.73
	.3445		8.75
	.3465		8.8
	.3480	S	
	.3504		8.9
	.3543		9.0
	.3580	T	
	.3583		9.1
23/64	.3594		9.12
	.3622		9.2
	.3642		9.25
	.3661		9.3
	.3680	U	
	.3701		9.4
	.3740		9.5
3/8	.3750		9.52
	.3770	V	
	.3780		9.6
	.3819		9.7
	.3839		9.75
	.3858		9.8
	.3860	W	
	.3898		9.9
25/64	.3906		9.92
	.3937		10.0
	.3970	X	
	.4040	Y	
13/32	.4062		10.31
	.4130	Z	
	.4134		10.5
27/64	.4219		10.71

Inch	Decimal	mm
	.4331	11.0
7/16	.4375	11.11
	.4528	11.5
29/64	.4531	11.51
15/32	.4688	11.90
	.4724	12.0
31/64	.4844	12.30
	.4921	12.5
1/2	.5000	12.70
	.5118	13.0
33/64	.5156	13.09
17/32	.5312	13.49
	.5315	13.5
35/64	.5469	13.89
	.5512	14.0
9/16	.5625	14.28
	.5709	14.5
37/64	.5781	14.68
	.5906	15.0
19/32	.5938	15.08
39/64	.6094	15.47
	.6102	15.5
5/8	.6250	15.87
	.6299	16.0
41/64	.6406	16.27
	.6496	16.5
21/32	.6562	16.66
	.6693	17.0
43/64	.6719	17.06
11/16	.6875	17.46
	.6890	17.5
45/64	.7031	17.85
	.7087	18.0
23/32	.7188	18.25
	.7283	18.5
47/64	.7344	18.65
	.7480	19.0
3/4	.7500	19.05
49/64	.7656	19.44
	.7677	19.5
25/32	.7812	19.84
	.7874	20.0
51/64	.7969	20.24
	.8071	20.5
13/16	.8125	20.63
	.8268	21.0
53/64	.8281	21.03
27/32	.8438	21.43
	.8465	21.5
55/64	.8594	21.82
	.8661	22.0
7/8	.8750	22.22
	.8858	22.5
57/64	.8906	22.62
	.9055	23.0
29/32	.9062	23.01
59/64	.9219	23.41
	.9252	23.5
15/16	.9375	23.81
	.9449	24.0
61/64	.9531	24.2
	.9646	24.5
31/32	.9688	24.6
	.9843	25.0
63/64	.9844	25.0
1	1.0000	25.4

Index

Chilton's Repair & Tune-Up Guides

The Complete line covers domestic cars, imports, trucks, vans, RV's and 4-wheel drive vehicles.

Car and truck model names are listed in alphabetical and numerical order

Model Name	RTUG Title	Part No.
Accord	Honda 1973–84	6980
Alliance	Renault 1975–85	7165
AMX	AMC 1975–82	7199
Aries 1981–82	Chrysler K-Car 1981–82	7163
Arrow	Champ/Arrow/Sapporo 1978–83	7041
Arrow Pick-Ups	D-50/Arrow Pick-Up 1979–82	7032
Aspen 1976–80	Aspen/Volare 1976–80	6637
Astre 1975–77	GM Subcompact 1971–80	6935
Barracuda 1965–72	Barracuda/Challenger 1965–72	5807
Bavaria	BMW 1970–82	6844
Bel Air 1968–75	Chevrolet 1968–83	7135
Belvedere 1968–70	Roadrunner/Satellite/ Belvedere/GTX 1968–73	5821
Biscayne 1968–71	Chevrolet 1968–83	7135
Blazer 1969–82	Blazer/Jimmy 1969–82	6931
Bobcat 1975–80	Pinto/Bobcat 1971–80	7027
Bonneville 1975–83	Buick/Olds/Pontiac 1975–83	7308
BRAT	Subaru 1970–84	6982
Bronco 1966–83	Ford Bronco 1966–83	7140
Bronco II 1984	Ford Bronco II 1984	7408
Brookwood 1968–72	Chevrolet 1968–83	7135
Brougham 1974–75	Valiant/Duster 1968–76	6326
B-210 1974–78	Datsun 1200, etc. 1973–84	7197
Caballero 1964–82	Chevrolet Mid-Size 1964–84	6840
Camaro 1967–81	Camaro 1967–81	6735
Camaro 1982–83	Camaro 1982–83	7317
Camry 1983–84	Toyota Corona, etc. 1970–84	7004
Capri 1970–77	Capri 1970–77	6695
Capri 1979–83	Mustang/Capri 1979–83	6963
Caprice 1975–83	Chevrolet 1968–83	7135
Caravan 1984–85	Caravan/Voyager 1984–85	7482
Carina 1972–73	Toyota Corolla, etc. 1970–84	7036
Catalina 1975–83	Buick/Olds/Pontiac 1975–83	7308
Cavalier 1982	GM J-Car 1982	7059
Celebrity 1982–83	GM A-Body 1982–83	7309
Celica 1971–83	Toyota Celica/Supra 1971–83	7043
Century, front wheel drive 1982–83	GM A-Body 1982–83	7309
Century, rear wheel drive 1975–83	Century/Regal 1975–83	7307
Challenger 1965–72	Barracuda/Challenger 1965–72	5807
Challenger 1977–83	Colt/Challenger/Vista 1971–83	7037
Champ	Champ/Arrow/Sapporo 1978–83	7041
Charger 2.2 1982–84	Omni/Horizon 1978–84	6845
Cherokee 1974–84	Jeep Wagoneer, etc. 1962–84	6739
Chevelle 1964–77	Chevrolet Mid-Size 1964–84	6840
Chevette 1976–84	Chevette/T-1000 1976–84	6836
Chevy Pick-Ups 1970–84	Chevrolet/GMC Pick-Ups/ Suburban 1970–84	6936
Chevy Vans 1967–84	Chevy/GMC Vans 1967–84	6930
Chevy II 1962–68	Chevy II/Nova 1962–79	6841
Cimarron 1982	GM J-Car 1982	7059
Citation 1980–83	GM X-Body 1980–83	7049
Civic	Honda 1973–84	6980
Colt	Colt/Challenger/Vista 1971–83	7037
Comet 1971–77	Maverick/Comet 1971–77	6634
Commando 1971–73	Jeep Wagoneer, Commando, Cherokee, Truck 1962–84	6739
Concord	AMC 1975–82	7199
Continental 1982–85	Ford/Mercury Mid-Size 1971–85	6696
Corolla 1968–70	Toyota 1966–70	5795
Corolla 1970–84	Toyota Corolla, etc. 1970–84	7036
Corona 1966–70	Toyota 1966–70	5795
Corona 1970–81	Toyota Corona, etc. 1970–84	7004
Corsa	Corvair 1960–69	6691
Corvair 1960–69	Corvair 1960–69	6691
Corvette 1953–62	Corvette 1953–62	6576
Corvette 1963–84	Corvette 1963–84	6843
Cosmo	Mazda 1971–84	6981
Cougar 1967–71	Mustang/Cougar 1965–73	6542
Cougar 1972–85	Ford/Mercury Mid-Size 1971–85	6696
Country Sedan 1968–81	Ford/Mercury/Lincoln 1968–85	6842
Country Squire 1968–83	Ford/Mercury/Lincoln 1968–85	6842
Courier 1972–82	Ford Courier 1972–82	6983
Cressida 1978–84	Toyota Corona, etc. 1970–84	7004
Crown 1966–70	Toyota 1966–70	5795
Crown 1970–84	Toyota Corona, etc. 1970–84	7004
Crown Victoria 1981–85	Ford/Mercury/Lincoln 1968–85	6842
Cutlass 1970–82	Cutlass 1970–82	6933
Cutlass Ciera 1982–83	GM A-Body 1982–83	7309
Dart 1968–76	Dart/Demon 1968–76	6324
Dasher	VW Front Wheel Drive 1974–83	6962
Datsun Pick-Ups 1961–72	Datsun 1961–72	5790
Datsun Pick-Ups 1970–83	Datsun Pick-Ups 1970–83	6816
Demon 1971–76	Dart/Demon 1968–76	6324
deVille 1967–84	Cadillac 1967–84	7462
Dodge Pick-Ups 1967–84	Dodge/Plymouth Trucks 1967–84	7459
Dodge Vans	Dodge/Plymouth Vans 1967–84	6934
Duster 1971–76	Valiant/Duster 1968–76	6326
D-50 Pick-Up 1979–81	D-50/Arrow Pick-Ups 1979–81	7032
Eagle	AMC 1975–82	7199
El Camino 1964–82	Chevrolet Mid-Size 1964–84	6840
Eldorado 1967–84	Cadillac 1967–84	7462
Electra 1975–84	Buick/Olds/Pontiac 1975–85	7308
Elite 1974–76	Ford/Mercury Mid-Size 1971–85	6696

Model Name	RTUG Title	Part No.
Encore	Renault 1975–85	7165
Escort, EXP 1981–85	Ford/Mercury Front Wheel Drive 1981–85	7055
Fairlane 1962–70	Fairlane/Torino 1962–75	6320
Fairmont 1978–83	Fairmont/Zephyr 1978–83	6965
FF-1	Subaru 1970–84	6982
Fiat, all models	Fiat 1969–81	7042
Fiesta	Fiesta 1978–80	6846
Firebird 1967–81	Firebird 1967–81	5996
Firebird 1982–83	Firebird 1982–83	7345
Firenza 1982	GM J-Car 1982	7059
Fleetwood 1967–84	Cadillac 1967–84	7462
Ford Pick-Ups 1965–84	Ford Pick-ups 1965–84	6913
Ford Vans	Ford Vans 1961–84	6849
Fuego	Renault 1975–85	7165
Fury 1968–76	Plymouth 1968–76	6552
F-10 1977–78	Datsun F-10, etc. 1977–82	7196
F-85 1970–72	Cutlass 1970–82	6933
Galaxie 1968–81	Ford/Mercury/Lincoln 1968–85	6842
GLC	Mazda 1971–84	6981
GMC Pick-Ups 1970–84	Chevrolet/GMC Pick-Ups/ Suburban 1970–84	6936
GMC Vans	Chevrolet/GMC Vans 1967–84	6930
Gordini	Renault 1975–85	7165
Granada 1975–82	Granada/Monarch 1975–82	6937
Grand Am 1974–80	Pontiac Mid-Size 1974–83	7346
Grand Coupe, Gran Fury, Gran Sedan	Plymouth 1968–76	6552
Grand Prix 1974–83	Pontiac Mid-Size 1974–83	7346
Grand Safari 1975–85	Buick/Olds/Pontiac 1975–85	7308
Grand Ville 1975–83	Buick/Olds/Pontiac 1975–83	7308
Greenbriar	Corvair 1960–69	6691
Gremlin	AMC 1975–82	7199
GTO 1968–73	Tempest/GTO/LeMans 1968–73	5905
GTO 1974	Pontiac Mid-Size 1974–83	7346
GTX 1968–71	Roadrunner/Satellite/Belvedere/ GTX 1968–73	5821
GT6	Triumph 1969–73	5910
G.T.350, G.T.500	Mustang/Cougar 1965–73	6542
Horizon 1978–84	Omni/Horizon 1978–84	6845
Hornet	AMC 1975–82	7199
Impala 1968–78	Chevrolet 1968–83	7135
Jeep CJ	Jeep CJ 1945–84	6817
Jeep Pick-Ups	Jeep Wagoneer, Commando, Cherokee, Truck 1962–84	6739
Jeepster 1966–70	Jeep Wagoneer, Commando, Cherokee, Truck 1962–84	6739
Jetta	VW Front Wheel Drive 1974–83	6962
Jimmy 1970–82	Blazer/Jimmy 1969–82	6931
Kingswood 1968–81	Chevrolet 1968–83	7135
Lakewood	Corvair 1960–69	6691
Lancer	Champ/Arrow/Sapporo 1977–83	7041
Land Cruiser 1966–70	Toyota 1966–70	5795
Land Cruiser 1970–83	Toyota Trucks 1970–84	7035
LeBaron 1982	Chrysler K-Car 1981–82	7163
LeCar	Renault 1975–85	7165
LeMans 1968–73	Tempest/GTO/LeMans 1968–73	5905
LeMans, Grand LeMans 1974–83	Pontiac Mid-Size 1974–83	7346
LeSabre 1975–85	Buick/Olds/Pontiac 1975–85	7308
Lincoln 1968–85	Ford/Mercury/Lincoln 1968–85	6842
LTD 1968–81	Ford/Mercury/Lincoln 1968–85	6842
LTD II 1977–79	Ford/Mercury Mid-Size 1971–85	6696
LUV 1972–81	Chevrolet LUV 1972–81	6815
Lynx, LN-7 1981–85	Ford/Mercury Front Wheel Drive 1981–85	7055
Mach I 1968–73	Mustang/Cougar 1965–73	6542
Malibu	Chevrolet Mid-Size 1964–84	6840
Matador	AMC 1975–82	7199
Maverick 1970–77	Maverick/Comet 1970–77	6634
Maxima 1980–84	Datsun 200SX, etc. 1973–84	7170
Mercury (Full-Size) 1968–85	Ford/Mercury/Lincoln 1968–85	6842
MG	MG 1961–81	6780
Mk.II 1969–70	Toyota 1966–70	5795
Mk.II 1970–76	Toyota Corona, etc. 1970–84	7004
Monaco 1968–77	Dodge 1968–77	6554
Monarch 1975–80	Granada/Monarch 1975–82	6937
Monte Carlo 1970–84	Chevrolet Mid-Size 1964–84	6840
Montego 1971–78	Ford/Mercury Mid-Size 1971–85	6696
Monza 1960–69	Corvair 1960–69	6691
Monza 1975–80	GM Subcompact 1971–80	6935
Mustang 1965–73	Mustang/Cougar 1965–73	6542
Mustang 1979–83	Mustang/Capri 1979–83	6963
Mustang II 1974–78	Mustang II 1974–78	6812
Nova	Chevy II/Nova 1962–79	6841
Omega 1980–81	GM X-Body 1980–83	7049
Omni 1978–84	Omni/Horizon 1978–84	6845
Opel	Opel 1964–70	5792
	Opel 1971–75	6575
Pacer	AMC 1975–82	7199
Patrol 1961–69	Datsun 1961–72	5790
Peugeot	Peugeot 1970–74	5982
Phoenix 1980–83	GM X-Body 1980–83	7049
Pinto 1971–80	Pinto/Bobcat 1971–80	7027

Model Name	RTUG Title	Part No.
Plymouth Vans 1974–84	Dodge/Plymouth Vans 1967–84	6934
Polara 1968–77	Dodge 1968–77	6554
Prelude	Honda 1973–84	6980
PV-444, 544	Volvo 1956–69	6529
P-1800	Volvo 1956–69	6529
Quantum 1974–84	VW Front Wheel Drive 1974–84	6962
Rabbit	VW Front Wheel Drive 1974–84	6962
Ramcharger	Dodge/Plymouth Trucks 1967–84	7459
Ranchero 1967–70	Fairlane/Torino 1962–70	6320
Ranchero 1971–78	Ford/Mercury Mid-Size 1971–85	6696
Ranch Wagon	Ford/Mercury/Lincoln 1968–85	6842
Ranger Pick-Up 1983–84	Ford Ranger 1983–84	7338
Regal 1975–85	Century/Regal 1975–85	7307
Reliant 1981–85	Chrysler K-Car 1981–85	7163
Roadrunner 1968–73	Roadrunner/Satellite/Belvedere/GTX 1968–73	5821
RX-2, RX-3, RX-4	Mazda 1971–84	6981
RX-7	RX-7 1979–81	7031
R-12, 15, 17, 18, 18i	Renault 1975–85	7165
Sapporo 1977–83	Champ/Arrow/Sapporo 1978–83	7041
Satellite 1968–73	Roadrunner/Satellite/Belvedere/GTX 1968–73	5821
Scamp 1971–76	Valiant/Duster 1968–76	6326
Scamp 1982	Omni/Horizon 1978–84	6845
Scirocco	VW Front Wheel Drive 1974–83	6962
Scout 1967–73	International Scout 1967–73	5912
Scrambler 1981–84	Jeep CJ 1981–84	6817
Sentra 1982–84	Datsun 1200, etc. 1973–84	7197
Seville 1967–84	Cadillac 1967–84	7462
Skyhawk 1975–80	GM Subcompact 1971–80	6935
Skyhawk 1982	GM J-Car 1982	7059
Skylark 1980–83	GM X-Body 1980–83	7049
Spirit	AMC 1975–82	7199
Sport Wagon	Renault 1975–85	7165
Stanza	Datsun F-10, etc. 1977–82	7196
Starfire 1975–80	GM Subcompact 1971–80	6935
Starlet 1981–84	Toyota Corolla, etc. 1970–84	7036
Suburban 1968–76	Plymouth 1968–76	6552
Suburban 1970–84	Chevy/GMC Pick-Ups/Suburban 1970–84	6936
Sunbird 1975–80	GM Subcompact 1971–80	6935
Super 90	Audi 1970–73	5902
Supra 1979–84	Toyota Celica/Supra 1971–84	7043
SX-4	AMC 1975–82	7199
S-10 Blazer, S-15 Jimmy 1982–85	Chevy S-10 Blazer/GMC S-15 Jimmy 1982–85	7383
S-10, S-15 Pick-Ups 1982–85	Chevy S-10/GMC S-15 Pick-Ups 1982–85	7310
TC-3 1978–82	Omni/Horizon/Rampage 1978–84	6845
Tempest 1968–73	Tempest/GTO/LeMans 1968–73	5905
Tempo 1984–85	Ford/Mercury Front Wheel Drive 1981–85	7055
Tercel 1980–84	Toyota Corolla, etc. 1970–84	7036
Thunderbird 1977–83	Ford/Mercury Mid-Size 1971–83	6696
Topaz 1983–85	Ford/Mercury Front Wheel Drive 1981–85	7055
Torino 1968–71	Fairlane/Torino 1962–75	6320
Torino, Gran Torino 1971–76	Ford/Mercury Mid-Size 1971–83	6696
Townsman 1968–72	Chevrolet 1968–83	7135
Toyota Pick-Ups 1966–70	Toyota 1966–70	5795
Toyota Pick-Ups 1970–83	Toyota Trucks 1970–83	7035
Toyota Van 1984	Toyota Corona, etc. 1970–84	7004
Trail Duster 1974–84	Dodge/Plymouth Trucks 1967–84	7459
Triumph, all models	Triumph 1969–73	5910
Turismo 1982–84	Omni/Horizon 1978–84	6845
T-37 1971	Tempest/GTO/LeMans 1968–73	5905
Vega 1971–77	GM Subcompact 1971–80	6935
Ventura 1974–79	Pontiac Mid-Size 1974–83	7346
Versailles 1978–80	Ford/Mercury Mid-Size 1971–83	6696
VIP 1969–74	Plymouth 1968–76	6552
Vista Cruiser 1970–72	Cutlass 1970–82	6933
Volare 1976–80	Aspen/Volare 1976–80	6637
Voyager 1984	Caravan/Voyager 1984	7482
VW All models 1949–71	VW 1949–71	5796
VW Types 1, 2, 3	VW 1970–81	6837
Wagoneer 1962–84	Jeep Wagoneer, Commando, Cherokee, Truck 1962–84	6739
XL 1968–75	Ford/Mercury/Lincoln 1968–83	6842
XR-7 1977–83	Ford/Mercury Mid-Size 1971–83	6696
Zephyr 1978–80	Fairmont/Zephyr 1978–83	6965
Z-28 1967–81	Camaro 1967–81	6735

Model Name	RTUG Title	Part No.
Z-28 1982–83	Camaro 1982–83	7317
4-4-2 1970–80	Cutlass 1970–82	6933
024 1978–84	Omni/Horizon 1978–84	6845
3.0S, 3.0Si, 3.0CS	BMW 1970–82	6844
6.9 1978–79	Mercedes-Benz 1974–84	6809
88, 98	Buick/Olds/Pontiac 1975–83	7308
99 1969–75	SAAB 99 1969–75	5988
100 LS, 100GL	Audi 1970–73	5902
122, 122S	Volvo 1956–69	6529
142, 144, 145, 164	Volvo 1956–69	6529
	Volvo 1970–84	7040
190E, 190D 1984	Mercedes-Benz 1974–84	6809
190C, 190DC 1961–66	Mercedes-Benz 1959–70	6065
200, 200D	Mercedes-Benz 1959–70	6065
200SX 1977–84	Datsun 200SX, etc. 1973–84	7170
210 1979–81	Datsun 1200, etc. 1971–84	7197
220D, 220B, 220Sb, 220SEb	Mercedes-Benz 1959–70	6065
220/8 1968–73	Mercedes-Benz 1968–73	5907
230 1974–78	Mercedes-Benz 1974–84	6809
230S, 230SL	Mercedes-Benz 1959–70	6065
230/8 1968–69	Mercedes-Benz 1968–73	5907
240D 1974–79	Mercedes-Benz 1974–84	6809
240Z, 260Z, 280Z, 280ZX, 300ZX	Datsun Z & ZX 1970–84	6932
242, 244, 245, 262, 264, 265	Volvo 1970–84	7040
250C, 250/8	Mercedes-Benz 1968–73	5907
250S, 250SE, 250SL	Mercedes-Benz 1959–70	6065
280, 280C, 280S/8, 280SE, 280SE/8, 280SEL, 280SEL/8, 280SL	Mercedes-Benz 1968–73	5907
280, 280C, 280CE, 280E, 280S, 280SE, 300CD, 300D, 300SD	Mercedes-Benz 1974–84	6809
300SE, 1961–63	Mercedes-Benz 1959–70	6065
300SEL, 3.5, 4.5, 6.3, 300SEL/8	Mercedes-Benz 1968–73	5907
300TD 1979	Mercedes-Benz 1974–84	6809
304	Peugeot 1970–74	5982
310, 311 1962–69	Datsun 1961–72	5790
310 1979–82	Datsun F-10, etc. 1977–82	7196
320i	BMW 1970–82	6844
350SL 1972	Mercedes-Benz 1968–73	5907
380SL, 380SL, 380SLC, 380SEL	Mercedes-Benz 1974–84	6809
400 1982	Chrysler K-Car 1981–82	7163
410, 411, 1963–68	Datsun 1961–72	5790
411, 412	VW 1970–81	7081
450SLC 1973	Mercedes-Benz 1968–73	5907
450SE, 450SEL, 450SEL 6.9, 450SL, 450SLC	Mercedes-Benz 1974–84	6809
500SEC, 500SEL	Mercedes-Benz 1974–84	6809
504	Peugeot 1970–74	5982
510 1968–71	Datsun 1961–72	5790
510 1973, 1978–80	Datsun 200SX, etc. 1973–84	7170
528i, 530i	BMW 1970–82	6844
600	Honda 1973–84	6980
610 1973–76	Datsun 200SX, etc. 1973–84	7170
626	Mazda 1971–84	6981
630 CSi, 633 CSi	BMW 1970–82	6844
710 1974–77	Datsun 200SX, etc. 1973–84	7170
733i	BMW 1970–82	6844
760, 760GLE	Volvo 1970–84	7040
808 (1300, 1600)	Mazda 1971–84	6981
810 1977–80	Datsun 200SX, etc. 1973–84	7170
900, 900 Turbo 1976–85	SAAB 900 1976–85	7572
911, 914	Porsche 1969–73	5822
924, 928	Porsche 924/928 1976–81	7048
1000 1981–84	Chevette/1000 1976–84	6836
1200 1500, 1600, 2000	Datsun 1961–72	5790
1200 1973	Datsun 1200, etc. 1973–84	7197
1400, 1600, 1800 GL/DL/GF	Subaru 1970–84	6982
1500, 1600, 1600–2, 1800	BMW 1970–82	6844
1800, 1800S	Volvo 1956–69	6529
2000, 2002, 2002Ti, 2002Tii, 2500, 2800	BMW 1970–82	6844
2000 1982	GM J-Car 1982	7059
4000, 5000	Audi 4000/5000 1978–81	7028
6000 1982–83	GM A-Body 1982–83	7309

Spanish Language Repair & Tune-Up Guides

Chevrolet/GMC Pick-ups 1970–82	Part No. 7468
Ford Pick-ups 1965–82	Part No. 7469
Toyota 1970–79	Part No. 7467
Chevrolet 1968–79	Part No. 7082
Datsun 1973–80	Part No. 7083
Ford 1968–79	Part No. 7084
Rabbit/Scirocco 1975–78	Part No. 7089
Volkswagen 1970–79	Part No. 7081

Chilton's Repair & Tune-Up Guides are available at your local retailer or by mailing a check or money order for **$11.95** plus **$1.75** to cover postage and handling to:

Chilton Book Company
Dept. DM
Radnor, PA 19089

NOTE: When ordering be sure to include your name & address, book part No. & title.